Microsoft® Expression Web

ILLUSTRATED

COMPLETE

Julie Riley

COURSE TECHNOLOGY
CENGAGE Learning

Australia • Brazil • Japan • Korea • Mexico • Singapore • Spain • United Kingdom • United States

COURSE TECHNOLOGY
CENGAGE Learning™

Microsoft® Expression® Web—Illustrated Complete
Julie Riley

Executive Editor: Marjorie Hunt

Senior Product Manager: Christina Kling Garrett

Product Manager: Jane Hosie-Bounar

Associate Product Manager: Rebecca Padrick

Editorial Assistant: Michelle Camisa

Director of Marketing: Cheryl Costantini

Marketing Manager: Ryan DeGrote

Marketing Specialist: Jennifer Hankin

Developmental Editor: MT Cozzola

Production Editor: GEX Publishing Services

Content Project Manager: Jennifer Goguen McGrail

Art Director: Bruce Bond

Print Buyer: Fola Orekoya

Text Designer: Joseph Lee, Black Fish Design

Copy Editor: Gary Michael Spahl

Proofreader: Chris Clark

Indexer: Rich Carlson

QA Manuscript Reviewers: John Frietas, Danielle Shaw

Cover Designers: Elizabeth Paquin, Kathleen Fivel

Cover Artist: Mark Hunt

Composition: GEX Publishing Services

For product information and technology assistance, contact us at
Cengage Learning Customer & Sales Support, 1-800-354-9706

For permission to use material from this text or product, submit all requests online at **cengage.com/permissions**
Further permissions questions can be emailed to
permissionrequest@cengage.com

ISBN-13: 978-1-4239-0550-9
ISBN-10: 1-4239-0550-4

Course Technology
25 Thomson Place
Boston, MA 02210
USA

Cengage Learning products are represented in Canada by Nelson Education, Ltd.

For your lifelong learning solutions, visit **course.cengage.com**

Purchase any of our products at your local college store or at our preferred online store **www.ichapters.com**.

Figures A-1 and D-2 courtesy of Dave Shea, csszengarden.com & mezzoblue.com.
Figure H-7 courtesy of W3C®, the World Wide Web Consortium (www.w3.org).

Printed in the United States of America
1 2 3 4 5 6 7 13 12 11 10 09 08

About This Book

Welcome to *Microsoft® Expression® Web Illustrated Complete*! Since the first book in the Illustrated Series was published in 1994, millions of students have used various Illustrated texts to master software skills and learn computer concepts. We are proud to bring you this new Illustrated book on Microsoft Expression Web, Microsoft's exciting new professional Web design tool you can use to create professional, standards-based Web sites.

Microsoft Expression Web is part of Microsoft Expression Studio, a new suite of Web authoring tools from Microsoft designed to work seamlessly together to create professional Web sites as well as stunning electronic content delivered on the desktop or on the Web. As you probably have heard by now, Microsoft Expression Web has replaced Microsoft FrontPage. If you are a FrontPage user, you might be alarmed that FrontPage is going away—but don't be! Expression Web is a much more powerful tool that is getting rave reviews from professional Web designers. Unlike FrontPage, Expression Web lets you create standards-based Web sites that conform to the latest versions of XHTML and CSS. Microsoft Expression Web also features an easy-to-use interface and powerful CSS tools that let you generate beautiful layouts quickly.

This Complete edition is designed to teach students how to effectively use Microsoft Expression Web. It covers getting started with the software, how to create a simple Web site, how to add text and links, how to use Cascading Style Sheets (CSS) to organize and format text, how to work with pictures, how to enhance a design using CSS, how to design site navigation, and how to test and publish a Web site. It also includes more advanced units that cover working with tables, forms, and behaviors, using advanced CSS techniques for typography, page layouts, and other professional touches. The final unit introduces the Dynamic Web Template, a tool that lets you make changes to and update your Web design in a few simple steps.

The unique design of this book, which presents each skill on two facing pages, makes it easy for novices to absorb and understand new skills, and also makes it easy for more experienced computer users to progress through the lessons quickly, with minimal reading required. We hope you enjoy exploring the features of this exciting new Web development tool as you work through this book!

Author Acknowledgments

Julie Riley — I have had the pleasure to work with an unbelievably talented team to bring this book together. Thanks to Marjorie Hunt for giving me the opportunity to work on such a rewarding project. Quality assurance testers John Frietas and Danielle Shaw meticulously tested each chapter and greatly enhanced the accuracy and quality of what you hold in your hands. Jen Goguen and Jane Hosie-Bounar skillfully guided the book through development and production.

I am forever grateful to MT Cozzola, editor extraordinaire, for improving both my words and my mood with her intelligence, grace, and wit. Her ability to discern when we needed "more cowbell," coupled with her fantastic sense of humor, made this a truly fun process. MT, you are the best.

I am grateful for my supportive coworkers who have been generous and patient with me throughout this project. Thanks to my family for a lifetime of unconditional love and to my friends for putting up with my social hibernation while writing. My deepest appreciation goes to my husband Brian, who is unwavering in his belief in me.

Preface

Welcome to *Microsoft Expression Web, Illustrated Complete*. If this is your first experience with the Illustrated series, you'll see that this book has a unique design: each skill is presented on two facing pages, with steps on the left and screens on the right. The layout makes it easy to digest a skill without having to read a lot of text and flip pages to see an illustration.

This book is an ideal learning tool for a wide range of learners—the rookies will find the clean design easy to follow and focused with only essential information presented, and the hotshots will appreciate being able to move quickly through the lessons to find the information they need without reading a lot of text. The design also makes this a great reference after the course is over! See the illustration on the right to learn more about the pedagogical and design elements of a typical lesson.

Coverage

This text is organized into sixteen units. In these units, students learn how to use the Expression Web interface; plan and create a Web site and Web pages; add text and links; structure text with HTML and style text with Cascading Style Sheets; work with pictures; enhance a design with CSS; design site navigation; and test and publish a Web site. They also learn how to import files and work with list-based navigation, as well as CSS-based rollovers, scrolling sidebars, attached images, print style sheets, and Dynamic Web Templates.

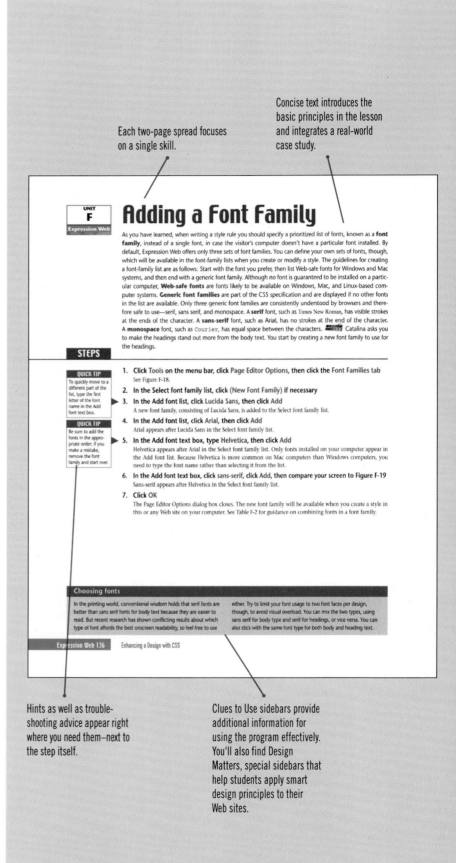

Each two-page spread focuses on a single skill.

Concise text introduces the basic principles in the lesson and integrates a real-world case study.

Hints as well as trouble-shooting advice appear right where you need them—next to the step itself.

Clues to Use sidebars provide additional information for using the program effectively. You'll also find Design Matters, special sidebars that help students apply smart design principles to their Web sites.

Assignments

The lessons use TradeWinds Café and Emporium, a fictitious company seeking a new Web site, as the case study. The assignments on the light purple pages at the end of each unit increase in difficulty. Data Files and case studies provide a variety of interesting and relevant business applications. Assignments include:

- **Concepts Reviews** consist of multiple choice, matching, and screen identification questions.
- **Skills Reviews** provide additional hands on, step-by-step reinforcement.
- **Independent Challenges** are case projects requiring critical thinking and application of the unit skills. In each Independent Challenge, students create a Web site that builds from unit to unit. The Independent Challenges increase in difficulty, with the first one in each unit being the easiest. Independent Challenges 2 and 3 become increasingly open-ended, requiring more independent problem solving.
- **Real Life Independent Challenges** are practical exercises in which students build a personal Web site using their own files and design ideas. No Data Files are supplied. This gives students the opportunity to apply the skills they learn on a higher cognitive level than by following specific step-by-step instructions. It also introduces the opportunity to develop critical thinking skills and encourages creativity.
- **Advanced Challenge Exercises** set within some Independent Challenges provide optional steps for more advanced students.
- **Visual Workshops** are practical, self-graded capstone projects that require independent problem solving. Students are shown a completed Web page and asked to recreate it using the skills they have learned.

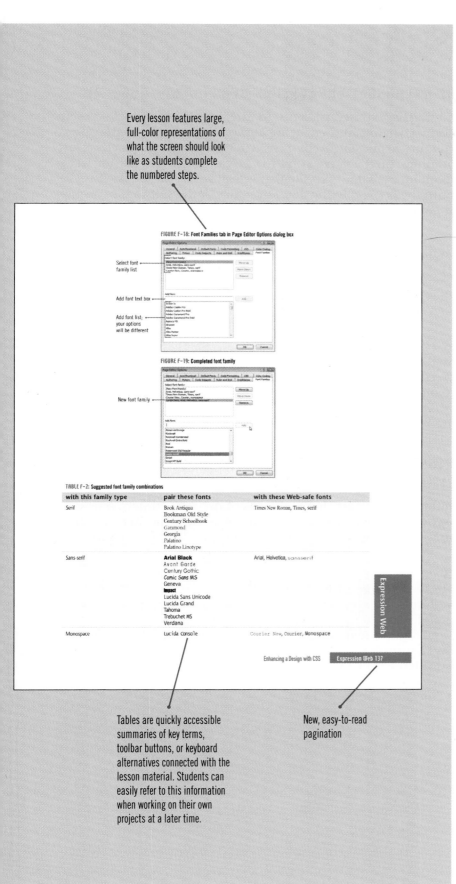

Every lesson features large, full-color representations of what the screen should look like as students complete the numbered steps.

Tables are quickly accessible summaries of key terms, toolbar buttons, or keyboard alternatives connected with the lesson material. Students can easily refer to this information when working on their own projects at a later time.

New, easy-to-read pagination

Other Training Solutions

A GUIDED TOUR OF MICROSOFT EXPRESSION WEB (1-4239-2568-8)

This CD of movie tutorials exposes students to the key features of Microsoft Expression Web quickly. Dynamic and engaging author Corinne Hoisington presents the highlights of using Expression Web to create a Web site in six movies totaling about forty-five minutes. All the movies on this CD feature the Web site for Trade Winds Café and Emporium, the same Web site that is featured in this book. This CD is a great supplement to the book, offering a fun overview of the software to inspire students and show them what is possible.

MICROSOFT EXPRESSION WEB ILLUSTRATED BRIEF (1-4239-0548-2)

The Brief edition contains the first four units that cover how to plan and create a Web site and work with cascading style sheets. It also includes an Appendix on Web publishing.

Table of Contents
Unit A: Getting Started with Expression Web
Unit B: Creating a Web site
Unit C: Adding Text and Links
Unit D: Structuring and Styling Text
Appendix: Publishing Your Web Site

MICROSOFT EXPRESSION WEB ILLUSTRATED INTRODUCTORY (1-4239-0549-0)

The Introductory edition includes the first four units of the Brief edition, plus four additional units on working with pictures, enhancing your design using cascading style sheets, designing site navigation, and testing and publishing your finished Web site.

Table of Contents
Unit A: Getting Started with Expression Web
Unit B: Creating a Web site
Unit C: Adding Text and Links
Unit D: Structuring and Styling Text
Unit E: Working with Pictures
Unit F: Enhancing a Design with CSS
Unit G: Designing Site Navigation
Unit H: Testing and Publishing Your Web Site

Instructor Resources

The Instructor Resources CD is Course Technology's way of putting the resources and information needed to teach and learn effectively into your hands. With an integrated array of teaching and learning tools that offers you and your students a broad range of technology-based instructional options, we believe this CD represents the highest quality and most cutting edge resources available to instructors today. Many of these resources are available at *www.course.com*. The resources available with this book are:

- **Instructor's Manual**—Available as an electronic file, the Instructor's Manual includes detailed lecture topics with teaching tips for each unit.

- **Sample Syllabus**—Prepare and customize your course easily using this sample course outline.

- **PowerPoint Presentations**—Each unit has a corresponding PowerPoint presentation that you can use in lecture, distribute to your students, or customize to suit your course.

- **Figure Files**—The figures in the text are provided on the Instructor Resources CD to help you illustrate key topics or concepts. You can create traditional overhead transparencies by printing the figure files. Or you can create electronic slide shows by using the figures in a presentation program such as PowerPoint.

- **Solutions to Exercises**—Solutions to Exercises contains every Web site file students are asked to create or modify in the lessons and end-of-unit material. This section also provides a document outlining the solutions for the end-of-unit Concepts Review, Skills Review, and Independent Challenges. An Annotated Solution File and Grading Rubric accompany each file and can be used together for quick and easy grading.

- **Data Files for Students**—To complete most of the units in this book, your students will need Data Files. You can post the Data Files on a file server for students to copy. The Data Files are available on the Instructor Resources CD, the Review Pack, and can also be downloaded from www.course.com. In this edition, we have included a lesson on downloading the Data Files for this book on page xvi.

Instruct students to use the Data Files List included on the Review Pack and the Instructor Resources CD. This list gives instructions on copying and organizing files.

- **ExamView**—ExamView is a powerful testing software package that allows you to create and administer printed, computer (LAN-based), and Internet exams. ExamView includes hundreds of questions that correspond to the topics covered in this text, enabling students to generate detailed study guides that include page references for further review. The computer-based and Internet testing components allow students to take exams at their computers, and also saves you time by grading each exam automatically.

CourseCasts—Learning on the Go. Always available...always relevant.

Want to keep up with the latest technology trends relevant to you? Visit our site to find a library of podcasts, CourseCasts, featuring a "CourseCast of the Week," and download them to your mp3 player at *http://coursecasts.course.com*.

Our fast-paced world is driven by technology. You know because you're an active participant—always on the go, always keeping up with technological trends, and always learning new ways to embrace technology to power your life.

Ken Baldauf, a faculty member of the Florida State University Computer Science Department, is responsible for teaching technology classes to thousands of FSU students each year. He knows what you know; he knows what you want to learn. He's also an expert in the latest technology and will sort through and aggregate the most pertinent news and information so you can spend your time enjoying technology, rather than trying to figure it out.

Visit us at *http://coursecasts.course.com* to learn on the go!

Brief Contents

Contents

Read This Before You Begin

Frequently Asked Questions

What are Data Files?

A Data File is a Web site, text file, image file, or other type of file that you use to complete the steps and exercises in the units to create the final Web site that you submit to your instructor.

Where are the Data Files?

Your instructor will provide the Data Files to you or direct you to a location on a network drive from which you can download them. Alternatively, you can follow the instructions on the next page to download the Data Files from this book's Web page.

What software was used to write and test this book?

This book was written and tested using a typical installation of Microsoft Expression Web installed on a computer with a typical installation of Microsoft Windows Vista.

The browser used for any steps that require a browser is Internet Explorer 7.

Do I need to be connected to the Internet to complete the steps and exercises in this book?

Some of the exercises in this book assume that your computer is connected to the Internet. If you are not connected to the Internet, see your instructor for information on how to complete the exercises. We recommend using Microsoft Internet Explorer 7.0 or later or Mozilla Firefox 2.0 or later.

Creating Web sites that have not been built through previous consecutive units

If you begin an assignment that requires a Web site that you did not create or maintain before this unit, you must perform the following steps:

1. Copy the Solution Files folder from the preceding unit for the Web site you wish to create on the hard drive, Zip drive, or USB storage device. For example, if you are working on Unit D, you need the Solution Files folder from Unit C. Your instructor will furnish this folder to you.

2. Start Expression Web, click File on the menu bar, then click Open Site.

3. Navigate to the location where you placed your Solution Files, then click the root folder for the site you are working on. For example, the root folder for the ConnectUp site is called connectup.

4. Click the local root folder, then click Open.

What do I do if my screen is different from the figures shown in this book?

This book was written and tested on computers with monitors set at a resolution of 1024 × 768. If your screen shows more or less information than the figures in the book, your monitor is probably set at a higher or lower resolution. If you don't see something on your screen, you might have to scroll down or up to see the object identified in the figures.

Downloading Data Files for This Book

In order to complete many of the lesson steps and exercises in this book, you are asked to open or insert Data Files. A **Data File** is a partially completed Web site, image, or text file that you use to complete the steps in the units and exercises. Your instructor will provide the Data Files to you or direct you to a location on a network drive from which you can download them. Alternatively, you can follow the instructions in this lesson to download the Data Files from this book's Web page.

1. Start Internet Explorer, type www.course.com in the address bar, then press [Enter]

2. When the Course.com Web site opens, click the Student Downloads link

3. On the Student Downloads page, click in the Search text box, type 9781423905509, then click Go

4. When the page opens for this textbook, in the left navigation bar, click the Download Student Files link, then, on the Student Downloads page, click the Data Files link

5. If the File Download – Security Warning dialog box opens, click Save. (If no dialog box appears, skip this step and go to Step 6.)

6. If the Save As dialog box opens, click the Save in list arrow at the top of the dialog box, select a folder on your USB drive or hard disk to download the file to, then click Save

7. Close Internet Explorer and then open My Computer or Windows Explorer and display the contents of the drive and folder to which you downloaded the file

8. Double-click the file 905509.exe in the drive or folder, then, if the Open File – Security Warning dialog box opens, click Run

9. In the WinZip Self-Extractor window, navigate to the drive and folder where you want to unzip the files to, then click Unzip

10. When the WinZip Self-Extractor displays a dialog box listing the number of files that have unzipped successfully, click OK, click Close in the WinZip Self-Extractor dialog box, then close Windows Explorer or My Computer

You are now ready to use the required files.

Getting Started with Microsoft Expression Web

Microsoft Expression Web is a Web design program for creating modern, standards-compliant Web sites. You recently have been hired by Catalina Romero, the owner of TradeWinds, a store and café in Florida, to redesign the existing Web site for her business. She wants a more visually interesting site that will draw visitors in and better reflect the fun spirit of TradeWinds. You begin by familiarizing yourself with Expression Web. Expression Web is part of a suite of programs called Expression Studio. The other programs in Expression Studio include Expression Design (for creating graphics), Expression Blend (for designing Web-based user interfaces), and Expression Media (for organizing digital photos and video).

OBJECTIVES

Understand Web design software

Start Microsoft Expression Web

Explore the Expression Web workspace

Open a Web page and preview it in
   a browser

Work with views and task panes

View Web page elements and visual aids

Get help

Print and close a page and exit
   Expression Web

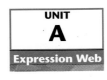
Understanding Web Design Software

Microsoft Expression Web allows you to design, publish, and manage professional-looking, modern Web sites. ▰▰▰▰ You decide to learn more about Expression Web and what it can do.

Using Expression Web, you can:

- **Create Web pages and Web sites**
  You can use Expression Web to create a single Web page or an entire Web site. A **Web page** is essentially a text file, usually written in a language called **HTML** (**HyperText Markup Language**). The code within the file often references images and other multimedia files that appear in the page. In Expression Web, HTML Web pages are saved by default with the file extension ".htm." A **Web site** is a collection of related Web pages, linked together. Web pages are viewed through a **Web browser**, software that interprets HTML code and displays it as the text and images you see on a Web page. Popular browsers include Microsoft Internet Explorer, Mozilla Firefox, Netscape Navigator, and Apple Safari.

- **See what your site will look like as you design it**
  Expression Web is a **WYSIWYG** program (pronounced WIZ-EE-WIG), which stands for "What You See Is What You Get." WYSIWYG programs make Web design much faster by showing you what your page will look like in a Web browser as you are designing it. They also allow you to create Web pages without knowing any HTML code. Before WYSIWYG programs existed, Web designers had to type HTML code, save the file, and then open the file in a browser to see what it looked like.

- **Add text, images, multimedia files, and scripts to your Web pages**
  Web pages today are much more than just text. Expression Web allows you to add images and JavaScript behaviors to add interactivity and interest to your site.

- **Create Web sites that adhere to Web standards**
  The Internet thrives because almost any computer with any browser can view any Web site. This flexibility is a result of organizations developing recommendations for creating Web pages, called **Web standards**. Designing a Web page is similar to writing; if you want readers to understand what you write, you must use proper grammar and spelling. But Web browsers are less forgiving than readers of a written document; if the syntax in an HTML file is wrong, the browser won't be able to display it at all—or at least not in the way you expected. Expression Web works behind the scenes to write code that correctly follows Web standards.

- **Create Cascading Style Sheets to format and lay out your pages**
  The HTML language is used to describe the structure of a Web page. **Cascading Style Sheets** (**CSS**), often called just **style sheets**, are rules that describe the presentation and visual design of a page, including fonts, colors, and often the layout and positioning of elements on the page. See Figure A-1 for an example of how style sheets change the appearance and layout of a Web site. Expression Web has outstanding tools to help you design and manage styles.

- **Manage your Web site**
  Keeping a Web site in good working order requires you to manage many files. Larger Web sites may have thousands of files to keep track of, including the HTML files, CSS files, image and other multimedia files, and scripts. When you create a Web site in Expression Web, the program helps you to organize the files and to make sure that any links you create between files are not broken if you move them to different folders.

- **Publish your Web site**
  People will not be able to visit your Web site until you publish it to a Web server. A **Web server** is a computer connected to the Internet that stores Web pages and other Web content and displays it to a Web browser. When you **publish** your site, you copy the Web pages and related files from your computer to a Web server. Expression Web makes it easy to publish your site.

FIGURE A-1: A Web page with and without a style sheet applied

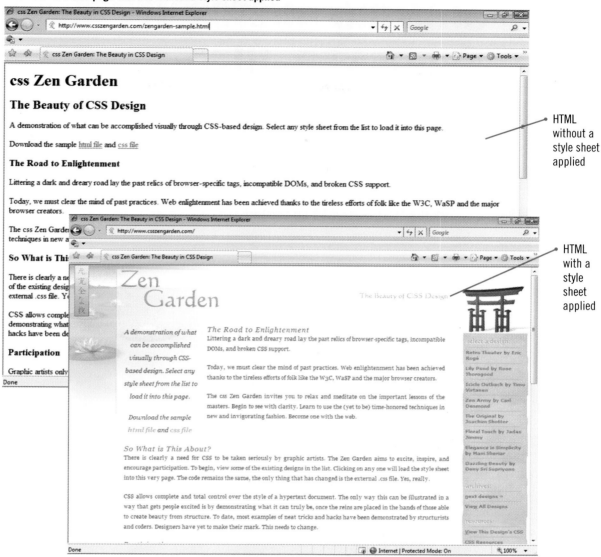

HTML without a style sheet applied

HTML with a style sheet applied

Courtesy of Dave Shea, csszengarden.com & mezzoblue.com

Understanding Web standards

In the early days of the Web, designers would use HTML code that was optimized for certain browsers. Many Web sites displayed "Best Viewed in Internet Explorer" or "Best Viewed in Netscape" banners and encouraged visitors to only use that particular browser to view the site. Thankfully those days, known as the "browser wars," are past. The modern way to design sites is to create code that complies with standards set by the **World Wide Web Consortium (W3C)** and other organizations, rather than code that targets a specific browser.

The advantages to this approach include knowing that your Web pages will be viewable by future versions of browsers, increasing their accessibility to visitors with disabilities, and making your site more visible and friendly to search engines. That's why it's so important that Expression Web creates standards-compliant code. For more information on Web standards, visit the Web Standards Project (WaSP) Web site at www.webstandards.org.

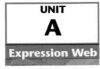

Starting Microsoft Expression Web

Your first step in using Expression Web is to start the program. You can start Expression Web by using the Start button on the Windows taskbar or by double-clicking a shortcut located on the Windows desktop. If you need additional assistance, contact your instructor or technical support person. You decide to launch Expression Web so you can explore the interface.

STEPS

1. **Click the Start button on the taskbar**
   The Start menu opens.

2. **Point to All Programs on the Start menu**
   The All Programs menu opens, listing the programs installed on your computer in alphabetical order.

3. **Click Microsoft Expression on the All Programs menu**
   The Microsoft Expression Studio programs installed on your computer appear, as shown in Figure A-2.

4. **Click Microsoft Expression Web on the Programs menu; if a dialog box opens asking if you want Expression Web to be your default Web editor, click No; if a Privacy Options dialog box opens, click OK**
   The Expression Web program window opens, as shown in Figure A-3.

5. **If necessary, click the Maximize button on the Expression Web program window**
   The program window is maximized.

Starting Expression Web quickly

Windows provides several options to quickly start Expression Web. One method is via the Recently Opened Programs pane on the Start menu. When you open the Start menu, the programs you recently opened are listed in the left pane. If you use Expression Web frequently, it may show up in this list, allowing you to open it without scrolling to the Microsoft Expression folder on the All Programs menu. You can also set Expression Web to always show up at the top of the Start Menu. To do this, right-click the program name in the Start menu, then click Pin to Start Menu. A third way is to add a shortcut to your Windows desktop. To do this, click the Start button, point to All Programs, click the Microsoft Expression folder, then right-click Microsoft Expression Web. Point to Send To, then click Desktop (create shortcut). The shortcut is added to the Windows desktop, and you can double-click it to start the program.

FIGURE A-2: Starting Microsoft Expression Web

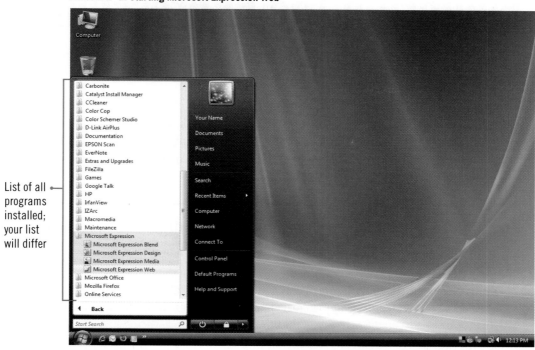

List of all programs installed; your list will differ

FIGURE A-3: Expression Web program window

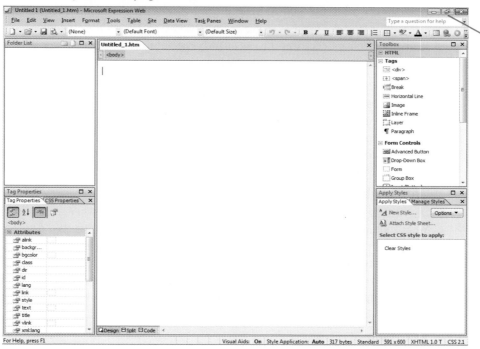

If program window is not maximized, Maximize button instead of Restore Down button appears here

Expression Web

Exploring the Expression Web Workspace

The Expression Web workspace is where you create and edit Web pages. The program window consists of a title bar, menu bar, Common toolbar, editing window, task panes, and a status bar. The workspace can look slightly intimidating, but as you work in the program, you'll see that all the elements work together to provide an integrated approach to designing and organizing your site. 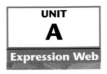 You spend some time exploring the Expression Web workspace.

DETAILS

Using Figure A-4 as a guide, familiarize yourself with the following elements:

- **Title bar**

  The **title bar** appears at the very top of the program window. It shows the title of the current Web site (if a site is open) or the current Web page (if only a page is open), the file path of the current site or page enclosed in parentheses, and the name of the program. Buttons for minimizing, resizing, and closing the program window are located on the right side of the title bar.

- **Menu bar**

  The **menu bar**, located under the title bar, includes all Expression Web commands organized into menus such as File and Edit. Many of these commands are also available in other locations in the program, such as in a task pane or toolbar, or can be activated through keyboard shortcuts.

- **Common toolbar**

  The **Common toolbar**, located under the menu bar, provides access to common tasks in Expression Web. Tasks include creating a new page, saving and opening files, and common text formatting options such as font, font size, bold, and italic. You can also insert a table, picture, or hyperlink using the Common toolbar. This toolbar is one of many available in Expression Web, but it's the only toolbar displayed by default. To open other toolbars, click **View** on the menu bar, point to **Toolbars**, then click the name of the toolbar you want to open. For a description of the toolbars available in Expression Web, see Table A-1.

- **Task panes**

  Task panes are small, resizable windows that provide access to tools for specific tasks. They appear on either side of the Expression Web window. Four task panes are displayed by default: Folder List in the top left, Tag Properties in the bottom left, Toolbox in the top right, and Apply Styles in the bottom right. Many task panes contain more than one tab. For example, the Tag Properties pane contains both a Tag Properties tab and a CSS Properties tab. The task pane title bar displays the name of the currently active tab.

- **Editing window**

  The **editing window** is the large area under the Common toolbar where you do most of your design work. A tab appears at the top of the editing window to indicate that one Web page (with the default name Untitled_1.htm) is currently open. If you open additional Web pages, additional tabs appear here. If you open a Web site, an additional tab appears here. The **quick tag selector bar** is located just below the tab area; it allows you to easily select and edit specific HTML tags on your Web page. In the bottom-left corner of the editing window, you can access the **Show Design View**, **Show Split View**, and **Show Code View** buttons, which allow you to view the Web page you are editing in different ways.

- **Status bar**

  The **status bar** is located along the bottom of the program window. It provides helpful information such as the current location of the insertion point, instructions for getting help, and current settings such as Visual Aids mode and Style Application mode—features that help you to place and format elements on a Web page. For the page you are currently editing, the status bar also indicates the file size, the page dimensions, and which versions of HTML and CSS are being used to create your Web page.

FIGURE A-4: The Expression Web workspace

Title bar
Menu bar
Web page tab
Quick tag selector bar

Common toolbar
Task panes
Editing window
Status bar

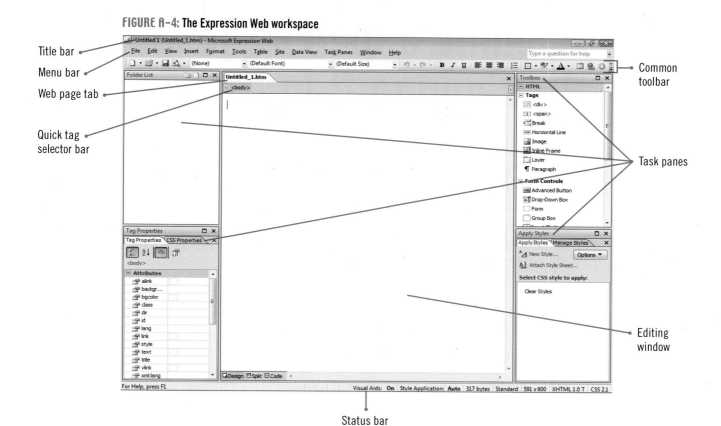

TABLE A-1: Toolbars available in Expression Web

toolbar	use to
Standard	Perform basic functions such as Open, New Document, Undo, Redo, and Spell Check
Formatting	Format text
Code View	Work directly in the HTML code
Common	Easily access commonly used tools from Formatting and Standard toolbars
Dynamic Web Template	Quickly navigate within a Dynamic Web Template
Master Page	Navigate in and edit Master Pages
Pictures	Change the appearance of pictures in your Web page
Positioning	Set size and positioning of page elements
Style	Apply, rename, and remove styles
Style Application	Control how styles are applied manually to page elements
Tables	Create and modify tables within a Web page

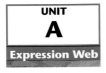

Opening a Web Page and Previewing It in a Browser

You can open either individual Web pages or an entire Web site at once in Expression Web. Opening a Web page opens a single page and displays it in the editing window. Opening a Web site displays the list of files included in that site in the Folder List task pane and also opens a Web site tab in the editing window. A frustrating aspect of Web design is the fact that your designs do not look the same in every browser. Expression Web does a good job at approximating what your page will look like in a Web browser, but you will want to check the appearance of your page in different browsers that your visitors might be using. You can use the **Preview** feature to check your pages as you work. You open the TradeWinds home page to view the current design, and preview it in a browser.

STEPS

1. **Click File on the menu bar, then click Open**

   The Open File dialog box opens.

2. **In the Open File dialog box, navigate to the drive and folder where you store your Data Files**

   See Figure A-5. Many students store files on a flash drive or Zip drive, but you can also store files on your computer, a network drive, or any storage device indicated by your instructor or technical support person.

3. **Double-click the Unit A folder**

   The folder opens, displaying a list of files. Web site files need to be named in a certain way so that they can be used on any type of Web server. When you name any file that is part of a Web site, including HTML files, CSS files, and image files, you should use only lowercase letters, numbers, or underscores. Don't use spaces, capital letters, or special characters such as # or *. By following these rules, you ensure that your site will function on any server.

4. **Click the file a_1.htm, then click Open**

   The TradeWinds home page opens in Expression Web, as shown in Figure A-6. This is the home page of the Web site you have been hired to redesign. Catalina is unhappy with this design and wants a look that is more fun and appealing to visitors.

QUICK TIP

If you are editing a Web page, you must save it before you preview it. You haven't made any changes to this page, so you don't need to save it first.

5. **Click the Preview button list arrow 🔍▾ on the Common toolbar**

   A menu of options for opening installed browsers in different window sizes opens, as shown in Figure A-7. Your list of options varies depending on which browsers are installed on your computer; you may see more or fewer options than those in the figure, and your default browser and window size might vary. The window size options represent common screen resolutions that site visitors may be using. The most common screen resolution used today is 1024 × 768, with 800 × 600 being the second most common. Web pages look different in different browsers and at different resolutions, so you should preview a page in several combinations as you work on a design.

QUICK TIP

To add a browser to the Preview list, click the Preview button list arrow, choose Edit Browser list, click Add, click Browse, navigate to the .exe file for the browser you wish to add (likely located in the Program Files folder), click Open, then click OK twice.

6. **Click the first option in the list**

   The TradeWinds home page opens in a browser window. You can return to Expression Web and choose another option from the list to view your page using a different available browser and window size. If more than one browser is installed on your computer, you can also choose the option to Preview in Multiple Browsers. If you choose this option, Expression Web previews the current page in all available browsers at once by opening multiple browser windows. If you click directly on the Preview button instead of on the list arrow, your page opens in the last option you chose.

7. **Click the Close button on the browser title bar**

   The browser window closes and you return to the Expression Web workspace.

FIGURE A-5: Open File dialog box

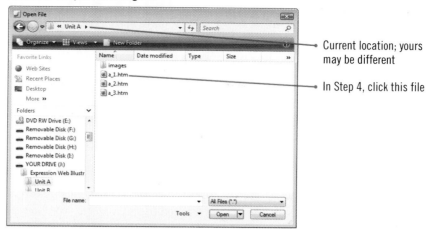

Current location; yours may be different

In Step 4, click this file

FIGURE A-6: Current TradeWinds home page

FIGURE A-7: Preview button list

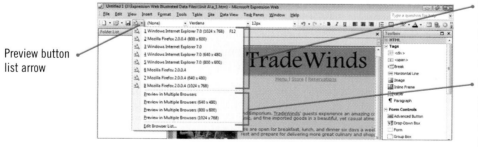

Preview button list arrow

Options to open page in any installed browser at different window sizes; your list may differ

Options to open page in multiple installed browsers at once; your list may differ

Thinking like a designer

Becoming a good Web designer involves more than learning the tools of a program like Expression Web. You also learn to think the way a designer thinks. As you visit Web sites, evaluate what you like or don't like about them. Notice the color scheme, font and typography, images, content, layout, and navigation. Does the visual design appeal to you? Is the type easy to read?

How easily can you find what you're looking for? What exactly is it about the design, content, or site structure that is successful or not successful? If it's a site you visit often, what aspects of the site draw you back for another visit? By thinking critically about Web sites, you'll start to develop an eye for details that you can use when you create your own sites.

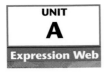

Working with Views and Task Panes

Expression Web includes three views for working with a page: Design, Code, and Split. **Design view** shows what a page will look like when viewed in a browser. This is the default view in Expression Web and the view you work in most often. **Code view** displays the HTML code that the page is written in, so it's useful if you are writing or revising code, or identifying trouble spots in a page. **Split view** is a combination view; it displays both a Code pane and a Design pane so that you can see both views at once when necessary. Task panes appear in all views; they include essential tools for building your Web site. The task panes consolidate tools related to very specific tasks such as modifying styles or selecting HTML tag properties in one convenient area. Task panes can be opened, closed, expanded, collapsed, and rearranged to suit your working style. ▄▄▄▄ You experiment with viewing Web pages in different ways and opening and closing task panes.

STEPS

1. **Click the Show Code View button at the bottom of the editing window**

   The HTML code for the open Web page appears, as shown in Figure A-8. When using Expression Web, you do not need to actually write any HTML code, but any time you make an edit in the editing window in Design View, Expression Web generates the HTML code for the page.

   > **QUICK TIP**
   > Split view is helpful for debugging or finding problems with your Web page; you can make changes in the Design View window and see the resulting code in the Code View window.

2. **Click the Show Split View button at the bottom of the editing window**

   Split view shows a combined view of the current page in Code view at the top of the editing window and in Design view at the bottom.

3. **Click the Show Design View button at the bottom of the editing window**

   The page now appears in Design view, the default view.

4. **Click the Maximize Window button on the Tag Properties task pane, as shown in Figure A-9**

   The Tag Properties task pane expands to take up the entire left side of the window, and the Folder List task pane collapses. On the maximized task pane, a Restore Window button replaces the Maximize button so that you can restore the task pane to the default size.

   > **QUICK TIP**
   > You can also drag the border between two task panes to resize the panes manually; to do so, point to a border until the pointer changes to ⬍; then drag up or down.

5. **Click the Restore Window button 🗗 on the Tag Properties task pane**

   The Tag Properties task pane partially collapses to half its previous length, and the Folder List task pane expands to its previous size. You can maximize and minimize task panes to suit your needs as you work. For example, maximizing the Folder List task pane can be helpful if your Web site contains a lot of files and you need more space to see the entire list at once.

6. **Click the Close Window button ☒ on the Toolbox task pane**

   The Toolbox task pane closes immediately, and the Apply Styles task pane expands to take up the entire right side of the window.

7. **Click Task Panes on the menu bar, then click Toolbox**

   The Toolbox task pane is now restored to its original position.

   > **TROUBLE**
   > If you release the mouse button while the Apply Styles task pane is directly on top of the Toolbox task pane, the tabs of the two task panes merge into one task pane; if this happens, just proceed to Step 9.

8. **Point to the title bar of the Apply Styles task pane until the move pointer ✛ appears, as shown in Figure A-10, click and drag the Apply Styles task pane up until it appears just above the Toolbox task pane, then release it**

   The Apply Styles task pane moves to the top-right part of the screen, and the Toolbox moves to the bottom right. You can also drag task panes to the middle of the editing window to create floating panes that are not attached to the sides.

9. **Click Task Panes on the menu bar, then click Reset Workspace Layout**

   The task panes return to their original positions. The Reset Workspace Layout command restores all panes to their default locations and sizes. It does not affect menus or toolbars.

FIGURE A-8: Code view

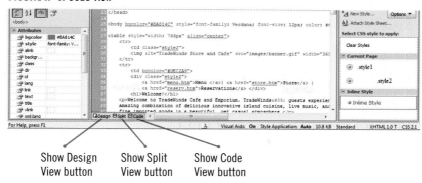

Show Design View button   Show Split View button   Show Code View button

FIGURE A-9: Task pane elements

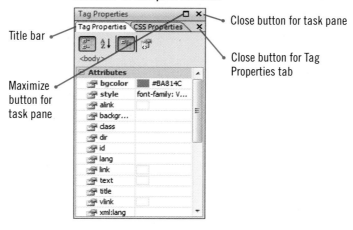

Title bar

Maximize button for task pane

Close button for task pane

Close button for Tag Properties tab

FIGURE A-10: Dragging a task pane

In Step 8, drag up to move the task pane

Using Split view to learn HTML

Expression Web automatically generates code as you work in Design view, so you can create an entire Web site without knowing any HTML. However, if you plan to do much work with Web pages, it helps to know the basics of the HTML language. A good way to ease into learning HTML is to work in Split view. As you edit in the Design pane, watch the code that Expression Web generates in the Code pane. You can pick up a surprising amount of knowledge about the underlying code just by observing. For example, if you insert a hyperlink to the Microsoft home page in Design pane, the Code pane shows <a href="http://www.microsoft.com">Microsoft Web Site</a>. The <a></a> tags indicate that you have inserted an anchor element, which is used to define a hyperlink. The "Microsoft Web Site" text between the tags is the text that will be linked from the Web page, and http://www.microsoft.com is the Web address that visitors will go to when they click the link.

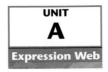

Viewing Web Page Elements and Visual Aids

Most Web pages are made up of many different elements, including the HTML page itself, images, tables, and text. Many of these elements are not normally visible in Design view or in a browser. The **visual aids** in Expression Web allow you to see and modify empty or invisible elements of your page while in Design view so you do not have to work in Code view. When you select certain elements, Expression Web outlines them and displays a tab indicating what type of element it is. Any element margins, padding, or styles are also indicated. Visual aids do not affect the content of your files, only the way that you view them on screen. ▰▰▰ You decide to examine how the current TradeWinds home page is constructed and what elements the page uses.

STEPS

TROUBLE ➤

If a visual aid does not appear, click View in the menu bar, point to Visual Aids, then click Show; make sure that Block Selection, Visible Borders, and Empty Containers display an orange square next to them, indicating they are selected (otherwise, click in the boxes to select each item).

1. **Click anywhere within the first paragraph of text, click the <table> tag on the quick tag selector bar, then scroll to the top of the page**

   Clicking anywhere within an element on a page displays the visual aids for that element. Clicking the <table> tag highlights the table and displays a visual aid indicating that this is a table, as shown in Figure A-11. Expression Web also outlines the table with visible dashed borders so you can see the structure. The Tag Properties task pane on the left side of the screen now displays the properties of the selected table, including the width and alignment. From this, you determine that the entire page is laid out using a table. A **table** is a grid-like container with rows and columns. It can be used to display data or to lay out elements on a page. The preferred method of laying out pages uses CSS, not tables. You decide that when you redesign this site, you want to change the page to a CSS-based layout.

2. **Click anywhere within the text Welcome! at the top of the page, then click the h1 tab on the visual aid that appears**

   See Figure A-12. The visual aid "h1" indicates that this text is a Heading 1. HTML provides six levels of **headings**. Heading 1 is the highest level and text at this level is usually the largest in size; Heading 6 is the least important and text at this level is usually the smallest in size. You can change the size and other attributes of headings by using CSS. The diagonal stripes above and below the heading show the margins that have been applied and indicate that the top margin is larger than the bottom margin. This information can be useful when troubleshooting layout issues.

3. **Click inside the text Email Address**

   A visual aid appears indicating that this text is contained inside a form and outlining the boundaries of the form. Without the visual aid, you would have to estimate where the form element stopped and started. A **form** is an HTML element that allows visitors to send information from a Web site.

4. **Click the underlined word Menu directly under the TradeWinds image**

   This is a hyperlink. A **hyperlink**, also called a link, is text or an image that visitors click to open another Web page, Web site, or file.

5. **Click the image of the fish fountain**

   A visual aid appears around the image. The "img" indicates that it is an image, and the ".style1" indicates that a style, named style1, has been applied to it. See Figure A-13. The Tag Properties change to display the properties of this image and style.

FIGURE A-11: Table selected showing visual aid

Table tag selected in quick tag selector bar

Tab indicates table element is selected

Table tag indicates that Tag Properties displayed apply to selected table

Scroll bar

First paragraph of text

Shaded area is the selected table; because the entire Web page is contained in the table, the full page is shaded

FIGURE A-12: h1 element selected on page

h1 tag selected in quick tag selector bar

h1 tab on visual aid

Shading shows area of page occupied by h1 element

h1 tag indicates that Tag Properties displayed apply to the h1 element selected

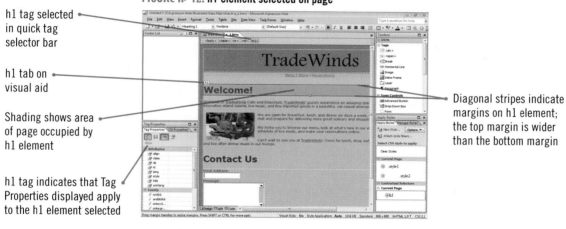

Diagonal stripes indicate margins on h1 element; the top margin is wider than the bottom margin

FIGURE A-13: img element selected on page

img tag is selected in quick tag selector

Tab indicates an img (image) element is selected and that a style named style1 has been applied to it

Properties of selected image, including the file path and styles applied

Shaded area outlines boundaries of selected image

Combining software programs for Web design

Expression Web and other Web design software programs can create HTML pages and Cascading Style Sheets. However, Web sites rarely consist of only pages of text. Almost all sites include images, and some also feature video, animation, and sound. This is why Web designers and developers use several software programs to create a site. For example, you might use Expression Design to create an illustration, Adobe Flash to create an animation, and Corel Paint Shop Pro to enhance your digital photos. You can then use Expression Web to insert these elements into your Web page. It's not uncommon for Web designers to use four or five different software programs while developing a site.

Getting Help

Expression Web has a Help system that you can refer to if you have questions or problems. You can press [F1] or click Help on the menu bar to open the Help window, where you can search or browse for information within the Help feature. You can also get help by typing a question or term in the Type a question for help box in the upper-right corner of the program window. The Help menu includes additional help resources, such as a Community command, which you can use to access online communities of other Expression Web users. You can also access updates to the software and learn about available extensions that add functionality to Expression Web. ▰▰▰▰ You want to learn more about the features available on the status bar in Expression Web.

STEPS

1. **Click Help on the menu bar, then click Microsoft Expression Web Help**

   The Expression Web Help window opens, as shown in Figure A-14. This window includes a Help toolbar, a Search box, and a list of topics. You can use the Back, Forward, Stop, Refresh, and Home buttons on the toolbar to navigate the Help pages as you would in a Web browser. You can also use the toolbar buttons to print, change the font size, show or hide the table of contents, and keep the Help window on top of other open windows for easy access. To get help, you can either click a topic to browse or you can enter a word or term in the Search box.

2. **Type status bar in the Search box, then click Search**

   A list of topics relating to the term "status bar" appears under the Search box, as shown in Figure A-15. You can scroll down to see all the results. You can also click the Next button to open the next page of search results. The Page information to the left of the Next button indicates how many pages of help information are available.

3. **Click Status Bar in the list of search results**

   Information about the status bar appears, as shown in Figure A-16. Scroll down the page and review the information.

4. **Click the Print button 🖨 on the Help toolbar to print the information, then click Print in the Print dialog box**

   The page you were viewing prints. You decide you want to see more information about the entire workspace in Expression Web.

5. **Click Workspace in the breadcrumb trail below the search box**

   A table of contents for the Workspace section of the Help feature appears. **Breadcrumbs** or **breadcrumb trails** are a popular navigation feature on the Web. They are named for the trail of breadcrumbs left by Hansel and Gretel in the Grimm fairy tale. Breadcrumbs usually appear horizontally above the page content and under the page's navigation. They allow visitors to backtrack one level or several levels and to see the path to the content they are currently viewing. Clicking any link in a breadcrumb trail opens that page.

6. **Click Task Panes under Subcategories, then click Toolbox Task Pane**

   Information about the Toolbox task pane appears.

7. **Click the Home button 🏠 on the Help toolbar**

   The Expression Web Help home page appears.

8. **Click the Show Table of Contents button 📖 on the Help toolbar**

   An expanded table of contents appears on the left side, as shown in Figure A-17. Using the table of contents is helpful when you want to browse for information. You can click a topic to expand it and display any subtopics in that area, and you can also click any subtopic.

9. **Click the Close button ✕ on the Help window title bar**

   The Help window closes and you return to the Expression Web workspace.

TROUBLE
If you see a message that says "Download Microsoft Visual Basic Help," click the down arrow next to the Search button, click Expression Web Help, then click the Search button again.

TROUBLE
If your computer is not connected to a printer, you will not be able to complete this step. Contact your technical support person for assistance.

QUICK TIP
You can make the text larger by clicking the Change Font Size button A̅ on the Help toolbar, then clicking Larger or Largest.

QUICK TIP
You can click the Hide Table of Contents button 📖 when you don't want to see the table of contents, and click the Show Table of Contents button 📖 when you want to display it.

FIGURE A-14: Expression Web Help window

Back button

Forward button

Search box

Home button

Print button

Show Table of Contents button

Search button

Change Font Size button

Help topics

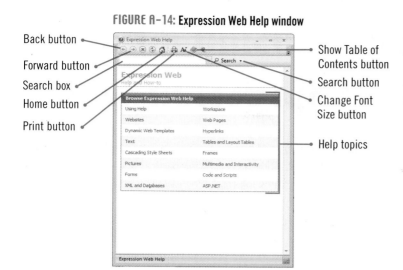

FIGURE A-15: Results for search on "status bar"

Words searched on

Next button

Page information indicates 2 pages of help are available, and Page 1 is currently displayed

Number of topics found for search term

In Step 3, click this topic

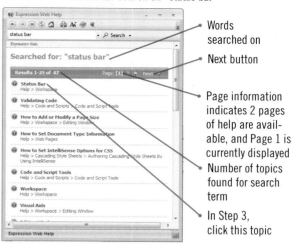

FIGURE A-16: Status Bar help topic

In Step 5, click the Workspace link in this breadcrumb trail

Status Bar information

Links to related topics

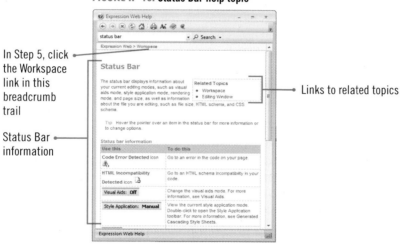

FIGURE A-17: Showing the table of contents in the Help window

Hide Table of Contents button

Table of Contents

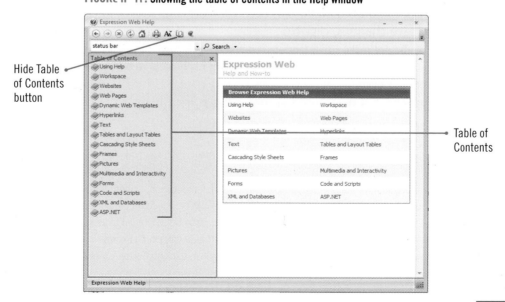

Expression Web

Printing and Closing a Page and Exiting Expression Web

Expression Web lets you print a Web page as it will look when printed in a browser. Printing is useful if you want to be able to mark up a page with design comments. When printing from Expression Web or from a browser, background colors and images do not print. (Printing a copy of the page as it looks in Design view or when previewed in a browser would strain your printer's ink resources.) When you launch Expression Web, it opens the last Web page or site you were working on, so it's a good idea to close your Web page or site before you exit Expression Web. That way if you are sharing a computer with others, Expression Web won't try to open files that might no longer be available (if, for instance, the files are stored on a flash drive that's been removed from the computer). 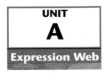 You are finished reviewing the TradeWinds site, so you decide to print and close the TradeWinds home page and exit Expression Web.

STEPS

1. **Click File on the menu bar, then point to Print**

   The Print submenu opens displaying the commands Print, Print Preview, and Page Setup, as shown in Figure A-18. Clicking Print opens the Print dialog box and prints the Web page as it would print from the Internet Explorer browser. Clicking Print Preview shows you what the page will look like when printed. Clicking Page Setup gives you options to change the page margins and the header and footer. By default, the page title prints in the header and the page number prints in the footer. You can replace these with your own text if you'd like.

2. **Click Print Preview on the Print submenu**

   The Print Preview window opens, displaying a preview of the Web page, as shown in Figure A-19. This view shows you what your page will like when printed. In this mode, background colors and background images do not appear, although regular images such as the fish fountain do appear. Using the buttons on the Print Preview toolbar, you can print the page, close Print Preview, navigate between pages if the Web page will span more than one printed page, and zoom in on the page.

3. **Click Print at the top of the Print preview window**

   The Print dialog box opens.

4. **Click OK in the Print dialog box**

   The page prints. Print Preview closes and you return to the editing window in Design view.

5. **Click File on the menu bar, then click Close as shown in Figure A-20; if you are prompted to save changes, click No**

   You did not make any intentional changes to this page, so you do not need to save changes. The Web page closes. The title bar now displays "Microsoft Expression Web," indicating that no Web page or Web site is currently open.

6. **Click File on the menu bar, then click Exit**

   Expression Web closes.

Saving and closing files

If you try to close a Web page that you have made changes to, a message box opens asking if you want to save your changes. If you click Yes and the page has been saved previously, Expression Web saves your changes to the file. If you click Yes and the file has not been saved previously, Expression Web opens the Save As dialog box so that you can save a copy of the file with a different filename, in a different location, or both. This is useful when you want to create a new Web page that contains text or design elements from a previous page but you need to keep the original file intact. If you click No in the message box, Expression Web closes the file, and any changes are lost. Clicking Cancel cancels the closing of the Web page and returns you to the Expression Web workspace.

FIGURE A-18: Print submenu

Print submenu

FIGURE A-19: Print preview of TradeWinds home page

Close button

Print button

Page title prints
in header by
default

Zoom In button

Page is white
because background
colors and images
do not print

Page number
prints in footer
by default

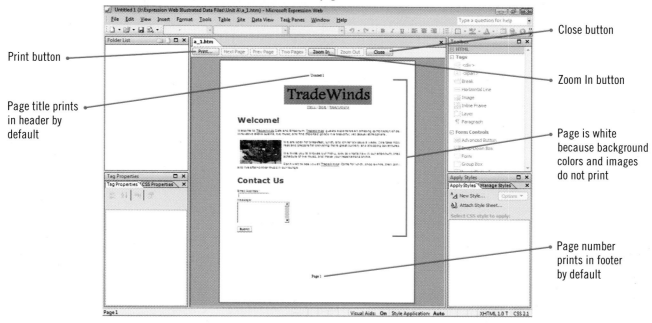

FIGURE A-20: File menu

Close command

Practice

If you have a SAM user profile, you may have access to hands-on instruction, practice, and assessment of the skills covered in this unit. Log in to your SAM account (http://sam2007.course.com/) to launch any assigned training activities or exams that relate to the skills covered in this unit.

▼ CONCEPTS REVIEW

Label each element in the Expression Web workspace shown in Figure A-21.

FIGURE A-21

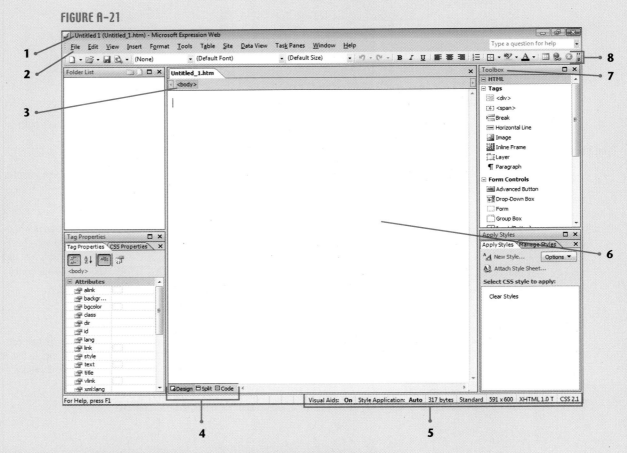

Match each term with the statement that best describes it.

9. **Task pane**

10. **Menu bar**

11. **Editing window**

12. **Common toolbar**

13. **Code View**

14. **Quick tag selector bar**

15. **Design View**

a. Displays the HTML code for the active Web page

b. Displays the active Web page as it will look in a Web browser

c. Allows you to select individual HTML tags

d. Small window that provides access to tools for specific tasks

e. Includes all the Expression Web commands

f. Provides access to common tasks and formatting options

g. Main area where you edit Web pages

Select the best answer from the list of choices.

16. **The ability to see what your Web page would look like in a browser as you edit it is called:**
    a. Cascading Style Sheets.
    c. WYSIWYG.
    b. Visual aids.
    d. Editing window.

17. **The name of the toolbar that is open by default in Expression Web is:**
    a. Formatting.
    c. Code View.
    b. Common.
    d. Standard.

18. **Copying Web site files from your computer to a Web server is called:**
    a. Publishing.
    c. Code View.
    b. Developing.
    d. Hyperlinking.

19. **A computer that stores and displays Web pages and other content is a:**
    a. Web browser.
    c. Web site.
    b. Web standard.
    d. Web server.

20. **Rules that describe the presentation and formatting of a Web page are:**
    a. Cascading Style Sheets.
    c. HTML files.
    b. JavaScript files.
    d. Image files.

▼ SKILLS REVIEW

1. **Start Microsoft Expression Web and explore the Expression Web workspace.**
   a. Launch Expression Web.
   b. If a Web site opens automatically, close it.
   c. Locate the title bar.
   d. Locate the menu bar.
   e. Locate the Common toolbar.
   f. Locate the editing window.
   g. Locate the status bar.

2. **Open a Web page and preview it in a browser.**
   a. Open the Open File dialog box.
   b. Navigate to the drive and folder where you store your your Data Files, then double-click a_2.htm in the Unit A folder. Your screen should resemble Figure A-22.
   c. Preview the page in the Internet Explorer browser in an 800 × 600 window. If this option is not available on your computer, choose a different resolution.

3. **Work with views and task panes.**
   a. Switch to Code view.
   b. Switch to Split view.
   c. Switch to Design view.
   d. Maximize the Tag Properties task pane.
   e. Restore the Tag Properties task pane.

4. **View Web page elements and visual aids.**
   a. Click anywhere in the first paragraph, then click the div#column_l tab on the quick tag selector bar.
   b. Click inside the text Why we're different.
   c. Click the word Home near the top of the page.
   d. Click the photo of the man.

FIGURE A-22

Expression Web

▼ SKILLS REVIEW (CONTINUED)

5. Get help.

a. Open Expression Web Help.

b. Search for information on tables.

c. Click the Tables (Help >Tables and Layout Tables >Tables) link.

d. Read the information on the page.

e. Close the Expression Web Help window.

6. Print and close a page and exit Expression Web.

a. Use Print Preview to preview the page.

b. Print the page.

c. Close the Web page; do not save changes to the page.

d. Exit Expression Web.

▼ INDEPENDENT CHALLENGE 1

As part of your redesign of the TradeWinds Web site, you decide to review the music page. You need to view the current music page and start considering what changes you want to make.

a. Start Expression Web.

b. Open file a_3.htm from the drive and folder where you store your Data Files. Your screen should resemble Figure A-23.

c. Select elements on the page and notice the visual aids that appear. Select a table, an image, and an HTML heading.

FIGURE A-23

d. Close the Tag Properties task pane.

e. Move the Manage Styles task pane to the bottom-left of the screen.

f. Restore the workspace to its original layout.

g. Change the view to Split View.

h. Change the view to Design View.

i. Write down three changes you would make to improve the appearance and functionality of this page. These can include changes to the design, graphics, or content.

j. Close the Web page, then exit Expression Web.

▼ INDEPENDENT CHALLENGE 2

Note: This Independent Challenge requires an Internet connection.

You have been hired as a Web designer for *Get Real*, an online news magazine. Your manager, Rex Treger, has asked you to find ways to reduce the costs of running the Web site by making it easier to maintain. You have read a little about Web standards and think that redesigning the site to be more standards-compliant could help the company meet this goal. You also think that the company could benefit in other ways from applying Web standards.

a. Go to your favorite search engine and search on the term **Web standards business case**.

b. Find at least two good articles that describe the "business case" for Web standards—in other words, articles that describe how businesses can save money or benefit in other ways by building standards-compliant sites.

c. Write at least two paragraphs for your manager, explaining all the business benefits of using Web standards.

Advanced Challenge Exercise

■ Find additional articles explaining the reasons organizations don't build sites that comply with Web standards.

■ Based on your additional research, write a paragraph explaining why companies sometimes resist using Web standards. Write a paragraph expressing why you do or do not feel these are good arguments against using Web standards.

▼ INDEPENDENT CHALLENGE 3

Note: This Independent Challenge requires an Internet connection.

Designers today are creating beautiful sites using Cascading Style Sheets to control the design and layout. Many Web sites feature sample CSS-based designs, and Web designers often visit these gallery sites for inspiration. Most galleries feature snapshots of the sites and allow visitors to comment on the design. Hone your design skills by visiting some CSS-based Web sites and evaluating them.

  a. Go to your favorite search engine and type CSS design gallery.
  b. Follow some of the links until you find one or two sites that are galleries of CSS-based Web site designs. You may have to click a page called "gallery," "showcase," or something similar to find the Web site examples.
  c. Browse the thumbnail images and find two that catch your interest.
  d. Read any comments that visitors have written about both of the sites that you chose.
  e. Click the thumbnail images to visit both sites.
  f. Take notes about what you like or don't like about the design and content of both sites.
  g. Write a paragraph about each site that includes the topic of the site, who you feel the intended audience is, and what you liked and didn't like about the design.

Advanced Challenge Exercise

  ■ For each Web site, write a paragraph describing why you think the sites either deserve or don't deserve to be showcased in a CSS gallery.
  ■ For each Web site, write a description of the changes you would make if you were redesigning the site.

▼ REAL LIFE INDEPENDENT CHALLENGE

Note: This Independent Challenge requires an Internet connection.

Developing a Web site is a great way to publicize your business or hobby. For this challenge, you will build a Web site of your choosing. You will pick not only the topic but also the audience. You will start by evaluating the design of sites that cover the same subject or audience. Throughout this book, you will design and build the site.

This Real Life Independent Challenge will build from unit to unit, so you must complete the Real Life Independent Challenge in each unit to complete your Web site.

  a. Write down the topic and the audience for your Web site. Describe the audience's demographics—age, gender, interests, and any other important characteristics.
  b. Go online and find at least two sites that cover the same topic as the one you plan to design.
  c. Evaluate the page layout, navigation, content, color scheme, typography, and use of images, video, or animations.
  d. Write a paragraph describing which elements of the sites (from the preceding list) you felt were well-designed and which were poorly designed, and why.
  e. Find at least two sites that target the same audience as yours but cover a different topic. For example, if you are planning to develop a music site for women over age 40, find sites targeting this group but covering topics other than music.
  f. For the two sites with similar audiences, write two paragraphs discussing whether the color, layout, content, navigation, and use of imagery and multimedia were appropriate for the sites' intended audiences. Explain why they were appropriate or inappropriate for the audience.

▼ VISUAL WORKSHOP

Launch Expression Web. Create a new Web page. Rearrange your workspace to match Figure A-24. When you have finished, press [Print Screen], paste the image into a word-processing program, add your name at the top of the document, print the document, close the word processor without saving changes, then exit Expression Web. If you are prompted to save your changes, click No.

FIGURE A-24

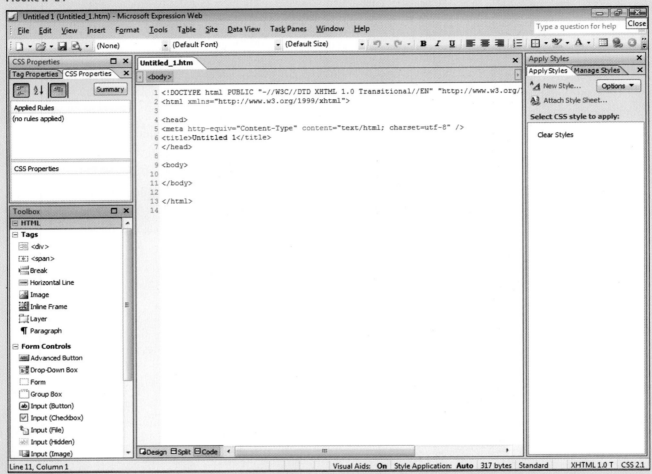

Creating a Web Site

Creating a Web site is a little like taking a trip. You could jump in the car and start driving, and hope you end up somewhere interesting. But if you have a particular goal in mind, like relaxing in a beachfront hut, you need to plan ahead; otherwise you could end up in a motel beside the highway, 500 miles from the nearest beach. The same holds true when creating a Web site. If you want the site to accomplish certain goals, such as selling products or sharing family photos, you need to do some planning and research up front. In this unit, you learn about the Web planning process and its role in developing a successful Web site. You also learn how to use the tools in Expression Web to create and manage a Web site and an individual Web page. You meet with Catalina Romera to discuss her expectations and goals for the TradeWinds site redesign, and begin developing the new site.

OBJECTIVES

Research and plan a Web site

Plan the page layout

Create a Web site

Create a Web page and set
   CSS options

Add a title, page description, and
   keywords

Manage Web pages

Add a folder to a Web site

Change the Web site view

Researching and Planning a Web Site

The Web site development process can be organized into six phases: research and plan, design, build, test, launch, and market, as shown in Figure B-1. By researching and planning a site before you begin building it, you can use the information to guide your design decisions along the way. ▓▓▓▓▓ You meet with Catalina several times to better understand her business goals. After some additional research, you create a plan for the site.

DETAILS

Developing a Web site involves these steps:

- **Research and plan the site**

  Identifying the goals for your Web site drives the entire research and planning process. To identify your goals, you need to consider the goals of the site owner and those of the site visitor. For example, your new design should satisfy Catalina's goals to promote live entertainment and new products, and her visitors' goals of getting directions and contact information.

  Next, learn as much as possible about your intended audience. Table B-1 describes some methods you can use to gather information about your audience before, during, and after the design process. While not every visitor to the TradeWinds Web site shares identical traits, Catalina's market research reveals that most site visitors are age 30 to 55, and that many access the site using a dial-up connection.

  Based on your analysis of the site's goals and audience, decide what features are important. You decide the TradeWinds site will include the following features: a section on the store page highlighting new products, a schedule of live music, and a section on the home page to promote products and/or events.

- **Design the site**

  You should consider the characteristics of both the business and the audience when designing a site's look and feel. For example, an insurance company site is likely to use a conservative design, while a music site geared toward teens might have a wild color scheme and an irreverent tone. You want the TradeWinds design to look polished and worldly, yet fun and casual.

  The next stage involves creating a **site map**, a diagram depicting how a Web site's pages are related within the site. The TradeWinds site map is shown in Figure B-2. Finally, design the **page layout**, the placement of content, graphics, and navigation on each page in the site.

- **Build and test the site**

  If you've followed a thoughtful planning process, you should be in good shape when you actually create the site and each page within Expression Web. Site building also includes writing the content and creating or gathering graphics.

  It is critical to test your site before you publish it. Although Design view in Expression Web approximates the way a site will look in a browser, the only way to really know how it looks is to view the site in each individual browser. You should test it on different browsers, different screen sizes, and different operating systems (Mac and PC), at different connection speeds, and, if possible, on handheld devices and cell phones.

- **Publish and market the site**

  When you are satisfied that your site is ready, you publish it to a Web server so visitors can access the site.

  After your site has been published, you can promote it so that you attract visitors. Registering the site with search engines, placing ads online or in print, and asking for links from other sites are all effective ways to market a Web site.

FIGURE B-1: Steps in the Web site development process

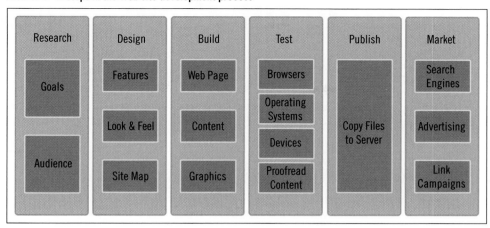

FIGURE B-2: TradeWinds site map

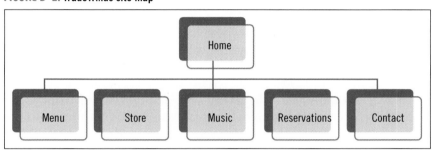

Organizing your site

Most sites are organized based on topic, audience, task, or date. Don't be too inventive when organizing your site; familiarity usually serves your purposes here better than originality. You want to use a structure that orients visitors right away, so they can find what they need easily. It can be helpful to visit similar sites and see how they are structured before you develop your site map. Be sure to include navigation that allows visitors to easily move back and forth between sections and pages of the site as well as a link back to the home page.

TABLE B-1: Methods of profiling a Web site audience

method	description	good for finding out...
Focus group	In-person discussion with a small group of current or potential Web site visitors	Subjective information about visitors' attitudes and initial reactions to site designs and features
Visitor survey	Questionnaire distributed to site visitors	Demographics and technology use, like/dislike of site features and design
Market research	Research published by companies describing a particular target market or trends in a specific industry	Big-picture data about the market or audience
Traffic analysis	Use of traffic analysis software to track how visitors interact with your site	How visitors use your site, what areas of your site are the most popular, what browsers and screen sizes visitors use

Expression Web

Planning the Page Layout

Once you have planned the overall structure, design, and content of the entire Web site, you need to plan the layout of the individual pages. Your design of each page should reflect and support your goals for the site. ▨▨▨▨ Catalina is pleased with the Web site plan you developed. Now she wants to see what the individual Web pages will look like. You reach for a paper and pencil and start sketching potential layouts for the TradeWinds site.

DETAILS

When designing the Web page layout:

QUICK TIP

After you've sketched your design on paper, you can use a graphics editing program to draw your sketch electronically, and use the file as the basis for designing the images for your site.

- **Sketch it on paper first**

  It can be tempting to immediately start Expression Web and begin laying out a page, but the best tools for planning your page layout are paper, pen or pencil, and your brain. Turn the paper sideways to approximate a computer screen and start drawing. By sketching on paper first, you can quickly and easily refine your ideas. Once you're happy with the design, you can start working in Expression Web to create the layout. Figure B-3 shows your planned layout for the TradeWinds home page.

- **Draw on existing conventions**

  When people pick up a book, they don't have to think about how the book works. They expect it to be bound on the left, to have page numbers at the top or bottom, to have a table of contents in the front and an index in the back. Research has shown that people have developed certain expectations of Web sites, too. They expect to find the logo and the link to the home page in the top left, internal links and navigation on the left, the search engine in the top right, and Contact us link, which usually contains copyright and contact information, at the bottom, as shown in Figure B-4. You can instantly make people feel comfortable in your site by using these design conventions and placing elements where visitors expect them to be.

QUICK TIP

Very large sites sometimes do vary their color schemes from section to section, essentially creating several smaller sites within the larger one. But for small to medium-sized sites, it's best to be consistent.

- **Be consistent**

  Using a consistent design and navigation scheme helps visitors quickly learn to use your site. Place elements in the same spot on every page, and maintain a consistent color scheme. Your site should "hang together" visually.

- **Keep it simple**

  Work toward a simple, clean design that shows off your content and lets visitors accomplish their tasks.

- **Focus on navigation**

  If visitors can't find what they want on your site, they will leave. With so many sites online, they may find a competitor's site and never come back to yours. Design effective navigation that orients your visitors and helps them find what they need. Label your navigation clearly with terms that visitors will understand.

- **Decide on a size**

  There are essentially two approaches to Web page size—fixed and liquid. A **fixed page design** means that the page is the same width on every visitor's computer no matter how large their screen is. A **liquid page design** shrinks or expands to fit the size of the visitor's screen. Each option has its pros and cons, but liquid designs can be more difficult to implement. If you want to use a fixed design, you need to decide what screen resolution to target.

Using basic page layouts

The Web is a very boxy place. Because of the rectangular nature of HTML elements and digital images, Web page layouts are almost always based on a grid pattern. Some basic layouts are used repeatedly because they work well and are easy to navigate. For example, most Web pages include a masthead running along the top of the page, internal navigation in a column on the left, content in the middle, and perhaps a third column on the right. A footer at the bottom often contains copyright information and text links to contact information, privacy policies, and other information. Even sites that look very different at first glance usually use an embellished version of this same basic layout.

FIGURE B-3: Sketch of TradeWinds Web page layout

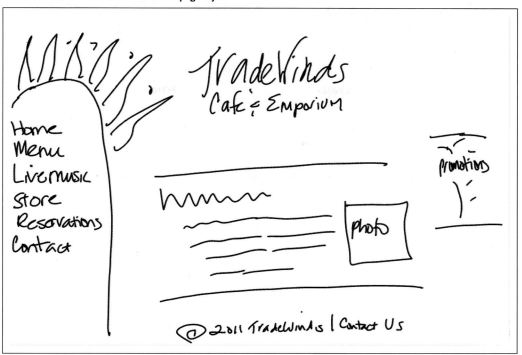

FIGURE B-4: Basic page layout structure familiar to Web visitors

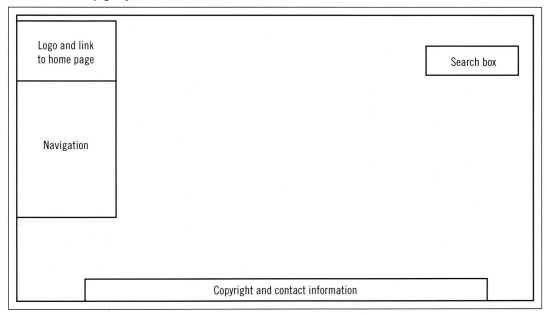

Avoiding a dated design

It can be fun to jump on the latest design fad to give your site that up-to-the-minute look. But trendy designs often don't wear well. What is cool today could be considered "so 2010" in just a few years. Some Web design crazes that have come and gone include blinking text, hit counters, rainbow-colored horizontal bars, heavily beveled buttons, heavy drop shadows, "splash" pages that open before the actual home page, distracting background patterns, "under construction" signs, and pages with tiny fonts and dashed content borders. Ouch. Don't let this happen to you. For a professional-looking site that's easy to use, stick to clean, simple, attractive designs that stand the test of time. If you want to step back in Internet time, visit the Wayback Machine at http://www.archive.org where you can see literally billions of archived Web pages dating from 1996 to the present.

Creating a Web Site

The first step in building your site is to create a Web site in Expression Web to organize your files, including HTML files, CSS files, and images, into a root folder. The **root folder** is a folder on your hard drive, USB drive, or network drive that stores all the files that make up your site. Expression Web includes three options for creating sites. You can create a simple Web site with one blank page, an empty Web site to which you can add your own pages, or an entire Web site at once based on templates that generate all the pages of the site for you. ▰▰▰▰ You look through the Web site templates in Expression Web and decide they don't fit your needs for the TradeWinds site. You create a new empty Web site and root folder in Expression Web for the TradeWinds site, to which you can add your own pages later.

STEPS

TROUBLE

If a Web site is already open in Expression Web, click File on the menu bar, then click Close Site.

1. **Start Expression Web, click File on the menu bar, point to New, then click Web Site**

   The New dialog box opens. See in Figure B-5. It includes a Web Site tab for creating a new Web site and a Page tab for creating a new Web page. Because you clicked the Web Site command, the Web site tab is in front.

2. **Click General in the list on the left, if it is not already selected**

   The left area lists two categories, General and Template. The right area lists the types of new sites available for the current category. The General category includes three types of sites: a One Page Web Site, an Empty Web Site, and the Import Web Size Wizard, which lets you import an existing set of Web site files. If you click the Templates category, you can create a Web site using one of the available templates.

3. **Click Empty Web Site in the list in the middle of the dialog box**

   The Description in the right area explains that this option creates an empty Web site, with nothing in it.

QUICK TIP

If you store your Web site files on a USB drive, remember to back them up somewhere else, too, such as onto your home computer, a second USB drive, or a school server, so that if you lose your drive or it fails, you have a copy of the files.

4. **Click Browse next to the Specify the location of the new Web site box**

   The New Web Site Location dialog box opens.

5. **In the New Web Site Location dialog box, navigate to the location where you store your Data Files, then click Open**

   You return to the New dialog box.

6. **Click at the end of the text in the Specify the location of the new Web site box, type tradewinds, then compare your screen to Figure B-6**

   When naming any files or folders that are part of your Web site, use all lowercase, no spaces, and no characters except numbers, letters, or underscores. If you don't follow these rules, your Web pages may not work when you publish them to the server.

7. **Click OK**

   Expression Web creates a folder named tradewinds in the location you specified and a new Web site within the new tradewinds folder. The Create New Web Site window opens, then closes quickly. The new Web site files appear in the Folder List task pane, and a Web Site tab is added to the editing window, as shown in Figure B-7.

Using Expression Web templates to build a site

The Templates category in the Create New Web Site dialog box includes 19 Web site templates that allow you to build a complete site in a matter of minutes. Expression Web includes six templates for sites for organizations such as clubs, seven for personal sites, and six for small business sites. Each template adds different types of pages that are appropriate to the site's purpose, such as news and calendar pages for the organization site, or resume and photo gallery pages for a personal site. Creating a template-based site can be a good way to learn more about Expression Web. Be aware that the templates included with Expression Web are all based on **Dynamic Web Templates**, which help maintain a consistent design across the pages in a site and allow you to make changes across several pages in a site at once. However, working with them requires some familiarity with additional concepts and tools. To learn more about working with Dynamic Web Templates, refer to Expression Web Help.

FIGURE B-5: New dialog box

Page tab includes options for creating a new Web page

Web Site tab includes options for creating a new Web site

General category

Templates category

Location of root folder for Web site

Description of the type of Web site that will be created

Browse button

FIGURE B-6: New dialog box after choosing Web site type and location

General category selected

Your path will vary, but \tradewinds should appear at the end of the path

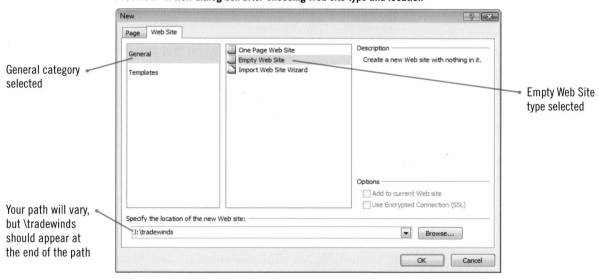

Empty Web Site type selected

FIGURE B-7: Creating a new Web site

Path to root folder

Folder List task pane showing path to tradewinds root folder

Web Site tab

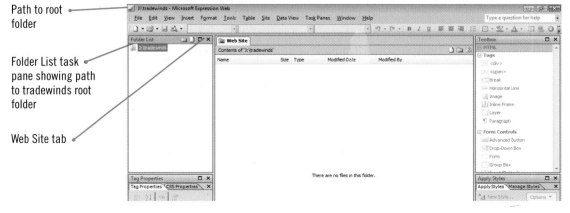

Expression Web

Creating a Web Page and Setting CSS Options

While creating the basic layout structure of Web pages is probably the least glamorous part of designing a Web site, it provides the foundation for the rest of your design. Structure can be created using layout tables, frames, or CSS positioning. Layout tables and frames are not recommended because they can cause problems for visitors with disabilities and those using handheld devices or cell phones. When you use **CSS positioning**, you create div elements in your HTML document, and then use style sheets to position them on the page. **Divs** are rectangular areas you can position on the page to hold your content, including text and images. It can be difficult to come up with a design that works well in all browsers, but Expression Web takes much of the work out of this process by including prestructured, browser-tested CSS page layouts. You are ready to create the page and decide to explore the available CSS layouts to see if there is one that works for your design. You also want to change some CSS options to make working with the style sheets more convenient as you build the rest of the site.

STEPS

TROUBLE
Be sure to click the first Header, nav, 2 columns, footer option and not the second one.

1. **Click File on the menu bar, point to New, then click Page**
   The New dialog box opens, with options for choosing a type of page, specific options for different page types, and a link for changing Page Editor Options.

2. **Click CSS Layouts in the list on the left, then click the first Header, nav, 2 columns, footer option in the list of layouts, as shown in Figure B-8**
   When you click a layout, the area on the right displays a description and preview of the current selection.

QUICK TIP
You can also access the CSS options by clicking Tools on the menu bar, clicking Page Editor Options, then clicking the CSS tab.

3. **Click the Page Editor Options link, click the CSS tab, then click Reset Defaults, as shown in Figure B-9**
   By resetting the defaults on the CSS tab of the Page Editor Options dialog box, you ensure that the only changes you make to these settings are the intended ones. When you change the Page Editor Options, all future sites you create in Expression Web will use those settings unless you change them.

QUICK TIP
You can also set the CSS Page Editor Options by right-clicking Style Application on the status bar, then click-ing CSS Options.

4. **Click the Page properties on the <body> tag list arrow, then click CSS (rules)**

5. **Click the Sizing, positioning, and floating list arrow, click CSS (classes), click OK, then click OK in the New dialog box**
   Expression Web creates two new files: an HTML file named Untitled_1.htm and a CSS (style sheet) file named Untitled_1.css. The HTML file contains the divs to hold the page content, while the CSS file contains style rules that describe how those divs should be positioned on the page. Expression Web also creates a link from the HTML file to the style sheet.

TROUBLE
If the page opens in Code view, click the Switch to Design View button.

6. **Click in the page_content div on the Untitled_1.htm page, as shown in Figure B-10, then type Welcome to TradeWinds**
   A visual aid appears when you click in the div, indicating that this div is named page_content.

7. **Click File on the menu bar, click Save, navigate to the folder and drive where you created your root folder, click the root folder (named tradewinds), click Open, then click Save**
   Expression Web recognizes that this is the first page you are saving in the Web site, so it fills in default.htm in the File name box, indicating that this will be saved as the **home page**, the first page a visitor sees when enter your Web site address in a browser. You could change this, but since you want this file to be your home page, you don't need to. Expression Web also recognizes that the Untitled_1.css file is linked to your page, so it prompts you to save that as well. You don't want to use the default file name for this file.

8. **Type twstyles.css in the File name box, then click Save**
   Expression Web saves the default page and the twstyles style sheet in your root folder, and the Save As dialog box closes.

FIGURE B-8: New dialog box

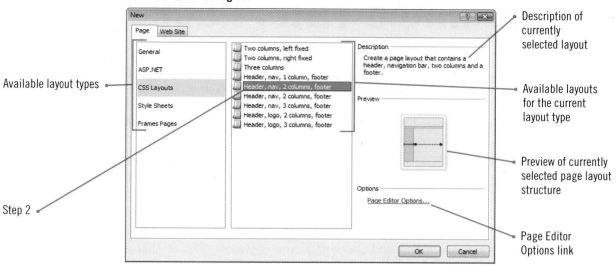

Description of currently selected layout

Available layout types

Available layouts for the current layout type

Step 2

Preview of currently selected page layout structure

Page Editor Options link

FIGURE B-9: Page Editor Options dialog box with CSS tab open

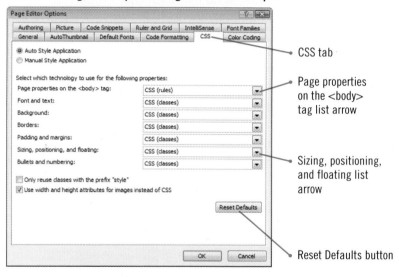

CSS tab

Page properties on the <body> tag list arrow

Sizing, positioning, and floating list arrow

Reset Defaults button

FIGURE B-10: Finished page with page_content div selected

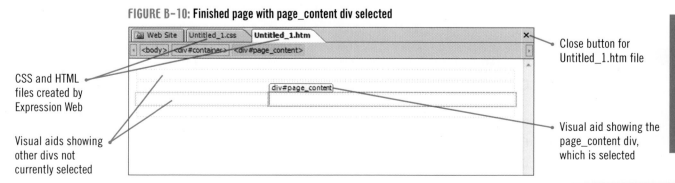

Close button for Untitled_1.htm file

CSS and HTML files created by Expression Web

Visual aids showing other divs not currently selected

Visual aid showing the page_content div, which is selected

Adding a Title, Page Description, and Keywords

The title, description, and keyword elements help visitors find your Web site. The contents of the **title** element are not displayed on the page itself; they appear in the title bar of the visitor's browser and as the title in a browser's list of favorites or bookmarks if a visitor has added it to that list. The description and keywords are used by some search engines to help determine what your site is about. Search engine results often display the contents of the title element as the link to your site and the **description** element as the description below the link. The description should be a brief explanation of what visitors can find at your site. It should motivate them to visit. **Keywords** are a list of terms, separated by commas, that describe the content of your site. You should try to anticipate which search terms related to your site visitors would enter in a search engine, and use those as your keywords. After consulting with Catalina and researching potential search terms, you come up with a description and keywords for the TradeWinds site. You use the Page Properties feature in Expression Web to add them to your basic Web page.

STEPS

TROUBLE

Select the page's tab in the editing window, not the page in the Folder List task pane.

1. **Click the default.htm tab in the editing window to make it the active tab**

2. **Click File on the menu bar, then click Properties.**

   The Page Properties dialog box opens, as shown in Figure B-11. In the General tab of this dialog box, you can set properties such as a title, a description, and keywords for a page. You can use other tabs, such as Formatting and Advanced, to change additional aspects of the page, including the background and link colors, margins, and page language. In general, it is best to let style sheets manage most of these settings, rather than setting the options here.

QUICK TIP

You can also open the Page Properties dialog box by right-clicking in the editing window of an open page in Design View, then clicking Page Properties.

3. **Select the text Welcome to TradeWinds in the Title text box, press [Delete], then type TradeWinds Cafe and Emporium**

   The new text replaces the default title. When you save a file, Expression Web gives it a title based on the first text that appears on the page. However, you usually want to change this to a more useful page title. Unlike a file name, you can use spaces and capital letters in the title. File names are read by computers, so they need to follow the naming rules. Titles are read by people, so they should be reader-friendly and descriptive.

4. **Click in the Page description text box, then type Experience an amazing combination of delicious island cuisine, live music, and fine imported goods in a beautiful yet casual atmosphere.**

   This short yet interesting description will be displayed as the "blurb" under the site name on the search results page for some search engines.

5. **Type African art, global imports, beads, steel drum music, seafood in the Keywords text box, compare your screen to Figure B-12, then click OK**

   These are the keywords you and Catalina decide to focus on to bring visitors to the site.

6. **Click the Show Code View button at the bottom of the editing window**

   The title, description, and keywords do not show up on the page itself in Design view or when viewed in a browser. But when you look at the code view, as shown in Figure B-13, you see that they have been added to the HTML code, which means that search engines will be able to see them.

QUICK TIP

It's important to save your work frequently as you design a Web site. To save time, use the keyboard shortcut [Ctrl][S] to save the page you are currently editing.

7. **Click the Show Design View button at the bottom of the editing window**

   The page is displayed in Design view. An asterisk appears on the tab next to the file name, indicating that changes have been made to the page since the last time you saved it.

8. **Click the Save button 🖫 on the Common toolbar**

   Expression Web saves your changes to the file, and the asterisk next to the file name on the tab is removed.

FIGURE B-11: Page Properties dialog box

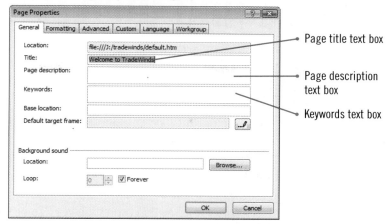

Page title text box

Page description text box

Keywords text box

FIGURE B-12: Page Properties dialog box with page properties added

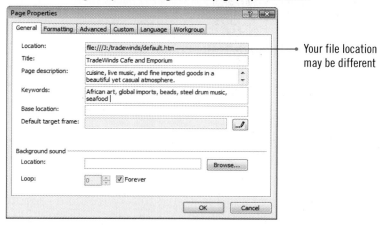

Your file location may be different

FIGURE B-13: Code view of TradeWinds home page

Title tag

Keywords tag

Description tag

Div tags created in the HTML by Expression Web

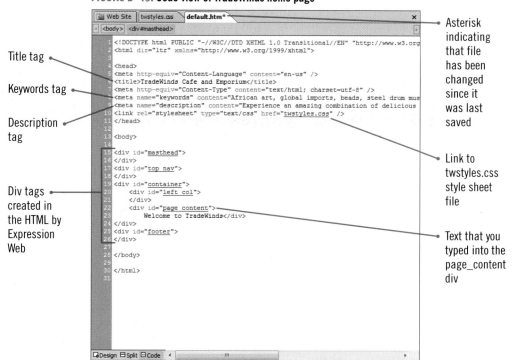

Asterisk indicating that file has been changed since it was last saved

Link to twstyles.css style sheet file

Text that you typed into the page_content div

Expression Web

Managing Web Pages

As you work with a Web site, you'll often find you need to create, delete, and rename pages. You should always perform these Web page management tasks within Expression Web rather than in Windows Explorer. You have learned to create a new page by using the Page command on the New submenu of the File menu. You can also create a copy of an existing page by using the **New From Existing Page** command. One of the advantages to creating an entire Web site in Expression Web, rather than just individual Web pages, is that Expression Web warns you if you delete files that have links to other pages, and will fix any links you may break by renaming or moving files. If you use Windows Explorer to move, delete, or rename any of your Web site files, you could end up with a messy site full of broken links that can take hours to fix. When you create, delete, or rename a page using Expression Web, you are making changes to the actual files on your disk, not just within Expression Web, so be careful when using these file management features. You have only created one page of the TradeWinds site, and the site map calls for several more pages to be developed. You decide to create the remaining pages for the TradeWinds site from the existing home page, since all the pages are structured like the home page.

STEPS

1. **Right-click default.htm in the Folder List task pane, then click New From Existing Page**
   A new page named Untitled_1.htm opens in the editing window, as shown in Figure B-14. The page is not saved in your Web site yet. Notice that the page has the same structure and text as the home page. There are now three pages open in the editing window. You can click the tabs at the top of the window to switch back and forth between the open pages.

2. **Click File on the menu bar, click Save, navigate to and open the root folder if necessary, click in the File name text box, type menu.htm to replace the text in the box, then click Save**
   Expression Web saves the file as menu.htm to your Web site, and the tab for this page displays the new file name.

3. **Repeat Steps 1 and 2 five times to add five more pages to the Web site, and save the pages to the root folder with the following file names: store.htm, lounge.htm, reservations.htm, contact.htm, and specials.htm**
   The editing window now shows eight open files, as shown in Figure B-15. If there are more tabs open than can fit on your screen, a torn edge appears on the leftmost tab to indicate there are additional open pages. You can use the Scroll Left and Scroll Right buttons to move among all the tabs.

4. **Click the Close button in the top-right corner of the editing window**
   The current page in the editing window, specials.htm, closes. Clicking the Close button on the editing window closes only the currently open page. Clicking the Close button on the program window closes the entire Web site.

5. **Click the Close button on the editing window seven more times**
   Each of the remaining open pages closes, and the Web site tab appears in the editing window in Folders view, as shown in Figure B-16. Catalina has just decided she does not want a Specials page on the Web site, so you need to delete the specials.htm file.

6. **Right-click specials.htm in the Folder List task pane, click Delete, then click Yes in the warning box**
   The specials.htm page is no longer listed in the Web site tab or the Folder List task pane, and the file is deleted from your disk or hard drive. You can also delete a file by right-clicking it in the Web site tab of the editing window. Files can be open or closed when you rename or delete them. You check the Web site plan and see that the page featuring live music should be named music.htm not lounge.htm, so you decide to rename the file.

7. **Right-click lounge.htm in the Folder List task pane, click Rename, type music.htm, then press [Enter]**
   The file is renamed to music.htm.

FIGURE B-14: New page open in editing window

Folder List task pane

default.htm

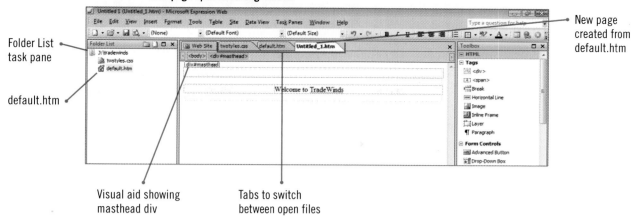

New page created from default.htm

Visual aid showing masthead div

Tabs to switch between open files

FIGURE B-15: Multiple pages open in editing window

New files created and saved in TradeWinds site

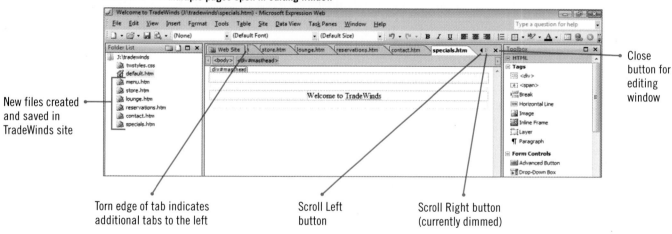

Close button for editing window

Torn edge of tab indicates additional tabs to the left

Scroll Left button

Scroll Right button (currently dimmed)

FIGURE B-16: Web Site tab open in editing window

lounge file

specials file

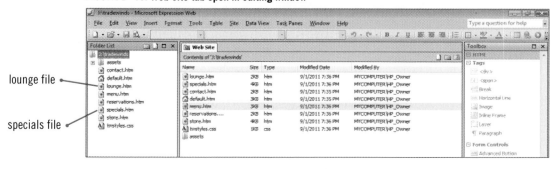

Adding a Folder to a Web Site

As you build a Web site, you accumulate many files. In addition to the HTML files for the Web pages themselves and the CSS files, you may have image files, animation files, video files, sound files, and more. These media files are known as **assets**. It's smart to create a subfolder in the root directory to hold assets and keep them separate from your HTML files. A good start is to create one general assets folder. Large sites may have several assets folders, each named differently—one for images, another for video files, another for sounds, and so on, but for a small site, one assets folder is usually sufficient. As with other Web page management tasks, you should always create new folders for your Web site in Expression Web rather than in Windows Explorer. You plan to add images and other media files to the TradeWinds Web site, so you decide to create an assets folder for these files.

STEPS

QUICK TIP
You can also create a new folder by clicking the New Folder icon. First be certain you have used the Folder List task pane to select the location in which you want the new folder to be created.

1. **Right-click the path of the root folder in the Folder List task pane, as shown in Figure B-17**

2. **Point to New, then click Folder**
   A new folder is created and the temporary name New_Folder is highlighted so that you can immediately replace it by typing a new name. Whenever you add a new folder, Expression Web creates it within the folder you have selected on the Folder List task pane.

TROUBLE
If the temporary folder name is not highlighted, right-click the new folder, click Rename, then type the new name.

3. **Type assets, then press [Enter]**
   The assets folder now appears in the Folder List task pane, as shown in Figure B-18, and in the list in the Web site tab of the editing window. As you build your site, you will save any files that are not HTML, CSS, or dynamic page files in this folder. See Table B-2 for a description of the typical files in a Web site and their file extensions.

TABLE B-2: Web site file types

file type	description	common file extensions
HTML	HTML pages	.htm, .html
CSS	Cascading Style Sheets	.css
Dynamic	Pages that use a combination of HTML and other languages to display information from a database within a Web page	.aspx, .asp, .jsp, .php, .cfm
Graphics	Photos, illustrations, or other images for a Web site	.jpg, .jpeg, .gif, .png
Audio	Files that play sound when a page loads or that visitors can click to play or download to their computers	.mp3, .mp4, .wav, .ram, .rm, .mid, .midi
Video	Files that play video when a page loads or that visitors can click to play or download to their computers; video files may also include audio	.avi, .mov, .qt, .mpg, .mpeg, .ram, .rm, .flv, .wmv, .mp4
Animation	Animated images such as blinking ad banners or moving illustrations; animated images don't include audio	.swf, .gif

Expression Web

FIGURE B-17: Create new folder in Folder List task pane

Path to root
directory;
your path
will differ

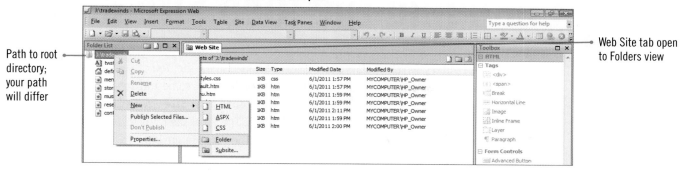

Web Site tab open
to Folders view

FIGURE B-18: Folder List task pane with assets folder

List of all files currently
saved in TradeWinds
Web site

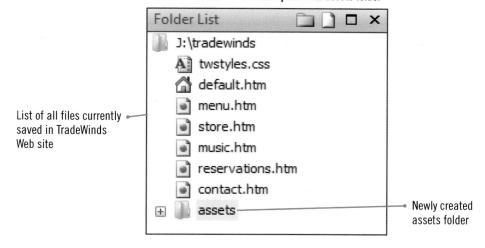

Newly created
assets folder

Understanding Web site addresses

Web site addresses are also known as URLs. The term **URL** stands for Uniform Resource Locator. A URL is made up of a domain name, a file name, and sometimes folder names. A **domain name** is a name that identifies a particular Web site. For example, the Web site for a school named Central University might be centraluniversity.edu. The three letters after the period indicate what type of site it is or from what country the site originates. For example, .edu indicates an educational institution, .org indicates a nonprofit organization, and .ca

indicates that the site originates in Canada. If the Web page with information about library hours at Central University was named hours.htm and was in a subfolder named library, the entire URL for that page would be www.centraluniversity.edu/library/hours.htm. Because file and folder names make up part of the URL, it's important to choose short file names that are descriptive. Try to avoid unnecessarily long URLs such as www.centraluniversity.edu/maincampuslibraryfiles/hours_we_are_open.htm.

Changing the Web Site View

When the Web Site tab is open in the editing window, you can view the current Web site four different ways. The default view is **Folders**, which displays a list of files and folders in the site. You can use this to navigate your site to locate files. It looks similar to the Folder List task pane but includes some additional information such as the file size and type as well as the last modified date. The **Remote Web Site** view displays a dual list of files, those on the local Web site and those on the remote Web site. The **local** site is the folder on your hard drive, USB drive, or network drive that contains your Web site files. The **remote** site is the folder on the Web server that contains your Web site files once you publish them. You must have a remote connection set up to use this view. The **Reports** view provides an overview of available Web site reports, with links to some reports to allow you to drill down for more details. You can view reports of broken hyperlinks, slow pages, recently changed pages, and more. The **Hyperlinks** view illustrates how one file is linked to other files in your site. ▓▓▓▓ You explore the different Web site views to learn more about the TradeWinds site.

1. **Click the Remote Web Site View button at the bottom of the editing window, as shown in Figure B-19**

   You switch to Remote Web Site View. Because you have not set up a remote Web site for this site, the message Click "Remote Web Site Properties…" to set up a remote Web site appears. This view is useful only after you have set up a remote site.

   > **TROUBLE**
   > If you do not see the Site Summary report, another report may have opened instead. If this happens, click the list arrow next to the current report name, then click Site Summary.

2. **Click the Reports View button**

   You switch to Reports view, as shown in Figure B-20. This view displays a Site Summary report, which lists basic information such as the number of files in the report. Many items in the list are links to more detailed reports. The report name, Site Summary, is shown just below the Web Site tab, and displays a small list arrow. You can click any of the links to view that particular report, or you can click the list arrow next to the report name to open a menu of all available reports. These reports will be more useful later, when the TradeWinds site is more fully developed.

3. **Click the Recently added files link in the Site Summary report**

   The Recently Added Files report opens, showing all files in the TradeWinds site created within the last 30 days. You can double-click any of the files to open them for viewing or editing.

   > **QUICK TIP**
   > The first time you use Reports view during a session, it opens to the Site Summary; the next time during the session you switch to Reports view, it opens to the last report you viewed.

4. **Click the list arrow next to the Recently Added Files report name, point to Problems, then click Unlinked Files**

   A report opens showing all files in the TradeWinds site that are not linked to any other pages in the site. As a general rule, you do not want any pages in your site that are not linked to the others, because visitors will not be able to access them. You take note that you will need to create links between all the Web site pages and run this report again later to make sure none were forgotten.

5. **Click the Hyperlinks View button at the bottom of the editing window**

   You switch to Hyperlinks view.

6. **Click the file twstyles.css in the Folder List task pane**

   The twstyles.css file opens in Hyperlinks view, as shown in Figure B-21. The TradeWinds style sheet is in the center, with the other Web site files on the left, pointing to the style sheet. This illustrates that all the pages in the site link to the style sheet.

7. **Click the Folders View button**

   You return to Folders view, which is the default view for the Web Site tab.

8. **Click File on the menu bar, click Close Site, click File on the menu bar, then click Exit**

   The Web site closes, and Expression Web closes.

FIGURE B-19: Switching Web site views

Hyperlinks View button

Reports View button

Remote Web Site View button

Folders View button

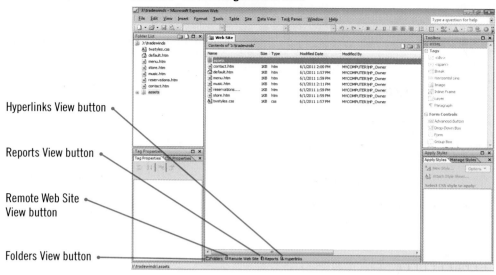

FIGURE B-20: Site Summary report open in Reports view

Current report name appears here

Links to more detailed reports

List arrow appears next to current report name (click to navigate among all reports)

Recently added files link

Reports View button is highlighted, indicating it is the active view

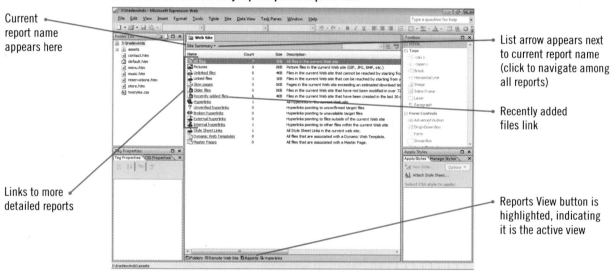

FIGURE B-21: Hyperlinks view

Indicates you are viewing hyperlinks for twstyles.css

twstyles.css file is selected

Arrows indicate links from HTML files to twstyles.css

Hyperlinks View button is highlighted, indicating it is the active view

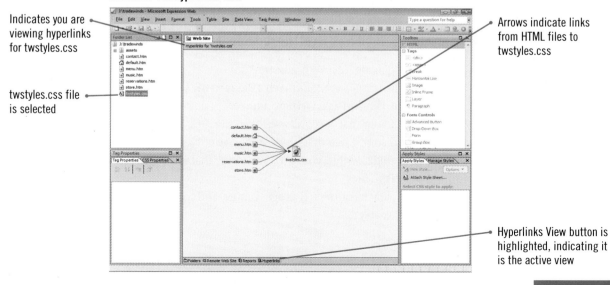

Practice

If you have a SAM user profile, you may have access to hands-on instruction, practice, and assessment of the skills covered in this unit. Log in to your SAM account (http://sam2007.course.com/) to launch any assigned training activities or exams that relate to the skills covered in this unit.

▼ CONCEPTS REVIEW

Label each element in the Expression Web window shown in Figure B-22.

FIGURE B-22

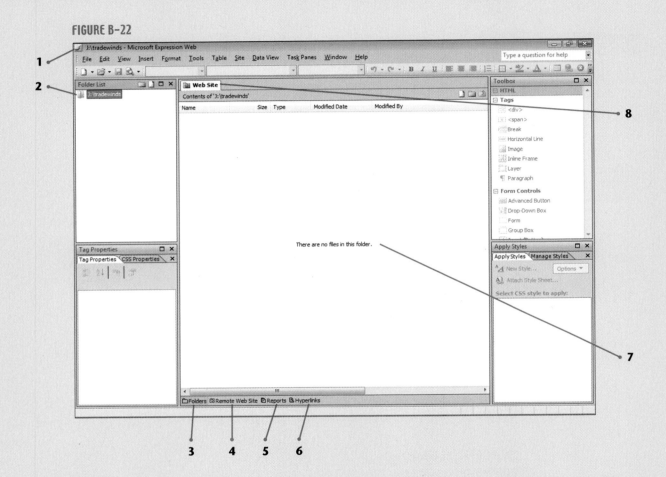

Match each term with the statement that best describes it.

9. URL
10. Div
11. Site map
12. Root folder
13. Asset folder
14. Demographics
15. default.htm

a. A diagram of a Web site structure
b. The name Expression Web assigns to the home page file of a Web site
c. Also known as a Web site address
d. A folder that holds all your Web site files
e. An empty area that holds Web page content
f. A folder within your Web site folder that holds image, sound, video, and other non-HTML files
g. Characteristics such as age, gender, and income level that identify a likely audience or market

Select the best answer from the list of choices.

16. What do visitors expect to find at the bottom of a Web site?

  a. Search box

  b. Home page link

  c. Contact us link

  d. Advertisements

17. In which Web site view can you see a report showing all the slow pages in your site?

  a. Hyperlinks view

  b. Reports view

  c. Folders view

  d. Remote Web Site view

18. What is the preferred method for creating a Web page layout?

  a. Tables

  b. CSS positioning

  c. JavaScript

  d. HTML

19. What is the first phase of the Web site development process?

  a. Build

  b. Design

  c. Test

  d. Research

20. A design that is the same width no matter what size screen the visitor's computer monitor has is called a:

  a. Fixed design.

  b. Narrow design.

  c. Liquid design.

  d. Table layout.

21. Which of the following are *not* allowed in a Web site file name?

  a. Lowercase letters

  b. Spaces

  c. Numbers

  d. Underscores

▼ SKILLS REVIEW

1. Create a new Web site.

  a. Launch Expression Web.

  b. Open the New dialog box.

  c. Switch to the Web Site tab if necessary, then click the General category if necessary.

  d. Create an Empty Web site in the drive and folder where your Data Files are stored. Name the root folder **careers**, then click OK to close the New dialog box.

2. Create a Web page and set CSS options.

  a. Open the New dialog box, then switch to the Page tab.

  b. Create a new page based on the second Header, Nav, 2 columns, footer layout in the CSS Layouts category. This is the layout with the narrower right column.

  c. Open the Page Editor Options dialog box, click the CSS tab, then click the Reset Defaults button.

  d. Change the Page properties on the <body> tag setting to CSS (rules). Change the Sizing, positioning, and floating setting to CSS (classes).

  e. Click OK to close the Page Options dialog box, then click OK to close the New dialog box.

  f. Click in the page_content div, then type **Welcome to Careers Guaranteed**. (*Hint*: The visual aid reads "div#page_content.") Compare your screen to Figure B-23.

  g. Save the Web page as **default.htm** and the style sheet as **cgstyles.css**.

3. Add a title, page description, and keywords.

  a. Open the Page Properties dialog box for the default.htm file.

  b. Click the General tab if necessary, then change the title to **Careers Guaranteed**.

FIGURE B-23

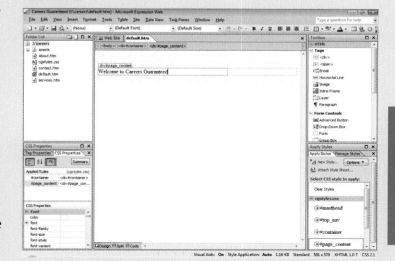

Expression Web

   c. Add the following page description: **At Careers Guaranteed, we only work with the best. We guarantee we will match you to a job position or we will refund your money.**.

   d. Add the following keywords: **careers, guaranteed jobs, job placement, career networking**. Click OK to close the Page Properties dialog box.

   e. View the page in Code view and find the title, keywords, and description tags.

   f. Switch back to Design view.

   g. Save your changes to the file.

4. Manage Web pages.

   a. Create pages based on the home page, using the New from Existing Page command. Save the new pages as **contact.htm**, **about.htm**, **jobs.htm**, and **history.htm**.

   b. Close all open files.

   c. Delete the history.htm file.

   d. Rename the jobs.htm file as **services.htm**.

5. Add a folder to a Web site.

   a. Create a new folder within the root folder.

   b. Name the new folder **assets**.

6. Change the Web site view.

   a. View the site in Remote Web Site view.

   b. View the site in Reports view.

   c. View the Recently Added Files report.

   d. View the Unlinked Files report.

   e. Switch to Hyperlinks view, then view the cgstyles.css file in hyperlinks view.

   f. Switch to Folders view, then compare your screen to Figure B-24.

   g. Close the Web site, then exit Expression Web.

FIGURE B-24

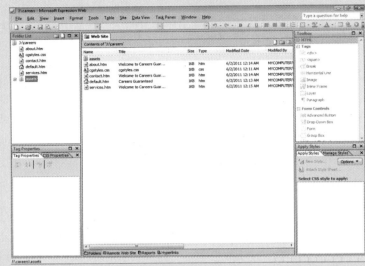

▼ INDEPENDENT CHALLENGE 1

You have been hired by Tiffany Harris, the marketing manager of a social networking business called ConnectUp, to design the ConnectUp Web site. The site's audience is made up of hip young professionals who want to network with people who can help them advance their careers and also become part of their social network. Tiffany wants a fresh look that will be attractive to their young and trendy audience.

a. Launch Expression Web, then create a new empty Web site in the folder and drive where your Data Files are stored. Name the root folder **connectup**.

b. Create a new Web page based on the Header, nav, 1 column, footer CSS layout.

c. Make this page the home page, and save the stylesheet as **custyles.css**.

d. Open the Page Editor Options dialog box for this page. Reset the defaults and change the Page properties on the <body> tag setting to CSS (rules). Change the Sizing, positioning, and floating setting to CSS (classes).

e. Add the text **ConnectUp** to the page_content div. (*Hint*: Use the visual aids to find the right div.)

f. Open the Page Properties dialog box using a command on the File menu. Change the page title to **ConnectUp**, add **Join thousands of young professionals who are Connecting Up to a better career and social life.** as the page description, and add **networking, careers, social networking, young professionals** as keywords. Save your changes to the page.

g. Create new pages for the site based on the home page. Name the new pages **joinup.htm**, **faq.htm**, and **contact.htm**.

h. Create an assets folder for the Web site.

i. Compare your screen to Figure B-25, then save changes to your files, close the Web site, and exit Expression Web.

FIGURE B-25

▼ INDEPENDENT CHALLENGE 2

You have been hired to create a Web site for Memories Restored, a company in Alberta, Canada that specializes in digital restoration of family photographs. Brian Edwards, the owner of the company, would like a site that showcases their photo restoration work and customer testimonials, educates visitors about the process of submitting a scanned or physical photo, and broadens their market reach beyond Alberta to other parts of Canada, the United States, and Europe. Many people are nervous about turning over their family photos to a stranger, so the Web site needs to present the business as credible and trustworthy. After doing some research and planning, you create a site map, shown in Figure B-26.

FIGURE B-26

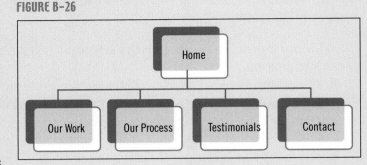

a. Create a Web site and root folder named **memories** in Expression Web for Memories Restored.

b. Create a new page based on the Header, logo, 2 columns, footer CSS layout. Change the Page Editor options to reset the defaults, then change the Page properties on the <body> tag setting to CSS (rules) and the Sizing, positioning, and floating setting to CSS (classes).

c. Click in the page_content div and type **Memories Restored**.

d. Save this page as the home page, and save the style sheet with an appropriate name.

e. Give the page a descriptive title. Add keywords and descriptions of your choosing.

f. Create four additional pages based on the default page. Use the site map as a guide in naming the pages, but remember to follow correct file naming rules.

Advanced Challenge Exercise

■ Create an additional page for the site that will feature tips for people who want to try to restore digital photos at home.

■ Save it with an appropriate name.

■ Give it an appropriate title, description, and keywords.

g. Create an assets folder.

h. Save your work, close the Web site, then exit Expression Web.

▼ INDEPENDENT CHALLENGE 3

Note: This Independent Challenge requires an Internet connection.

A local nonprofit organization, Technology For All, needs to redesign their Web site. The organization collects cast-off computers, repairs and upgrades them, and then donates the refurbished machines to low-income students. You have volunteered to help the organization by conducting a design audit. As part of the audit, you decide to research some new ways to organize the site. You posted a survey for Web site visitors, and many people wrote that the site was poorly organized and difficult to navigate. You know that the four most common ways to organize a Web site are based on topic or category, audience, task, and date. You want to examine some real-world examples of how designers implement these structures. You decide to start by more closely examining sites that you visit frequently.

a. Make a list of at least 10 Web sites you like to visit. Try to think of a mix of sites, including educational sites, news sites, shopping sites, entertainment sites, and corporate sites.

b. Visit the sites and spend a few minutes analyzing how each site is structured and how the navigation is organized. Write down which category of site organization the site fits into. Some sites may use a combination of methods.

c. Write a site survey based on your research. Choose one site from each site organization category you researched. For each site chosen, write the site name, URL, and one paragraph explaining why you think the site designer chose that method for organizing the site. Your document should include descriptions of four sites.

Advanced Challenge Exercise

■ Choose one of the sites that you think was poorly structured or could use improvement.

■ Write a paragraph explaining what is lacking in the structure and navigation.

■ Draw a site map or create an outline illustrating how you would restructure the site.

d.   Add your name to the document and print it.

▼ REAL LIFE INDEPENDENT CHALLENGE

This assignment builds on the personal Web site you started planning in Unit A. In this project, you will create a Web site in Expression Web, create your site pages, and add titles, keywords, and descriptions to your pages.

a. Write down at least three goals for your site.

b. Sketch a site map and page layout for your site.

c. In Expression Web, create a Web site and root folder.

d. Create a new Web page for your site, using one of the CSS layout options, and save it as the home page.

e. Add a title, description, and keywords to your home page.

f. Create the additional pages you will need based on your site map.

g. Create an assets folder to hold additional Web site files.

h. Begin collecting or creating content and images for your site.

i. When you are finished, close the Web site, then exit Expression Web.

▼ VISUAL WORKSHOP

Launch Expression Web. Create an empty Web site in the drive and folder where your Data Files are stored. Name the root folder **ecotours**. Create a Web page based on the Header, nav, 1 column, footer CSS Layout. Add a title, keywords, and a description. Save your home page and style sheet with the names shown in Figure B-27. Create the other Web pages with the file names shown, create an assets folder, then close all Web pages so your editing window matches the figure. When you have finished, press [Print Screen], paste the image into a word-processing program, add your name at the top of the document, print the document, close the word processor without saving changes, then exit Expression Web.

FIGURE B-27

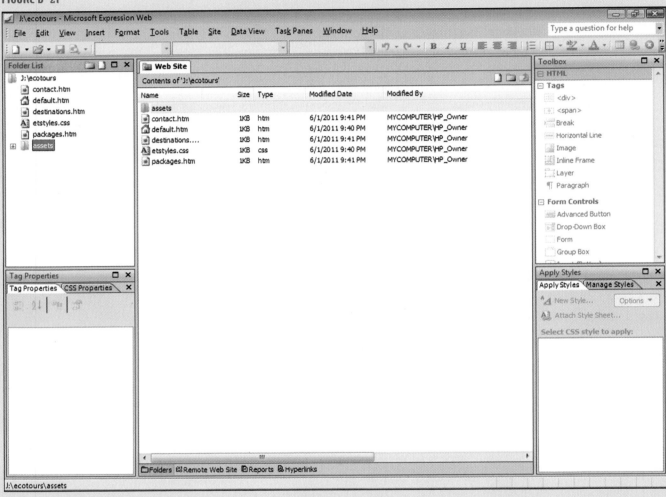

Adding Text and Links

Beneath the sophisticated layouts, colorful graphics, and engaging video, Web pages have a solid supporting foundation of text and links. You can add text to your Web page by typing it, by inserting the contents of a file, or by copying and pasting from another file. Text might not seem as exciting as other Web page elements, such as pictures or videos, but it's the work-horse of the Web. Whether your goal is to sell a product or provide information, text is still the simplest and most common way to communicate with Web site visitors. In fact, the Web originated as a way for scientists and researchers to exchange text-based documents. The inventors of the Web also came up with a way to navigate from one document to another— hyperlinks, also known simply as links. Links allow you to surf from one Web site to another or among pages in a single site; they're the glue that holds the Web together. Catalina has e-mailed you some content for the new TradeWinds site. You decide to add it to the Web pages you laid out earlier.

OBJECTIVES

Insert a text file into a Web page

Paste text into a Web page

Type text and insert symbols

Check spelling and use the thesaurus

Create an internal link

Create an external link

Create and link to a bookmark

Create an e-mail link

Copy and paste content between

pages

Inserting a Text File into a Web Page

You can save time by inserting the contents of an entire text file into your page. A **text file** has a .txt file extension and consists of basic text without formatting such as font faces, colors, and sizes; bold; or italics. This is an advantage when creating your Web page because you want to be able to control formatting through style sheets in Expression Web, rather than relying on the formatting generated in another program such as Microsoft Word.  You need to add several text files to the appropriate Web pages in the TradeWinds site.

STEPS

QUICK TIP

You should work in Design view when you add text, so you have more control over how text is added to the page.

1. **Launch Expression Web, open the** tradewinds **Web site from the location where you store your Data Files, then switch to Design view if necessary**

   The tradewinds Web site you created in Unit B opens in Design view.

2. **Double-click** default.htm **in the Folder List task pane or the Web site tab, then click in the** page_content div

   The page_content div is the main content container for your page. Any content or graphics that are not part of the navigation, footer, or masthead should be inserted in this div. See Figure C-1.

TROUBLE

Be careful when you add content to ensure that you add it to the correct div; use the visual aids and the quick tag selector to help verify that your cursor is correctly placed.

3. **Point to** <div#page_content> **on the quick tag selector bar, click the** <div#page_content> **list arrow, then click** Select Tag Contents

   This selects the contents of the div but not the div itself. Only the words should be highlighted.

4. **Press** [Delete]

   The text is deleted.

QUICK TIP

An asterisk appears next to the file name on the default.htm tab above the editing window, indicating that you have changed the file but not yet saved the changes.

5. **Click** Insert **on the menu bar, click** File, **then navigate to the drive and folder where you store your Data Files, as shown in Figure C-2**

6. **Open the** Unit C **folder, click the** Files of Type **list arrow (currently reads HTML Files (*.html,*.htm)), click** All Files (*.*), **then double-click** tw_home.txt

   The Paste Text dialog box opens. When you insert a text file, or when you copy and paste text, you can choose from five different options for how Expression Web brings the text in, as shown in Table C-1.

7. **Click** Normal paragraphs without line breaks **in the list of options, then click** OK

   The text is inserted into the Web page, as shown in Figure C-3.

TROUBLE

You can use Steps 2–7 as a guide when inserting this additional content.

8. **Replace the text in the page_content div of the following pages with the following files, using the Normal paragraphs without line breaks option:**

page	insert file
contact.htm	tw_contact.txt
music.htm	tw_music.txt
reservations.htm	tw_reservations.txt
store.htm	tw_store.txt
store.htm	tw_store.txt

9. **Click** File **on the menu bar, then click** Save All

   This command saves changes to all open files in the Web site.

FIGURE C-1: TradeWinds home page

Insert menu

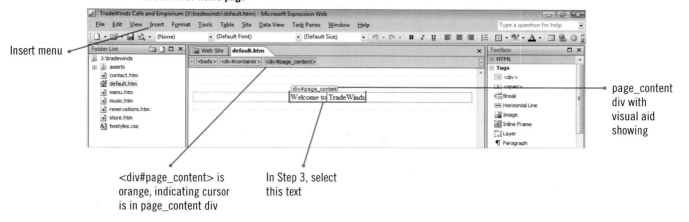

page_content div with visual aid showing

<div#page_content> is orange, indicating cursor is in page_content div

In Step 3, select this text

FIGURE C-2: Select File dialog box

Unit C folder

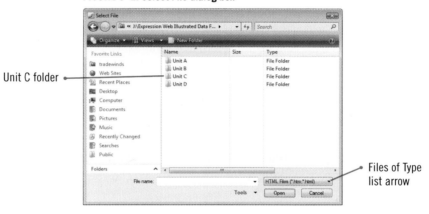

Files of Type list arrow

FIGURE C-3: The tw_home.txt file pasted as Normal paragraphs without line breaks

You will correct this error in a later lesson

TABLE C-1: Options for pasting text

option	what it does
Plain text	All text is pasted as one block with no line or paragraph breaks
One <pre> formatted paragraph	Places text in one paragraph surrounded by the <pre> HTML tag, which preserves all spacing within the paragraph; to avoid significant formatting conflicts, this option is not recommended
Many <pre> formatted paragraphs	Places text in more than one paragraph, each surrounded by the <pre> HTML tag, which preserves all spacing within the paragraph; to avoid formatting conflicts, this option is not recommended
Normal paragraphs with line breaks	Pastes text and replaces paragraph breaks with line breaks; to avoid formatting conflicts, this option is not recommended
Normal paragraphs without line breaks	Pastes text and preserves paragraph breaks but not line breaks; usually the safest option

Expression Web

Pasting Text into a Web Page

It's common for Web site content to be created in a Word processing program such as Microsoft Word and saved as a .doc or .docx file rather than as plain text. You can use Expression Web to insert a Word file into a Web page just as you insert a plain text file, but any formatting that was created in Word will also be inserted. This may seem like a time-saving step, but in fact, bringing Word formatting into your Web page can cause problems later. Word uses style sheets and HTML code to create the formatting; this can conflict with the styles you create and apply to your Web pages, causing unpredictable or undesirable results. The safest way to bring content from Word into a Web page is to copy it directly from the Word document and paste it into the Web page in Expression Web. When you paste text into a Web page, the **Paste Options button** offers several options for controlling how much, if any, formatting you wish to include with the text. Inserting a Word document using the File option on the Insert menu does not give you this same degree of control. ▓▓▓▓ Catalina has sent you a file with the content for the menu page in Microsoft Word format. You copy and paste the content from Word into Expression Web.

STEPS

1. **Open the menu page by double-clicking the menu.htm file name in either the Web Site tab or Folder List task pane**

   The menu page becomes the active page in the editing window.

TROUBLE

If Microsoft Word is not installed on your computer, consult your technical support person.

2. **Click in the page_content div, point to <div#page_content> on the quick tag selector bar, click the <div#page_content> list arrow, click Select Tag Contents, then press [Delete]**

   The page_content div is now empty.

3. **Launch Microsoft Word, open the Open dialog box, navigate to the drive and folder where you store your Data Files, double-click the Unit C folder, then double-click cafe_menu.doc**

   The cafe_menu.doc file opens in Microsoft Word. See Figure C-4. The text is heavily formatted with different font colors and sizes.

4. **Press [Ctrl][A] to select the text on the page, press [Ctrl][C] to copy the text, then click the Close button ☒ on the Word program window to exit Word**

   The text is copied to the **Windows clipboard**, a temporary storage area in your computer's memory. The formatting is copied along with the text. The cafe_menu.doc file closes and you return to the Expression Web workspace.

QUICK TIP

You can also paste by clicking Edit on the file menu, then clicking Paste, or by pressing [Ctrl][V].

▶ 5. **Right-click in the page_content div on the menu page, then click Paste**

   See Figure C-5. The text, along with the formatting, is pasted into the page_content div on the Web page. Notice the icon that appears under the pasted text. This is the Paste Options button.

TROUBLE

If you don't see the Paste Options button, click the Tools menu, click Page Editor Options, click the General tab, then check the box next to Show Paste Options buttons.

▶ 6. **Click the Paste Options button 📋, click Keep Text Only, click Normal paragraphs without line breaks, then click OK**

   See Figure C-6. The formatting is removed from the pasted text. The Paste Options button displays options that determine how much formatting is pasted along with the text; the available options depend on the program you copied the text from and the format of the text where you are pasting. See Table C-2 for information on commonly available options. Choosing Keep Text Only opens the Paste Text dialog box you used in the last lesson. Choosing Normal paragraphs without line breaks preserves the structure of your text by creating paragraph containers, but strips away the formatting. Later, you will create and apply styles in Expression Web to format the text.

7. **Save the page**

FIGURE C-4: cafe_menu.doc open in Microsoft Word

Text is heavily formatted with different sizes and font colors

Word program window Close button

FIGURE C-5: Content from cafe_menu.doc pasted into menu.htm

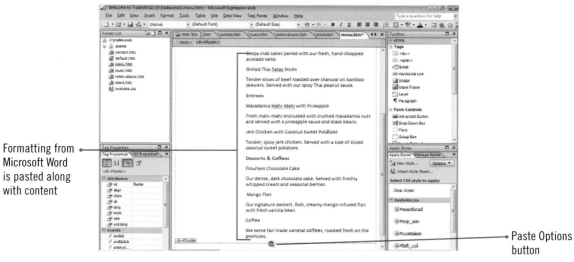

Formatting from Microsoft Word is pasted along with content

Paste Options button

FIGURE C-6: Content pasted from cafe_menu document

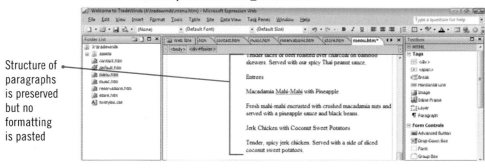

Structure of paragraphs is preserved but no formatting is pasted

TABLE C-2: Common Paste Options

option	what it does	when to use it
Match Destination Formatting	Pastes selection with formatting of the destination page, but also pastes some leftover formatting code from the source page	Only if you will not be adding your own styles
Keep Source Formatting	Pastes the selection with formatting of the source page	Only if you will not be adding your own styles
Remove Formatting	Removes most formatting and pastes selection as plain text; may leave behind some unintended code	Not recommended; can leave behind code that causes formatting conflicts
Keep HTML Only	Pastes the selection with any HTML code that was copied with it	Only if you are familiar with how the HTML was coded, since the extra code can create conflicts
Keep Text Only	Pastes the selection as plain text, and opens Paste Text dialog box	The safest option to use when you want to paste text with no formatting

Expression Web

Typing Text and Inserting Symbols

In addition to inserting files and copying and pasting from other files or programs, you can type and edit text directly in the page in Expression Web. You sometimes need to insert symbols in addition to regular text. For example, many Web sites include an area at the bottom of each page called the **footer**, which usually contains contact information and a copyright statement. Certain symbols and special characters, such as the copyright symbol, foreign letters, and scientific notation, cannot be typed using a standard keyboard; you can use the Symbol command on the Insert menu to easily add the characters to your page. Although you plan to add navigation buttons along the left side of the page, you want to add some text in the footer of the home page that will serve as text-based navigation. You also need to add a copyright statement to the page and fix the spelling of "café".

STEPS

TROUBLE

If you can't see the default.htm tab, click the Left Scroll Arrow until it comes into view.

1. **Click the default.htm tab to make that page active in the editing window**

2. **Insert your cursor in the footer div, type Home | Menu | Live Music | Store | Reservations | Contact Us, press [Enter], then type 2011 TradeWinds**

   Pressing [Enter] creates a new line. Compare your screen to Figure C-7. The vertical lines between the words are called **pipes**; usually, this symbol shares a key with the backslash symbol.

3. **Insert your cursor in front of the text 2011 you just typed, click Insert on the menu bar, then click Symbol**

   The Symbol dialog box opens, as shown in Figure C-8. The Font is automatically set to the font surrounding the insertion point, in this case Times New Roman. More symbols are available than are visible in the dialog box; you can use the scroll bar to find more symbols. To jump more quickly among sets of symbols, you can click the Subset list arrow and click a different subset.

TROUBLE

If the Symbol dialog box is in the way, click and hold the title bar of the Symbol dialog box, then drag it out of the way until you can see the text.

4. **Scroll down until you see the copyright sign (©), click ©, then click Insert**

   The symbol is inserted into your page. The Symbol dialog box remains open and the Cancel button changes to a Close button.

5. **Click Close on the Symbol dialog box, then press [Spacebar]**

   The Symbol dialog box closes and a space is added between the copyright symbol and 2011.

6. **In the first line of text in the page content div, select the e in Cafe, press [Delete], click Insert on the menu bar, then click Symbol**

   The "e" is deleted and the Insert Symbol dialog box opens.

QUICK TIP

Be sure to choose the lowercase e acute symbol and not the uppercase one.

7. **Scroll down and find the Latin small letter e with acute (é), click é, click Insert, click Close, then compare your screen to Figure C-9**

8. **Save the page**

Text-based navigation

Many Web sites use images linked to internal pages for navigation, often along the side or top of the page. It's also a good idea to include text-only navigation links at the bottom of each page that duplicate the image-based navigation found elsewhere. This text-based navigation can be helpful to visitors with disabilities and those accessing the site with handheld devices or cell phones. It also provides a convenient way to move to another page without having to scroll back up to the top of the current page. Text-only links also help search engines to find all the pages on your Web site so they show up in search results.

FIGURE C-7: TradeWinds home page with footer text added

In Step 3, insert cursor here

Text added to footer

FIGURE C-8: Symbol dialog box

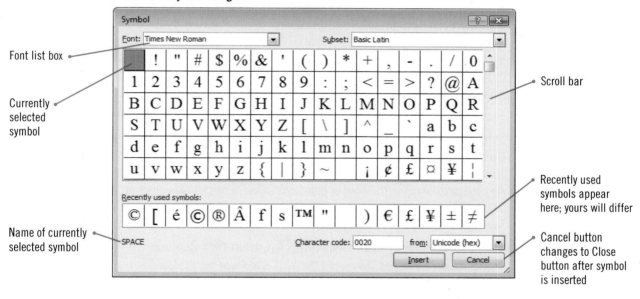

Font list box

Currently selected symbol

Name of currently selected symbol

Scroll bar

Recently used symbols appear here; yours will differ

Cancel button changes to Close button after symbol is inserted

FIGURE C-9: Home page after symbols are inserted

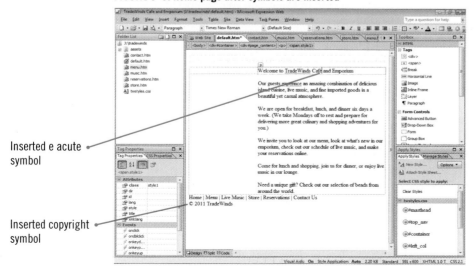

Inserted e acute symbol

Inserted copyright symbol

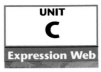

Checking Spelling and Using the Thesaurus

Visitors judge the credibility of a Web site not only on the design, but also on the quality and accuracy of the content. Expression Web has a robust spelling feature that can help you identify and correct spelling errors either on individual pages or in an entire Web site. If you have used the spell checking tools in Microsoft Office, you will be familiar with the Spelling feature in Expression Web. When you add text to a page, a wavy red line appears under any words that are not in Expression Web's dictionary, indicating a potential spelling error. The Thesaurus feature allows you to look up synonyms of a word or phrase and substitute them for your text. ▆▆▆▆▆ You noticed a few errors in the home page text, so you use the Spelling feature in Expression Web to correct them. You also decide to use the Thesaurus feature to help add variety to the wording of the text.

STEPS

1. **Right-click the word experince in the page_content div, as shown in Figure C-10**
   The shortcut menu offers alternatives to the misspelled word. It also displays options to Ignore All (if you want Expression Web to stop flagging this word as misspelled) and Add (if you would like to add this word as it is spelled to the custom dictionary). By default, Expression Web shares a custom dictionary with Microsoft Office, so any words you add to the dictionary in Office programs such as Word will also be used by the Expression Web dictionary and vice versa.

2. **Click experience on the shortcut menu**
   The shortcut menu closes and the word "experience" replaces the misspelled word.

QUICK TIP
You can also open the Thesaurus dialog box by using [Shift][F7].

3. **Select the words look at in the phrase look at our menu, click Tools on the menu bar, then click Thesaurus**
   The Thesaurus dialog box opens, as shown in Figure C-11. The Meanings list displays words or phrases that are close in meaning to the word or phrase you selected, in this case, "look at." When you choose an option in the Meanings list, more words and phrases with meanings similar to the selected word appear in the Replace list. You can choose one to replace the phrase.

QUICK TIP
To remove an added word from the custom dictionary, click Tools, point to Spelling, click Spelling Options, click Custom Dictionaries, click Edit Word List, select the word, click Delete, then click OK three times in the dialog boxes.

4. **Click explore (verb) in the Meanings list, then click Replace**
   The Thesaurus dialog box closes, and "look at" is replaced by "explore."

5. **Right-click the word TradeWinds, then click Add**
   Your page should look like Figure C-12. The word "TradeWinds" is added to the custom dictionary and will no longer be flagged as misspelled in Expression Web or any Office programs.

6. **Save your page**

Checking the spelling in an entire Web site

In addition to checking individual words on a page, you can check the spelling in a Web page or in an entire Web site at once. To check spelling in the current page, click Tools on the menu bar, point to Spelling, then click Spelling. To check spelling throughout all pages in a site, click the Web site tab to select it, click Tools on the menu bar, point to Spelling, then click Spelling. The Spelling dialog box opens, giving you the option of checking the spelling for selected pages or the entire site. If you choose the entire site, Expression Web displays a list of pages containing errors. Double-click the page name and Expression Web will open it and step through each possible error, allowing you to choose a replacement, ignore it, or add it to the custom dictionary. In addition to using the Spelling feature, you should always proofread each page in a site to check for any errors that were not recognized by the Spelling feature.

FIGURE C-10: Spelling shortcut menu

Red, wavy underlines indicate words that are possibly misspelled

Shortcut menu with spelling options

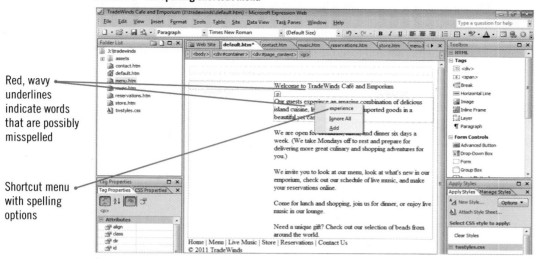

FIGURE C-11: Thesaurus dialog box

Text that was selected when Thesaurus dialog box opened

Meanings list displays synonyms for selected text

Selected meaning is highlighted

Word or phrase that will replace selected text if Replace button is clicked

Synonyms or equivalent meanings for currently selected meaning

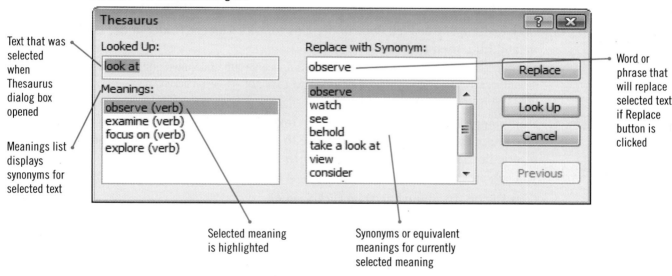

FIGURE C-12: TradeWinds home page after checking spelling and using the Thesaurus

The word "TradeWinds" is no longer flagged as possible misspelling

The word "explore" replaces "look at"

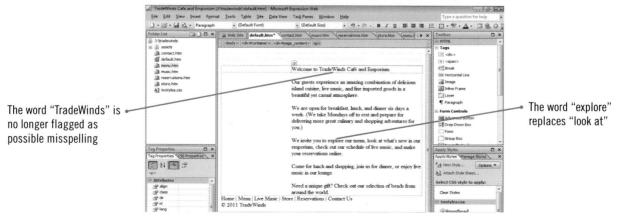

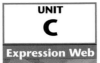
Creating an Internal Link

You can create both internal and external links in Expression Web. **Internal links** are links between pages or files within the same Web site. **External links** are links to Web pages or files on a different Web site. A working link has two parts, called **anchors**. The first part is the **source anchor**, which is the word, phrase, or image on a Web page that, when clicked, leads to another page or file. The second part is the **destination anchor**, which is the file or page that opens when a visitor clicks the link. In Expression Web, you can link to any type of file, including Web pages, images, movies, PDF files, Word documents, and PowerPoint files. If you link to any type of file besides an image or Web page, visitors must have the necessary software installed on their computers in order to view the file. 　　　 You create the internal links for your text-based navigation at the bottom of the home page.

QUICK TIP

To quickly select a word, double-click it.

1. **Select the word** Home **in the footer**

   Make sure to select only the word and not the space on either side, or the link underline will extend past the word (it will still work, but will look a bit sloppy).

QUICK TIP

You can also click the Insert Hyperlink button 🔗 on the Common toolbar to open the Insert Hyperlink dialog box.

2. **Right-click the selected word, then click** Hyperlink **on the shortcut menu**

   The Insert Hyperlink dialog box opens, as shown in Figure C-13. The text you selected, "Home," appears in the Text to display box.

3. **Click** Existing File or Web Page **under Link to, click** Current Folder **under Look in, click** default.htm, **then click** OK

   The Insert Hyperlink dialog box closes. Home is now blue and underlined, indicating that it is a link. The default style is blue and underlined for links that have not yet been clicked and purple and underlined for links that have already been clicked.

TROUBLE

If you do not see your Web site files listed, click the down arrow next to Look in, navigate to your root folder, then open it.

4. **Using Steps 1 and 2 as a guide, link the text** Menu **in the footer to** menu.htm, **the text** Live Music **to** music.htm, **the text** Store **to** store.htm, **the text** Reservations **to** reservations.htm, **and the text** Contact Us **to** contact.htm

   Your links are created, but you cannot test them in Design view. Testing links requires a Web browser.

5. **Click** File **on the menu bar, then click** Save All

6. **Click the** Preview in Browser **button** 🔍▾ **on the Common toolbar**

   The home page opens in a browser window, as shown in Figure C-14. Your browser type and window size may differ from the one shown.

7. **Click the** Store **link at the bottom of the page**

   The Store page opens in the same browser window, indicating that the link is working.

8. **Close the browser, then return to Expression Web**

Maintaining your links

Creating an entire Web site in Expression Web, rather than just individual pages, makes it much easier to manage your Web site files. When you create links between pages, the file location and name are both part of the link URL. Normally, this means that if you move the file or rename it, the link will break and will no longer work.

However, if you rename and move your files within Expression Web, its site management features will update the links for you automatically. So be sure to always do your file management in Expression Web and not in Windows Explorer.

FIGURE C-13: Insert Hyperlink dialog box

Text that was selected when Insert Hyperlink button was clicked; it will become the linked text

Existing File or Web Page button

Current Folder button

Selected text

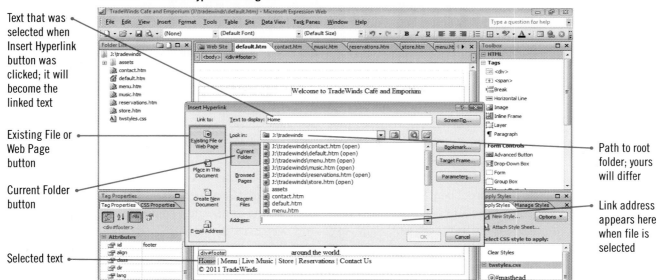

Path to root folder; yours will differ

Link address appears here when file is selected

FIGURE C-14: Music page in browser with internal links in page footer

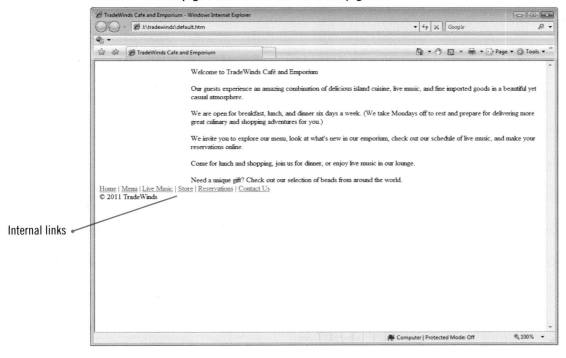

Internal links

Understanding absolute and relative URLs

A URL defines the location of a file. External files use **absolute URLs** containing a path that describes the protocol (such as http://), the domain name (such as centraluniversity.com), and the file path (such as /library/hours.htm) to make up a complete URL such as http://centraluniversity.com/library/hours.htm. Internal links use **relative URLs**, which contain a path that describes only the location of the file being linked relative to the source file. An example of a relative URL would be ../contact.htm. This URL indicates that the file being linked to is one folder up (../) and is named contact.htm. Notice that no protocol or domain name are included. To grasp the concept of absolute versus relative URLs, consider the different ways you might give people directions to your house. You might give a neighbor relative directions, telling her to turn right out of her driveway, take a right at the next street, then turn in to the second house on the left. Those directions are relative to her starting point, in this case your house. On the other hand, you might give a different friend absolute directions, telling her you live at 134 Chestnut Street. She would be able to find your house no matter where she started because this is an absolute address and it is not relative to her starting point.

Creating an External Link

In addition to defining the source and the destination of a link, you can also determine a link's target. The **target** is the browser window or frame in which the destination file opens. You can target internal or external links but not e-mail links. With the increasing amount of advertising on the Web, many people now use software known as a **pop-up blocker** that prevents new browser windows from opening. Some pop-up blockers only block windows that open automatically without user intervention, such as those annoying ads, but others are more restrictive and prevent any new windows from opening, even when a visitor clicks the link. Many designers still target links to open in new windows, but you should be aware of this issue when you make decisions about opening links in new browser windows. When in doubt, play it safe and don't open the link in a new window. ▓▓▓▓ Catalina requests that you create a link to a museum site about Kentucky quilts and link to it from the store page. She has provided the URL and you have added the text to the store page, so you just need to create the link. She is concerned, however, that visitors will get lost and will not return to the TradeWinds site, so you decide to create the link so it opens in a new browser window. This will leave the TradeWinds page open so a visitor can easily return after visiting the quilt museum site.

STEPS

1. **Click the store.htm tab to make it the active page**

2. **Select the text Museum of the American Quilter's Society toward the middle of the page under Americana, right-click the selection, then click Hyperlink**
   The Insert Hyperlink dialog box opens. See Figure C-15. You can type a URL in the Address box to create a link to an external Web site. All external links must start with http://, but Expression Web will fill it in for you if you forget.

3. **In the Address box, type http://www.quiltmuseum.org, then click Target Frame**
   The Target Frame dialog box opens. See Figure C-16. The left area lists any frames-based pages currently in the site. Since you aren't using frames to construct your Web pages, this list is empty. The right area lists options for targeting the link. Same Frame, Whole Page, and Parent Frame only apply to frames-based pages. New Window can be used on any type of page and opens the destination link in a new browser window. Page Default (none) resets the target to the default, meaning that it opens as a regular link would—in the same browser window as the source page.

TROUBLE
If you accidentally close the window before clicking the Target Frame button, right-click the link in Design view, then click Hyperlink Properties on the shortcut menu.

4. **Click New Window in the Common targets list**
   The text "_blank" appears in the Target setting box, indicating that the link will open in a blank, or new, browser window.

5. **Click OK, then click OK again**
   The dialog boxes close and you return to the store.htm tab in the editing window. The text "Museum of the American Quilter's Society" is blue and underlined, indicating a link.

QUICK TIP
If you need to make changes to an existing hyperlink, right-click the link in Design view, then select Hyperlink Properties from the shortcut menu.

6. **Save changes to the page, then click the Preview in Browser button 🔍 ▾ on the Common toolbar**
   The Store page opens in a browser window, as shown in Figure C-17. Your browser type and size may be different from the one shown; this is not a problem. Any browser type and size works fine for testing the links.

7. **Click the link Museum of the American Quilter's Society near the middle of the page**
   The Museum of American Quilter's Society Web site opens in a new browser window. The TradeWinds Store page is still open in the first browser window. (You may have to minimize the Museum browser window to see it.)

8. **Close both browser windows, then return to Expression Web**

FIGURE C-15: Insert Hyperlink dialog box

Selected text

Address text box

Browse the Web button

Bookmark button

Target Frame button

FIGURE C-16: Target Frame dialog box

New window option

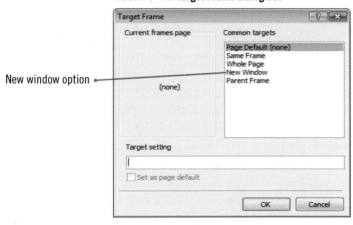

FIGURE C-17: Store page open in browser

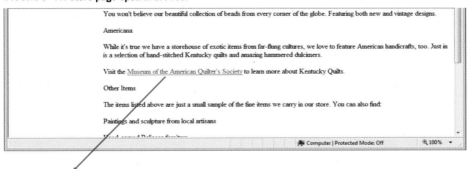

Link to http://www.quiltmuseum.org

Ensuring accuracy of URLs

Accurately typing a URL can be tricky—and if one character is wrong, the link won't work. To ensure that your link URLs are accurate, you can use one of two methods. You can visit the site in a browser and copy the URL from the browser's address window, then paste it into the Address text box when you insert the hyperlink in Expression Web. Or, you can save time by using the Browse the Web button in the Insert Hyperlink dialog box. Click the button to open your default browser. Surf to the page you want to link to, then leave the browser open and return to Expression Web. The Insert Hyperlink dialog box is displayed again and the address of the site automatically appears in the Address text box—like magic!

Creating and Linking to a Bookmark

A **bookmark**, also known as a **named anchor**, is a marker at a specific spot on a Web page that can be used as a destination anchor. One common use of bookmarks is to create a table of contents at the top of a long, scrolling page so that when visitors click a link, they jump down the page to that particular section. Bookmarks can also be used to link from one page to a specific section of a different page. Creating a bookmark is a two-part process: first you create a bookmark for the text that will serve as the destination anchor; then you create the link to the bookmark. ▰▰▰▰ You want to link the information about beads on the home page to the bead section of the store page. First you need to create the bookmark on the store page, and then you can create the link on the home page to the bookmark.

STEPS

1. **If necessary, click the store.htm tab to make it the active page**

QUICK TIP
Your bookmark name may have an extra underscore at the end (World_Bead_ Collection_) if you also selected the space after Collection; this is fine.

2. **Select the text World Bead Collection approximately one-third of the way down the page, click Insert on the menu bar, then click Bookmark**
   The Bookmark dialog box opens, as shown in Figure C-18. The Bookmark name text box displays a suggested name for the bookmark based on the text you selected. You decide the name World_Bead_Collection is fine. A bookmark name cannot contain any spaces or special characters, and no two bookmarks on the same page can have the same name.

3. **Click OK**
   The Bookmark dialog box closes. A visual aid consisting of a dashed line appears under the text World Bead Collection, indicating that this is a bookmark. See Figure C-19. The visual aid is only to help you see the bookmark, which would otherwise be invisible. The dashed line will not appear when the page is viewed in a browser.

4. **Save the changes to store.htm, make default.htm the active page, then select the text selection of beads in the last sentence**
   This is the text you wish to link to the World_Bead_Collection bookmark on the Store page.

5. **Right-click the selection, click Hyperlink on the shortcut menu, click Existing File or Web Page under Link to, click Current Folder under Look in, then click store.htm**

TROUBLE
If you do not see your Web site files listed, click the down arrow next to Look in, navigate to your root folder, and open it.

6. **Click Bookmark, click World_Bead_Collection, then click OK**
   The Bookmark dialog box closes. See Figure C-20. The relative URL shows up in the Address box. Links to bookmarks are constructed by adding # and the name of the bookmark to the end of the file name in which the bookmark is inserted.

7. **Click OK**
   The Insert Hyperlink dialog box closes. The text "selection of beads" is now linked.

8. **Save your changes, click the Preview in Browser button 🔍 ▾ on the Common toolbar, then click the selection of beads link**
   The Store page opens in your Web browser. Because the link is to the bookmark, the page opens so that World Bead Collection is at the top of the page.

9. **Close the browser and return to Expression Web**

FIGURE C-18: Bookmark dialog box

Bookmark name text box

If there were other bookmarks on this page, they would be listed here

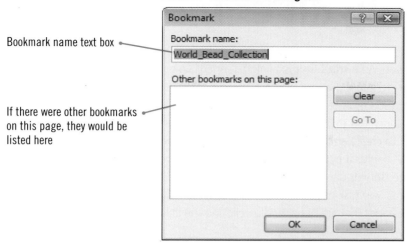

FIGURE C-19: Store page after bookmark is inserted

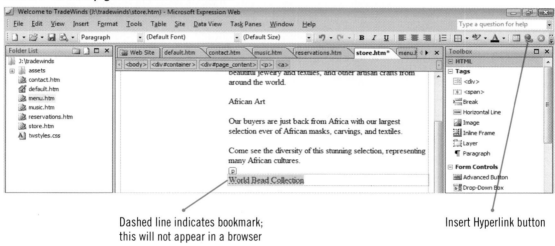

Dashed line indicates bookmark; this will not appear in a browser

Insert Hyperlink button

FIGURE C-20: Creating a link to the bookmark

Text that will display in link

Address or URL of World Bead Collection bookmark on Store page

Bookmark button

Selected text

Creating an E-mail Link

Including an e-mail link on your contact page or elsewhere on your Web site makes it easy for visitors to communicate with you. An **e-mail link** is a link that opens an e-mail message in the visitor's default e-mail program, with your designated e-mail address already entered in the To line. Visitors to a site often use e-mail links to ask questions, note problems, or request additional information. While putting an e-mail link on a Web page can increase the amount of **spam**, or bulk unsolicited e-mail, received, many Web sites include e-mail links. To create an e-mail link, you select the text or image that you want visitors to click, and then format the selection as a hyperlink. ▇▆▅ Catalina is eager to receive feedback from visitors to the TradeWinds Web site, so you decide to create an e-mail link on the contact page. The page already contains text for the link, you just need to format it as a hyperlink and specify the information that should appear in e-mail messages that are generated by clicking the link.

STEPS

1. **Click the contact.htm tab to make that page active in the editing window**

2. **Select the text info@tradewindsemporium.com at the bottom of the page, right-click the selection, then click Hyperlink**

   The Insert Hyperlink dialog box opens, as shown in Figure C-21. For link text, you can use a phrase such as "Email us" instead of the address; however, using the e-mail address as the link text ensures that people can read the address even if there's a problem opening the link with their e-mail program or if they print the page.

3. **Click the E-mail Address button under Link to**

QUICK TIP

Creating a subject line for the e-mail message makes it easy for the person who receives the messages to see e-mails that have originated from the Web site; however, visitors can change the subject line in their e-mail program.

4. **Type @info@tradewindsemporium.com in the E-mail address text box, type Web Site Contact in the Subject text box, then compare your screen to Figure C-22**

   The "mailto:" protocol, which needs to be inserted before the actual e-mail address, is filled out for you.

5. **Click OK**

   The Insert Hyperlink dialog box closes. The e-mail address is linked and appears as blue, underlined text. When visitors click the e-mail link, a new e-mail outgoing message window will open on their computer, with the e-mail address and subject line already filled in. They can then complete the message and send it.

6. **Save changes to the page**

Writing good link text

Writing good link text is an art. Clear, accurate link text minimizes any distraction from the content and lets the visitor know what to expect when they click a link. Some general guidelines to follow include:

- Write naturally, but plan for placement of the link.
- When possible, place link text toward the end of a sentence.
- Make the link text meaningful and obvious.
- Don't use "click here" in link text.

This last point deserves special attention. Avoid using "click here" because:

- When out of context, it is meaningless. If visitors are scanning the page and "click here" repeatedly catches their eye, the phrase provides no additional information about the page.

- It is device-dependent. Not all users "click" to follow a link; navigation varies with different devices.
- It lowers search engine rankings for your site. Search engines give weight to link text, and "click here" offers no clue to help the search engine software decide what your site is all about.
- It makes your site less accessible to those who have visual impairments and who use screen readers to hear content, including links. A series of links labeled "click here" doesn't clarify the surrounding context for a screen reader system, making navigation difficult.

FIGURE C-21: **Creating an e-mail link**

E-mail Address
button

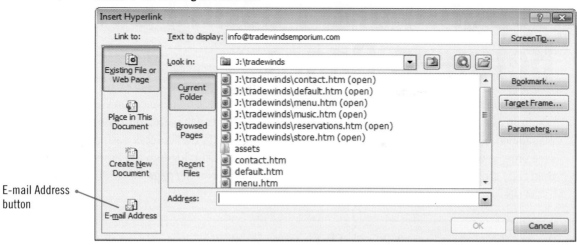

FIGURE C-22: **Creating the e-mail link**

E-mail Address
text box

Subject text
box

E-mail Address
button

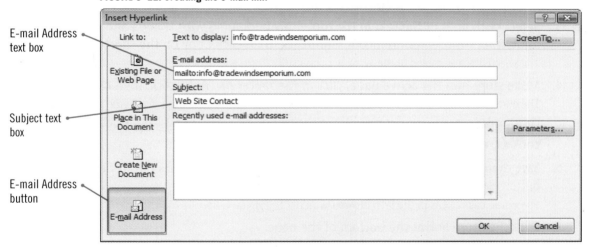

Avoiding spam generated by e-mail links

While it is convenient for both you and your visitors to have an
e-mail link on your Web site, it can be an open invitation for a flood
of spam. Spammers use software called "harvesters" to crawl
through Web pages and find linked e-mail addresses. They then add
those addresses to their mailing lists, and the unfortunate recipient
can begin to receive hundreds or thousands of unwanted e-mails a
day. To protect yourself from spam, consider using an HTML form
instead of providing a direct link to your e-mail address.

Copying and Pasting Content Between Pages

It is common to have text that repeats on every page of a Web site. Using Expression Web, it's easy to copy text from one page and paste it into another. When you paste between pages, the formatting and links are maintained. ▰▰▰ You want to create a set of navigation links in the footer of each page in the site. To save time, you decide to copy the e-mail address from the contact page into the home page footer, and then copy the complete navigation and copyright notice from the home page footer to all the other pages in the site.

STEPS

TROUBLE
Be sure to right-click the highlighted text. If you click outside the text, it will be deselected. If this happens, select it again, then right-click the selected text.

1. **On the contact.htm page, select the** info@tradewindsemporium.com **link, right-click, then click** Copy **on the shortcut menu**
   The text is copied to the Windows clipboard.

2. **Click the** default.htm **tab, click at the end of the copyright line in the footer div, press [Spacebar], type [|], press [Spacebar] again, right-click after the space, then click** Paste
   The text is pasted with the default Paste Option of "Keep Source Formatting," as shown in Figure C-23. Because no formatting was applied to the original text, this is fine. The home page now has a complete footer with a top row of text-based navigation and a bottom row containing the copyright notice and e-mail address separated by a vertical pipe. You want this same footer on every page, but you don't want to have to type it into every page and re-create all the links.

QUICK TIP
Remember to use the visual aids and quick tag selector bar to make sure the cursor is in the correct div.

3. **Select both lines of the text in the footer div beginning with** Home | **and ending with** info@tradewindsemporium.com, **right-click, then click** Copy **on the shortcut menu**
   The selected text is copied to the Windows clipboard.

4. **Make** store.htm **the active page, click in the** footer div, **right-click, then click** Paste
   The entire footer from the home page, with links intact, is on the store page. See Figure C-24.

TROUBLE
If one or more of these pages are not open, double-click the file name in the Folder List task pane or Web site tab.

5. **Using Step 4 four as a guide, paste the footer text and links into the footer of the** contact, menu, music, **and** reservations **pages**

6. **Save changes to all pages, make** music.htm **the active page, then click the** Preview in Browser **button** 🔍 ▾ **on the Common toolbar**
   The music page opens in the Web browser window. See Figure C-25.

7. **Click the** Store **link at the bottom of the page**
   The store page opens in the browser window, indicating that the link is working.

8. **Close the browser, then return to Expression Web**

9. **Save any changes to your pages, close the Web site, then exit Expression Web**

FIGURE C-23: Home page with e-mail address link pasted into page

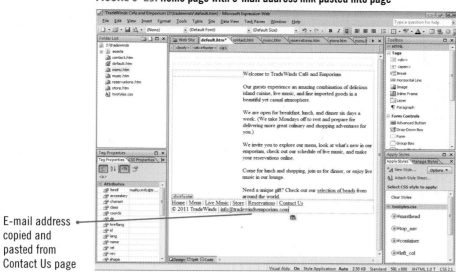

E-mail address copied and pasted from Contact Us page

FIGURE C-24: Store page

Footer text pasted in footer div

FIGURE C-25: Music page with footer open in browser

Text and links copied and pasted from home page

Practice

▼ CONCEPTS REVIEW

Use Figure C-26 to answer the following questions.

FIGURE C-26

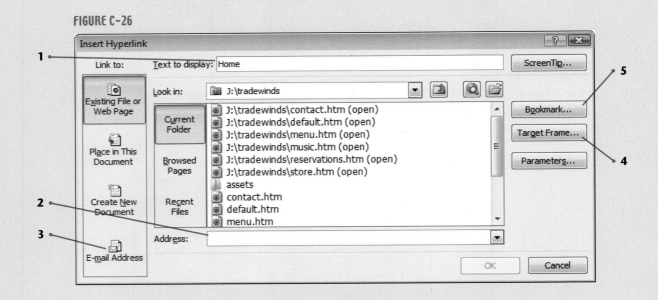

1. Which element do you click to create a link that will allow visitors to contact you from your Web site?
2. Which element do you type in to create an external link?
3. Which element do you click to change in which browser window a link opens?
4. Which element displays the text that will be in the source link?
5. Which element do you click to link to a particular area on a page?

Match each term with the statement that best describes it.

6. Bookmark
7. Internal link
8. External link
9. Spam
10. E-mail link

a. Allows visitors to send e-mail from a Web site
b. Use absolute URLs
c. Use relative URLs
d. Also known as a named anchor
e. Unsolicited bulk e-mail

Select the best answer from the list of choices.

11. The safest option to choose when pasting text if you want to avoid conflicts later with CSS styles is:
   a. Match Destination Formatting
   b. Keep Source Formatting
   c. Keep HTML Only
   d. Keep Text Only

12. The spelling tools in Expression Web allow you to:
   a. Check the spelling in an entire Web site
   b. Check the spelling on a single Web page
   c. Add your own words to the custom dictionary
   d. All of the above

13. If you create a link from your personal Web site to the Microsoft Web site, this would be considered:

a. An internal link

b. A source anchor

c. An external link

d. A destination anchor

14. Which of the following are *not* allowed as part of a bookmark name?

a. Spaces

b. Uppercase letters

c. Special characters

d. Both a and c are correct

▼ SKILLS REVIEW

1. Insert a text file into a Web page.

a. Launch Expression Web, then open the careers Web site.

b. Open the home page. Insert the cursor in the page_content div. (*Hint*: It's on the left side of the page.)

c. Use the quick tag selector to select the contents of the page_content div, then delete the content.

d. Open the Insert File dialog box, navigate to the drive and folder where you store your Data Files, open the Unit C folder, then insert the cg_home.txt file. (*Hint*: Remember to set the File list box to All Files.)

e. Paste the file as Normal paragraphs without line breaks into the page_content div.

FIGURE C-27

f. On the about.htm page, use the quick tag selector to select the contents of the page_content div, delete the contents, then insert the cg_about.txt file into the div as Normal paragraphs without line breaks. (*Hint*: You must first click in the div.)

g. On the contact.htm page, use the quick tag selector to select the contents of the page_content div, delete the contents, then insert the cg_about.txt file into the div as Normal paragraphs without line breaks.

h. Save your pages.

2. Paste text into a Web page.

a. Open the services.htm page, use the quick tag selector to select the contents of the page_content div, then delete the contents.

b. Launch Microsoft Word, open the Open dialog box, navigate to the folder where you store your Data Files, open the Unit C folder, then open the cg_career_services.doc file.

c. Select all the text, then copy it to the Windows clipboard.

d. Close Microsoft Word and return to Expression Web.

e. Paste the text into the page_content div in the services.htm page as Keep text only and as Normal paragraphs without line breaks.

f. Save the page.

3. Type text into a Web page and insert symbols.

a. Switch to the home page in the editing window. In the footer div, type **Home | Services | About | Contact**.

b. Press [Enter], then type **2011 Careers Guaranteed**.

c. Insert a copyright symbol and a space in front of the text 2011.

d. Save your changes to the file.

▼ SKILLS REVIEW (CONTINUED)

4. **Check spelling and use the thesaurus.**
   a. Correct the spelling error on the home page.
   b. Use the Thesaurus feature to find another word or phrase to replace the word **work** in the sentence "You know how those other career sites work." (*Hint*: You will have many options; be sure to choose one that makes sense in the context of the sentence.)
   c. Save your changes to the file.

5. **Create an internal link.**
   a. Create a link from the word **Home** in the footer div of the home page to the same page, default.htm. (*Hint*: You want the option to link to an existing page.)
   b. Create a link from the word **Services** in the footer div of the home page to the services.htm page.
   c. Create a link from the word **About** in the footer div of the home page to the about.htm page.
   d. Create a link from the word **Contact** in the footer div of the home page to the contact.htm page.
   e. Save your changes to the page, then preview the home page in a browser and check each link.

6. **Create an external link.**
   a. Switch to the about page.
   b. In the paragraph under Tina Russo, Chief Technology Officer, link the text **vintage synthesizers** to **http://www.synthmuseum.com** and make the link open in a new window.
   c. Save your changes.
   d. Preview the about page and click the link to test it.

7. **Create a bookmark and link to it.**
   a. Switch to the services page.
   b. Select the text **Help with career planning:** and insert a bookmark.
   c. Save the page.
   d. Switch to the home page.
   e. Select the text **career exploration tools**, then create a link to the bookmark in the services.htm page.
   f. Save the page.
   g. Preview the home page in a browser and test the link.

8. **Create an e-mail link.**
   a. Switch to the contact page.
   b. Select the text **info@careersguaranteed.com**.
   c. Link the selected text as an e-mail link to info@careersguaranteed.com with a subject line of **Web site visitor**.
   d. Save the page.

9. **Copy and paste content between pages.**
   a. In the contact page, select the **info@careersguaranteed.com e-mail** link, then copy it to the Clipboard.
   b. Switch to the home page.
   c. In the last line of the footer div, click after the word Guaranteed, press [Spacebar], type [|], then press [Spacebar] again.
   d. Paste the e-mail link at the location of the insertion point.
   e. Select the entire contents of the footer. This includes both lines of text, the navigation, and the copyright notice with e-mail link.
   f. Paste this into the footer div on all pages of the site.
   g. Save all pages.
   h. Preview the Home page in a browser, then test the links. Your page should look similar to Figure C-27.
   i. Close the browser window, close the Web site, then exit Expression Web.

▼ INDEPENDENT CHALLENGE 1

In this project, you continue your work on the ConnectUp Web site. Tiffany has provided you with content that you need to add to the site. You also want to add some navigation links at the bottom of the pages.

a. Launch Expression Web, then open the connectup Web site.

b. Open the home page, then delete the contents of the page_content div.

c. Insert the cu_home.txt file from the location where you store your Data Files into the page_content div, using the Normal paragraphs without line breaks option.

d. On the contact page, replace the contents of the page_content div with the contents of the cu_contact.txt file.

e. On the faq page, replace the contents of the page_content div with the contents of the cu_faq.txt file.

f. On the joinup page, delete the contents of the page_content div, then copy the content of cu_join_up.doc from within Microsoft Word and paste it as text only, Normal paragraphs without line breaks, into the page_content div.

g. Switch to the home page, then add the following text as your text-based navigation in the footer div: **Home | Join Up | FAQ | Contact Us**.

h. On a new line under the new text, add a copyright statement that includes a copyright symbol.

i. Check the spelling on the home page and correct any misspellings. Add ConnectUp to the custom dictionary so it is no longer flagged as a misspelled word.

j. Use the Insert Hyperlink function to link the name of each page in the footer div of the home page to the appropriate Web page in the site.

k. On the faq page, link the words **Charity Navigator** to http://www.charitynavigator.org; target the link to open in a new window.

l. On the faq page, select the word Membership, insert a bookmark, then save the page.

m. On the joinup page, link the text **Frequently Asked Questions** to the bookmark you created on the faq page.

n. On the contact page, select the text **info@connectupyourlife.com**, then create an e-mail link with a subject line of your choosing.

o. Copy the e-mail link from the contact page into the footer of the home page after the copyright statement. (*Hint*: Add some space and a pipe to separate the two and make them easier to read.)

p. Copy and paste the content of the footer div on the home page into the other pages. (*Hint*: You should have two lines of text to paste.)

q. Save changes to all pages, then preview the joinup page in a browser and check all the links. Your screen should look similar to Figure C-28.

r. Close the browser windows, close the Web site, then exit Expression Web.

FIGURE C-28

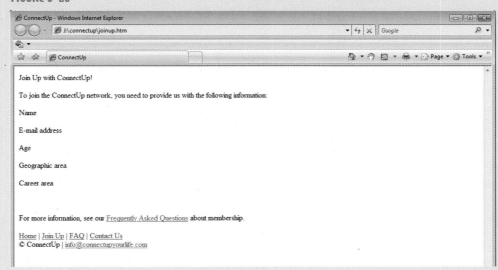

▼ INDEPENDENT CHALLENGE 2

In this project, you continue your work on the Memories Restored Web site. Brian has sent you the content so that you can start adding it to the pages.

a. Launch Expression Web, then open the Memories Restored Web site.

b. Add the contents of the following files, located in the drive and folder where you store your Data Files, to the appropriate pages: mr_contact.txt, mr_home.txt, mr_process.txt, mr_testimonials.doc, and mr_our_work.doc. (*Hint*: Insert text files and copy and paste content from Word files. Be sure to choose your paste options wisely to avoid bringing in formatting along with the text.)

c. Check the spelling and correct any errors. If you like, use the Thesaurus feature to make changes to the text.

d. Link the e-mail address on the contact page.

e. On the home page, create a footer that contains links to all pages in the site, a copyright statement, and an e-mail link.

f. Copy the footer and paste it into the footer of all other pages in the site.

g. Add an external link that opens in a new window to a page of your choosing. (*Hint*: Check the process page for an idea for an external link relating to payment for services.)

h. Add a bookmark to a page, then create a link to the bookmark either from the same page or a different one. (*Hint:* One method is to link from the home page to the testimonials from organizations text at the bottom of the testimonials page.)

Advanced Challenge Exercise

- Insert the file mr_ace_tips.txt into the tips page you created.
- Enter **photo restoration tips** into your favorite search engine, and look through the results to find a site you like that provides advice on restoring photos.
- Under the inserted text in the page_content div, type **Resources**, then add text describing the site you found and an external link to the site.

i. Save your work, then preview your pages in a browser and check the links. When you are finished, close the Web site, then exit Expression Web.

▼ INDEPENDENT CHALLENGE 3

Note: This Independent Challenge requires an Internet connection.

Technology for All has asked you to research some guidelines their editors and writers can use when developing content for the company's Web site.

a. Enter the phrase **writing for the web** into your favorite search engine. From the search results, choose and read at least three articles from three different authors related to how to write for the Web. (*Hint*: You may need to go past the first page of search results to find three quality articles.) If you find an article that doesn't seem credible, find another. Take notes while you're reading.

b. Based on the information you read, create a summary that lists at least five principles the editors and writers at Technology for All can use when writing content for the Web. Briefly explain each principle. Add one paragraph explaining why writing for the Web is different from writing for a print publication.

Advanced Challenge Exercise

- Visit two of the four sites you wrote about in Unit B, and spend some time looking at how the content is written and structured.
- Evaluate the content based on the guidelines you created.
- Write a paragraph on each site evaluating how well it met or didn't meet your guidelines.

c. Add your name to the document, save it, and print it.

d. Close your Web browser and your word processing program.

▼ REAL LIFE INDEPENDENT CHALLENGE

This assignment builds on the personal Web site you started planning in Unit A and created in Unit B. In this project, you add text and links to your Web pages.

a. Add a heading describing the page (for example, About this Site) and at least one paragraph of text to each of your Web pages.

b. If you copy and paste the text from other sources, use the appropriate options to paste only the text and not the formatting.

c. Check the spelling of all your content to be sure you don't have any misspellings.

d. Create an e-mail link so visitors can contact you.

e. Add text-based navigation at the bottom of each page to link the pages together.

f. Add at least one external link and one bookmark link to your site.

g. Preview your pages in a browser, and test the links to be sure they work.

h. Begin collecting or creating images for your site.

i. Begin thinking of a color scheme for your site.

j. When you are finished, close the Web site, then exit Expression Web.

▼ VISUAL WORKSHOP

Launch Expression Web, then open the **ecotours** Web site. Add the content from the et_default.txt file, located in the drive and folder where you store your Data Files, to the home page. Make any necessary changes so that when you preview your page in a Web browser, it looks like Figure C-29. Save the page, close the Web site, then exit Expression Web.

FIGURE C-29

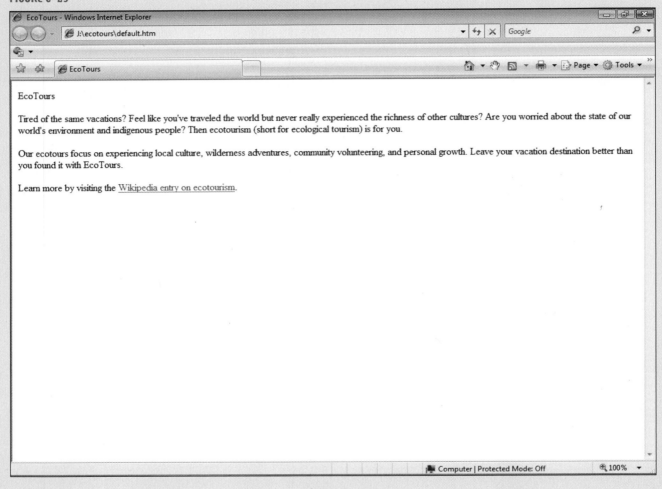

Structuring and Styling Text

Separating structure from visual design is a primary principle of standards-based Web design. The purpose of HTML is to meaningfully define a document's structure by identifying pieces of text as paragraphs, quotes, lists, headings, or other elements. Before CSS existed, HTML was also used to describe the look of the text, even though that was not its original purpose. Modern sites use HTML to control document structure, and use CSS to control visual properties such as fonts, colors, margins, and the position of elements on the page. By keeping the structure and presentation separate, you have more flexibility in how you use the content. For example, you can create a special style sheet to present a less heavily formatted version of your site to visitors accessing it through their cell phones. Updating a site is also easier with CSS. You can make a change to one style and apply it to all the pages in a site at once.  You have added all the text to the TradeWinds site. Now it's time to add structure to the text and to create styles to control its presentation.

OBJECTIVES

Structure content with HTML

Create paragraphs and line breaks

Create headings

Create lists

Understand Cascading Style Sheets

Create an element-based style rule

Modify a style rule

Create a class-based style rule

Apply and remove a class-based
 style rule

Structuring Content with HTML

Structuring your HTML documents properly is the key to a reliable, well-built Web site. If you take the time to use appropriate HTML markup, you will have more flexibility in the way you use your content later, fewer hassles when it comes to updating your site, and an easier time creating and applying CSS styles. A sound document structure starts when you import text files without any accompanying formatting, or type the text within Expression Web. This gives you a clean basis from which to work. ▓▓▓ You spend some time studying the way HTML documents are structured so you can logically structure the content for the TradeWinds site.

To understand HTML document structure, review the following concepts:

- **HTML tags and elements**

  Using HTML allows you to add tags to a document to denote meaning and structure. **HTML tags** are simply text enclosed in angle brackets that surround pieces of Web page content. For example, in the code `<li>study for test</li>`, the `<li>` tags indicate that "study for test" is a list item. Most HTML tags surround the content they define with an opening tag and a closing tag. The closing tag is the same as the opening tag with the addition of a "/" before the tag name. The combination of an opening tag, content, and a closing tag is known as an **element**. Elements can also have **attributes**, which describe other properties of the element. For example, in Figure D-1, the attribute class specifies that the element belongs to the style class "important." While it's helpful to understand the concept behind how HTML works, the tools in Expression Web allow you to create well-structured content without knowing how to write HTML tags. Lucky you! The use of tags to describe the structure of a document is known as **markup**. This accounts for the "M" in HTML (HyperText Markup Language).

- **Semantic markup**

  Following principles of **semantic markup**—that is, using HTML tags to mark up elements in a meaningful and descriptive way—is important. See Figure D-2 for an example of a well-structured document. Because semantic markup was used to create the Web page, the structure is clear even without applying a style sheet. Although people who visit your site don't see your code, the devices they use do. Browsers, search engines, and assistive devices for people with disabilities all use HTML code to help interpret your Web page.

  The concept of meaningful markup is probably easiest to understand by considering some examples of nonsemantic markup, or markup that is used solely for presentation rather than for structure or meaning. One example of nonsemantic markup is to misuse HTML elements by relying on them to force content to display in a certain way rather than using them for meaning. For example, the HTML element <blockquote> is intended to be used to identify a piece of text as a quotation. But because most browsers display a <blockquote> element as being indented on the left and right sides, it's common for people to put <blockquote> tags around content that's not a quote, just so it will display as indented text. The correct way to handle this is to put the text in an ordinary paragraph tag, then use a style sheet to display it as indented.

  Another example of nonsemantic markup is to use a style to make text display a certain way without using an HTML tag to denote its meaning. An example would be the first line of text on a Web page, which usually serves as a heading. A nonsemantic approach to marking up the text would be to create a style to display it as bold and red, without also applying an <h1> tag to mark the text as a first-level heading. The text may look like a heading, but it has no structural meaning without the HTML tag.

- **Common text elements**

  All content on a Web page should be contained in an element, so that it can be controlled using CSS. The elements used most often are shown in table D-1.

FIGURE D-1: HTML element

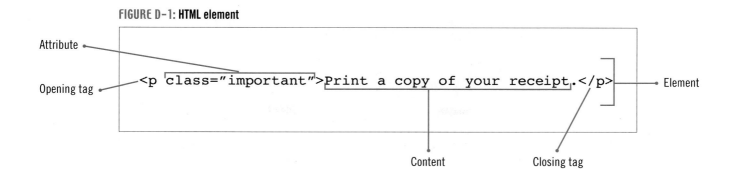

Attribute

Opening tag

`<p class="important">Print a copy of your receipt.</p>`

Element

Content

Closing tag

FIGURE D-2: A well-structured HTML document with styles disabled

Body text and three levels of headings are apparent even without style sheet applied

TABLE D-1: Common HTML text elements

element	tag	purpose
paragraph	<p>	Creates a paragraph of text
line break	 	Creates a line break to force text to the next line, while still keeping it in the same paragraph
unordered list	<ul>	Creates a bulleted list
ordered list	<ol>	Creates a numbered list
headings <h1> through <h6>	<h1>, <h2>, <h3>, <h4>, <h5>, <h6>	Creates headings with <h1> being the highest level and <h6> being the lowest

Understanding screen readers

People who are blind or have severely impaired eyesight use software called a **screen reader** to help them use a computer. Screen readers use a synthesized voice to read aloud the text that is on the screen. Built-in controls on most screen readers allow the user to navigate through the content. However, these controls rely on the document being well structured. When a screen reader encounters a tag indicating the presence of a list, for example, it activates controls that allow the user to skip to the next list item. If the structural HTML tags are absent or incorrectly applied, it makes it difficult or impossible for visitors who use screen readers to navigate through the content.

Creating Paragraphs and Line Breaks

The most basic structural element of any written content is a paragraph, and Web pages are no different. In HTML, the <p> tag denotes a paragraph element. Browsers usually display text contained in a <p> tag with no indentation and with top and bottom margins that create white space above and below the paragraph. All text within a paragraph element wraps automatically according to the size of the page, so there's no need to hyphenate text on the Web. The <br /> element is used to create a new line of text within an existing paragraph without creating a new paragraph. You don't need to use line breaks often, but they can come in handy when you want to force text to the next line within a paragraph. ▰▰▰ You notice that the TradeWinds address on the contact page is not listed on separate lines. You decide to add line breaks to make it more readable.

STEPS

1. **Launch Expression Web, open the tradewinds site, then open contact.htm**

2. **Click the Show Split View button at the bottom of the editing window, click View on the menu bar, point to Formatting Marks, then click Show**

   Using Split view, you can continue to work in the Design pane and see the code generated by Expression Web. Showing Formatting Marks allows you to see paragraph and line break marks in Design view.

3. **In the Design pane, click in front of the text 239 in the TradeWinds address**

   See Figure D-3. The Code pane shows that all the address text is contained in a single paragraph tag with no line breaks. The Design pane shows that the address text runs together, breaking to the next line only when it reaches the right edge of the editing window.

4. **Press [Enter]**

   A new paragraph element is inserted and the resulting text displays with an extra line of white space above it, as shown in Figure D-4. A visual aid appears with a p in the tab, indicating the new paragraph. Expression Web creates a new paragraph any time you press [Enter] while in Design view when the insertion point is in a paragraph. Although you want the text to break to a new line, you do not want it to create a new paragraph.

5. **Click Edit on the menu bar, then click Undo Insert**

   The paragraph element is removed.

6. **Press [Shift][Enter]**

   The street address appears on a new line with no extra white space, and a <br /> tag appears in the Code pane. Expression Web inserts a line break whenever you press [Shift][Enter] rather than [Enter]. A line break has no visual aid or closing tag, since it doesn't hold any content and is considered an empty element.

7. **Click in front of the word Shell in the Design pane, then press [Shift] [Enter]**

   In the Design pane, the city, state, and zip code appear on a new line. In the Code pane, a <br /> tag is inserted. See Figure D-5.

8. **Click the Show Design View button, click View on the menu bar, point to Formatting Marks, then click Show**

   You return to Design view and Formatting Marks no longer appear. You can insert HTML tags without working in Split view. Sometimes it helps to be able to see the code, but it's your choice as to how you want to work.

9. **Save your changes**

FIGURE D-3: Viewing the text in Split view

Entire address enclosed in one paragraph with no break tags

Address does not display with line breaks

Show Split View button

FIGURE D-4: Results of inserting a paragraph break

Pressing [Enter] creates a new paragraph

Visual aid tab

Visual aid showing new paragraph

Paragraph mark

FIGURE D-5: Results of inserting a line break

Break tags

Line break

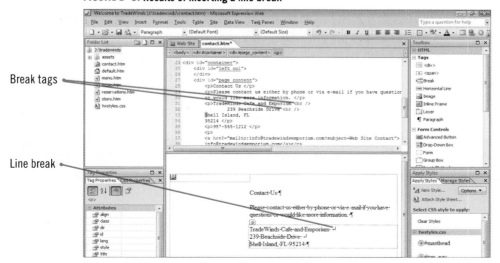

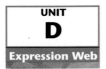

Creating Headings

Using the tools in Expression Web, you can easily add HTML tags to create structure in your document without having to write code. The Style list box on the Common toolbar allows you to choose from a list of common structural elements and apply them to your content. Don't be confused by the name of the Style list box; it actually applies HTML tags, not CSS, to your content. Although HTML has six levels of headings, you generally won't use more than three or four levels unless you have very long, highly structured documents on your site. ▟▟▟▟▟ You review the pages in the TradeWinds site and notice that some text on the pages is meant to serve as page headings and subheadings. You add markup to create the headings.

STEPS

1. **Select the text Contact Us on the contact page**
   See Figure D-6. The text is selected and the p in the tab on the visual aid indicates that this text is contained in a paragraph element.

2. **Click the Style list arrow, then click Heading 1 <h1>**
   See Figure D-7. The text is now large and bold. The tab on the visual aid changes to h1, indicating that the text is now contained in an <h1> element. Design view displays text the way it will look in most browsers. Browsers generally display <h1> elements as very large and bold, with subsequent lower level headings decreasing in text size. If you prefer smaller text for a heading, it's better to write a style to change the text size than to mark up the main heading with an <h2> tag, which is intended to mark up subheadings. Remember that the purpose of the markup is to describe this text as a first-level heading, not to dictate the display properties.

3. **Open default.htm, select the text Welcome to TradeWinds Café and Emporium, click the Style list arrow, then click Heading 1 <h1>**

4. **Open menu.htm, select the text TradeWinds Menu, click the Style list arrow, then click Heading 1 <h1>**

5. **Open music.htm, select the text Live Music at TradeWinds, click the Style list arrow, then click Heading 1 <h1>**

6. **Open reservations.htm, then apply the Heading 1 <h1> tag to the text Reservations**

7. **Open store.htm, then apply the Heading 1 <h1> tag to the text What's New in the TradeWinds Emporium**

8. **Select the text African Art, click the Style list arrow, then click Heading 2 <h2>**
   The text is now larger and bolder than the body text but not as large as the text in the <h1> element. The tab on the visual aid changes to h2, indicating that the text is now contained in an <h2> element.

9. **Apply the Heading 2 <h2> tag to the text World Bead Collection, Americana, Other Items, and Our Prices on this page, compare your screen to Figure D-8, then save your changes to all open pages**

Creating a visual hierarchy

You can use CSS to override any style, including, for example, making your sixth-level headings larger than your third-level headings. This is a bad idea, though. Part of an aesthetically pleasing and user-friendly design is creating a **visual hierarchy** on the page. This means varying the size of text elements in relationship to their importance. So first-level headings should be the largest and most eye-catching, with second-level headings being less visually prominent. This helps readers quickly scan the page and grasp the structure of the content.

FIGURE D-6: Contact page with text highlighted

Style list box

Style list arrow

Selected text

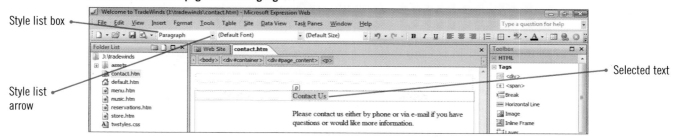

FIGURE D-7: Text with <h1> tag applied

Heading 1 style results in <h1> tag

Visual aid indicating <h1> tag has been applied

Quick tag selector indicating <h1> tag

Heading 1 text

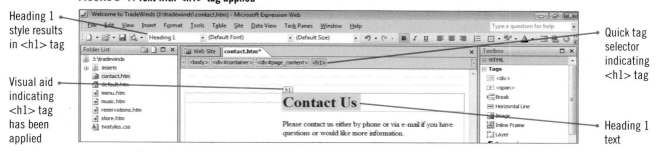

FIGURE D-8: Text with <h2> tag applied

Heading 2 style results in <h2> tag

Heading 2 text

Visual aid indicating <h2> tag has been applied

Quick tag selector indicating <h2> tag

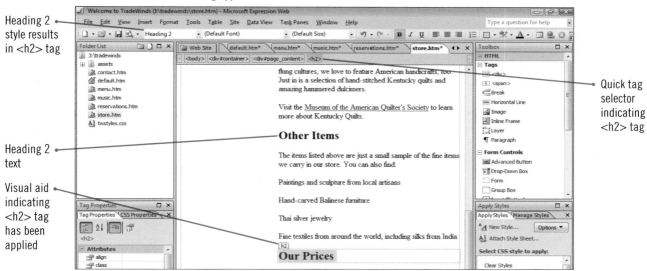

Introducing XHTML

In this book, we refer to HTML as the primary Web development language. By default, Expression Web actually uses **XHTML** (Extensible HyperText Markup Language) when generating code for your Web pages. XHTML is a newer version of HTML that has slightly different rules and tags; however, XHTML files still use the ".htm" or ".html" extension. It's fine to refer to both languages as HTML, but if you want to impress your geeky friends, you can start referring to your code as XHTML.

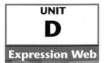

Creating Lists

Any text that is a list of items should be marked up as a list with HTML tags. HTML provides three types of list elements: ordered list, unordered list, and definition list. Items in **ordered lists** appear numbered by default. Items in **unordered lists** appear with bullets beside them by default. **Definition lists** are used to list terms and their definitions; they are not used as often as the other types. When marking up text, choose the list type based on the purpose of the list rather than how it might initially look; you can always adjust the formatting later. The store page contains text that is marked up as paragraphs but intended to be a list of items. You decide to fix this. Catalina has also requested that you add an item to the list.

STEPS

1. **On the store page, select the four lines of text starting with Paintings and sculpture and ending with silks from India**

   See Figure D-9. No visual aid appears because you have selected more than one element. Visual aids only appear when you select a single element. Each line of text is currently contained within its own <p> element.

2. **Click the Style list arrow, then click Ordered List <ol>**

   See Figure D-10. The visual aid tab changes to ol, indicating an ordered list. The items are now listed numerically on the page. You decide to change this to an unordered list, since these items aren't in any particular sequence.

3. **Click the Style list arrow, then click Unordered List <ul>**

   The tab on the visual aid changes to ul, indicating an unordered list. The list items now have bullets instead of numbers beside them. You now need to add the new item to the list.

4. **Click after the word India, then press [Enter]**

   See Figure D-11. The cursor appears on a new line with a bullet beside it. The li on the visual aid tab indicates that this is a list item. Lists are defined by marking up the entire list with the list tag (<ul>, for example), then marking up each item with an <li> tag.

5. **Type Mexican glassware**

6. **Press [Enter]**

   Expression Web created a new list item, but you are finished with this list and realize you don't need a new list item.

7. **Click [Backspace]**

   The bullet is removed.

8. **Click anywhere outside the list, then save your changes**

   To finish a list without creating a new list item, you can click anywhere outside the list.

Using lists for site navigation

Many Web designers mark up the navigation links on a Web site as a list. This makes sense, since the navigation is essentially a list of locations you can choose to visit. No one wants their navigation to actually look like a bulleted list, so this option wouldn't be very popular if designers could not override the default list style. Through the magic of CSS, designers can remove the bullets or numbers, make list items appear side-by-side rather than on separate lines, and add background colors and borders. By the time the lists have had the styles applied, they are unrecognizable as lists when viewed in a browser. However, the list markup is still in the HTML so screen readers and other devices can make use of it.

FIGURE D-9: Selected text

Selected text

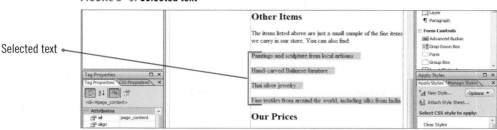

FIGURE D-10: Numbered list

Ordered list

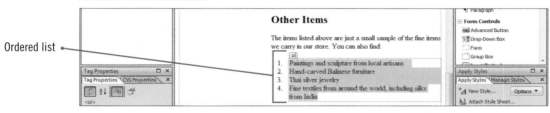

FIGURE D-11: Bulleted list with new list item

Unordered list

Visual aid indicating <li> tag

New list item

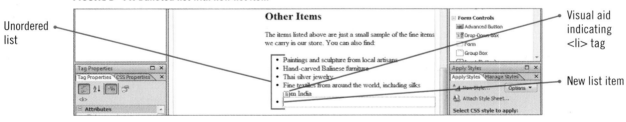

Understanding browser defaults

Each Web browser uses its own built-in styles to decide how to display HTML elements. These styles are commonly referred to as the **browser defaults**. The default displays are fairly consistent across all browsers. The <p> or paragraph tag is a good example. In printed materials, paragraphs are generally indented and don't have an extra line of white space between them. Almost all browsers, though, display any content that's wrapped in a <p> tag with top and bottom margins and no indentation. If you don't specifically apply a style to an element, it will display using the browser defaults of the visitor's Web browser. You can override any default by creating and applying your own style. You could, for example, write a style to display paragraphs with no margins, which would remove the extra space between them. While defaults have some consistency from browser to browser, there is enough variation that you want to be sure to check the way your pages display in several different browsers.

Expression Web

Understanding Cascading Style Sheets

The CSS tools in Expression Web make it easy to create sophisticated styles and apply them to elements on your page. It can be great fun to play with the style tools because they can instantly add color and visual interest to your design. However, understanding some basic concepts about CSS can keep your enjoyable endeavor from turning into frustration. ▓▓▓▓ You decide to take some time and learn about how Cascading Style Sheets work.

DETAILS

To use CSS effectively, it is important to understand:

- **What a CSS style rule is**

  CSS, as you know, stands for Cascading Style Sheets. A style sheet is a collection of style rules. A **style rule**, often referred to simply as a style, describes how a particular element or piece of content should be displayed.

- **What CSS can do**

  When CSS appeared on the scene, it opened up a whole new world of possibilities for Web designers. If you use only HTML to design Web pages, your design options are limited since HTML works best for describing document structure, not the visual design. A good example is the current state of the TradeWinds pages. While they are structurally sound, they're not very visually exciting. With CSS, you can control almost every aspect of your site's visual design. You can create styles that dictate what text looks like, where images are displayed, how the pages are laid out, and more. You can even create styles that hide content and keep it from appearing on the page. CSS works with HTML to send instructions to the browser about how the page should be displayed. Refer to Table D-1 for an overview of the CSS tools available in Expression Web.

- **How CSS style rules work**

  Style rules are written in the CSS language, which is different from HTML. A style rule has two parts, the selector and the declaration. A **selector** tells the browser what the style should apply to. CSS provides three basic types of selectors—IDs, elements, and classes. An ID selector can only be used once on a page and is usually used in conjunction with a <div> tag to style layout elements of a page. You learn more about element and class selectors later in this unit. The **declaration** part of the rule describes what properties you want to change and how you want to change them. Each declaration has a **property**, describing what to change, and a **value**, indicating how to change the property. For example, you want to change the background color to yellow. Figure D-12 shows a style rule within a style sheet.

- **Options for placing style rules**

  As the Web designer, you must choose where to place your style rules. You can direct Expression Web to create them directly in your HTML file, enclosed in the head of the document in a special <style> tag, which is called an **internal style sheet**. This is convenient but it limits you to only being able to use the styles in the page where they reside. Your second option is to create an **external style sheet**, which is a separate file with a .css extension, and direct Expression Web to create the style rules in that file. Once that file is created and attached to all your HTML pages, you can use those styles in any page of the site. This also means that if you change a style in the external style sheet, the changes will be reflected in all your pages at once. This is one of the best features of CSS and can save you lots of time. See Figure D-13 for an example of an external style sheet. A third option is to create **inline styles** that are placed directly around content similar to HTML tags. This is rarely a good option, since they cannot be reused at all, even in the same page, but WYSI-WYG editors such as Expression Web sometimes write inline styles and apply them when you use formatting tools in the program. When you set the CSS options in the Page Editor options in Unit B, you chose options that will prevent Expression Web from adding inline styles to the body tag or layout divs.

  The set of rules that guide the display of your pages is always known as a style sheet, whether it's written into the HTML file or whether it's a separate file.

FIGURE D-12: Parts of a style rule

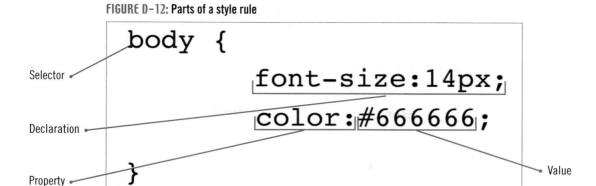

Selector

Declaration

Property

Value

FIGURE D-13: External style sheet generated by Expression Web

```
/* CSS layout */
#masthead {
}

#top_nav {
}

#container {
    position: relative;
    width: 100%;
}

#left_col {
    width: 200px;
    position: absolute;
    left: 0px;
    top: 0px;
}

#page_content {
    margin-left: 200px;
}

#footer {
}
body {
    font-family: Arial, Helvetica, sans-serif;
    font-size: 14px;
    color: #890120;
}
.highlight {
    font-weight: bold;
    background-color: #FFE9BB;
}
```

TABLE D-1: CSS tools available in Expression Web

tool	use to
Apply Styles task pane	Apply, remove, modify, rename, and delete styles; attach or detach external Cascading Style Sheets (CSS); select all instances of a style; and go to the code that contains a style's rule set
Manage Styles task pane	Perform all the functions of the Apply Styles task pane; move styles between external and internal style sheets; and move the location of a style within a style sheet
CSS Properties task pane	View all styles of current selection, the order of precedence of those styles, and all properties and values of the styles
Style toolbar	Apply, rename, and remove styles
Style Application toolbar	Control how styles are applied manually to page elements
CSS reports	View reports of style errors and styles that are in use on your page or site

Creating an Element-Based Style Rule

An **element-based style rule** essentially redefines the look of an HTML element. For example, you could write a rule to make all unordered lists have a special icon beside them. It's very common to create a style rule based on the <body> element. Style rules have **inheritance**, which means that a style applied to an element on the page is also applied to any elements it contains. The <body> tag surrounds all the page content—by creating a style rule for this element and placing the rule in an external style sheet, you affect all the content on every page of the site with one step. ▨▨▨▨ The default font displayed on the TradeWinds Web pages strikes you as being in need of some pizzazz. You create a style rule based on the <body> element to change the font face.

STEPS

1. **Click the Maximize button on the Apply Styles task pane**

   See Figure D-14. The Apply Styles task pane provides access to all of the tools you need to create, modify, and apply styles. By default, styles are organized according to where they reside. Styles available only on the current page are listed first, then styles available in attached external style sheets are listed.

2. **Click the New Style button**

   The New Style dialog box opens, where you can access every property for constructing a style rule. The properties are organized by categories, listed under Category. Clicking one displays all the properties for that category in a series of lists and text boxes.

3. **Click the Selector list arrow, then click body**

   The Selector list displays all HTML elements so you can choose the one for which you wish to create a style rule.

4. **Click the Define in list arrow, then click Existing style sheet**

   The Define list lets you choose whether you want to define this style rule in an internal or external style sheet. If you did not already have a style sheet attached to the page, you could create one here and attach it.

5. **Click the URL list arrow, then click twstyles.css**

6. **Click the font-family list arrow, then click Arial, Helvetica, sans-serif**

   Compare your screen to Figure D-15. Expression Web includes a long list of available font families, but to ensure consistency across browsers, you should limit yourself to the first three options. In order for a font to appear in a visitor's browser, it must be installed on their computer. When choosing a font for a style rule, it's common practice to define not just one but an entire list of fonts. The visitor's computer will go down this list until they find one that is installed.

7. **Click OK**

   See Figure D-16. The font face on the page changes to Arial, and the twstyles.css tab on the editing window indicates the file is open, with an asterisk beside the file name indicating that changes have been made. When you use any of the style tools to create rules that affect an external style sheet, Expression Web opens that file. No changes have been made to the HTML file, since the style was created in the external style sheet.

8. **Switch to each open page, using the tabs on the editing window**

   The change in the font face reflects that the new style has been applied to the <body> element on all pages.

9. **Save your changes to all open pages**

   This saves changes to the CSS file and any open Web pages.

FIGURE D-14: TradeWinds store page

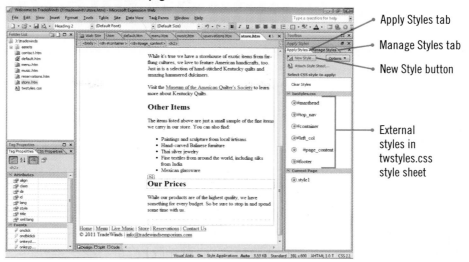

Apply Styles tab

Manage Styles tab

New Style button

External styles in twstyles.css style sheet

FIGURE D-15: New Style dialog box after choosing options

Selector list arrow, Step 3

Define in list arrow, Step 4

Preview box displays Arial font

Description of options chosen

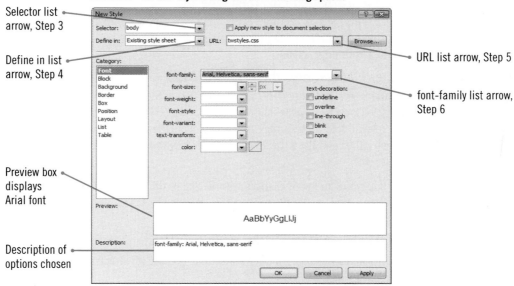

URL list arrow, Step 5

font-family list arrow, Step 6

FIGURE D-16: Editing window after creation of new body style

New style rule applied to body text

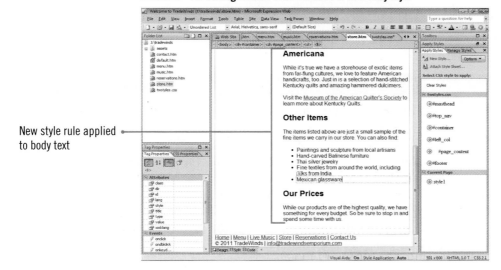

Modifying a Style Rule

Once you create a style rule, you're not stuck with it forever. You can easily modify it if, for example, you decide you want to change an attribute such as the font size or color, or add an attribute such as a margin. If the style rule is defined in an external style sheet, changes will be reflected in all attached Web pages. ▄▄▄▓▓ You decide that the text color and size that are currently displayed on the TradeWinds pages should be changed to work better with your proposed design and color palette.

STEPS

1. **Make** store.htm **the active page, then click the** Manage Styles tab **in the Apply Styles task pane**

   The task pane title bar changes to display the name of the active tab, Manage Styles.

   > **QUICK TIP**
   >
   > Element-based rules are shown only in the Manage Styles task pane, not in the Apply Styles task pane.

2. **Right-click the** body style, **then click "Modify Style..."**

   The Modify Style dialog box opens. It includes the same options as the New Style dialog box, except that you cannot modify the location of the style sheet. You would not change the selector unless you wanted the rule to apply to a different element.

3. **Click in the** font-size text box, **then type** 14

   The font-size units list box becomes active after you type a number into the font-size text box, with px selected as the default. The px stands for pixels. A **pixel** is the basic unit of measurement for anything displayed on a computer screen.

   > **QUICK TIP**
   >
   > You can also choose a color by clicking the color swatch, clicking a color in the More Colors dialog box, then clicking OK. Expression Web will fill in the hex value for you.

4. **Click in the** color text box, **then type** #890120

   Compare your screen to Figure D-17. The swatch beside the color text box turns dark red. The strange characters you typed are a **hex value** (short for hexidecimal code), a sequence of six numbers and/or letters used to define a specific color in CSS rules. In this case, you knew the hex value of the color you wanted, but you could also click the color list arrow to choose a color without knowing the hex value.

5. **Click** OK

   The dialog box closes and your changes are reflected in the page, as shown in Figure D-18. No changes were made to the store.htm code, only to the external style sheet, so only the twstyles.css tab above the editing window displays an asterisk.

6. **Make** reservations.htm **the active page**

   Even though you only changed the style sheet file, because it's attached to every HTML page on the site, all pages reflect the changes.

7. **Save your changes to all open pages**

Working with CSS font measurement units

If you enter the term "CSS font size" into a search engine, you'll find many passionate, detailed, and technical articles about which measurement system is best to use when specifying font sizes. The font-size units list box lets you choose from 10 different measurement units, including px for pixel, but many of these options are unreliable in the way they display fonts on different systems. Avoid using points (pt), picas (pc), inches (in), centimeters (cm), and millimeters (mm). The remaining systems fall into two categories. The first is to specify relative sizing using keywords (such as small or x-large), ems, or percentages. In theory, this is a great way to choose font sizes because it allows your text size to be scalable by setting the relative rather than absolute sizes of a font. You could declare that, say, a first-level heading should be twice as large as the body text. In practice, though, you have to be quite skilled in CSS to make this work reliably. That leaves you with an absolute measurement, pixels, as the best option. The default setting for text in browsers is 16 px. So if the default size looks too large, you can specify a smaller number such as 12 or 14.

FIGURE D-17: Modify Style dialog box

font-size text box

color text box

Preview of style being modified

Description of style being modified

font-size units list box

body style rule

color swatch

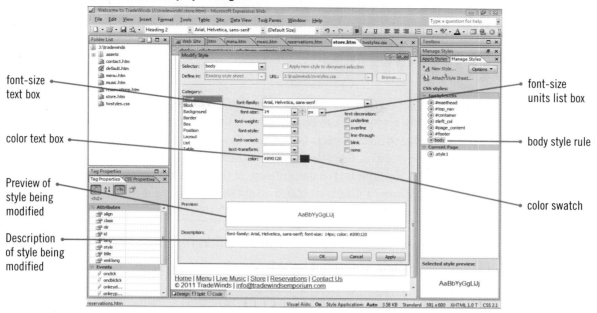

FIGURE D-18: Store page after body style is modified

Changes to style rule applied

Style sheet is now open, with asterisk indicating file has been changed

No asterisk, indicating that HTML page has not been changed

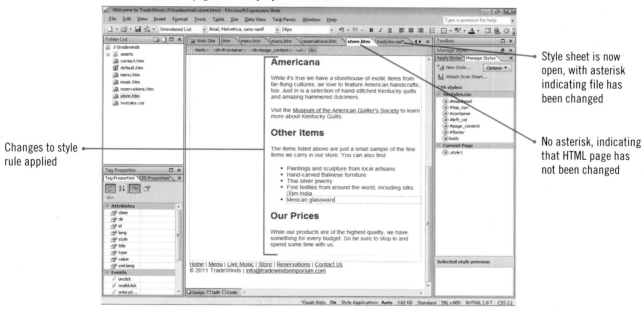

Taking control of your styles

Once you begin to create and apply your own styles in Expression Web, you should avoid using the Font, Font Size, Font Color, Highlight, Align Text Left, Center, and Align Text Right tools on the Common toolbar. If you use the toolbar options rather than creating and applying styles using the Apply Styles task pane, Expression Web will make and apply a style for you and add the style rule to the HTML page. This can present several problems. First, Expression Web names the styles incrementally as .style1, .style2, etc. These aren't very descriptive names, and it becomes difficult to sort them out. The second issue is that because Expression Web inserts the styles into the HTML document, you cannot use these styles on other pages in your site. Finally, because of the cascade, these applied styles can override any styles you place in the external style sheet later, causing frustration when the styles aren't acting as you expected. The CSS Properties task pane can be helpful when troubleshooting these issues as it shows all styles applied to a selection and the order of precedence.

Expression Web

Creating a Class–Based Style Rule

Element-based rules are unbeatable if you want an element to appear the same way on every page of a site. But what if you need a style that can be applied to a single instance of an element or only part of an element? Use a class-based style. A **class-based rule** is a style rule that can be created and applied to any selected content or element. Class-based styles must be manually applied to content. ⬛⬛⬛ Catalina wants to be able to highlight text in certain areas of the site with a subtle shade of yellow. You create a class-based style to display a bold text against a light yellow background.

STEPS

1. **Make the store.htm tab page active in the editing window**

2. **Click the New Style button on the Manage Styles task pane**
   The New Style dialog box opens.

TROUBLE
Be sure not to type over the period before the class name. If you do, retype the period. The style will not show up as an available style to use unless you start it with a period.

3. **Click in the Selector text box, then type highlight to replace the selected name**
   The new class is named .highlight. The period in front of the name is required and indicates that this is a class-based rule. When naming a class, do not use a number as the first character. It's common to avoid using spaces, but they are allowed. You should choose class names based on meaning, not on appearance. For example, you plan to use this style to call attention to certain text on the site, so "highlight" is appropriate. "YellowBackground" would be less appropriate since it describes the intended appearance rather than the purpose of the class. There's a practical reason for this. If Catalina changes her mind and decides she wants to highlight text by putting a blue border around it instead of using a yellow background, the name of the class still makes sense.

4. **Click the Define in list arrow, then click Existing style sheet**

5. **If twstyles.css does not appear in the URL list, click the URL list arrow, then click twstyles.css**
   The new style rule will be added to the external style sheet for this site.

6. **Click the font-weight list arrow, then click bold**
   Compare your screen to Figure D-19.

QUICK TIP
Hex values are not case sensitive; typing either #FFE9BB or #ffe9bb is acceptable and results in the same color.

7. **Click Background in the Category list, click in the background-color text box, type #FFE9BB, then compare your screen to Figure D-20**
   The new background-color swatch displays a pale shade of yellow. Notice that the Font category is in bold, indicating that style options have been selected in that category.

8. **Verify that your screen matches Figure D-20, then click OK**
   The New Style dialog box closes. Nothing has changed on the page because the style has not yet been applied to any content. In the Manage Styles task pane, a red dot indicates an id-based style, a green dot indicates a class-based style, a blue dot indicates an element-based style, and a yellow dot indicates an inline style. A circle around the dot means that the style is used in the current page.

9. **Save your changes to all open pages**

FIGURE D-19: New Style dialog box with Font options selected

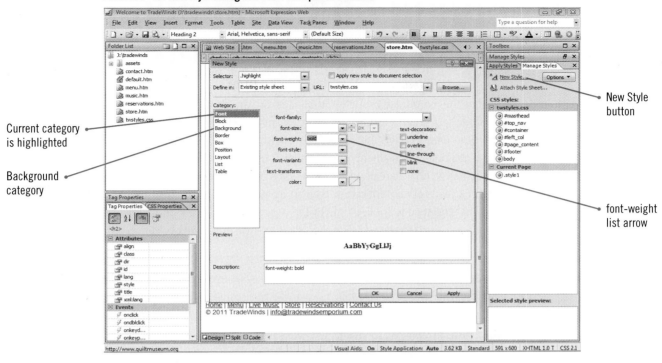

Current category is highlighted

Background category

New Style button

font-weight list arrow

FIGURE D-20: Background category of New Style dialog box

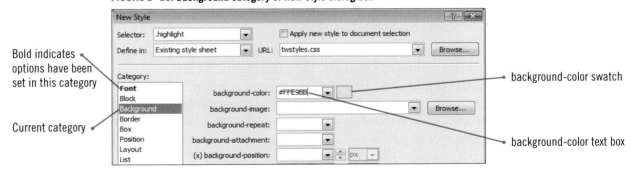

Bold indicates options have been set in this category

Current category

background-color swatch

background-color text box

Understanding the cascade in Cascading Style Sheets

Style rules are applied in a particular order, called the **cascade**. The cascading order is only important when two or more rules could possibly apply to an element. When troubleshooting styles in Expression Web, it's helpful to know that inline styles take precedence over internal styles, which take precedence over external styles, which take precedence over the browser default styles. The simplest way to avoid worrying about this is to be sure you put all your styles in the external style sheet for your site. This keeps conflicts to a minimum and makes it easier to fix any problems that might arise.

Expression Web

Applying and Removing a Class-Based Style Rule

In order for Web pages to display properly, HTML and CSS must work together. A style rule must be connected to an HTML tag as an attribute. So you can apply a class-based style in two ways. The first is to select an element in Design view, then apply the class to an existing element, such as a paragraph. The class applies to that single <p> element, and the style is only displayed on that element. The second way is to select content that is only part of an element (such as a sentence within a paragraph) and apply the style. If you select a piece of content rather than an element, Expression Web inserts a <span> tag around the content, so that the style is applied only to the desired text. ▚▚▚▚ You apply the class to some text on the Store page to call attention to TradeWind's wide range of product prices.

STEPS

QUICK TIP
Clicking the visual aid tab selects the entire element, including the HTML tags, not just the text.

1. **Verify that store.htm is the active page, click anywhere in the last paragraph, then click the visual aid tab**

   The paragraph element is selected.

2. **Click the Apply Styles tab in the Manage Styles task pane, then point to .highlight**

   See Figure D-21. When you point to a style, a list arrow and ScreenTip appear. The ScreenTip displays the style rule as it is written in CSS language. Clicking the list arrow opens a menu of options for applying and modifying styles.

3. **Click .highlight to apply the style, then click anywhere inside the selected text**

   The text is now bold with a light yellow background, as shown in Figure D-22. The quick tag selector and the visual aid tab display <p.highlight>, indicating that the <p> element now has a .highlight class applied to it. The store.htm tab has an asterisk on it, indicating that a change has been made to the page. The CSS file has not been changed because you applied an existing style. In this case, the changes are made to the page itself when Expression Web applies the class attribute to the paragraph tag. You decide that highlighting the entire paragraph is too visually distracting.

4. **Click the <p.highlight> tab on the visual aid, point to .highlight in the Apply Styles tab, click the .highlight list arrow, then click Remove Class**

   The text now looks the same as the surrounding body text. The quick tag selector and the visual aid tab display <p>, indicating that the .highlight class has been removed. Notice that the class is still available in the Apply Styles task pane for you to use. You have only detached the class from the element; you have not deleted the style rule.

5. **Select the text something for every budget**

6. **Click .highlight in the Apply Styles tab, then click anywhere inside the selection**

   Compare your screen to Figure D-23. The quick tag selector and the visual aid tab indicate that the text is now part of a <span> element with a .highlight class applied to it.

7. **Save all changes, close the tradewinds site, then exit Expression Web**

Using multiple style sheets

You are not limited to using one style sheet on your site. Many sites now include a special style sheet that determines how a Web page will look when printed. These print style sheets often remove some of the design elements and format the text to make it more readable in print. Some sites also use a style sheet to serve up a different design to visitors using handheld devices. Multiple style sheets can also be used in conjunction with JavaScript code to enable visitors to display the site with a different layout or color scheme or, more important, to allow them to increase the text size to make it easier to read.

FIGURE D-21: Highlight class style

Apply Styles tab

highlight class style

highlight list arrow

ScreenTip

<p> element selected

FIGURE D-22: Style highlight applied to <p> element

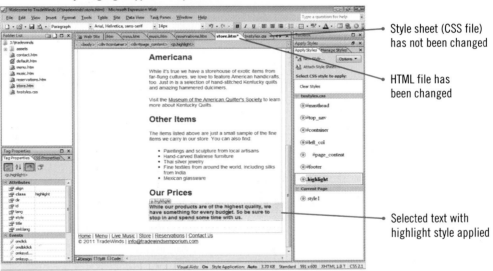

Style sheet (CSS file) has not been changed

HTML file has been changed

Selected text with highlight style applied

FIGURE D-23: Style highlight applied to selected text

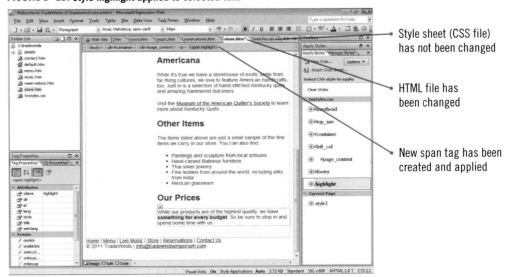

Style sheet (CSS file) has not been changed

HTML file has been changed

New span tag has been created and applied

Practice

If you have a SAM user profile, you may have access to hands-on instruction, practice, and assessment of the skills covered in this unit. Log in to your SAM account (http://sam2007.course.com/) to launch any assigned training activities or exams that relate to the skills covered in this unit.

▼ CONCEPTS REVIEW

Label each element in the Expression Web window shown in Figure D-24.

FIGURE D-24

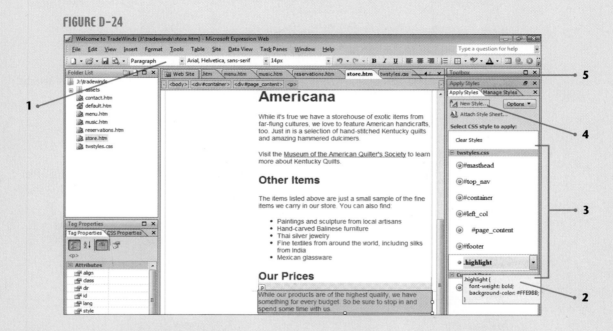

Match the HTML element with the statement that best describes when to use it.

6. **\<p\>**
7. **\<br /\>**
8. **\<h1\>**
9. **\<h2\>**
10. **\<ol\>**
11. **\<ul\>**
12. **\<span\>**

a. Create an element so a class can be applied to it
b. Create a new paragraph
c. Create a first-level heading
d. Add a line break within a paragraph
e. Create a subheading
f. Create a list of unordered items
g. Create a list of ordered items

Select the best answer from the list of choices.

13. **Pressing [Shift][Enter] while in Design view inserts a(n):**
    a. \<p\> tag.
    b. \<li\> tag.
    c. \<br /\> tag.
    d. \<span\> tag.

14. **Placing your style rules in a CSS file is known as using:**
    a. An internal style sheet.
    b. Inline styles.
    c. An external style sheet.
    d. Semantic markup.

15. **If you want to create a style rule that you can apply to only a few paragraph elements in your site, you would use:**
    a. The \<body\> tag.
    b. The \<br /\> tag.
    c. An element selector.
    d. A class selector.

16. A hex value is used to:

- **a.** Define a color in a style rule.
- **b.** Attach a style sheet to an HTML file.
- **c.** Determine the font size.
- **d.** Remove an applied style.

▼ SKILLS REVIEW

1. Create paragraphs and line breaks.

- **a.** Launch Expression Web, then open the careers Web site.
- **b.** Open the contact page.
- **c.** Click in front of the text **9283** at the bottom of the page, then switch to Split view.
- **d.** Create a paragraph break at the location of the insertion point.
- **e.** Undo your last action.
- **f.** Create a line break at the location of the insertion point.
- **g.** Create a line break in front of the word **Avon**.
- **h.** Switch back to Design view, then save your page.

2. Create headings.

- **a.** Select the text **Contact Careers Guaranteed** at the top of the contact page.
- **b.** Using the Style list box, apply the <h1> tag to the selected text.
- **c.** Open the home page, then apply the <h1> tag to the text **Your Career. Guaranteed**.
- **d.** On the home page, apply the <h2> tag to the text **Why we're different**.
- **e.** On the home page, apply the <h2> tag to the text **Testimonial**.
- **f.** Open the about page, then apply the <h1> tag to the text **About Careers Guaranteed**.
- **g.** On the about page, apply the <h2> tag to the text **Our Management Team**.
- **h.** Open the services page, then apply the <h1> tag to the text **Careers Guaranteed Services**.
- **i.** On the services page, apply the <h2> tag to each line of text that begins **Help with**.
- **j.** Save all open pages.

3. Create lists.

- **a.** On the services page, select the text beginning with **Career exploration** and ending with **future earnings** and potential.
- **b.** Use the Style list box options to create an ordered list of the selected text.
- **c.** Use the Style list box options to change it to an unordered list.
- **d.** Create a new list item at the end of the list, then type **Online career library**.
- **e.** Save your changes to the page.

4. Create an element-based style rule.

- **a.** Open the New Style dialog box.
- **b.** Choose the body element as a selector, and define the rule in the cgstyles.css style sheet.
- **c.** Set the font-size to 14 px.
- **d.** Click the OK button to close the New Style dialog box.
- **e.** View another page in the site to verify that text size changed on all pages.
- **f.** Save all open pages.

5. Modify a style rule.

- **a.** On the Manage Styles tab, right-click the body style, then open the Modify Style dialog box.
- **b.** Change the font-family to Arial, Helvetica, sans-serif, and the color to #663300.
- **c.** Click OK to close the Modify Style dialog box.
- **d.** View another page to verify that the font face and color changed on all pages.
- **e.** Save all open pages.

6. Create a class-based style rule.

- **a.** Switch to the home page, then open the New Style dialog box.
- **b.** Type **testimonial** in the Selector text box. (*Hint*: Be careful not to type over the period.)
- **c.** Define the style in an existing style sheet (cgstyles.css).

d. Switch to the Background category, then set the background-color to #CCDDFF.

e. Click the OK button to close the New Style dialog box.

f. Save your changes to the style sheet.

7. **Apply and remove a class-based style rule.**

a. Select the word **Testimonial** on the home page, then apply the testimonial style to the selected word.

b. Click the visual aid tab to select the heading element you just applied the style to.

c. Point to the testimonial style in the Apply Styles task pane, click the list arrow, then remove the class.

d. Click in the last paragraph of text, and click the visual aid tab to select the element.

e. Apply the testimonial style by clicking the style in the Apply Styles task pane, then click anywhere inside the testimonial paragraph.

f. Compare your screen to Figure D-25, save all open pages, close the Web site, then exit Expression Web.

FIGURE D-25

> **Testimonial**
>
> p.testimonial
> I'd been looking for the right job for more than four months when a friend told me about Careers Guaranteed. They had matched me with the perfect job within six weeks. I've never been happier with my career! --Antoine D.
>
> Home | Services | About | Contact
> © 2011 Careers Guaranteed | info@careersguaranteed.com
>
> ☐Design ☐Split ☐Code ◀
>
> Visual Aids: **On** Style Application: **Auto** 2.91 KB Standa

▼ INDEPENDENT CHALLENGE 1

In this project, you continue your work on the ConnectUp Web site. Tiffany e-mailed you to ask about progress on the Web site. You decide your next step should be to mark up the text and create some styles for the site.

a. Launch Expression Web, then open the connectup Web site.

b. Open the contact page and add line breaks after each line of the address.

c. Select the text **Contact ConnectUp** and apply an <h1> tag.

d. Open the home page, then apply the <h1> tag to the text ConnectUp to a Better Career and Life.

e. Open the joinup page, then apply the <h1> tag to the text Join Up with ConnectUp!.

f. Open the faq page, then apply the <h1> tag to the text Frequently Asked Questions about ConnectUp. Apply the <h2> tag to the lines Services, Pricing, Membership, Privacy, and About the Company.

g. Select the four lines of text under the first answer, beginning with **friends** and ending with **neighborhood**, and create an unordered list.

h. Create a new style; use the body element as a selector and define it in the custyles.css external style sheet. Set the font-family as Arial, Helvetica, sans-serif. Click OK to close the New Style dialog box.

i. Modify the body style to make the font-color #666666 and the font-size 14 px. (*Hint*: You must use the Manage Styles pane to modify an element-based rule.)

j. Create a class-based style rule named **.qa** that sets the font-color to #FFFFFF and the background-color to #FF8800.

k. On the faq page, apply the qa style to the text Q: before each question and A: before each answer. (*Hint*: Be careful not to select the space after the colon.)

l. Modify the qa style to change the font-size to 16px.

m. Save changes to all open files, then preview the faq page in a browser.

n. Compare your screen to Figure D-26, save your work, close the Web site, then exit Expression Web.

FIGURE D-26

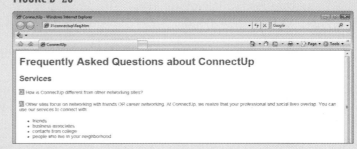

▼ INDEPENDENT CHALLENGE 2

In this project, you continue your work on the Memories Restored Web site. You are ready to mark up your content, then start creating some styles that will work with your design concept and color scheme.

a. Launch Expression Web, then open the memories Web site.

b. Go through each page and add <h1> and <h2> tags as appropriate. (*Hint*: On the contact page, you first need line breaks before the text 1579, Banff, T1L, and 403-555-1212.)

c. Mark up the services on the home page as an unordered list.

d. In the external style sheet, define a style using the body element as a selector, with a font-size of 12 px and a font-color of #663333.

e. In the external style sheet, create a class-based style named **testimonialname**, then apply the style to each name on the testimonial page. You can choose how to style it, but include the color #316A72 or #CDE6EA.

Advanced Challenge Exercise

- Open the tips page and create a class-based style named **.resources**. Give the style a solid, thin, dark brown border.
- Apply the <h2> tag to the word Resources, then apply the .resources style to the h2 element.

g. Save your work, close the Web site, then exit Expression Web.

▼ INDEPENDENT CHALLENGE 3

Note: This Independent Challenge requires an Internet connection.

The staff at Technology for All is most interested in developing a new graphical look for their new Web site. You, however, understand that the way the content is structured and styled is very important, too. You decide to research some sites you admire to see how they structure and style their content so you can provide some recommendations to Technology for All.

a. Visit at least three Web sites that you think are well-designed. Notice the way text is visually displayed on each site.

b. Use the View Source function of your browser to look at the underlying code. Try to identify any semantic markup. The page will include a lot of code but don't be intimidated or try to understand it all. Just focus on looking for the tags you learned about in this unit. (*Hint*: The View Source command is usually located on the View menu; it might be called Page Source, Source, or something similar.)

c. Write a paragraph on each site that evaluates how readable the text is, how well-structured it is, and whether the content is easy to scan for structure.

Advanced Challenge Exercise

- For each site, identify one piece of text that is displayed as a heading. (For example, it's larger and a different color from the body text.) Find that text in the code in View Source, and note whether it is marked with HTML heading tags.
- Write a paragraph explaining the results of your research and discussing why the sites did or did not do a good job with marking up the content.

d. Add your name to the document, save it, and print it.

▼ REAL LIFE INDEPENDENT CHALLENGE

This assignment builds on the personal Web site you have worked on in previous units. In this project, you add structure and styles to the text on the pages.

a. Review your text and add any necessary line breaks or paragraphs to complete the structure of the page.

b. Apply appropriate HTML heading tags to the text headings and subheadings (if used) on your pages.

c. Review your text and create lists where appropriate. Add content to create at least one list if necessary; it can be either an ordered or an unordered list.

d. Create at least one element-based rule in the external style sheet for your site that changes the look of your site's text in some way.

e. Create at least one class-based style rule in the external style sheet, name it according to its function rather than its appearance, then apply the class-based style rule where appropriate.

f. When you are finished, save changes to all pages, preview the site in a Web browser, then close the site and exit Expression Web.

Expression Web

▼ VISUAL WORKSHOP

Launch Expression Web, then open the ecotours Web site. Modify the home page and the external style sheet so that your screen matches Figure D-27. To accomplish this, you'll need to add text as necessary, structure the text, create an element-based style, and create and apply a class-based style. (*Hint*: The color used in the element-based style has the hex value #666666 and the color used in the class-based style has the hex value #D2FFD2.) When you are finished, save your changes, close the Web site, then exit Expression Web.

FIGURE D-27

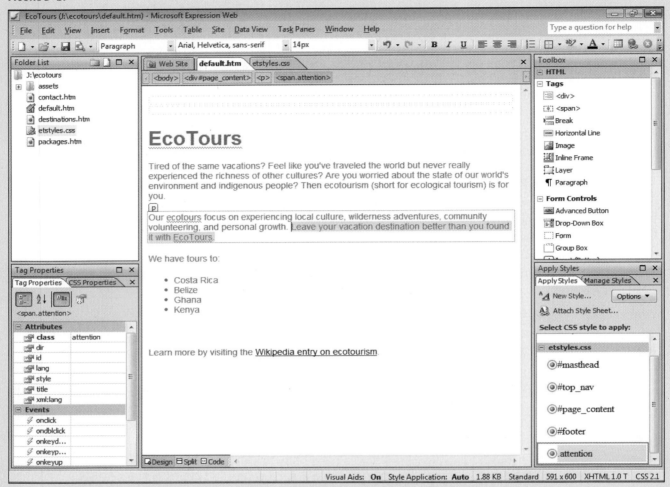

Working with Pictures

Pictures, also called **images** or **graphics**, add visual interest to any Web site, helping to draw visitors into the site's content. For some types of sites, such as online stores, portfolios, or photo galleries, pictures are an essential part of the content. Using Expression Web, you can add pictures to your Web pages, resize and enhance pictures, adjust the margins and alignment of a picture, and create small pictures that link to larger ones. Now that you have created a solid foundation for the TradeWinds site and added all the text, you decide to add pictures to the site.

OBJECTIVES

Understand Web graphics

Insert a picture

Resize and resample a picture

Edit a picture

Set wrapping style and margins

Set Auto Thumbnail options

Create a thumbnail picture

Style a thumbnail picture

Understanding Web Graphics

Learning to create and use Web graphics can be one of the most fun and yet most frustrating aspects of learning Web design. The possibilities for creativity are endless, but learning the terminology and tools involved in creating and editing images requires time and patience. Web graphics is an entire field unto itself and, in fact, many sites are designed by one person or team who works on the code and another who creates the graphics. However, with a little education about how digital graphics work, you can be comfortable working with pictures in Expression Web. 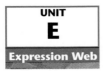 You decide to learn more about Web graphics.

DETAILS

To work successfully with pictures in Expression Web, it's important to understand:

- **Image measurements**

    The size of an image can be measured in two ways. The **dimensions** of an image are its height and width, usually measured in pixels. These dimensions determine how large the picture looks on a screen. The **file size** of an image is measured in kilobytes (KB) and affects how long it takes the picture to display in a visitor's browser. In general, the larger an image's dimensions, the larger its file size. However, the file format and the amount of color and detail in the image also affect the file size.

- **Page download times**

    The **download time** of a page is the amount of time it takes the page to load into a browser. Download time is determined by two factors: the file size of the page and its referenced files (including image files), and the speed of the visitor's Internet connection. You have no influence over a visitor's Internet connection speed, but you can control the size of your Web page files. Keeping your pages lean is critical to a successful Web site. Research has shown that people will wait an average of eight seconds for a page to load before surfing away to a different site.

    The status bar in Expression Web shows the total file size for a page. See Figure E-1. It's a good idea to keep an eye on this as you're working to make sure your page size doesn't become too large. There is no ideal file size for a page, but as a rule of thumb, 50–100 KB is a safe range. A 100 KB page downloads in about 14 seconds on a 56k dial-up connection and in 2 seconds on a high-speed connection. If most of your visitors are using a slower dial-up connection, aim for a smaller file size for your pages. You can keep the total page size down by using fewer images and using images that have smaller file sizes.

- **Image file formats**

    Digital images can be saved in dozens of different file formats. Only three of these file formats, JPEG, GIF, and PNG, can be used for Web pages. The golden rule when saving images for the Web is to produce the best-looking image with the smallest possible file size. The format in which the file is saved affects both image quality and file size. The **JPEG** (pronounced jay-peg) format is best used for photographs and other images that contain many different colors, such as detailed artwork. The **GIF** (pronounced jif or gif) format is best used for images that are drawings, simple graphics, navigation buttons, or that contain large areas of solid colors. A GIF can also be animated and can have a transparent background color. The **PNG** (pronounced ping) format was created specifically for Web graphics. It produces high-quality images with small file sizes. Unfortunately, many browsers still don't properly display PNG images, so it has limited practical usefulness. See Figure E-2 for examples of a JPG and a GIF.

FIGURE E-1: File size indicator on status bar

File size

FIGURE E-2: Examples of JPEG and GIF images

JPEG format is best
for photographs
and paintings

GIF format is best
for images with
fewer colors

Finding photographs for your site

If you're fortunate enough to be a talented photographer, you can shoot your own digital photos to use for your Web site. Or you could hire a professional photographer, but that can get expensive. It can be tempting to copy pictures off other Web sites, but unauthorized use violates copyright laws and leads to legal problems. A better option is to purchase stock photography, or to use photos that fall within the public domain. **Stock photos** are photos taken by professional photographers and then offered for sale to Web designers, graphic designers, and others who need images for Web sites, print advertisements, and other projects. Stock photography used to be very expensive, but now there are many Web sites that offer high-quality photos for reasonable prices. **Public domain** is work that is not protected by copyright law and is free to use and copy. To learn more about stock photography, enter the term "stock photography" in your favorite search engine and look through the listings. To learn more about public domain photos, visit a site such as www.pdphoto.org, or enter a term such as "public domain photos" in a search engine.

Inserting a Picture

A picture in a Web page is not embedded in the HTML file. Rather, the image file is referenced in the page's HTML code. When you insert a picture into a page, Expression Web inserts an <img> tag in the Web page code. The <img> tag contains the path to the image file as well as the height, width, and other attributes of the image. The Web browser then locates the image file and displays it in the page for the visitor. Catalina has sent you a picture of a fountain in front of the TradeWinds Café that she would like to include on the home page.

STEPS

1. **Open the tradewinds Web site, then open the home page**

2. **Click just before the text Our guests experience, click Insert on the menu bar, point to Picture, then click From File**

TROUBLE
Make sure that a check mark appears in the Show this prompt when inserting images box.

3. **Navigate to the folder where you store your Data Files, click Fish Fountain.jpg, then click Insert**
   The Accessibility Properties dialog box opens, allowing you to set properties to improve the accessibility of your site. **Alternate text**, often referred to as alt text, is an attribute of the <img> tag that describes the image in words. Visitors who use screen reader software hear this text read aloud. Some people set their browsers to display alt text instead of images so pages load more quickly. A **long description** allows you to provide a more detailed description of the image, either by typing it in the box or by using the Browse button to link to an HTML file containing the description. This is necessary only for charts, graphs, and other data-intensive images. Neither of these properties is visible on the Web page; they are added to the code.

4. **Click in the Alternate text field, then type Fish fountain at TradeWinds**
   See Figure E-3. If the image itself contains text, such as a navigation button that reads About Us, enter that text as the alternate text. If an image is purely decorative, such as a bullet or dividing line, it's acceptable to not use alternate text.

QUICK TIP
You can move an image by clicking it, then dragging it to a new position on the page.

5. **Click OK, then click the Save button 🖫 on the Common toolbar**
   The Save Embedded Files dialog box opens. The picture you inserted was located outside the tradewinds root folder, so you can use this dialog box to save a copy of it in the root folder with your other Web site files. For more information on options available in this dialog box, see Table E-1. You want to save the image as prompted but the file name, Fish Fountain.jpg, contains spaces, which are not allowed in Web file names.

6. **Click Rename, type fishfountain.jpg, then press [Enter]**
   The new file name replaces the original name.

QUICK TIP
You can also move an image file by clicking the file name in the Folder List task pane, then dragging it into the correct folder.

7. **Click Change Folder, click assets, then click OK**
   See Figure E-4.

8. **Click OK again, then double-click the assets folder in the Folder List task pane**
   Both the home page and image file are saved. Notice that the file size of the page has increased to approximately 30 kilobytes. The fishfountain.jpg file is now in the assets folder. See Figure E-5.

TABLE E-1: Options in the Save Embedded Files dialog box

button	function
Rename	Rename the file before saving
Change Folder	Change the folder where the file is saved
Set Action	Allows you to choose an action based on what type of file you are saving; when saving a file you inserted from outside the root folder, allows you to leave the image in its original location.
Picture File Type	Change the file type to GIF, JPEG, PNG-8, or PNG-24; you normally want to leave the image file type the same.

FIGURE E-3: Accessibility Properties dialog box

Alternate text field

FIGURE E-4: Save Embedded Files dialog box

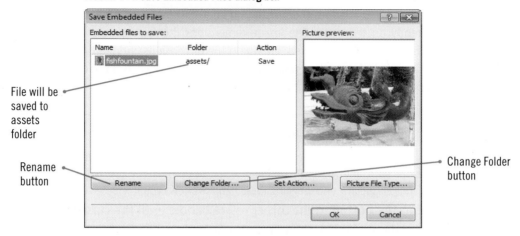

File will be saved to assets folder

Rename button

Change Folder button

FIGURE E-5: Page and embedded files are saved

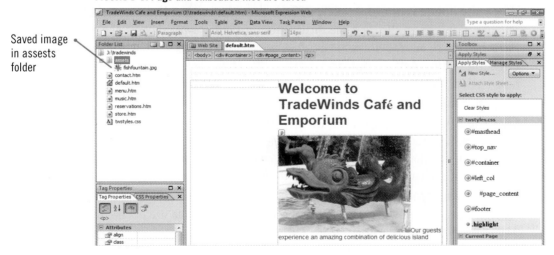

Saved image in assests folder

Writing meaningful alternate text

When creating alternate text, keep your descriptions brief. Think about what information the image conveys and use that as a description. Don't use the word "picture" or "button" in the alt text. For example, alt text for a navigation button that says "Services" on it should read "Services," not "Services button." For a company logo, use the company name. For other images, focus on describing what the image means, rather than what the image looks like. For example, suppose you're using a photo of a baseball player in a story about his game-winning grand slam. Instead of using "David Ortiz" for the alt text, use something like "Ortiz rounds third base after hitting a grand slam."

Resizing and Resampling a Picture

You can change the size of a picture in Expression Web by dragging the sides or a corner of the image until it's the right size. In general, reducing the image dimensions works well but enlarging them can result in a significant loss of quality and a grainy or blurry appearance. When changing the size of an image in Expression Web, you can simply resize it or you can resample it. **Resizing** the picture means that Expression Web changes the height and width attributes in the <img> tag to make the image display differently on the page. The image dimensions themselves don't change, nor does the file size. **Resampling** removes extra pixels, changing the dimensions and file size of the image. It improves the clarity, so it's usually better than resizing. Resampling also decreases the download time. ▓▓▓▓▓ The fish fountain picture is so large that it overwhelms the text. You decide to make it smaller.

STEPS

1. **Click the fish fountain picture to select it**

   See Figure E-6. The Tag Properties task pane displays the image attributes, including the alternative text, height, file path, and width. Resize handles appear on the right side, bottom side, and bottom-right corner of the image. Clicking and dragging these handles allows you to change the size of the image.

2. **Point to the bottom-right corner resize handle until the cursor changes to** ⬉

3. **Press and hold [Shift], then drag the resize handle up and to the left**

   A ScreenTip appears showing the dimensions of the image in pixels. The first measurement is the width and the second is the height. You can watch the dimensions change on the ScreenTip so you know when to release the image. By holding [Shift] as you drag, the height and width change in the same proportion.

4. **When the image is approximately 250 pixels wide, release the mouse button and [Shift]**

   The image appears smaller and the Picture Actions button appears below the picture, as shown in Figure E-7. The Picture Actions button provides the option of resizing or resampling the picture.

5. **Click the Picture Actions button list arrow 🖼, then click the Resample Picture to Match Size option button**

   The picture looks clearer.

6. **Click the Save button 💾 on the Common Toolbar**

   Because you have made changes to the image file, the Save Embedded Files dialog box opens, giving you options for saving the changes to the image file. You want to keep the original copy of the fish fountain just in case you need it later, so you decide to save the file with a different name.

7. **Click Rename, type fishfountain_small.jpg, then click OK**

   See Figure E-8. Two image files are now in the assets folder. The file size has decreased to approximately 3 kilobytes, so the page will load more quickly in a visitor's browser.

8. **Preview your page in a browser, close the browser window, then return to Expression Web**

Thinking in pixels

After spending your life thinking in inches or centimeters, it can be difficult to adjust to thinking in pixels. As you work more with pixel measurements, you will get better at knowing, for example, how large a 200X400 pixel image looks on the page. Until then, here are some tips to help you visualize:

- On most monitors, 75 pixels is about an inch and 30 pixels is about a centimeter.

- If you're not sure how wide an image should be, start at 200 pixels and adjust from there.
- Think of the measurement in relationship to your target screen resolution. If you're designing for a screen that's 1024 pixels wide, a picture that's 500 pixels wide takes up half the width of the screen.

FIGURE E-6: Fish fountain picture selected

Resize handles

In Step 2, drag this resize handle

File size has increased to 30.6 kilobytes

Attributes of fish fountain image

FIGURE E-7: Resized fish fountain picture

Picture Actions button

File size has not changed

Height and width have changed

FIGURE E-8: Resampled fish fountain picture

assets folder contains both images

File size has decreased to 2.77 kilobytes

Editing a Picture

Expression Web includes many image editing functions, available on the Pictures toolbar. These tools allow you to make simple changes to a picture, such as cropping or increasing contrast, without having to open it in a graphics editing program. **Cropping** a picture trims or removes unwanted parts of the picture. The image editing tools don't have the same capabilities as a full-blown graphics program, so for any significant changes in size, color, or tone, you'll want to use a graphics editing program to edit the image and then use Expression Web to insert it in the page. ▓▓▒▒ You are pleased with the size of the fish fountain image, but think a few enhancements would improve its appearance. You decide to edit the picture to remove the bottom area showing the pipes under the fish, brighten the image, and flip it so the fish points to the right.

STEPS

QUICK TIP

If the toolbar opens on top of the picture, drag the top of the toolbar down until it's below the picture.

1. **Right-click the fish fountain picture on the home page, then click Show Pictures Toolbar on the shortcut menu**

   The Pictures toolbar opens as a floating toolbar near the picture. See Table E-2 for a description of the buttons on this toolbar.

2. **Click the Crop button ⊹ on the Pictures toolbar**

   A cropping area appears within the image, surrounded by eight crop handles. To crop the image, you can drag any or all crop handles to change the cropping area, then press [Enter].

3. **Drag the crop handles until your cropping area matches Figure E-9, then press [Enter]**

   The picture is cropped so the pipes no longer show at the bottom.

4. **Click the More Brightness button ⊠⃒ on the Pictures toolbar four times**

   Each time you click the More Brightness button, the picture becomes brighter. You decide you've taken it a bit too far and would like to decrease the brightness.

5. **Click the Less Brightness button ⊠⃒ on the Pictures toolbar two times**

   The picture's brightness decreases and the appearance improves.

6. **Click the Flip Horizontal button ◢◣ on the Pictures toolbar**

   The picture flips horizontally so that the head is pointing to the right.

7. **Click the Close button ✖ on the Pictures toolbar, then compare your screen to Figure E-10**

   The Pictures toolbar closes. The fish fountain image is now cropped, brightened, and faces right instead of left.

8. **Save the page**

   The Save Embedded Files dialog box opens. The edits to the picture were made to the file itself, so you need to save the file.

9. **Click Rename, type fishfountain_edited.jpg to replace the highlighted text, then click OK**

   You now have three versions of the fish fountain image in the assets folder: the original image, the resized image, and the resized and edited image.

Using the Pictures toolbar

The Pictures toolbar is packed with simple image editing tools. Using the features on the toolbar, you can change a picture from color to grayscale, wash out the color on a picture, rotate pictures, create multiple hotspots on a single picture that link to different pages, or add a beveled edge to your picture. A bevel is an angled edge that adds a three-dimensional look to an image. It's worth spending some time experimenting with the tools on the Pictures toolbar to see how they can enhance your Web site graphics.

FIGURE E-9: Fish fountain picture with crop marks

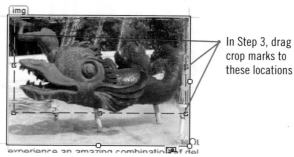

FIGURE E-9: Fish fountain picture with crop marks

In Step 3, drag crop marks to these locations

FIGURE E-10: Cropped, brightened, and flipped picture

TABLE E-2: Buttons on the Pictures toolbar

button	use to	button	use to
Insert Picture From File	Insert a new picture or replace selected picture	More Brightness	Increase brightness of selected picture
Auto Thumbnail	Create a reduced-size version of selected picture and link it to a full-size version	Less Brightness	Decrease brightness of selected picture
Bring Forward	Set selected picture to display on top of surrounding content	Crop	Trim unwanted areas from selected picture
Send Backward	Set selected picture to display beneath surrounding content	Set Transparent Color	Make a specific color in selected picture transparent
Rotate Left 90°	Rotate selected picture 90° counterclockwise	Color	Make colors of selected picture grayscale or washed out
Rotate Right 90°	Rotate selected picture 90° clockwise	Bevel	Create an angled edge on selected picture
Flip Horizontal	Flip selected picture horizontally	Resample	Increase or decrease pixel dimensions and physical file size of selected picture
Flip Vertical	Flip selected picture vertically	Select Hotspot / Rectangular Hotspot / Circular Hotspot / Polygonal Hotspot / Highlight Hotspots	Select and create hotspot areas in selected picture that can be linked to files or pages
More Contrast	Increase contrast of selected picture	Restore	Undo all actions on selected picture since you last saved the Web page
Less Contrast	Decrease contrast of selected picture		

Expression Web

Setting Wrapping Style and Margins

Controlling a picture's wrapping style and margins helps you ensure that pictures and text work together to create a harmonious, easy-to-read design. You have three choices, called **wrapping styles** in Expression Web, for dictating how a picture will be positioned relative to its surrounding text. With the default wrapping style, None, the text does not flow around the picture, but starts at the bottom edge. This usually isn't the best look for a page layout. The other options are Left, which displays the picture on the left side with text wrapping around it on the right, or Right, which displays the picture on the right side with text wrapping around it on the left. If you wrap text around your image, you also want to create margins around your picture so the text doesn't flow to the edge of the picture. Expression Web includes several ways to set these properties, but the most convenient is using the Picture Properties dialog box. You want the image to appear on the left with text flowing on the right, and some white space around the image.

STEPS

1. **Double-click the fish fountain picture**
   The Picture Properties dialog box opens, as shown in Figure E-11. In the General tab, which is in front by default, you can change the image's file path, alternate text, and long description, and add or edit a hyperlink from the image.

2. **Click the Appearance tab**
   In the Appearance tab, you can set the wrapping style; determine layout options such as alignment, border thickness, and margins; and change the size of the image. The Alignment property determines the vertical alignment of the image. If you're applying a wrapping style, it is not necessary to set this property. By default, no border is added to an image when it is inserted, but if you'd like a border, you can add one here by typing a number for the width in the box.

3. **Click Left under Wrapping style**

4. **Select the text in the Horizontal margin box, type 10, select the text in the Vertical margin box, type 10, then compare your screen to Figure E-12**
   The horizontal margin controls the left and right margins, while the vertical margin controls the top and bottom margins. These settings determine how much white space is displayed between the picture and surrounding text.

5. **Click OK, then point to .style2 in the Apply Styles task pane**
   Expression Web created a class-based style rule, .style2, and applied it to the <img> tag to control the alignment and margins. The style rule declares that the picture should float to the left margin and should have a 10-pixel margin all around it. The img visual aid reflects the 10-pixel margins by showing a pink, diagonally striped area all around the image. You can change the margin by dragging on the edge of the visual aid. You decide you want the right margin to be larger than the left.

6. **Click the right edge of the visual aid box until the pointer changes to ⟺, drag to the right until the ScreenTip reads margin-right: 25px, then release the mouse button**
   The right margin is now larger than the left, as shown in Figure E-13.

7. **Point to .style2 in the Apply Styles task pane**
   The style has been revised to reflect the change in the right margin.

8. **Save the page, preview it in a Web browser, close the browser, then return to Expression Web**

FIGURE E-11: Picture Properties dialog box

Appearance tab

File path to picture

Alternate Text field

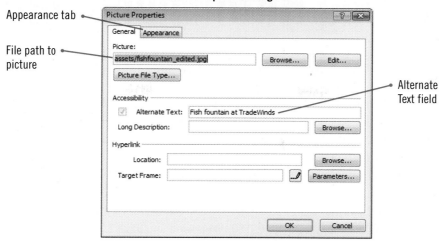

FIGURE E-12: Appearance tab of Picture Properties dialog box

Wrapping style options

Horizontal margin box

Vertical margin box

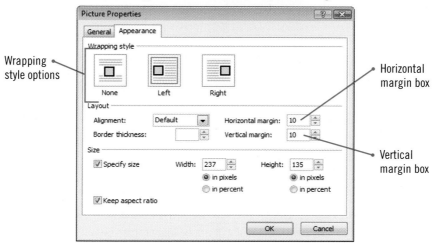

FIGURE E-13: Fish fountain picture after right margin is enlarged

Pink striped areas indicate margins

ScreenTip

Click and drag this edge

.style2 rule

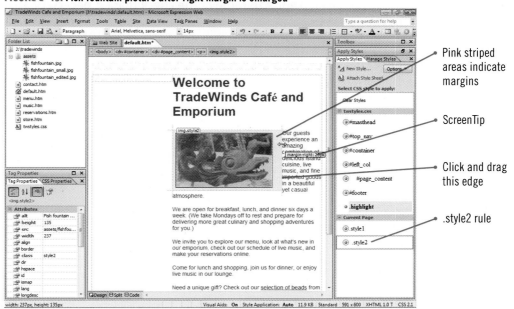

Expression Web

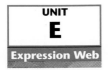
Setting Auto Thumbnail Options

Sometimes you may want to display a series of smaller images and link them to a larger version of the same image. Using smaller images, called thumbnail pictures or **thumbnails**, saves space on the page and minimizes download time. Product galleries, sets of vacation pictures, and portfolios are all examples of pages that work well with thumbnail images. Expression Web includes an Auto Thumbnail tool that can help save time. It creates a thumbnail image and automatically links it to the larger image. Without this feature, you would have to resize the image in a graphics program and then use Expression Web to insert the thumbnail into the page and create a link to the larger image. Expression Web's default styles for thumbnails create images that are 100 pixels wide and have a 2-pixel border. If you want to create thumbnails with properties that differ from the default, you should change the Auto Thumbnail settings in the Page Editor options *before* you create the thumbnail. Catalina has sent you a picture for the products page that you think would work best as a thumbnail. You want the thumbnail picture to be no longer or wider than 150 pixels and you don't want it to include a border.

STEPS

1. **Click** Tools **on the menu bar, then click** Page Editor Options
   The Page Editor dialog box opens.

2. **Click the** AutoThumbnail tab
   In the AutoThumbnail tab, you can set options that control the dimensions of the thumbnail, the size of the thumbnail's border, and whether a bevel is applied to the thumbnail.

3. **Click the** Set list arrow
   The Set options allow you to choose the dimensions of the width, the height, the longest side, or the shortest side.

QUICK TIP
Setting the longest or shortest side is useful if you have some images that are horizontal and some that are vertical; it ensures that while all thumbnails will not have the exact same dimensions, they will be more consistent in size.

4. **Click** Longest side, **then type** 150 **in the pixels box**
   The longest side of any thumbnail will not be longer than 150 pixels.

5. **Type** 0 **in the** Border thickness pixels **box**
   The thumbnail will not display a border.

6. **Click the** Beveled edge **to remove the check mark if necessary, then compare your screen to Figure E-14**
   The thumbnail will not display a bevel.

7. **Click** OK
   All new thumbnails you create in the Web site will be formatted with the new settings. When you change AutoThumbnail settings, all thumbnails you create afterward are affected, but previously created thumbnails will not change.

FIGURE E-14: Thumbnail tab of Page Editor Options dialog box

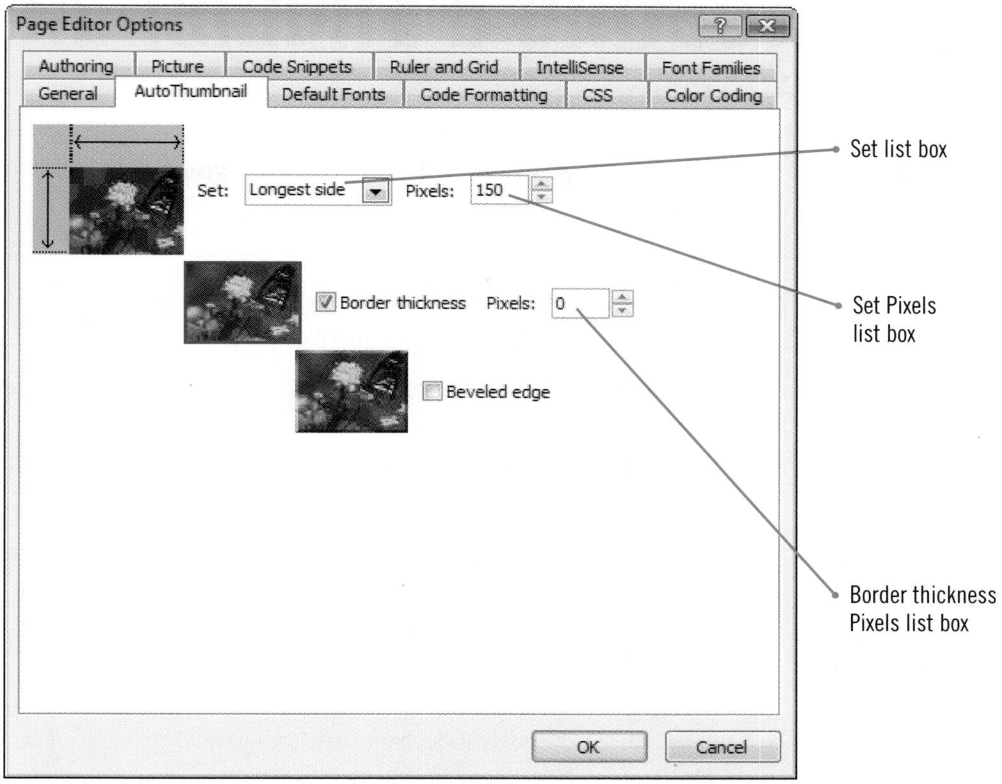

Maintaining a consistent graphical style

When deciding what graphics to use on your Web site, it's best to choose one style and stick with it. If you decide to use cartoon-like images, use them throughout the site. If you use photographs, don't mix them with illustrations. And if you use black-and-white photos, use them consistently rather than adding color images. Using a consistent style gives your site a polished and professional appearance.

Creating a Thumbnail Picture

After you have set the options for your thumbnail pictures, the next step is to insert the image into the page. You can then use the Auto Thumbnail command to create the thumbnail image as well as the link to the full-sized image. ▨▨▨▨ Now that you have set the appropriate options for your thumbnail image, you decide to insert the image and create the thumbnail.

1. **Open the store page, click just before the heading** African Art, **click** Insert **on the menu bar, point to** Picture, **then click** From File

2. **Navigate to the folder where you store your Data Files, click** Elephant Sculpture.jpg, **then click** Insert

QUICK TIP

If you want to make changes to an existing thumbnail, delete it, change the properties, then insert the picture again and re-create the thumbnail.

3. **Type** African Elephant Sculpture **in the Alternate text field, then click** OK
   The elephant sculpture picture is displayed in the page.

4. **Right-click the** elephant sculpture picture, **click** Auto Thumbnail **on the shortcut menu, then click anywhere on the page outside the picture**
   See Figure E-15. The picture is converted to a smaller thumbnail.

QUICK TIP

If you want to be able to see the entire file name, you can click the border between Name and Folder, then drag to the right to make the Name column wider.

5. **Save the page**
   The Save Embedded Files dialog box opens. Two files are listed. One is the thumbnail created by Expression Web and the other is the original elephant sculpture image. Depending on your screen size, you may not be able to see the entire file name of the image until you click the Rename button.

6. **Click the** first file name, **click** Rename, **then type** elephant_sculpture_thumb.jpg
   By default, Expression Web names the thumbnail image with the original file name plus "_small." Because the original file name had spaces in it, you need to change the entire file name.

7. **Click the** second file name, **click** Rename, **then type** elephant_sculpture.jpg
   Compare your screen to Figure E-16.

8. **Click** OK, **preview your page in a browser, then click the** elephant sculpture picture **in the browser window**
   See Figure E-17. The thumbnail links directly to the large image. Because it links directly to the image and not to a Web page, nothing displays except the image.

9. **Close the browser window, then return to Expression Web**

FIGURE E-15: Auto thumbnail of elephant sculpture

Auto thumbnail

FIGURE E-16: Renamed files in the Save Embedded Files dialog box

FIGURE E-17: Larger image displayed when thumbnail is clicked

Styling a Thumbnail Picture

The AutoThumbnail settings in the Page Editor Options control the dimensions, border size, and beveled edges on the thumbnail. To change the wrapping styles, alignment, or margins, you use the Picture Properties options. ▓▓▓▓ You are satisfied with the size of the thumbnail, but would like for it to wrap to the left and have some white space around it.

STEPS

1. **Double-click the elephant sculpture thumbnail picture**

   The Picture Properties dialog box opens.

2. **Click the Appearance tab, click Left under Wrapping style, type 10 in the Horizontal margin box, type 10 in the Vertical margin box, then compare your screen to Figure E-18**

3. **Click OK**

   See Figure E-19. The tab on the thumbnail's visual aid indicates that a style, style 2, has been applied. The visual aid also shows the 10-pixel margins surrounding the image.

4. **Save your changes to the page**

   The Save Embedded Files dialog box does not open because you only made changes to the styles on the page, and not to the image itself.

5. **Preview the page in a browser, then compare your screen to Figure E-20**

6. **Close the browser window, then return to Expression Web**

7. **Close the Web site, then exit Expression Web**

Understanding automatically generated styles

When you use toolbars or dialog boxes to change image or text properties, Expression Web will usually generate a style rule in that page's internal style sheet and attach it to the element. The styles are named incrementally (style1, style2, and so on). The styles appear in the Apply Styles and Manage Styles task panes, allowing you to modify or delete the style properties if you wish. For example, if you choose to have Expression Web add a border when an auto thumbnail is created, a style is generated and applied to the thumbnail. You can then modify the style later to change the border color or size.

FIGURE E-18: Appearance tab of Picture Properties dialog box

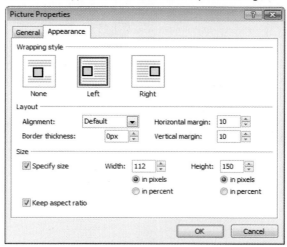

FIGURE E-19: Thumbnail Picture with styles applied

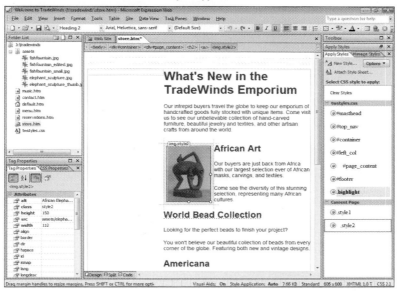

FIGURE E-20: Store page displayed in browser

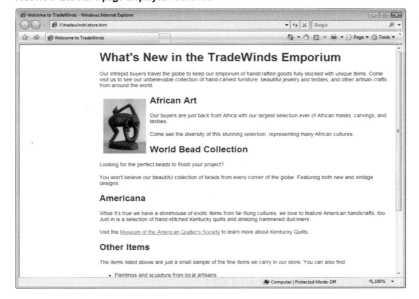

Practice

▼ CONCEPTS REVIEW

Refer to Figure E-21 to answer the following questions:

FIGURE E-21

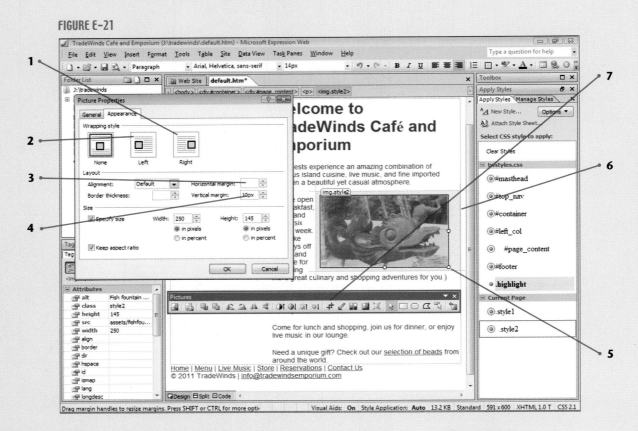

1. **Which element do you click to crop a picture?**
2. **Which element do you drag to change the margin size?**
3. **Which element do you drag to change the image size?**
4. **Which element do you click to make the text wrap on the right of a picture?**
5. **Which element do you click to make the text wrap on the left of a picture?**
6. **Which element do you use to set the top and bottom margins of a picture?**
7. **Which element do you use to set the left and right margins of a picture?**

Match each term with the statement that best describes it.

8. **Resizing**
9. **Resampling**
10. **JPEG**
11. **GIF**
12. **PNG**
13. **Thumbnail**

a. File format not well-supported by current browsers

b. File format best used for simple drawings and artwork with fewer colors

c. File format best used for photographs and detailed artwork

d. Changes the height and width attributes in the <img> tag but not the file dimensions

e. A small version of an image that links to a larger version of the image

f. Changes the image dimensions and file size

Select the best answer from the list of choices.

14. **Which of these controls the way text flows around a picture?**
    a. Margins
    b. Wrapping style
    c. Alignment
    d. Brightness

15. **If your Web site visitors use a slow dial-up connection, your Web page file sizes should be less than:**
    a. 1000 kilobytes.
    b. 100 kilobytes.
    c. 50 kilobytes.
    d. 5 kilobytes.

16. **Tools for cropping a picture and changing its brightness can be found on the:**
    a. Page Properties dialog box.
    b. Apply Styles task pane.
    c. Status bar.
    d. Pictures toolbar.

17. **For which type of image is it preferable to leave the Alternate text box empty?**
    a. Decorative image, such as a bullet
    b. Company logo
    c. Pictures accompanying text
    d. Navigation buttons

18. **Which of the following does *not* affect the download time of a Web page?**
    a. Number of images used on the page
    b. Speed of visitor's Internet connection
    c. File size of images used on the page
    d. Speed of the Web designer's Internet connection

19. **When resizing an image by dragging its resize handles, which key do you press to maintain the image's proportion while changing the width and height?**
    a. [Shift]
    b. [Alt]
    c. [Ctrl]
    d. [Tab]

▼ SKILLS REVIEW

1. **Insert a picture.**
   a. Launch Expression Web, then open the careers Web site.
   b. Open the home page, then click before the word Testimonial.
   c. Open the Picture dialog box, navigate to where you store your Data Files, then insert Testimonial Picture.jpg.
   d. Add the following alternate text when prompted: **Antoine is smiling about his new job.**
   e. Save the page. When the Save Embedded Files dialog box opens, change the folder to assets and rename the file to **testimonial_pic.jpg**. Click OK.
   f. Double-click the assets folder in the Folder List task pane to verify that testimonial_pic.jpg is in the folder.
   g. Preview your page in a browser, close the browser, then return to Expression Web.

2. **Resize and resample a picture.**
   a. Click the testimonial picture to select it.
   b. Click the bottom-right corner resize handle, hold down [Shift], then drag up and to the left until the width is approximately 270 pixels.
   c. Use the Picture Actions button to resample the picture.
   d. Sav your changes. When the Save Embedded Files dialog box opens, rename the image file to **testimonial_pic_small.jpg**. Click OK.
   e. Preview your page in a browser, close the browser, then return to Expression Web.

3. **Edit a picture.**
   a. Open the Pictures toolbar.
   b. Flip the picture horizontally.
   c. Close the Pictures toolbar.
   d. Save your changes. When the Save Embedded Files dialog box opens, rename the file to **testimonial_pic_edited.jpg**. Click OK.

4. **Set wrapping style and margins.**
   a. Double-click the testimonial picture to open the Picture Properties dialog box.
   b. Use the Appearance tab to set the Wrapping style to Right and all margins to 15.
   c. Click OK to close the Picture Properties dialog box.

d. Point to the .style2 rule in the Apply Styles task pane and verify the style properties.

e. Drag the left side of the image's visual aid to create a 40-pixel-wide left margin.

f. Point to the .style2 rule in the Apply Styles task pane and note the change in the size of the left margin.

g. Save the page, preview in a browser, compare your screen to Figure E-22, close the browser window, and return to Expression Web.

5. Set Auto Thumbnail options.

a. Open the Page Editor Options dialog box. On the AutoThumbnail tab, change the properties to a width of 75 pixels, a border of 0 pixels, and no beveled edge.

b. Click OK to close the Page Editor Options dialog box.

6. Create a thumbnail picture.

a. Open the contact page, then click just before the text **Careers Guaranteed** on the first line of the address.

b. Open the Picture dialog box, navigate to where you store your Data Files, then insert Careers Map.jpg. Add the following alternate text when prompted: **Map of Careers Guaranteed office location**.

c. Create an Auto Thumbnail from the map image.

d. Save the page. When the Save Embedded Files dialog box opens, rename the first image file to **careers_map_thumb.jpg** and the second to **careers_map.jpg**.

e. Preview the page in a browser, click the thumbnail image, close the browser window, and return to Expression Web.

7. Style a thumbnail picture.

a. Double-click the map image.

b. In the Appearance tab of the Picture Properties dialog box, set the Wrapping style to Left and the margins to 15 pixels each.

c. Save the page.

d. Preview the contact page in your browser and compare it to Figure E-23.

e. Close the Web site, then exit Expression Web.

FIGURE E-22

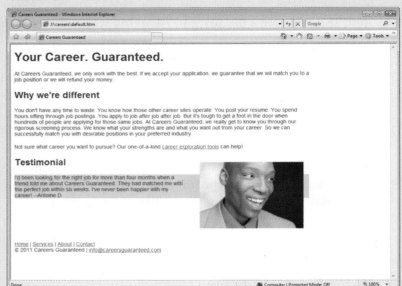

FIGURE E-23

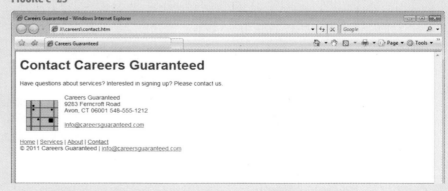

▼ INDEPENDENT CHALLENGE 1

In this project, you continue your work on the ConnectUp Web site. Tiffany is happy with the text on the site but wants to see some progress on the visual design. You decide to add some images to the site in preparation for your next meeting with her.

   a. Launch Expression Web, open the connectup Web site, then open the home page.

   b. Click just before the text You don't separate, then insert Connected Badge.jpg from the drive and folder where you store your Data Files. Add the Alternate text **Get Connected**!

   c. Save the page, then save the image in the assets folder as **connected_badge.jpg**. Preview the page in a browser, close the browser window, then return to Expression Web.

   d. Use the [Shift] key to maintain proportions as you resize the image to approximately 150 pixels wide.

   e. Resample the resized picture.

   f. Save the page, then save the image in the assets folder as **connected_badge_small.jpg**.

   g. Open the Pictures toolbar, then use the Crop button to trim as much white space from around the button without trimming any of the orange badge. When you are finished, close the Pictures toolbar.

   h. Save the page, then save the image in the asset folder as **connected_badge_cropped.jpg**.

   i. Use the Picture Properties tools to set the Wrapping style of the image to Left and all margins to 25 pixels.

   j. Drag the visual aid to decrease the top margin to approximately 10 pixels, then save the page.

   k. Select the badge image and drag it to move it right before the heading ConnectUp to a Better Career and Life.

   l. Save your changes, preview the home page in the browser, then compare your screen to Figure E-24.

   m. When you are finished, close the browser window, return to Expression Web, close the site, then exit Expression Web.

FIGURE E-24

▼ INDEPENDENT CHALLENGE 2

In this project, you continue your work on the Memories Restored Web site. You are ready to add some pictures that showcase the high-quality work of the photo restoration experts at Memories Restored.

    a. Launch Expression Web, then open the memories Web site.

    b. Open the home page, then insert the picture Car Couple.jpg from the drive and folder where you store your Data Files. Place the image anywhere in the page_content div on the home page that you think looks good. Add appropriate alternate text when prompted.

    c. Resize and edit the image as you'd like, using the Pictures toolbar.

    d. Save the page, saving the images in the assets folder and renaming them appropriately.

    e. Use the Picture Properties dialog box to adjust the margins and wrapping style as you'd like, then save the page.

    f. Open the work page, click beneath Example One, then insert the Example One.jpg file. Repeat this process to insert Example Two.jpg under the Example Two header, and Example Three.jpg under the Example Three header. Add appropriate alternate text when prompted.

    g. Save your page, renaming the images appropriately and saving them within the assets folder.

    h. Open the AutoThumbnail tab on the Page Editor options, and set the options as you'd like. (*Hint*: Because the images are so large, you might want to make these wider than normal thumbnails.)

    i. Create an AutoThumbnail from each of the example images you inserted on the work page. Save your page and rename all images as you're saving. (*Hint*: If you're not happy with them, delete each one, go back and change the Page Editor options, reinsert the images, then re-create the AutoThumbnails.)

Advanced Challenge Exercise

    ■ Open the tips page, click after the text **Photo Restoration** Tips, then insert the Tips Banner.jpg image.

    ■ Use the Pictures toolbar to rotate the image and change it to a grayscale image.

    ■ Save the page, and save the embedded image with an appropriate name.

    j. Preview your page in a browser, click each thumbnail, close the browser windows, return to Expression Web, close the Web site, and exit Expression Web.

▼ INDEPENDENT CHALLENGE 3

Note: This Independent Challenge requires an Internet connection.

Your client at Technology for All would like to use some photographs on the new Web site. The organization doesn't have any of their own photographs, and you don't have time to take photos yourself. You decide to look at some stock photography sites to see what your options are.

a. Go to your favorite search engine and enter **stock photography** as the search term.

b. Visit at least three of the sites that come up. At each site, search for images that would be suitable for Technology for All. Remember that the organization collects cast-off computers, repairs and upgrades them, and then donates the refurbished machines to low-income students.

c. Write a paragraph outlining what search terms you used while on the stock photography site to locate appropriate images.

d. Write a second paragraph describing at least five appropriate images you found for the site.

Advanced Challenge Exercise

■ Choose two similar images from two different sites and determine how much it would cost to purchase them. Assume that you plan to use the images on a Web site for at least five years at a size of at least 300x300 pixels. (*Hint:* You will have to look around the site for pricing information. You may have to add the images to a shopping cart to see the pricing, but you shouldn't need to enter any personal or payment information.)

■ Write a comparison of the costs for each image.

■ Write at least three sentences explaining whether you think any price difference between the images is justified and which image you would rather use, based on both appearance and price.

e. Add your name to the document, save it, and print it.

▼ REAL LIFE INDEPENDENT CHALLENGE

This assignment builds on the personal Web site you have worked on in previous units. In this project, you add pictures to your site.

a. Add at least three images to your site. You can use photographs you've taken, illustrations you've created, or other available graphics. Make sure that you own the copyright to the images or that they fall within the public domain.

b. Resize, resample, and/or move the images if necessary.

c. Make any edits to the pictures to improve their appearance, such as rotating them, changing the brightness or contrast, and so on.

d. Adjust the wrapping style and margins of each picture until you are pleased with the appearance of your pages.

e. Create at least one Auto Thumbnail and adjust the styles as you like.

f. Check the file size of each page in the status bar to make sure each of your pages has a reasonable download time. Document the file size of each page.

g. When you are finished, close the Web site, then exit Expression Web.

▼ VISUAL WORKSHOP

Launch Expression Web, then open the ecotours Web site. On the home page, insert the Rain Forest.jpg image from the drive and folder where you store your Data Files. Save the image, using an appropriate name, within the assets folder. Edit the image and properties as necessary so that your screen matches Figure E-25. (*Hint*: You'll need to add a border.) When you are finished, save your changes, close the Web site, then exit Expression Web.

FIGURE E-25

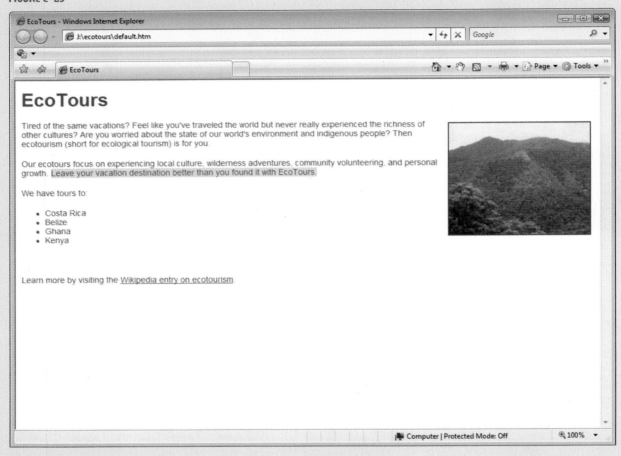

Enhancing a Design with CSS

Paying attention to design details can make the difference between a site that is merely acceptable to visitors and one that truly captures their attention. One of the tricks professionals use to enhance the appearance of a site is to add background colors, background images, borders, and appropriate white space to page elements and headings in ways that create a pleasing and cohesive visual identity for the site. You're ready to add some polish to the TradeWinds Web site by creating styles for the layout elements and headings.

OBJECTIVES

Understand CSS layouts

Add background images

Set a background color using
    the Eyedropper tool

Set a background color
    using a swatch

Add a border

Set margins and padding

Style the footer

Add a font family

Style headings

Understanding CSS Layouts

To take full advantage of the formatting capabilities of CSS, you need to understand the model that underlies it. In addition to understanding CSS principles, you should be familiar with the specific structure of the page you are designing. ▓▓▓▓▓ You decide to learn more about CSS layouts in general, and the TradeWinds page layout in particular.

Before you create styles for layout elements, it's important to understand:

- **The CSS Box Model**

  Familiar terms such as border and margin have particular rules and meanings in CSS. CSS presentation and layout is based on the **CSS box model**, which states that every element on a page is a rectangular box, including divs, images, headers, paragraphs, lists, and so on. Each box has one core component (the content area) and three optional components (borders, padding, and margins). The optional components do not appear unless specified in a style rule. Figure F-1 shows a diagram of the box model.

  Understanding the order in which these components appear allows you to create style rules that work as intended. The **content area** is the innermost box, which contains the text, image, or other content. The **padding area** creates space between the content and the border. **Borders** enclose both the padding and content areas. The **margin** area creates space surrounding the other three components (borders, padding, and content). Margins can also be thought of as providing space between separate elements. For every element, you can apply different padding, border, and margin properties to each of the four sides of the box.

- **CSS Layouts in Expression Web**

  When you create a Web page using one of Expression Web's CSS layouts, the new page is structured with the divs included in that layout, and the divs are placed according to the rules of the style sheet assigned to that page. The pages you created in Unit B for the TradeWinds site were based on the CSS layout Header, nav, 2 columns, footer—resulting in an HTML page with six divs arranged according to the style sheet for this layout.

  As you learned in Unit B, a div is a generic HTML container element that is often used for layout and positioning. Divs are usually assigned an id attribute, which is a unique and specific name. Unlike a class attribute, an id can only be used once on a page. While class-based rules are indicated by a period before the selector name (.highlight, for example), id-based rules are indicated with "#" (#masthead, for example).

  You must understand the structure of your page in order to make intelligent decisions about how and where to apply styles. Refer to Figure F-2 to review the placement of the following divs in the TradeWinds Web pages:
  - masthead: used for the main header and branding area for the site
  - top_nav: can be used for horizontal navigation; the tradewinds design does not use this area
  - left_col: a left-hand column; the tradewinds design uses this for site navigation
  - page_content: an area to the right of the column that holds the site content, both images and text
  - container: a div that contains both the left_col and the page_content divs
  - footer: a div at the bottom of the page that holds text-based navigation and copyright notice

FIGURE F-1: The CSS box model

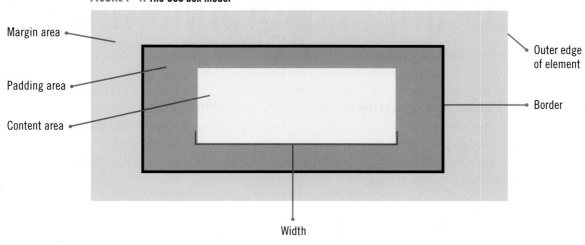

Margin area

Outer edge of element

Padding area

Border

Content area

Width

FIGURE F-2: Layout elements outlined on TradeWinds home page

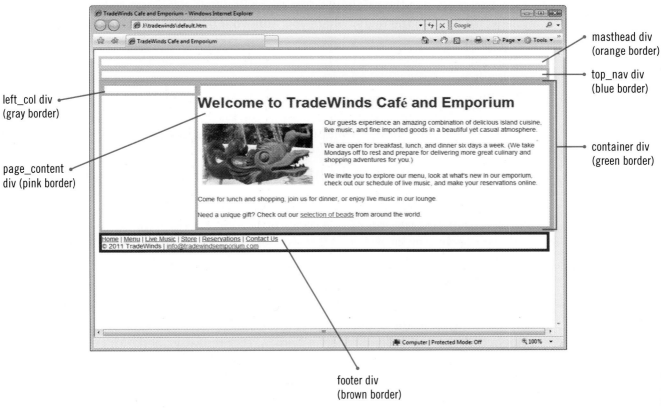

left_col div (gray border)

masthead div (orange border)

top_nav div (blue border)

container div (green border)

page_content div (pink border)

footer div (brown border)

Adding Background Images

Current Web design practices make extensive use of CSS background images to create a consistent look across all pages of the site. Background images are applied through a style rule instead of being directly inserted into an HTML page as other images are. Once you've created a style rule to have a background image display in a div, it shows up on all pages that have that div as part of their structure. When you add the background-image property to a style rule, you can specify values for four properties. **Background-repeat** controls whether and how the image repeats across the element. **Background-attachment** controls whether the image scrolls with the element's content or stays fixed as the content scrolls over it. **(X) background-position** and **(y) background-position** control where the image is placed relative to the element's left edge and top edge, respectively. See Table F-1 for a description of each value. Based on your design plans for the TradeWinds page layout, you decide to add a main header image as a background on the masthead div and a second image as a background on the container div.

STEPS

1. **Launch Expression Web, open the tradewinds site, open the home page, point to #masthead in the Apply Styles task pane, click the #masthead list arrow, then click Modify Style**

   The Modify Style dialog box opens. The #masthead style rule was created automatically when you created your page from Expression Web's CSS layouts.

   > **QUICK TIP**
   > Expression Web uses the file path to your data files folder until you save the page and embedded images to your site's root folder.

2. **Click Background in the category list, click the Browse button next to background-image, navigate to the folder where you store your data files, click tw_header.gif, then click Open**

   The file path to the image in your data file folder appears in the background-image text box, and the image displays as the background in the preview box.

   > **QUICK TIP**
   > An element can only have one background image; it's not possible to, for example, use one image at the top of an element and another at the bottom.

3. **Click the background-repeat list arrow, then click no-repeat**

   You want the TradeWinds header graphic to display only once. Boldly patterned and colored background images are best reserved for areas of the page that will not contain text, as they can make the text difficult to read.

4. **Click Position in the category list, type 235 in the height text box, then click OK**

   The header image is now visible along the top of the page. Elements that don't contain content or have any specified dimensions collapse and are not visible on the page. The background image is not considered content, because it's part of the style rule and not part of the HTML element. Specifying a height for the div that is the same height as the image prevents it from collapsing and allows the background image to be displayed.

5. **Point to #container in the Apply Styles task pane, click the #container list arrow, then click Modify Style**

   > **QUICK TIP**
   > A limitation of background images is that they cannot include a link. If you want an image to appear on every page but include a link, you must insert the image in each page individually.

6. **Click Background in the category list, click the Browse button next to background-image, navigate to the folder where you store your Data Files, click tw_page_bg.gif, click Open, click the background-repeat list arrow, click repeat-y, then click OK**

   See Figure F-3. In this case, you are setting a thin slice of an image as the background and want it to repeat the length of the element. Using this repeat method allows you to keep the image file size small and allows you to fill up the entire element without having to know its height.

7. **Click File on the menu bar, click Save All, then click OK in the Save Embedded Files dialog box**

   It's important to use the Save All command so that both the HTML file and the CSS file are saved to your site folder and all references to the images are maintained when you publish the site.

container
div repeating
background
image

masthead div
background
image

TABLE F-1: Background image properties and values

property	value	what it does
background-repeat	no-repeat	Background image does not repeat
	repeat	Background image repeats vertically and horizontally; this is the default
	repeat-x	Background image repeats horizontally only
	repeat-y	Background image repeats vertically only
	inherit	Uses same background-repeat value as containing element
background-attachment	fixed	Background image is fixed to element and scrolls with the content
	scroll	Background image stays fixed and content scrolls over it
	inherit	Uses same background-attachment value as containing element
(x) background-position	center	Horizontally centers background image in element
	left	Positions background image on left edge of element
	right	Positions background image on right edge of element
	inherit	Uses same horizontal position of background image as containing element
	(value)	Allows specification of a pixel value to dictate the distance from left edge of element to left edge of background image
(y) background-position	bottom	Positions background image on bottom edge of element
	center	Vertically centers background image in element
	top	Positions background image on top edge of element
	inherit	Uses same vertical position of background image as containing element
	value	Allows specification of a pixel value to dictate the distance from top edge of element to top edge of background image

Expression Web

Setting a Background Color Using the Eyedropper Tool

Specifying a background color for an element is a handy way to add color to a page without adding additional images. The background color displays across the entire element, including the margins. You have already learned how to specify colors in style rules by typing in a hex value. Expression Web offers several additional means of choosing colors, including using the **select** or **eyedropper tool**, which allows you to **sample** a color, or select it by clicking it on your screen. When you want to exactly match the color in an existing style rule or image, the eyedropper tool is your best bet. You want the background of the body element to be the same tan color as the background of the TradeWinds masthead graphic and the two tan stripes in the container background image. You decide to modify the body style rule to set a background color, and to specify the color using the eyedropper tool.

STEPS

1. **Confirm that the home page is the active page, click the Manage Styles tab in the Apply Styles task pane, right-click body, then click Modify Style**

   The Modify Style dialog box opens. Element-based styles such as the body style are not displayed in the Apply Styles task pane, so to modify the body style you use the Manage Styles task pane.

2. **Click Background in the category list, then click the background-color color swatch** ◻

   The More Colors dialog box opens, as shown in Figure F-4. On the left are swatches of all the Web-safe colors. **Web-safe colors** are colors that display reliably on all computer monitors that have 256 colors or less. They were more important in the early days of Web design than they are now, since most visitors' monitors now display millions of colors. Some designers still restrict their color choices to the Web-safe palette if they are designing for cell phones or handhelds, since these devices can display fewer colors than the typical computer monitor.

3. **Click Select**

   The cursor changes to an eyedropper 🖊, which you can use to select any color that is visible on the page.

4. **Point to the light tan stripe between the dark red and gold stripes in the background image, as shown in Figure F-5**

5. **Click the light tan stripe, click OK, then compare your screen to Figure F-6**

   The hex code #E5DFCB appears in the Value box, and the color swatch in the New box displays the color you sampled.

6. **Click OK**

   The Modify Style dialog box closes and the background color of the page now matches the tan stripe.

7. **Save changes to all open files**

8. **Preview the home page in a browser, then use navigation links at the bottom of the pages to view all pages in the site**

   Because you modified the styles in an external style sheet, all pages display the new background color for the body element.

9. **Close the browser window, then return to Expression Web**

> **TROUBLE**
>
> If the dialog boxes are in the way, click the Cancel button on the More Colors dialog box, drag and move the Modify Style dialog box out of the way, click the background-color color swatch, then click Select.

> **QUICK TIP**
>
> If you wanted a lighter or darker shade of the selected color, you could click Custom and use the slider on the right to change the color.

FIGURE F-4: More Colors dialog box

Web-safe colors

Select button

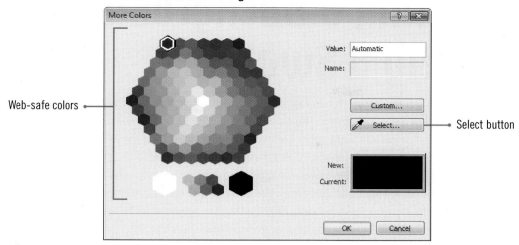

FIGURE F-5: Sampling a color with the Eyedropper tool

Hex value of selected color

Selected color

Eyedropper pointer

In Step 4, click this light tan stripe

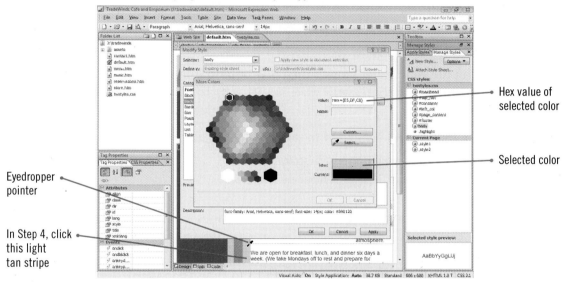

FIGURE F-6: Modify Style dialog box with sampled color as #body style background-color

Color selected with eyedropper

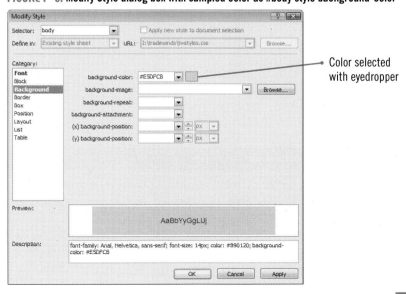

Expression Web

Setting a Background Color Using a Swatch

Another way to specify a color in Expression Web is to select one of the predefined swatches that appear when you click a color list arrow. The color swatches provide access to basic colors such as red, yellow, and gray. In most cases, you want more control over your color than this. For example, you probably would want to choose a certain shade of red rather than just using the generic swatch offered by default. However, these swatches work well for specifying basic black and white. The page_content div inherited the tan background color from the body, and you are concerned that the red text will be difficult to read on the new background color. You think white would work better as the background color for the page_content div, and decide to use a swatch to make this change.

STEPS

1. **Right-click #page_content in the Manage Styles task pane, then click Modify Style**
   The Modify Style dialog box opens.

2. **Click Background in the category list, then click the background-color list arrow**
   A palette of color swatches opens, as shown in Figure F-7.

3. **Click the white color swatch (first row, second from the left)**
   See Figure F-8. The hex value for white, #FFFFFF, is displayed in the background-color text box.

4. **Click OK**

5. **Use the Save All command to save changes to all open files**

6. **Preview the home page in a browser**
   The background of the page_content div is now white, and the readability of the dark red text is improved, as shown in Figure F-9.

7. **Use navigation links at the bottom of the pages to view all pages in the site**
   Because you modified the styles in an external style sheet, all pages display the new background colors for the page_content div.

8. **Close the browser window, then return to Expression Web**

Ensuring sufficient color contrast

When choosing a background color, be sure there is enough **contrast**, or perceived color difference, between an element's background color and any text that displays on the background. Older visitors or those with poor eyesight might have difficulty reading dark text on a dark background or light text on a light background. Background and text that are too similar in color can also cause readability problems. Several online tools allow you to check color contrast by providing the hex values for the desired text and the background colors; the tool then analyzes whether there is sufficient contrast between the two. Enter the term "color contrast tool" into your favorite search engine to learn more about available contrast-checking tools.

FIGURE F-7: Color swatches

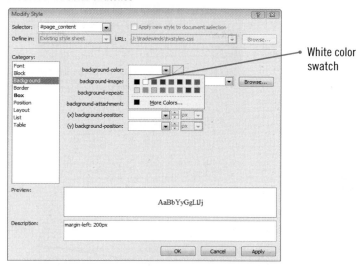

White color swatch

FIGURE F-8: background-color text box after white color swatch is selected

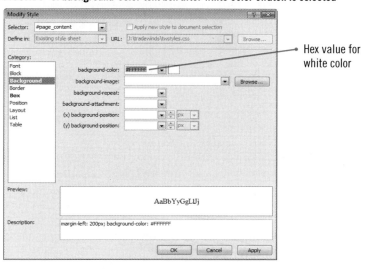

Hex value for white color

FIGURE F-9: Home page with background colors applied to body and page_content divs

Adding a Border

Colorful borders can serve to enhance the visual design of a site, draw attention to particular areas or content, and act as visual separators on the page. You can specify three border-related properties in CSS: border-style, border-width, and border-color. For the border-style property you can choose from 11 different options, but not all of them are well-supported by current browsers. When specifying border-width, you can use keywords (thin, medium, or thick) or specify a value in pixels. It's best to choose a specific value rather than using keywords because different browsers interpret the keywords differently, which can cause your design to display differently than you intended. You decide to add a gold border to the top and bottom of the page_content to subtly set it off from the rest of the page.

STEPS

1. **Make the home page the active page, right-click the #page_content div in the Manage Styles task pane, then click Modify Style**

   The Modify Style dialog box opens.

2. **Click Border in the category list**

3. **Click the Same for all check boxes under border-style, border-width, and border-color to remove the check marks**

   Because you want to define only a top and bottom border, it's necessary to deselect the same-for-all check boxes.

4. **Click the top list arrow under border-style, click solid, click the bottom list arrow under border-style, then click solid**

5. **Click in the top text box under border-width, type 4, click in the bottom text box under border-width, then type 4**

6. **Click in the top text box under border-color, type #E2CC7E, click in the bottom text box under border-color, type #E2CC7E, then compare your screen to Figure F-10**

   A gold color appears in the swatch beside top border-color and bottom border-color.

7. **Click OK, then compare your screen to Figure F-11**

8. **Save your changes to all open files, preview the home page in a browser, use navigation links at the bottom of the pages to view all pages in the site, then return to the home page**

   Leave the browser window open.

> **QUICK TIP**
>
> If you don't specify a value for border-style, the border won't display, even if you set the border-color and border-width properties.

FIGURE F-10: Completed Border options

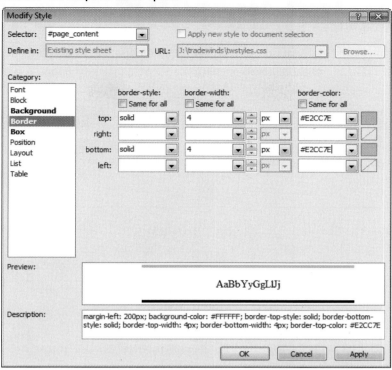

FIGURE F-11: Home page with border added to page_content div

Setting Margins and Padding

Sometimes what is absent from a design is just as important as what is present. Adding white space in the form of margins and padding can open up your design, making it appear less cluttered and improving the appearance as well as the readability of the content. Specifying margins can also solve the opposite problem—space appearing where you don't want it to. This is especially true on the body element. By default, browsers add margins to the body element; this can interfere with certain types of design. Setting all four body margins to zero removes any extra space on the edges of the page. In reviewing the current TradeWinds page layout, you notice a few problems you think can be solved through specifying margins and padding.

STEPS

1. **Observe the home page in the browser window**

   Compare your screen to Figure F-12. Notice that the text in the page_content div is too close to the edge of the element. Notice also that the TradeWinds header image is too far to the left, and does not stand out enough.

2. **Close the browser window, return to Expression Web, right-click body on the Manage Styles task pane, then click Modify Style**

   The Modify Style dialog box opens.

QUICK TIP

When the Same for all check box contains a check mark, all fields in the current setting change automatically when you enter a new value.

3. **Click Box on the category list, click in the top text box under margin, type 0, compare your screen to Figure F-13, then click OK**

   Now that all the body margins are set to zero, the header image is positioned directly against the top and left edge of the page, which is where you want it.

4. **Right-click page_content on the Manage Styles task pane, then click Modify Style**

   The Modify Style dialog box opens.

5. **Click Box on the category list, click in the top text box under padding, type 15, then compare your screen to Figure F-14**

   The 200-pixel left margin was created when Expression Web generated the original style sheet for the page layout.

6. **Click OK**

   A 15-pixel padding surrounds the content and separates it from the edges of the page_content div.

7. **Save your changes to all open files, preview the home page in a browser, use navigation links at the bottom of the pages to view all pages in the site, close the browser window, then return to Expression Web**

FIGURE F-12: Home page before margins and padding are applied

Space on top and left needs to be eliminated

Text is too close to edge of div

FIGURE F-13: Modifing the Box category of body style

top margin text box

Box model reference

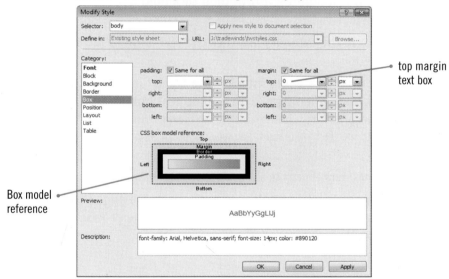

FIGURE F-14: Box category for #page_content style

Margin was set when Expression Web generated the style sheet

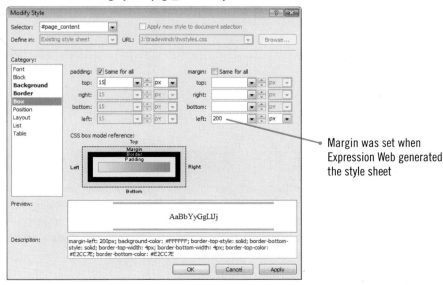

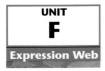

Styling the Footer

Like footers in a document, Web page footers include practical information, presented in a simple and succinct format. Web page footers generally feature text-only navigation, a copyright notice, and perhaps links to reference areas such as a privacy policy or contact information. Usually designers de-emphasize the footer by making the text smaller and less noticeable so it doesn't distract from other, more important content on the page. You want the TradeWinds page footer to have a smaller font size, to have the text centered in the div, and to have more white space between the top of the text and the bottom of the page_content div. To make these changes, you need to modify the #footer style.

STEPS

1. **Right-click #footer in the Manage Styles task pane, then click Modify Style**
   The Modify Style dialog box opens.

2. **Click in the font-size box, then type 10**
   While it's appropriate to make the footer font size small, a size below 10 pixels might be so small that it's unreadable.

3. **Click the font-weight list arrow, then click bold**
   See Figure F-15.

4. **Click Block in the category list, click the text-align list arrow, then click center**
   See Figure F-16.

5. **Click Box on the category list, click the Same for all check box next to margin to remove the check mark, then type 20 in the top text box**
   Because you only need to create space between the top of the text and the bottom of the page_content div, you only need to specify a top margin. The settings for the #footer style are complete, as shown in Figure F-17.

6. **Click OK**
   The footer text now appears smaller, centered, and with white space at the top.

7. **Save changes to all open files, preview the home page in a browser, use the bottom navigation to view the other site pages, close the browser window, then return to Expression Web**

Understanding semantic div ids

Unlike the list or paragraph element, the div element does not have a specific semantic meaning. However, divs are usually assigned an id attribute, which is a unique and specific name, and these id names are often semantic, reflecting the purpose of the div. When you use one of the CSS layouts in Expression Web, many of the divs have semantic ids, such as masthead, footer, or page_content, but some have non-semantic ids, such as left_col. You can feel free to use the divs for other purposes, though, such as using the masthead for horizontal navigation at the top of a page.

FIGURE F-15: Font category for #footer style

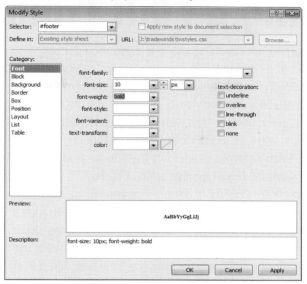

FIGURE F-16: Block category for #footer style

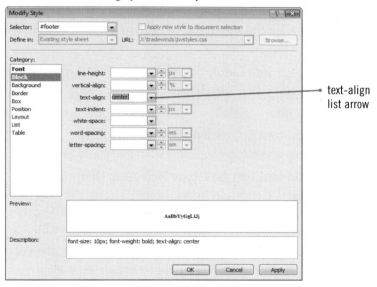

text-align list arrow

FIGURE F-17: Box category for #footer style

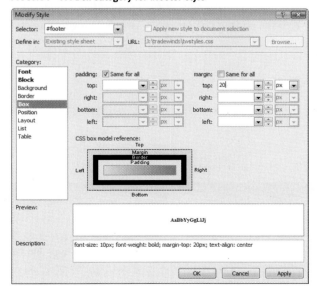

Expression Web

Adding a Font Family

As you have learned, when writing a style rule you should specify a prioritized list of fonts, known as a **font family**, instead of a single font, in case the visitor's computer doesn't have a particular font installed. By default, Expression Web offers only three sets of font families. You can define your own sets of fonts, though, which will be available in the font-family lists when you create or modify a style. The guidelines for creating a font-family list are as follows: Start with the font you prefer, then list Web-safe fonts for Windows and Mac systems, and then end with a generic font family. Although no font is guaranteed to be installed on a particular computer, **Web-safe fonts** are fonts likely to be available on Windows, Mac, and Linux-based computer systems. **Generic font families** are part of the CSS specification and are displayed if no other fonts in the list are available. Only three generic font families are consistently understood by browsers and therefore safe to use—serif, sans serif, and monospace. A **serif** font, such as Times New Roman, has visible strokes at the ends of the character. A **sans-serif** font, such as Arial, has no strokes at the end of the character. A **monospace** font, such as Courier, has equal space between the characters. ▨▨▨ Catalina asks you to make the headings stand out more from the body text. You start by creating a new font family to use for the headings.

QUICK TIP

To quickly move to a different part of the list, type the first letter of the font name in the Add font text box.

QUICK TIP

Be sure to add the fonts in the appropriate order; if you make a mistake, remove the font family and start over.

1. **Click Tools on the menu bar, click Page Editor Options, then click the Font Families tab**
   See Figure F-18.

2. **In the Select font family list, click (New Font Family) if necessary**

3. **In the Add font list, click Lucida Sans, then click Add**
   A new font family, consisting of Lucida Sans, is added to the Select font family list.

4. **In the Add font list, click Arial, then click Add**
   Arial appears after Lucida Sans in the Select font family list.

5. **In the Add font text box, type Helvetica, then click Add**
   Helvetica appears after Arial in the Select font family list. Only fonts installed on your computer appear in the Add font list. Because Helvetica is more common on Mac computers than Windows computers, you need to type the font name rather than selecting it from the list.

6. **In the Add font text box, click sans-serif, click Add, then compare your screen to Figure F-19**
   Sans-serif appears after Helvetica in the Select font family list.

7. **Click OK**
   The Page Editor Options dialog box closes. The new font family will be available when you create a style in this or any Web site on your computer. See Table F-2 for guidance on combining fonts in a font family.

Choosing fonts

In the printing world, conventional wisdom holds that serif fonts are better than sans serif fonts for body text because they are easier to read. But recent research has shown conflicting results about which type of font affords the best onscreen readability, so feel free to use either. Try to limit your font usage to two font faces per design, though, to avoid visual overload. You can mix the two types, using sans serif for body type and serif for headings, or vice versa. You can also stick with the same font type for both body and heading text.

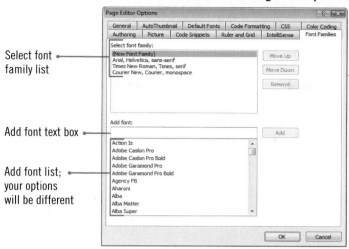

FIGURE F-18: Font Families tab in Page Editor Options dialog box

Select font family list

Add font text box

Add font list; your options will be different

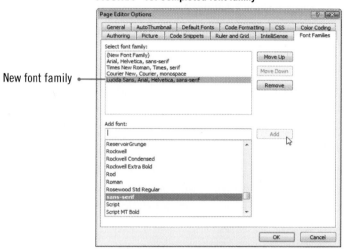

FIGURE F-19: Completed font family

New font family

TABLE F-2: Suggested font family combinations

with this family type	pair these fonts	with these Web-safe fonts
Serif	Book Antiqua Bookman Old Style Century Schoolbook Garamond Georgia Palatino Palatino Linotype	Times New Roman, Times, serif
Sans-serif	**Arial Black** Avant Garde Century Gothic Comic Sans MS Geneva **Impact** Lucida Sans Unicode Lucida Grand Tahoma Trebuchet MS Verdana	Arial, Helvetica, sansserif
Monospace	Lucida Console	Courier New, Courier, Monospace

Styling Headings

The CSS box model applies to headings, too, which means they can have the same properties applied to them as other elements, such as borders, margins, padding, and background colors and images. Creating interesting styles for headings is a great way to make your site more readable and more visually pleasing. ▰▰▰▰ To make the headings in the TradeWinds site stand out more, you decide the first-level headings should be the same dark red color as the body text, with a different font and a gold bottom border. You want the second-level headings to be gold and smaller than the first-level headings, with no border.

STEPS

1. **Click the** New Style button **on the Manage Styles task pane, click the** Selector list arrow, **click** h1, **click the** Define in **list arrow, click** Existing style sheet, **click the** URL list arrow, **then click** twstyles.css

   You are using an element-based selector, h1, to create the style rule, so that the changes will be reflected in all instances of that element throughout the site.

2. **Click the** font-family list arrow, **click** Lucida Sans, Arial, Helvetica, sans-serif, **type** 22 **in the** font-size box, **click the** font-weight list arrow, **click** bold, **then type** #890120 **in the color text box.**

3. **Click** Border **in the category list, then click the** Same for all check boxes **under border-style, border-width, and border-color to remove the check marks**

4. **Click the** bottom list arrow **under** border-style, **click** solid, **click in the** bottom text box **under** border-width, **type** 1, **click in the** bottom text box **under** border-color, **type** #C9A62D, **compare your screen to Figure F-20, then click** OK

5. **Click the** New Style button **on the Manage Styles task pane, click the** Selector list arrow, **click** h2, **click the** Define in **list arrow, click** Existing style sheet, **click the** URL list arrow, **then click** twstyles.css

   You are ready to create the heading 2 style.

6. **Type** 18 **in the** font-size box, **click the** font-weight list arrow, **click** bold, **type** #C9A62D **in the color text box, compare your screen to Figure F-21, then click** OK

7. **Use the Save All command to save changes to all open files, preview the home page in a browser, then click the** Store link

   See Figure F-22. The first- and second-level headings reflect the new style rules you created.

8. **Close the browser window, return to Expression Web, close the tradewinds site, then exit Expression Web**

FIGURE F-20: Border category for h1 style rule

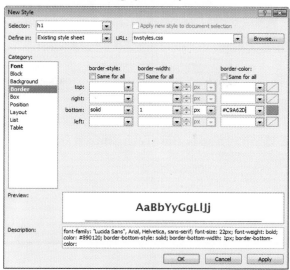

FIGURE F-21: Font category for h2 style rule

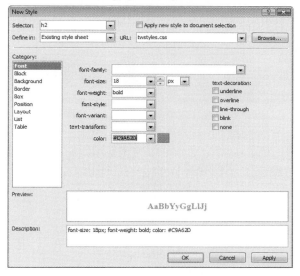

FIGURE F-22: Store page with new heading styles

First-level heading

Second-level headings

Practice

▼ CONCEPTS REVIEW

Label each element in the CSS box model diagram shown in Figure F-23.

FIGURE F-23

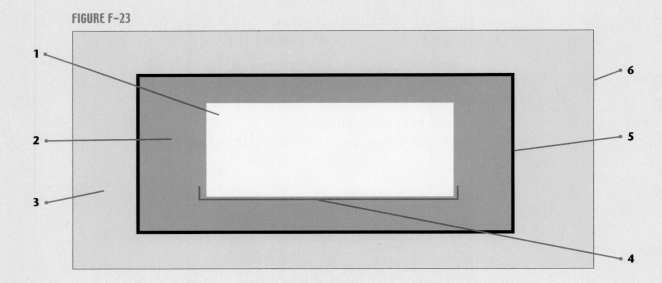

Match each term with the statement that best describes it.

7. (x) background-position
8. (y) background-position
9. sans serif fonts
10. serif fonts
11. monospace fonts

a. Arial and Helvetica
b. Times and Times New Roman
c. Property that controls where a background image is placed relative to the element's top edge
d. Property that controls where a background image is placed relative to the element's left edge
e. Courier and Courier New

Select the best answer from the list of choices.

12. **Which property creates space between two different elements?**
    a. Background
    b. Padding
    c. Margin
    d. Border

13. **Which property creates space between an element's content and its border?**
    a. Background
    b. Padding
    c. Margin
    d. Border

14. **Which property allows you to specify that a background image stays fixed while the element's content scrolls?**
    a. background-attachment
    b. background-repeat
    c. background-color
    d. background-scroll

15. **Which value of the background-repeat property causes a background image to repeat horizontally across the page?**
    a. repeat-x
    b. repeat-y
    c. auto
    d. repeat-h

16. **How many background images can you add to an element?**
    a. One
    b. Two
    c. Three
    d. As many as you'd like

17. **Which of the following is *not* a Web-safe font?**
    a. Courier
    b. Times New Roman
    c. Arial
    d. Copperplate Gothic

▼ SKILLS REVIEW

1. **Add background images.**
    a. Launch Expression Web, then open the careers site.
    b. Open the home page.
    c. Open the Modify Style dialog box for #masthead.
    d. In the Background category, specify cg_logo.gif (located in the drive and folder where you store your Data Files) as the background image, and set the background-repeat to no-repeat.
    e. In the Position category, set the height to **100 pixels**.
    f. Click OK to close the Modify Style dialog box.
    g. Use the Save All command to save your changes, confirm that you want to save embedded files, preview the home page in the browser, use navigation links at the bottom of the pages to view the other pages in the site, close the browser window, then return to Expression Web.

2. **Set a background color using the Eyedropper tool.**
    a. Using the Manage Styles task pane, open the Modify Style dialog box for the body style.
    b. In the Background category, click the background-color swatch, then use the Select eyedropper to sample a light brown shade from the man's jacket in the testimonial photo. (*Hint*: You might need to cancel out of the dialog boxes to adjust the photo location, then reopen the necessary dialog boxes and/or drag the Modify Style dialog box to a different location.)
    c. Click OK to close the More Colors dialog box, then click OK to close the Modify Style dialog box.
    d. Use the Save All command to save your changes, preview the home page in the browser, use the bottom text links to view the other pages in the site, close the browser window, then return to Expression Web.

3. **Set a background color using a swatch.**
    a. Open the Modify Style dialog box for the #masthead style.
    b. In the Background category, click the background-color list arrow, then choose the black swatch from the palette.
    c. Click OK to close the Modify Style dialog box.
    d. Open the Modify Style dialog box for the #container style.
    e. In the Background category, click the background-color list arrow, then choose the white swatch from the palette.
    f. Click OK to close the Modify Style dialog box.
    g. Use the Save All command to save your changes, preview the home page in the browser, use navigation links to view the other pages in the site, close the browser window, then return to Expression Web.

4. **Add a border.**
    a. Open the Modify Style dialog box for the #container style.
    b. Use the options in the Border category to create a solid border that is **2 pixels** wide with the color **#663300** on all four sides.
    c. Click OK to close the Modify Style dialog box.
    d. Use the Save All command to save your changes, preview the home page in the browser, use the navigation links at the bottom of the page to view the other pages in the site, close the browser window, then return to Expression Web.

5. Set margins and padding.

  a. Open the Modify Style dialog box for the body style.

  b. Use the options in the Box category to set all margins to **0 pixels**.

  c. Click OK to close the Modify Style dialog box.

  d. Open the Modify Style dialog box for the #page_content style.

  e. Use the options in the Box category to set padding on all four sides to **20 pixels**.

  f. Click OK to close the Modify Style dialog box.

  g. Use the Save All command to save your changes, preview the home page in the browser, use the navigation links at the bottom of the page to view the other pages in the site, close the browser window, then return to Expression Web.

6. Style the footer.

  a. Open the Modify Style dialog box for the #footer style.

  b. Use the options in the Font category to set the font-size to **12 pixels**.

  c. Use the options in the Block category to set the text-align to center.

  d. Use the options in the Box category to set only the top padding to **15 pixels**, then click OK to close the Modify Style dialog box.

  e. Use the Save All command to save your changes, preview the home page in the browser, use the navigation links to view the other pages in the site, close the browser window, then return to Expression Web.

7. Add a font family.

  a. Open the Page Editor Options dialog box, then switch to the Font Families tab if necessary.

  b. Select (New Font Family) in the Select font family list if necessary.

  c. Select Georgia in the Add font list, then add it to the font family.

  d. Select Times New Roman in the Add font list, then add it to the font family.

  e. Type **Times** in the Add font text box, then add it to the font family.

  f. Select serif in the Add font list, then add it to the font family.

  g. Click OK to close the Page Editor Options dialog box.

8. Style headings.

  a. Open the New Style dialog box, set the selector to h1, then create the style in the existing style sheet cgstyles.css.

  b. In the Font category, set the font-family to Georgia, Times New Roman, Times, serif; the font-size to **30 pixels**; the font-weight to bold; and the color to black.

  c. In the Border category, create only a bottom border with a border-style of dashed, a border-width of **1 pixel**, and a border-color of **#C0C0C0**.

  d. Click OK to close the New Style dialog box.

  e. Open the New Style dialog box, set the selector to h2, then create the style in the existing style sheet cgstyles.css.

  f. In the Font category, set the font-family to the Georgia, Times New Roman, Times, serif; the font-size to **20 pixels**; the font-weight to bold, and the color to black.

  g. Click OK to close the New Style dialog box.

  h. Use the Save All command to save your changes, preview the home page in a browser, then use the navigation links to view the other pages in the site.

  i. Compare your home page to Figure F-24, close the browser window, return to Expression Web, close the site, then exit Expression Web.

Careers Guaranteed

Your Career. Guaranteed.

At Careers Guaranteed, we only work with the best. If we accept your application, we guarantee that we will match you to a job position or we will refund your money.

Why we're different

You don't have any time to waste. You know how those other career sites operate. You post your resume. You spend hours sifting through job postings. You apply to job after job after job. But it's tough to get a foot in the door when hundreds of people are applying for those same jobs. At Careers Guaranteed, we really get to know you through our rigorous screening process. We know what your strengths are and what you want out from your career. So we can successfully match you with desirable positions in your preferred industry.

Not sure what career you want to pursue? Our one-of-a-kind career exploration tools can help!

Testimonial

I'd been looking for the right job for more than four months when a friend told me about Careers Guaranteed. They had matched me with the perfect job within six weeks. I've never been happier with my career! --Antoine D.

Home | Services | About | Contact
© 2011 Careers Guaranteed | info@careersguaranteed.com

▼ INDEPENDENT CHALLENGE 1

In this project you continue your work on the ConnectUp Web site. Tiffany has sent you some ideas for the types of colors she wants to use—bright, eye-catching colors that will appeal to the site's target audience. You get to work incorporating her suggestions to the site by adding styles to the divs and headings. As part of your design, you are using the top_nav div as your header, and the masthead div for navigation.

a. Launch Expression Web, then open the connectup Web site.

b. Open the home page.

c. Modify the #top_nav style with the following properties: set the background-image to cu_logo.jpg, which can be found in the location where you store data files. Set the background-repeat to no repeat, the (x) background-position to center, and the height to **200 pixels**.

d. Modify the #page_content style to set background-color to white and create a border on the left and right sides only that is solid, 1 pixel wide, and black.

e. Modify the #top_nav style to use the Select eyedropper to set the background-color to the same color as the cu_logo.jpg background.

f. Modify the body style to set margins on all sides to zero and the background-color to **#D8E0E4**.

g. Modify the #page_content style to set padding on all sides to **25 pixels**.

h. Create a new font family containing Trebuchet MS, Arial, Helvetica, sans-serif, in that order.

i. Create a new h1 style in the custyles.css stylesheet with the following properties: set the font-family to Trebuchet MS, Arial, Helvetica, sans-serif; set the font-size to **32 pixels**; set the font-weight to bold; set the color to **#6FD917**; and set margins on the top, left, and right sides to **0** and on the bottom to **10 pixels**.

j. Create a new h2 style in the custyles.css stylesheet with the following properties: set the font-family to Trebuchet MS, Arial, Helvetica, sans-serif,; set the font-size to **24 pixels**; and set the color to a shade of blue sampled from the ConnectUp logo.

k. Modify the #footer style to set the font-size to **10 pixels**, the font color to white, the margins on all sides to **15 pixels**, the text-align to center, and the background-image to cu_footer_bg.gif with repeat-x.

▼ INDEPENDENT CHALLENGE 1 (CONTINUED)

l. Use the Save All command to save your changes, preview the home page in a browser, then use the navigation links to view all pages.

m. Compare the upper portion of your faq page to Figure F-25, close the browser window, return to Expression Web, close the site, then exit Expression Web.

FIGURE F-25

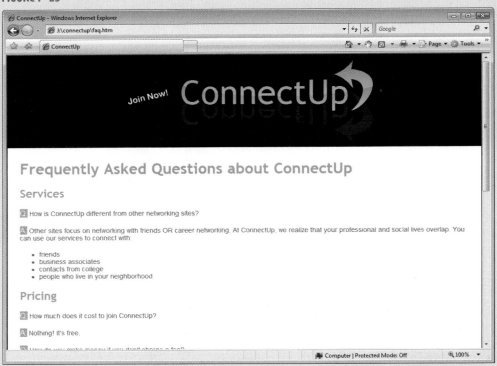

▼ INDEPENDENT CHALLENGE 2

In this project you continue your work on the Memories Restored Web site. You are ready to add visual interest to the site through the use of background images, colors, borders, and heading styles.

a. Launch Expression Web, then open the memories Web site.

b. Modify the #masthead style to add mr_logo.gif as the background image with the appropriate repeat. Set the height to **150 pixels**. Set the background color to match the background color of the mr_logo image.

c. Modify the body style to add mr_bg.gif as a repeating bg image.

d. Modify the #page_content div to add padding, borders, and a background color that makes the page text easy to read. You may need to experiment with different settings until you find a combination you like.

e. Modify the #footer div as you'd like.

f. Create a new font-family list using a beginning font of your choice, followed by a list of web-safe fonts, and the appropriate generic font family.

g. Create a style in the existing style sheet using h1 as a selector and using the font family you created. If you wish, change the size, color, border, or any other characteristics of the h1 style.

h. Create a style in the existing style sheet using h2 as a selector and using the font family you created. If you wish, change the size, color, border, or any other characteristics of the h2 heading.

Advanced Challenge Exercise

- Open the tips page.
- Modify the .resources style to create attractive spacing between the text and the border.
- Apply any other settings you'd like to change the appearance of the style.

i. Save your changes to all open files, preview the site in a browser, then use the navigation links to view all pages. When you are finished, close the browser, return to Expression Web, close the site, then exit Expression Web.

▼ INDEPENDENT CHALLENGE 3

Note: This Independent Challenge requires an Internet connection.

As part of your research for the Technology for All redesign, you want to explore the ways that designers are creating the striking designs you've seen accomplished through CSS. The css Zen Garden site uses one HTML file paired with different style sheets to display the same content with radically different appearances. The designs are accomplished using the same techniques you learned in this unit—use of divs styled with background images, background colors, and borders, and creative heading styles. In addition, you will notice that many designers use advanced CSS to position the divs in different locations on the page, something you have not learned yet.

a. Visit www.csszengarden.com, then click through the available designs to find two that you like but that differ from each other in look or feel.

b. View the sample HTML file on the site to see what the unstyled content looks like.

c. Analyze the two designs by comparing the appearance and location of each content area on the two designs. Note the use of colors, images, borders, and fonts.

d. Write at least three paragraphs describing what CSS techniques you think the designers used to create the visual design of the sites.

Advanced Challenge Exercise

- Using the same two designs, analyze what types of sites and audience the design would be appropriate for, and why.
- Write one paragraph giving an example of the type of site and audience that would be best suited to each design.

e. Add your name to the document, save it, and print it.

▼ REAL LIFE INDEPENDENT CHALLENGE

This project builds on the personal Web site you have worked on in previous units. You're ready to enhance your design with background images, background colors, borders, margins, and paddings. You will also style your headings.

a. Open your site in Expression Web, then carefully review the pages, identifying each div that makes up the layout. On a piece of paper, write down any design issues you think could be solved by adding background images, background colors, borders, margins, or padding.

b. Add a background image to at least one element.

c. Add a background color to at least one element.

d. Add a border to at least one element.

e. Add margins and/or padding as desired to create white space around at least one element. (*Hint*: You may need to add both margins and padding , or just one of these attributes, to the element.)

f. Create a new font-family list, then use it to create a new heading style for either the h1 element, the h2 element, or both.

g. Save your changes to all open files, preview the site in a browser, then use the navigation links to view all pages. When you are finished, close the browser, return to Expression Web, close the site, then exit Expression Web.

▼ VISUAL WORKSHOP

Open the ecotours Web site in Expression Web. Modify the home page and the external style sheet so that your screen matches Figure F-26. To accomplish this, you need to add background colors, borders, and padding to different divs as necessary. (*Hint*: The colors used are # #CCCCCC and #D2FFD2. The third color you need can be sampled from an element on the page.) When you are finished, save your changes, close the Web site, then exit Expression Web.

FIGURE F-26

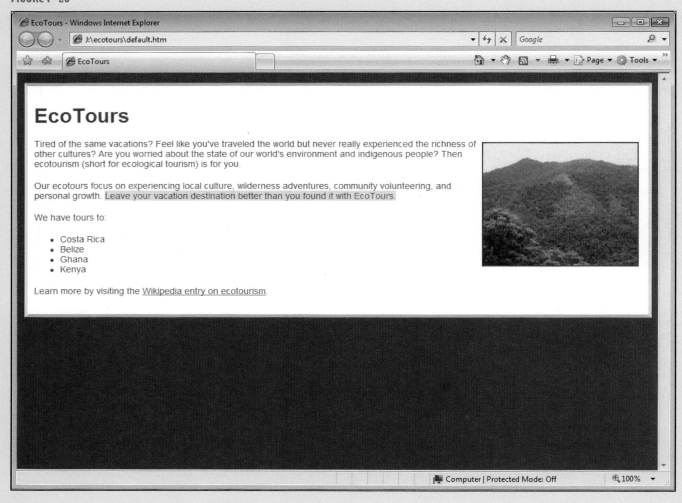

Designing Site Navigation

Navigation is an essential element of a successful site. No matter how compelling your site's design and content are, if the navigation is confusing, your visitors will not be able to find what they're seeking and will leave. By creating a system of links that is clear and logical, you ensure that visitors can navigate from page to page easily. Content, graphics, and styles are all in place on the TradeWinds site. Now it is time to add the navigation and style the links so they complement the look of the site.

OBJECTIVES

Understand effective navigation

Create an interactive button

Edit an interactive button

Create a navigation bar

Add a navigation bar to site pages

Understand link styles

Create link styles

Understanding Effective Navigation

A site's navigation should both orient the visitor and provide clear options for where the visitor can go next. Creating an effective navigation system for a Web site can be fairly straightforward for a small site focused on one topic. However, as a site's complexity and diversity of content increase, it becomes more challenging to design navigation that is simple and easy to use. Knowing some basic principles can help you create a user-friendly navigation system for any size Web site. ▟▟▟▟ Before creating the navigation for the TradeWinds Web site, you decide to review some design principles.

DETAILS

To design effective navigation, it helps to understand:

- **Guidelines for navigation**

   Good navigation is consistent, clearly labeled, and reflects the needs of the site's audience. Visitors can easily feel disoriented on sites they are not familiar with, but links that are similar on every page can help to build their sense of familiarity and encourage them to explore the entire site. Navigation labels are usually short, so there's no room to be clever with the wording—keep it clear and succinct. Above all, navigation should be designed for the needs of your site's visitors. A common mistake is to create navigation that corresponds with an organization's internal structure and jargon, rather than a visitor's goals. For example, a company might have three different departments that deal with customer service, due to its corporate structure; on the Web site, however, there should be just one area where visitors go for their customer service needs.

- **Types of navigation**

   Global navigation is the navigation that appears on each page, usually at the top or left side. Global navigation usually features each top-level section in a site; in a small site this can include every single page, but in a larger site this might not be feasible. **Local navigation** is used on large sites where there is so much content in a section that global navigation is inadequate. For example, a site that sells books, music, and movies would likely feature top-level categories in the global navigation, and feature local navigation in each section, such as links to different movie genres in the movies section. **Related navigation** usually appears within the content area and highlights content related to that page's information. For example, the page featuring a specific movie for sale might list movies by the same director in the related navigation. See Figure G-1 for an example of the three types of navigation.

- **Navigation elements**

   The elements that make up your navigation should be determined by the site's goals, the content of the site, and the target audience. For many years, most sites used graphics for navigation. In recent years, text links that are creatively styled with CSS have become popular. Pulldown menus, which feature list arrows that, when clicked, reveal a longer list of options, are convenient when space is at a premium and you have a long list of links to feature.

Architecting information

Did you know that there is an entire field devoted to the art and science of organizing and labeling Web content? **Information architects**, or **IAs** for short, are people whose job it is to create structures, navigation, and search systems for Web sites. IAs work as independent consultants or as part of in-house Web design teams within organizations. Working with an IA can be especially useful on complex sites that have thousands of pages of content or that deal with multiple audiences or topics. IAs understand how people look for information and are trained in specific research techniques that can help designers create and test site structures and navigation.

FIGURE G-1: **Global, local, and related navigation**

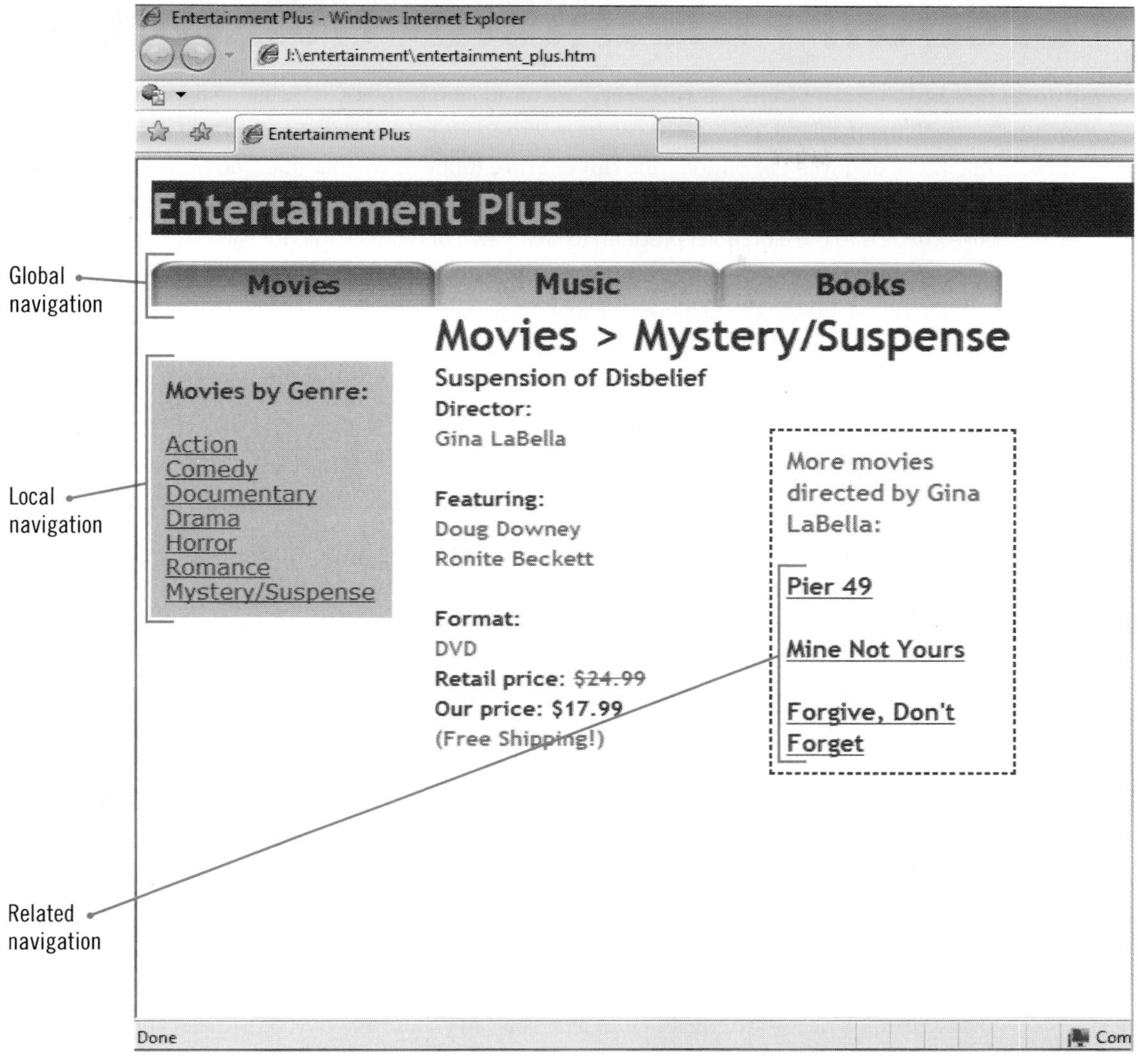

Learning how your visitors think

When designing a Web site that includes several pages, you might find that it pays to do some research before structuring your navigation. **Card sorting** is a technique you can use to involve actual or potential Web site visitors in this process. To perform a card sort, take a stack of index cards and on each card write the name of a topic, feature, or piece of content that is currently on your site or you are planning to have on your site. (Using about 25 cards works well for a small site. You may need more for a larger one.) Recruit 5 to 10 people who either use your site or are members of your site's target audience, and make an appointment with each. At the meeting, ask the person to read through the cards and to put cards they feel are related together into groups and to label each group. Record the results of each session on a spreadsheet. At the end of the process, review the information you gathered. Everyone thinks a bit differently, so you'll never have complete agreement, but look for trends that can help you decide how to group and label the content on the site.

Creating an Interactive Button

Interactive buttons, also known as **rollovers**, are navigation graphics that change appearance when a visitor interacts with them. Interactive buttons can have three different states: the **original state** (appears when a visitor is not interacting with the button), the **hover state** (appears when a visitor points to or hovers over the image), and the **pressed state** (appears while a visitor is clicking the button). The usual way to create this type of interactive image is to use a graphics program to create two or more images for each navigation element and then write some JavaScript code to control the change in appearance. But a much easier alternative is to use the predesigned interactive buttons included with Expression Web. Using the interactive button feature provides a variety of design choices and makes it a snap to create polished interactive navigation graphics. However, you are limited to choosing from Expression Web's list of buttons when you create an interactive button; if none of them work with your design, you will have to create your own buttons or use text links. You decide to create interactive buttons and place them in the left column of the TradeWinds home page.

STEPS

QUICK TIP
You can also link a button to an external Web page or an e-mail address.

1. **Launch Expression Web, open the tradewinds site, open the home page, click in the left_col div, click Insert on the menu bar, then click Interactive Button**

   The Interactive Buttons dialog box opens, as shown in Figure G-2. The dialog box includes three tabs—Button, Font, and Image—each of which allows you to control a different set of options for the button you are creating. In the Button tab, you can choose the graphic style of the button, the text that appears on the button, and the page to which the button links. When you click an option in the Buttons list, a preview of your choice appears in the Preview box. If you point to the Preview area, the image changes to a preview of the button's hover state.

2. **In the Buttons list click Braided Column 4, select the text in the Text field, press [Spacebar], then type Home**

   Inserting a space gives you some room between the left edge of the text and the right edge of the circular decoration on the button. The text " Home" will appear on the finished button.

TROUBLE
If you don't see default.htm listed, make sure that both Existing File or Web Page and Current Folder are selected.

3. **Click Browse next to the Link field**

   The Edit Hyperlink dialog box opens. From here you can choose any of your site files and Expression Web will create a link from the interactive button to the file.

4. **Click default.htm, click OK, then compare your screen to Figure G-3**

5. **Click the Font tab**

   The Font tab options allow you to change the font face, style, and size. You can also choose different font colors for each of the three button states and set the vertical and horizontal alignment of the button text in relationship to its background graphic.

QUICK TIP
Decide on your button type before you work in the Font tab; if you switch back to the Button tab after working in the Font tab, you lose any button type settings.

6. **Click Arial, Helvetica, sans-serif in the Font list, click Bold in the Font Style list, click 12 in the Size list, click the Horizontal Alignment list arrow, click Left, then compare your screen to Figure G-4**

TROUBLE
Make sure the assets folder is listed in the folder column; if it isn't, click the Change Folder button, navigate to the assets folder, click the assets folder, then click OK.

7. **Click OK, then save your changes**

   The Save Embedded Files dialog box opens. Three image files are listed in the Embedded files to save list. Expression Web has created three versions of the Home button, one for each state. The program has also added to the page all the HTML and JavaScript code necessary for the buttons to function.

8. **Click OK**

   The three image files are saved in the tradewinds assets folder.

9. **Preview the page in a browser, point to the Home button, click the Home button, close the browser window, then return to Expression Web**

   The button changes when you point to it and changes again when you click on it.

FIGURE G-2: Button tab of Interactive Buttons dialog box

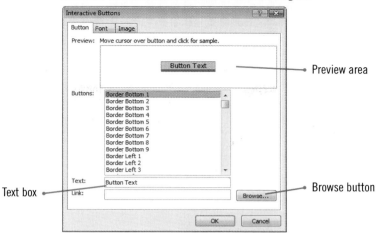

Preview area

Text box

Browse button

FIGURE G-3: Completed Button tab of Interactive Buttons dialog box

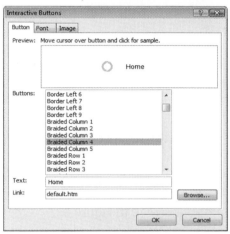

FIGURE G-4: Completed Font tab of Interactive Buttons dialog

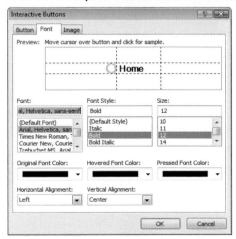

Choosing fonts for navigation buttons

Using graphics, such as interactive buttons, instead of text for navigation affords you much more flexibility in your font choices. Because Expression Web actually creates an image of the text, you are not limited to using Web-safe fonts. When creating interactive buttons, you can safely choose any font that appears in your font list. When choosing the font face, size, and color, make sure that the text is large enough to read and that it has enough contrast with the background color to be legible.

Editing an Interactive Button

Once you create an interactive button, Expression Web makes it easy to edit it or change the formatting. ▓▓▓ The navigation button you created is a good start, but you'd like for the background color to blend with the background image on the page, and for the font color to change when the visitor points to the button. You also want the button to be a bit larger.

STEPS

1. **Double-click the** Home button, **then click the** Font tab

2. **Click the** Original Font Color list arrow, **click** More Colors, **click in the** Value box, **select the text, press [Delete], type** #E2CC7E, **then click** OK

   See Figure G-5.

3. **Click the** Hovered Font Color list arrow, **click** More Colors, **delete the text in the Value box, type** #C9A62D, **then click** OK

   This option determines the color the text will appear when a visitor points to the button.

4. **Click the** Image tab

   See Figure G-6. The Image tab options allow you to change the height and width of the button. You can also control whether Expression Web creates a hovered and a pressed image. If you add a check mark to the Preload button images check box, Expression Web will generate code and add it to the page that causes the images for all states of the navigation images to load when the page loads. This prevents any delay between the time the visitor points to an image and the time the hover state of the image appears.

TROUBLE

Make sure you don't select the space in front of the text, just the text itself.

5. **Select the text in the** Width box, **press [Delete], then type** 120

   Because the Maintain proportions check box is selected, the height changes to 24 pixels to make the height larger in proportion to the increased width.

6. **Click the** Make the button a GIF image and use a transparent background. **option button, then compare your screen to Figure G-7**

   The preview area changes to show a checkerboard pattern. This indicates that the image will have a transparent background, so that it blends into the background color on which it is placed. The effect of this option varies slightly, depending on the button style. On some styles, including this one, this option makes the entire button background transparent; on other styles it changes only the white space around the button, such as that surrounding the rounded corners of a capsule-style button.

7. **Click** OK, **then save your changes**

   The Save Embedded Files dialog box opens, showing the file names of three images. Expression Web has created three new images to replace the existing home button images.

8. **Click** OK **in the Saved Embedded Files dialog box, preview the page in a browser, point to the** Home button, **click the** Home button, **close the browser window, then return to Expression Web**

FIGURE G-5: Completed More Colors dialog box

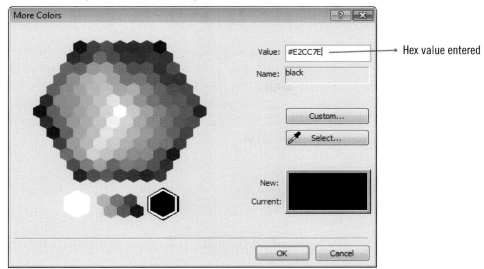

Hex value entered

FIGURE G-6: Image tab of Interactive Buttons dialog box

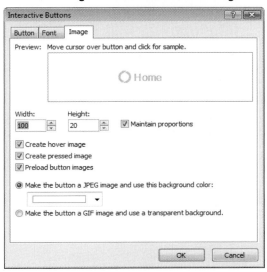

FIGURE G-7: Image tab of Interactive Buttons dialog box with transparent GIF option selected

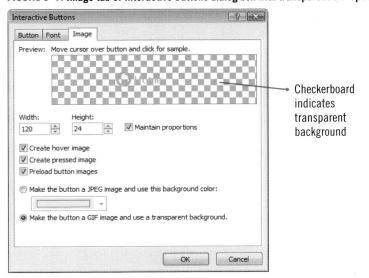

Checkerboard indicates transparent background

Creating a Navigation Bar

A set of related navigation links, whether text or images, is known as a **navigation bar**. Maintaining a consistent look among the buttons in a navigation bar makes a Web site easier to navigate and your design more cohesive. Once you have created one interactive button that you like, the easiest way to create the others is to copy and paste the original button and then change the text and link. Using this technique, all the buttons look similar. ▰▰▰ To finish the navigation bar on the home page, you create and modify several copies of the Home button.

STEPS

1. **Click the** <div#left_col> **list arrow on the quick tag selector bar, click** Select Tag Contents, **click** Edit **on the menu bar, then click** Copy

   The home button and related code are copied to the Windows clipboard.

2. **Click the** Home button, **press** [→]**, then press** [Shift][Enter]

   This inserts a <br /> tag and creates a line break after the Home button, as shown in Figure G-8.

3. **Click** Edit **on the menu bar, then click** Paste

   A second Home button is in place on the new line under the original Home button.

> **TROUBLE**
> Make sure you don't select the space in front of the text, just the text itself.

4. **Double-click the** bottom Home button, **in the Interactive Buttons dialog box select** Home **in the Text field, type** Menu, **click** Browse, **click** menu.htm, **click** OK, **then click** OK **again**

   You have created a second navigation button that reads " Menu" and links to the menu page. See Figure G-9.

5. **Click to the** right of the Menu button, **click** [Shift][Enter]**, click** Edit **on the menu bar, click** Paste, **double-click the** bottom Home button, **select** Home **in the Text field, type** Store, **click** Browse, **click** store.htm, **click** OK, **then click** OK **again**

> **QUICK TIP**
> When you create an interactive button, Expression Web also uses the button text as the alternate text attribute.

6. **Click to the** right of the Store button, **click** [Shift][Enter]**, click** Edit **on the menu bar, click** Paste, **double-click the** bottom Home button, **replace the text in the Text field with** Music, **click** Browse, **double-click** music.htm, **then click** OK

7. **Click to the** right of the Music button, **click** [Shift][Enter]**, click** Edit **on the menu bar, click** Paste, **double-click the** bottom Home button, **replace the text in the Text field with** Reservations, **click** Browse, **double-click** reservations.htm, **click** OK, **then compare your screen to Figure G-10**

   The navigation bar is almost complete, but the text on the Reservations button appears truncated because the word is too long to fit the button size.

8. **Double-click the** Reservations button, **in the Interactive Buttons dialog box click the** Font tab, **click** 11 **in the Font-size list, click** OK, **then save your changes**

   The Embedded Files dialog box opens with 12 files listed. Expression Web has created three versions for each of the four navigation buttons.

9. **Click** OK, **preview the page in a browser, point to the** Store button, **click the** Store button, **close the browser window, then return to Expression Web**

FIGURE G-8: Interactive Button placed on home page

New line created after
Home button

FIGURE G-9: Home page with Home and Menu buttons placed

FIGURE G-10: Home page with navigation bar in place

Truncated text on
Reservations button

Adding a Navigation Bar to Site Pages

Each page on a Web site should include a navigation bar, and this element should be consistent from page to page so that visitors can easily navigate the site. Once you have created a navigation bar on one page, it is a simple matter of copying and pasting to add it to each page of the site. ▨▨▨▨▨ You add the navigation bar from the TradeWinds home page to the other pages.

STEPS

QUICK TIP

Using the Select Tag Contents option ensures that you only select the navigation bar and not the containing div.

1. **Click anywhere in the left_col div, point to <div#left_col> on the quick tag selector bar, click the <div#left_col> list arrow, then click Select Tag Contents**
   See Figure G-11. Selecting the content of the left_col div selects all the interactive buttons and their corresponding code.

2. **Click Edit on the menu bar, then click Copy**
   The buttons and corresponding code are copied to the Windows clipboard.

3. **Open the store page, click in the left_col div, click Edit on the menu bar, then click Paste**
   See Figure G-12. The entire navigation bar and all links are now incorporated into the store page.

QUICK TIP

Instead of using the Edit menu, you can right-click where you would like to paste and then choose Paste from the shortcut menu.

4. **Open the contact page, then repeat Step 3**

5. **Open the menu page, then repeat Step 3**

6. **Open the music page, then repeat Step 3**

7. **Open the reservations page, then repeat Step 3**

8. **Save changes to all files, click OK each time the Save Embedded Files dialog box opens, then preview the reservations page in a browser**
   See Figure G-13.

9. **Use the links in the navigation bar to view all the pages in the site, then leave the browser window open**

FIGURE G-11: Selecting contents of div#left_col

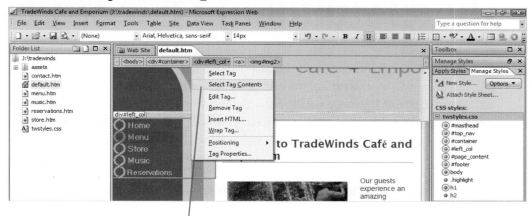

Select Tag Contents command

FIGURE G-12: Navigation bar pasted into store page

FIGURE G-13: Previewing the reservations page in a browser

Understanding Link Styles

In the early days of the World Wide Web, all linked text looked the same—it was blue and underlined on every Web site. This consistency made it instantly stand out to visitors as a clickable link. Today, thanks to CSS, designers have much more control over how links appear—they can be blue or not, underlined or not, and formatted almost any way you wish. But with this control comes a responsibility to create link styles that clearly indicate to a visitor that the link is clickable. Before styling the links on the TradeWinds site, you want to know more about the concepts and principles behind this area of Web design.

DETAILS

To understand link styles, you should be familiar with the following terms and guidelines:

- **Link states**

  So far you have learned about using classes, elements, and ids as selectors for creating style rules. Links can be styled by using the <a> or anchor tag as the selector, but links are unique in that you also have the option of attaching a pseudo-class to the tag. A **pseudo-class** defines properties for a particular state of the element. Links have four commonly used pseudoclass selectors: **a:link**, indicating the normal, unvisited state of a link; **a:visited**, meaning that the link has been clickn the visitor's browser and is present in the browser's history; **a:hover**, meaning that the visitor's cursor is pointing to the link; and **a:active**, meaning that the link has been clicked but not released. By default, normal links are blue and underlined and visited links are purple and underlined. See Figure G-14.

  It's best to create a style rule for at least the a:link, a:visited, and a:hover states so that each state looks different to visitors. The a:active state is seen for such a brief period (only during the actual click on the link) that creating a style for this state is not usually critical.

  In a Web page, these link pseudo-class styles are applied according to the order in which they are listed in the style sheet, so it's important that they be listed in the correct order. Expression Web writes styles rules in the style sheet in the order in which you create them, so always create your styles rules in this order: a:link, a:visited, a:hover, and a:active. A popular way to remember this order is to think of the phrase LoVe—HA.

- **Guidelines for creating link styles**

  Leave links underlined. You can remove underlines from your links by modifying the text-decoration property in CSS, but it's advisable to leave the underline on your links. Underlined text is almost universally understood to be a clickable link, and using underlines will make your site more user-friendly. See Table G-1 for available text-decoration options.

  Differentiate between visited and unvisited links. Creating different styles for visited and unvisited links helps visitors keep track of which areas of the site they have visited. In general, it's best to create styles that make unvisited links more noticeable and visited links less so. This can be accomplished through using a brighter color for unvisited links and a more subtle or less saturated color for visited links.

  Experiment with hover styles and colors. Creating a slightly more dramatic style for the hover state is an effective way to provide feedback to visitors that the link is indeed clickable. For example, you can add a background color for the hover state so the link appears to be highlighted, or use an overline to add emphasis. Feel free to use link colors that coordinate with your design; however, avoid purple to indicate normal links and blue to indicate visited links, since this reverses the normal color conventions and could confuse visitors.

Visited link   Unvisited link

TABLE G-1: Available text-decoration options

value	effect
underline	Displays a line under the text
overline	Displays a line above the text
line-through	Displays a line through the center of the text
blink	Displays text as blinking; not well-supported by browsers
none	Displays text with none of the preceding decorations; use when styling links to remove the default underline

Using more than one set of link styles on a site

Sites commonly need to include more than one set of link styles. For example, the designer may want the navigation text links to look different from the text links that are within the site's content. CSS makes this simple to accomplish through the use of descendent selectors. **Descendent selectors** define properties for all instances of an element that occur within a defined container. For example, if you want all links contained in the footer div to have a different style from other links on the site, create a new style and in the Selector box type #footer a:link, define it in your external style sheet, then choose your options. This will create a normal link style that only applies to links contained within your footer div. Create styles for the other states in the same manner by using #footer a: visited, #footer a:hover, and #footer a:active as the selectors. You can also use the same principle with any div and any element. For example, you could use the selector #masthead h1 to define a style that only applies to h1 elements that are within the masthead div.

Creating Link Styles

Once you've decided how you want each of your link states to look, you can use the New Style button in Expression Web to create the styles. Remember to follow the LoVe-HA order when creating them: a:link, a:visited, a:hover, and then a:active. ░░░░░ You are ready to create styles for the a:link, a:visited, and a:hover link states. You decide not to create a style for the a:active link states in this site.

1. **Close the browser window, return to Expression Web, make the** store page **the active page, then click the** New Style button **on the Manage Styles task pane**
   The New Style dialog box opens.

2. **Click the** Selector list arrow, **click** a:link, **click the** Define in list arrow, **click** Existing style sheet, **click the** URL list arrow, **then click** twstyles.css

3. **Click in the** color box, **type** #757E34, **compare your screen to Figure G-15, then click** OK
   You cannot see the link styles on the pages until you preview them in a browser.

4. **Click the** New Style button **on the Manage Styles task pane, click the** Selector list arrow, **click** a:visited, **click the** Define in list arrow, **then click** Existing style sheet

5. **Click in the** color box, **type** #BFC97C, **then click** OK
   By using a lighter shade of the color used for the a:link style, the visited links will not be as visually prominent on the page.

6. **Click the** New Style button **on the Manage Styles task pane, click the** Selector list arrow, **click** a:hover, **click the** Define in list arrow, **then click** Existing style sheet

7. **Click in the** color box, **type** #B1012A, **click the** overline check box **under text-decoration, click the** underline check box **under text-decoration, compare your screen to Figure G-16, then click** OK

8. **Save changes to all files, preview the store page in the browser as shown in Figure G-17, point to the** Museum of American Quilter's Society link, **close the browser window, return to Expression Web, close the tradewinds site, then exit Expression Web**

Rearranging your styles

You can see the order of your styles by looking at either the Manage Styles or Apply Styles task pane. The styles are listed in the order in which they appear in the style sheet. If your link styles get out of the proper LoVe-HA order, open the Manage Styles task pane, click the name of the style you want to move, then drag it to the correct location in the list.

FIGURE G-15: New Style dialog box for a:link style

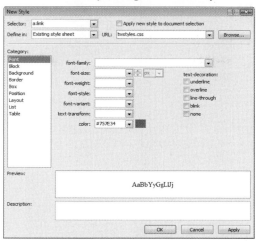

FIGURE G-16: New Style dialog box for a:hover style

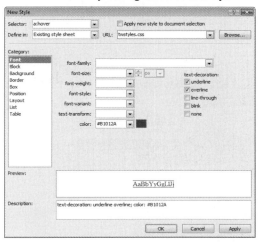

FIGURE G-17: Store page in browser with link styles

alink style

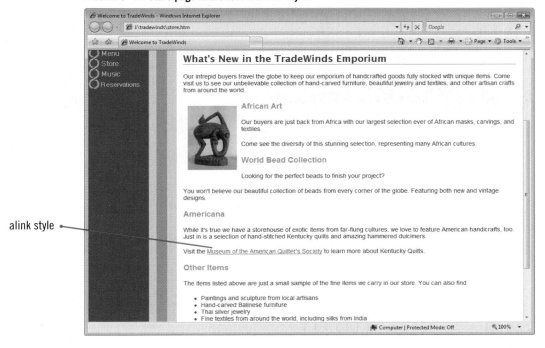

Expression Web

Practice

If you have a SAM user profile, you may have access to hands-on instruction, practice, and assessment of the skills covered in this unit. Log in to your SAM account (http://sam2007.course.com/) to launch any assigned training activities or exams that relate to the skills covered in this unit.

▼ CONCEPTS REVIEW

Refer to Figure G-18 to answer the following questions:

FIGURE G-18

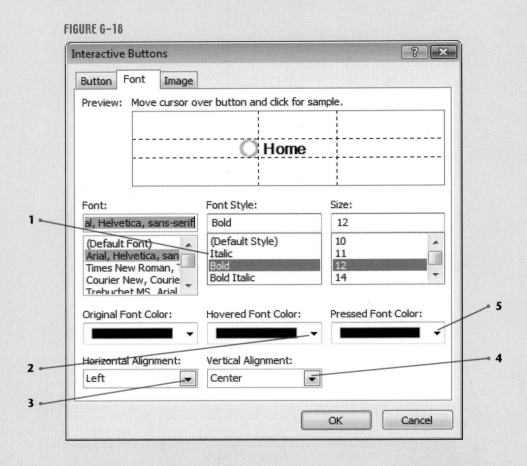

1. Which element would you click to change the color of the text when a visitor points to the button?
2. Which element would you click to change the color of the text when a visitor clicks a button?
3. Which element would you select to make the text align to the right edge of the button?
4. Which element would you select from to italicize the text on a button?
5. Which element would you click to make the text align to the bottom edge of the button?

Match each link state with the order in which it should appear in the style sheet.

6. a:active   **a.** First
7. a:link   **b.** Second
8. a:visited   **c.** Third
9. a:hover   **d.** Fourth

Select the best answer from the list of choices.

10. **The default style for a visited link is:**
    - **a.** Purple and underlined.
    - **b.** Blue and underlined.
    - **c.** Purple and bold.
    - **d.** Blue and bold.

11. **Which type of navigation area features links that are related to a particular section of a site?**
    - **a.** Global navigation
    - **b.** Local navigation
    - **c.** Utility navigation
    - **d.** Site map navigation

12. **Compared to normal unvisited links, visited links should be:**
    - **a.** More noticeable.
    - **b.** Less noticeable.
    - **c.** Underlined.
    - **d.** Overlined.

13. **A person who specializes in structuring and organizing content and navigation is called a(n):**
    - **a.** Structuralist.
    - **b.** Organizational designer.
    - **c.** Navigation specialist.
    - **d.** Information architect.

14. **Which link state occurs when a visitor points to a link?**
    - **a.** a:active
    - **b.** a:visited
    - **c.** a:unvisited
    - **d.** a:hover

15. **Which type of navigation feature links to each top-level section in the entire site?**
    - **a.** Global navigation
    - **b.** Local navigation
    - **c.** Utility navigation
    - **d.** Site map navigation

16. **The default style for a normal link that has not yet been visited is:**
    - **a.** Purple and underlined.
    - **b.** Blue and underlined.
    - **c.** Purple and bold.
    - **d.** Blue and bold.

17. **The technique of card sorting can be used to:**
    - **a.** Involve your audience in organizing your site content.
    - **b.** Create effective link styles.
    - **c.** Edit interactive buttons.
    - **d.** Design navigation graphics.

18. **If the visitor has clicked a link and the link is present in the visitor's history, which pseudoclass style is displayed?**
    - **a.** a:link
    - **b.** a:hover
    - **c.** a:active
    - **d.** a:visited

19. **The acronym LoVe-HA is used to help remember the order in which:**
    - **a.** Interactive buttons should be copied and pasted.
    - **b.** Navigation bars should be created.
    - **c.** Link pseudoclass styles should appear in a style sheet.
    - **d.** Navigation should appear on a page.

20. **Another term for interactive button is:**
    - **a.** Pressed button.
    - **b.** Rollover.
    - **c.** Graphic.
    - **d.** Link.

▼ SKILLS REVIEW

1. **Create an interactive button.**
   a. Launch Expression Web, then open the careers site.
   b. Open the home page.
   c. Click in the top_nav div, click Insert on the menu bar, then click Interactive Button.
   d. On the Button tab of the Interactive Buttons dialog box, choose Simple Block 1, replace the text with **Home**, then use the Browse button next to the Link field to link it to the home page.
   e. Click OK to close the Interactive Buttons dialog box.
   f. Save your changes, then click OK when the Save Embedded Files dialog box appears.

2. **Edit an interactive button.**
   a. Double-click the Home button.
   b. On the Font tab, set the font to Arial, Helvetica, sans-serif, the font-weight to Bold, and the size to 18.
   c. Set the Hovered Font Color to #CCDDFF and the Pressed Font Color to #663300.
   d. On the Image tab, set the width to 150 pixels while maintaining the proportions.
   e. Confirm that the Make the Button a JPEG image and use this background color option is selected, click the list arrow, then click the light tan swatch in the Document Colors section.
   f. Click OK to close the Interactive Buttons dialog box.
   g. Save your changes, preview the home page in a browser, point to the Home button, click the Home button, close the browser, then return to Expression Web.

3. **Create a navigation bar.**
   a. Select the Home button, click Edit on the menu bar, then click Copy.
   b. With the Home button selected, press [→], click Edit on the menu bar, then click Paste.
   c. Double-click the second Home button, then edit the properties so the text reads **Services** and the button links to the services page.
   d. Click to the right of the Services button, click Edit on the menu bar, then click Paste.
   e. Double-click the second Home button, then edit the properties so the text reads **About Us** and the button links to the about page.
   f. Save all the pages, click the Change Folder button in the Save Embedded Files dialog box that opens, navigate to the assets folder, click assets, click OK, then click OK again.
   g. Preview the home page in a browser, click the Services button in the navigation bar, close the browser window, then return to Expression Web.

4. **Add a navigation bar to site pages.**
   a. Click inside the top_nav div, click the <#top_nav> list arrow on the quick tag selector bar, then click Select Tag Contents.
   b. Click Edit on the menu bar, then click Copy.
   c. Open the services page, click in the top_nav div, click Edit on the menu bar, then click Paste.
   d. Open the about page, click in the top_nav div, click Edit on the menu bar, then click Paste.
   e. Open the contact page, click in the top_nav div, click Edit on the menu bar, then click Paste.
   f. Save your pages, preview the services page in a browser, close the browser, then return to Expression Web.

5. Create link styles.

a. Open the New Style dialog box.

b. Choose a:link as the selector and define the style in the cgstyles.css style sheet. Set the color to #002980, then click OK to close the New Style dialog box.

c. Open the New Style dialog box, choose a:visited as the selector, and define the style in the cgstyles.css style sheet. Set the color to #333333, then click OK to close the New Style dialog box.

d. Open the New Style dialog box, choose a:hover as the selector, and define the style in the cgstyles.css style sheet. Switch to the Background category, set the background-color to #FFFFCC, then click OK to close the New Style dialog box.

e. Save your pages, preview the home page in a browser, point to the career exploration tools link, then compare your screen to Figure G-19.

f. Close the browser, return to Expression Web, close the careers site, then exit Expression Web.

FIGURE G-19

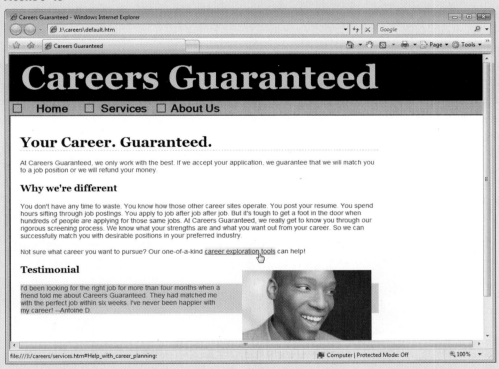

Expression Web

▼ INDEPENDENT CHALLENGE 1

In this project, you continue your work on the ConnectUp Web site. Tiffany likes your design so far, but she would like to see some visual elements that really make the site pop. You decide to create a tabbed navigation bar that coordinates with the green color used in the site headings.

a. Launch Expression Web, then open the connectup Web site.

b. Open the home page.

c. Click in the masthead div and insert an interactive button with the following properties: the Embossed Tab 2 button type, text that reads **Home**, a link to the default.htm page, and font settings of Trebuchet MS, bold, size 14. Set the Hovered Font Color to #FF6600 and the Pressed Font Color to #C0C0C0. On the Image tab, select the option to create a GIF with a transparent background.

d. Select the Home button and copy it. Click to the right of the Home button and paste it. Modify this button to read **F.A.Q.**, and to link it to the faq page.

e. Click to the right of the F.A.Q. button and paste. Modify this button to read **JoinUp**, and link it to the join up page.

f. Select the contents of the masthead div using the quick tag selector, then copy the contents.

g. Open the faq page and paste the contents into the masthead div. Repeat this step for the contact and joinup pages.

h. Save changes to all pages.

i. Create an a:link style in the existing style sheet. Set the color to #25B6FC and the font-weight to bold.

j. Create an a:visited style in the existing style sheet. Set the color to #666666 and the font-weight to bold.

k. Create an a:hover style in the existing style sheet. Set the color to #FC8F00 and the font-weight to bold.

l. Save the changes to all pages, preview the home page in a browser, and compare your screen to Figure G-20. Use the navigation tabs to click through to the other pages, close the browser, return to Expression Web, close the site, and exit Expression Web.

FIGURE G-20

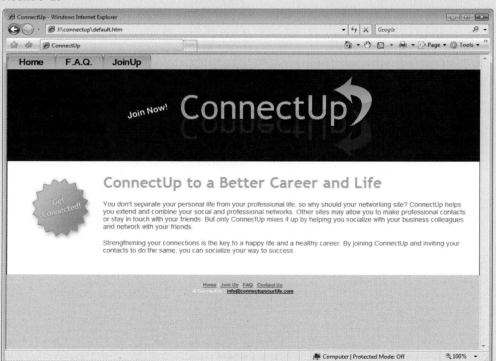

▼ INDEPENDENT CHALLENGE 2

In this project, you continue your work on the Memories Restored Web site. You are ready to add a navigation bar to the site and create styles for the links.

   a. Launch Expression Web, then open the memories Web site.

   b. Taking note of the shapes and colors used in the Memories Restored Web site, insert an interactive button in the left_col div that complements the site's design. The button should have the text **Home** on it and link to the home page.

   c. Edit the button as necessary until you are satisified. You may even need to delete the button and start over again a few times until you find a design you like.

   d. Copy, paste, and modify the finished button as necessary to create a navigation bar that links to all the site pages except the contact page.

   e. Add the navigation bar to all site pages, including the contact page.

   f. Save changes to all pages.

   g. Create link styles for a: link, a:visited, and a:active in the external style sheet, using settings that you think complement the overall site. Figure G-22 shows an example of one possible design; your project will differ.

Advanced Challenge Exercise

   ■ Create a style for a:hover.

   ■ Use the Manage Styles task pane to move this style to the correct position in the style sheet.

   h. Save your changes to all open files, preview the site in a browser, then use the links in the navigation bar to view all pages. When you are finished, close the browser, return to Expression Web, close the site, then exit Expression Web.

FIGURE G-21

▼ INDEPENDENT CHALLENGE 3

This Independent Challenge requires an Internet connection.

You've been attending some meetings at Technology for All related to the Web site redesign. The discussions have been difficult because several people have strong but conflicting opinions on how the navigation should be structured and how the content should be organized and labeled. Over coffee, a friend tells you about usability.gov, a Web site that features research-based guidelines on many aspects of Web site design. You decide to review the materials at usability.gov to see if perhaps the guidelines could be helpful in resolving some of the design arguments that have been brewing among the staff.

a. Visit the usability.gov Web site, then navigate to the Research-Based Web Design & Usability Guidelines, as shown in Figure G-22.

b. Read at least two chapters that interest you.

c. Write at least three paragraphs explaining what you learned from the guidelines and how such guidelines could be helpful in assisting Web design teams in making decisions.

Advanced Challenge Exercise

- Familiarize yourself with the research behind these guidelines by reviewing the Strength of Evidence scale (the higher the number, the stronger the evidence) and the references for two of the guidelines you read about.

- Write a paragraph explaining in what situations, if any, it would be appropriate to ignore these two guidelines in favor of relying on your own instincts in designing a site.

d. Add your name to the document, save it, and print it.

FIGURE G-22

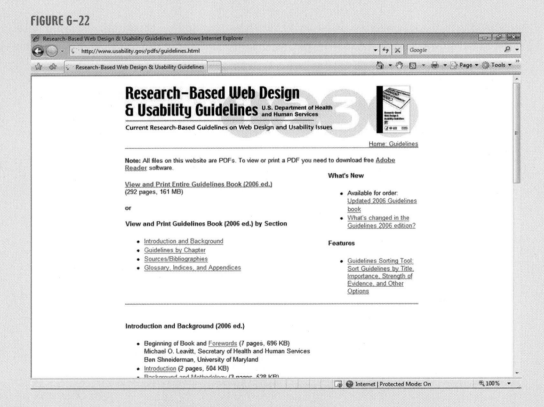

▼ REAL LIFE INDEPENDENT CHALLENGE

This assignment builds on the personal Web site you have worked on in previous units. In this project, you add a navigation bar to each page in your site and create link styles.

- **a.** Use the interactive button feature in ExpressionWeb to create one interactive button for your site. Choose fonts, colors, and sizes that complement your site.
- **b.** Edit the button as necessary until you are satisfied with the design.
- **c.** Use this button to build a navigation bar, and then add the navigation bar to each page in your site.
- **d.** Create styles for the following link states in your external style sheet: a:link, a:visited, a:hover, and a:active.
- **e.** Save your changes to all open files, preview the site in a browser, then use the navigation links to view all pages. When you are finished, close the browser, return to Expression Web, close the site, then exit Expression Web.

▼ VISUAL WORKSHOP

Launch Expression Web, then open the ecotours Web site. Modify the home page and the external style sheet so that your screen matches Figure G-23. To accomplish this, you need to add interactive buttons and create an a:link style. (*Hint*: The text on the buttons is a dark gray and the link text is a dark green; you can choose which dark gray and green you would like to use as long as it is similar to the figure.) When you are finished, save your changes, close the Web site, then exit Expression Web.

FIGURE G-23

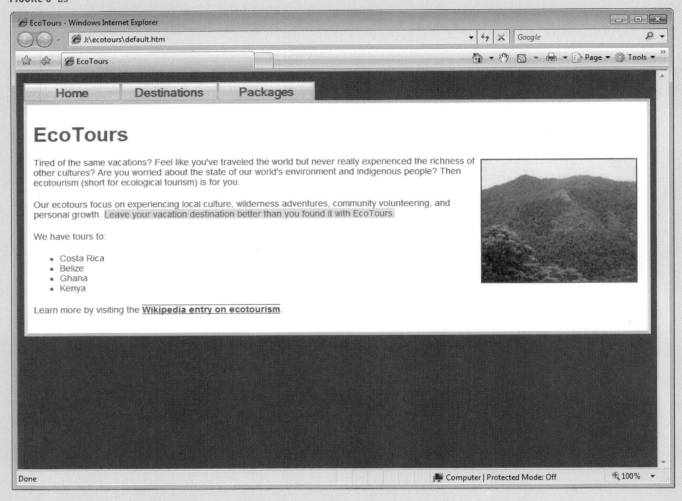

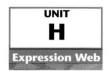
Testing and Publishing Your Web Site

Expression Web makes it easy to **publish** your Web site, placing a copy of the site files on a Web server so that people can visit it. Before you publish, you should test your site by viewing it in as many different browsers as possible, at different screen resolutions, and if possible on both Windows and Mac computers. In addition, check the spelling and grammar of all content. Once you've completed these steps, you're ready to use Expression Web reports to assist you in testing other features of the site, such as hyperlinks, accessibility, and page titles. You prepare the TradeWinds site for publication and learn to use the publishing feature in Expression Web to publish the site.

OBJECTIVES

Verify hyperlinks

View and edit page titles

Understand accessibility

Test accessibility

Understand Web server types

Set up and connect to a remote
  Web site

Publish a Web site

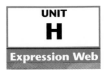
Verifying Hyperlinks

Expression Web includes a variety of reports to assist you in testing important features of the site, such as hyperlinks, accessibility, and page titles. As long as you use Expression Web to manage your Web site files, you are unlikely to have any broken internal hyperlinks, because Expression Web updates links between the pages in your site as needed. You are more likely to encounter broken external links, which can be caused by a change in a Web page address, removal of a Web page, or a mistake in typing the URL. If your site includes external links, you should verify these links before publishing your site. **Verifying links** means to check them to be sure they are working correctly. It's also a good idea to verify external hyperlinks on an ongoing basis, in case the page you have linked to is moved or removed. You must have an active Internet connection to be able to verify links. ▄▀▄▀ As part of your preparation for publishing the TradeWinds site, you verify the external hyperlinks on the site.

STEPS

1. **Launch Expression Web, then open the tradewinds site**

   The Web site tab opens in Folders view.

2. **Click the Reports View button at the bottom of the Web Site tab**

   The Site Summary report appears, as shown in Figure H-1. From here, you can link to more detailed reports. See Table H-1 for a list of these reports and the information provided by each. You notice that the Unverified hyperlinks report shows a count of 1, indicating that there is one unverified hyperlink in the site.

3. **Click the Unverified hyperlinks link**

   As shown in Figure H-2, the Reports View dialog box opens, asking if you would like to verify hyperlinks. Behind the dialog box, you can see that the unverified hyperlink is the link to the American Quilt Museum.

QUICK TIP

If you need to change a hyperlink, right-click the hyperlink in the report, choose Edit Hyperlink, then enter the correct URL in the Edit Hyperlink dialog box.

4. **Click Yes**

   The results are displayed in the Web Site tab, as shown in Figure H-3. To verify the hyperlinks, Expression Web visits each URL to make sure it is valid. If the hyperlink is not working, the word "broken" will appear beside it in the report.

5. **Click the Hyperlinks list arrow, then click Site Summary**

   You return to the Site Summary screen. The Count column of the Unverified hyperlinks report now says "0," indicating that there are no unverified hyperlinks in the site.

TABLE H-1: Reports available in Reports view

report name	lists...
All files	Every file in the site
Unlinked files	Files that are not linked to any other pages; these can often be deleted
Slow pages	Pages that take longer than 30 seconds to download at a connection speed of 56.6 Kbps
Older files	Files that have not changed in the past 72 days
Recently added files	Files added to site in the past 30 days
Hyperlinks	All hyperlinks in the site, both internal and external
Unverified hyperlinks	Hyperlinks that have not been checked to see if they are valid, working links
Broken hyperlinks	Hyperlinks that have been checked and were found to not be valid, working links
External hyperlinks	Links to Web pages outside of current site
Style sheet links	Links to style sheets in the current site
Dynamic Web Templates	All files that are associated with a Dynamic Web Template
Master Pages	All files that are associated with an ASP.NET Master Page

FIGURE H-1: Reports View in Web Site Tab

Unverified
hyperlinks
link

Reports View
button

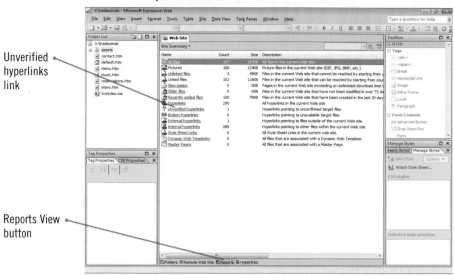

FIGURE H-2: Confirming hyperlink verification

Hyperlinks
list arrow

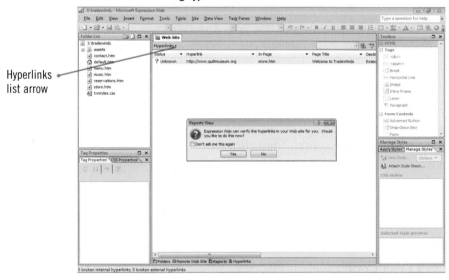

FIGURE H-3: Verified hyperlink

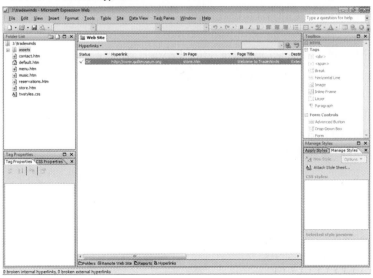

Expression Web

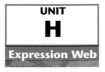

Viewing and Editing Page Titles

When you created the TradeWinds pages, you used the New from Existing Page feature. Expression Web gave the new pages titles based on the text on the page at the time of creation. Because all the pages were based on the home page, which contained the text "Welcome to TradeWinds," they all now have the same title. It's a good idea to give every page in a site its own unique title. Expression Web offers several ways to view and edit a page's title. Working in Hyperlinks view provides a helpful graphical display of each page's title as well as quick access for editing the title. ▓▓▓▓▓ You decide to use Hyperlinks view to view and edit each page's title in the TradeWinds site.

STEPS

TROUBLE
If Hyperlinks view does not show links to and from the home page, click Site, click Recalculate Hyperlinks, then click Yes.

1. **Click the Hyperlinks View button at the bottom of the Web Site tab, then click default.htm in the Folder List task pane**
   The Hyperlinks view of the Web Site tab is displayed with the home page in the center, as shown in Figure H-4. This view shows how the pages in the site are linked to the selected file—in this case, the home page.

2. **Right-click in any blank area of the Web Site tab, then click Show Page Titles**
   See Figure H-5. The title of the page, rather than the file name, is now displayed. Because all the pages in the TradeWinds site have the same title, it's difficult to tell them apart when only the page titles are displayed.

3. **Right-click in any blank area of the Web Site tab, then click Show Page Titles**
   Show Page Titles is now deselected, and Hyperlinks view once again displays the file name of each page.

4. **Right-click contact.htm, click Properties, type Contact TradeWinds in the Title box to replace the highlighted text, then click OK**
   The title changes to Contact TradeWinds.

QUICK TIP
You can't use symbols such as é in the page title.

5. **Right-click menu.htm, click Properties, type TradeWinds Cafe Menu in the Title box to replace the highlighted text, then click OK**
   The title changes to TradeWinds Cafe Menu.

6. **Right-click music.htm, click Properties, type Live Music at TradeWinds in the Title box to replace the highlighted text, then click OK**
   The title changes to Live Music at TradeWinds.

QUICK TIP
Remember that page titles show up in search engine results, in the browser's title bar, and as the title when a visitor adds the page to book-marks or favorites.

7. **Right-click store.htm, click Properties, type TradeWinds Emporium in the Title box to replace the highlighted text, then click OK**
   The title changes to TradeWinds Emporium.

8. **Right-click reservations.htm, click Properties, type Make a Reservation at TradeWinds in the Title box to replace the highlighted text, then click OK**
   The title changes to Make a Reservation at TradeWinds.

9. **Right-click in any blank area of the Web Site tab, click Show Page Titles, compare your screen to Figure H-6, right-click in any blank area of the Web Site tab, then click Show Page Titles to turn off this setting**

FIGURE H-4: Hyperlinks view with home page selected

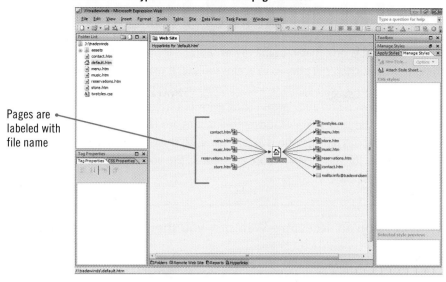

Pages are
labeled with
file name

FIGURE H-5: Hyperlinks view showing page titles

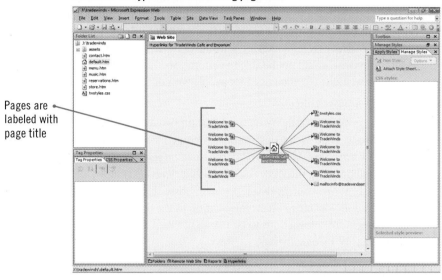

Pages are
labeled with
page title

FIGURE H-6: Hyperlinks view showing new page titles

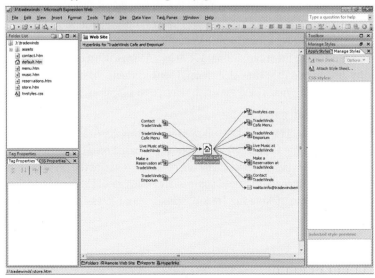

Expression Web

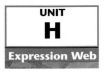

Understanding Accessibility

An accessible Web site is one that is usable by all visitors, including those with disabilities or those using nonstandard devices such as cell phones to access the site. It makes good business sense to design your site to be accessible to anyone who wants to visit. It could also help you avoid legal problems. Several lawsuits have been filed against companies whose sites were not accessible to people with disabilities. In many countries, including the United States, government sites are required to comply with accessibility guidelines. ▄▟▓▓ Catalina has a sister who is legally blind, so she is very aware of and concerned about accessibility. She would like for you to learn more about Web site accessibility so you can make the TradeWinds site accessible to all visitors.

DETAILS

In order to develop an accessible Web site, you should be familiar with:

- **Types of disabilities**

  Disabilities fall into four major categories. **Visual disabilities** include legal blindness, low vision, and color blindness. **Hearing disabilities** include deafness and hearing loss. People with **motor disabilities** have a condition that may affect their ability to use a standard-issue mouse and/or keyboard to navigate a site. **Cognitive disabilities** include learning disabilities, memory impairments, and intellectual impairments. People with disabilities usually use **assistive technologies** to help them use a computer and navigate the Internet. Assistive technologies are software or devices that help people with disabilities to perform functions they otherwise would not be able to perform. See Table H-2 for examples of these assistive devices as well as accommodations recommended for people with different disabilities.

- **Guidelines for accessibility**

  Expression Web generates accessibility reports based on two different sets of guidelines:

  - The W3C (World Wide Web Consortium) has created a set of international Web Content Accessibility Guidelines, known as **WCAG**. The WCAG are based on research, expert opinion, and observations of people with disabilities using the Web. The WCAG guidelines are grouped into three sets of priority levels.

    - Priority 1: A Web content developer *must* satisfy this checkpoint. Otherwise, one or more groups will find it impossible to access information in the document. Satisfying this checkpoint is a basic requirement for some groups to be able to use Web documents. See Figure H-7 for a partial checklist of Priority 1 Guidelines.

    - Priority 2: A Web content developer *should* satisfy this checkpoint. Otherwise, one or more groups will find it difficult to access information in the document. Satisfying this checkpoint will remove significant barriers to accessing Web documents.

    - Priority 3: A Web content developer *may* address this checkpoint. Otherwise, one or more groups will find it somewhat difficult to access information in the document. Satisfying this checkpoint will improve access to Web documents.

  - In addition to the international WCAG guidelines, most countries have developed their own accessibility requirements. The U.S. federal government has issued guidelines in Section 508 of the Rehabilitation Act. These are often referred to simply as **Section 508 guidelines**.

- **What you've already done**

  Several of the practices you have followed in creating the TradeWinds site also help make it accessible. For starters, just by using Expression Web, your site is based on well-written, standards-compliant code that will be readable by all types of devices. The use of CSS to separate the presentation of the pages from the content, the use of semantic markup to add appropriate structural HTML tags, and the use of alternate text for images have contributed to making the TradeWinds site more accessible to all visitors.

FIGURE H-7: WCAG Web site

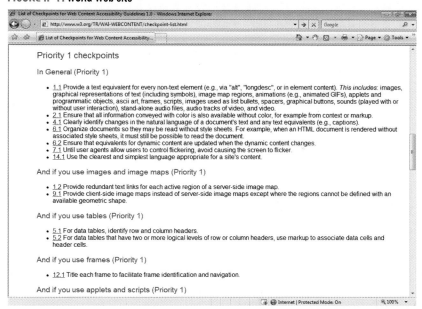

TABLE H-2: Assistive technologies and accommodations that help people with disabilities use computers

type of disability	available assistive technology	recommended accommodations
Visual	Screen magnifier software, screen reader software	• Provide alternate text for images • Ensure that link text is understandable out of context • Avoid using frames • Do not rely on color alone to convey meaning • Provide a means for users to skip links
Hearing	None usually needed	• Provide captions for audio and video
Motor	Mouth stick, head wand, breath-activated switches, voice-activated software, adaptive keyboards, eye-tracking software	• Ensure site is navigable via keyboard only without use of mouse
Cognitive	None	• Ensure content is clearly written • Provide clear and helpful error messages • Use white space, headings, subheadings, and bulleted lists to structure content
Seizure	None	• Avoid animations, graphics, or movies that strobe, flicker, or flash; these can induce seizures

Being visible to the search engines

Designing a site to be standards-compliant also makes your site more visible to search engines. However, ensuring that your pages rank near the top of search results takes more work. Each search engine uses its own **algorithm** or method of deciding which pages show up, say, on page one rather than page three when you search for "chocolate chip cookie recipes." The algorithms used by search engines are a closely guarded secret; they are very sophisticated, change frequently, and take into account factors such as the number of times the search term shows up in your content, where the search term occurs on your page, and how many other reputable sites link to your site. Search terms that are included in the title tag and in linked text usually cause a page to rank higher. Search engines drive a considerable amount of traffic to Web sites, so **search engine optimization**, the business of adjusting a Web site so it ranks higher than competing sites on search engine pages, has become a thriving industry. Companies pay thousands of dollars to firms that can tweak their Web site's code and content in such a way that the site is displayed on the first page of results on popular search engines.

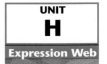

Testing Accessibility

Expression Web can generate accessibility reports that provide details of potential violations of the WCAG or Section 508 guidelines. Some accessibility issues may require additional research in order to be resolved, so Expression Web also provides a way for you to learn more about accessibility while viewing the report. You can also generate a formatted HTML version of the report which you can save and/or print for reference. You can generate accessibility reports for a single page, multiple pages, or an entire site. You decide to check the TradeWinds contact page for any accessibility issues. You want to print an accessibility report for Catalina, so that all potential issues can be resolved.

STEPS

1. **Click the Folders View button on the bottom of the Web site tab**

2. **Click contact.htm in the Web site tab to select it**

3. **Click Tools on the menu bar, then click Accessibility Reports**

   The Accessibility Checker dialog box opens. Here you can choose which pages to include in the report, which guidelines to include, and whether to include errors (serious issues which definitely need to be fixed), warnings (issues which should be fixed), or a manual checklist (a list of issues which can't be checked automatically; you can use this to manually check your site for any accessibility problems).

4. **Verify or select options in the Accessibility Checker dialog box so that your screen matches Figure H-8, then click Check**

   The Accessibility task pane opens at the bottom of the Web site tab with the report results listed, as shown in Figure H-9. Each line lists the page and file name where the error or warning was found, the line of code that resulted in the error, the issue type (error or warning), the specific WCAG or Section 508 checkpoint to which the warning or error refers, and a summary of the problem. You may have to scroll left to right to see all the information. If you point to a line in the report, a ScreenTip will display the summary of the problem.

5. **Right-click the second line of the report, then click Learn More, as shown in Figure H-10**

   A browser window opens and displays the guideline on the WCAG Web site that corresponds to that issue. This information can be helpful in deciding how to address the issue. Clicking the Techniques for checkpoint 6.1 link provides more information about how to fix this particular problem.

6. **Close the browser window, then return to Expression Web**

7. **Click the Generate HTML Report button** 🖹

   Expression Web generates and displays an HTML version of the report. You can use this report to research and check off each issue as it is resolved.

8. **Click File on the menu bar, point to Print, click Print on the Print submenu, then click OK**

   A copy of the report is printed.

9. **Click the Close Window button on the Accessibility task pane**

   The task pane closes.

FIGURE H-8: Accessibility Checker dialog box

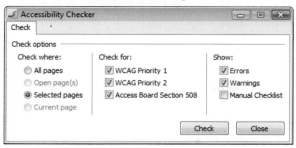

FIGURE H-9: Accessibility task pane showing results of Accessibility report

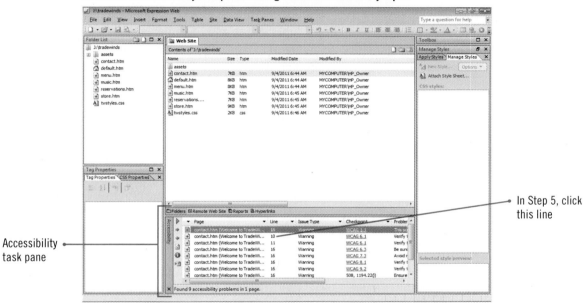

Accessibility task pane

In Step 5, click this line

FIGURE H-10: Shortcut menu

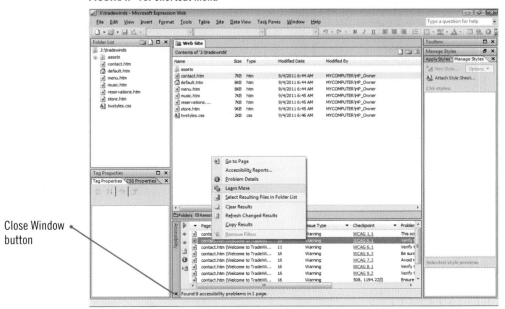

Close Window button

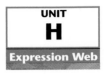

Understanding Web Server Types

Before you can publish your site, you must have space available on a server, along with an account so that you can access the space to log in and add files to it. The server that stores your Web site files is known as a **Web server**. Your Internet Service Provider (ISP) might include Web hosting space with your Internet service account; alternatively, you can purchase space from a Web hosting company. **Web hosting companies** provide server space for a monthly or annual fee. The server space where you post your Web files is known as your remote site. Expression Web supports publishing to four different server types, as shown in Figure H-11. When you define a remote site, you need to choose which type to use, and you need to provide certain account details such as your account user name and password. To find out which type of server you will be publishing to and to gather your account details, check with your Web hosting provider. To decide what type of Web server to use for TradeWinds, you review the server type options available in Expression Web.

DETAILS

Expression Web supports the following server type options for publishing a Web site:

- **FrontPage Server Extensions**

  FrontPage Server Extensions are files that are installed on a server and were used by Microsoft's legacy Web design program, FrontPage, to facilitate publishing and to support interactive Web features. FrontPage Server Extensions should be used only when converting an existing FrontPage site to Expression Web. If you use this method to publish, you first need to verify that your server has the extensions installed. To publish your files, you need to know the address to publish to and the user name and password for your account.

- **WebDAV**

  WebDAV stands for Web-based Distributed Authoring and Versioning. WebDAV allows groups to work on the same files by providing workflow and collaboration features such as file check-in and check-out and versioning of files (to facilitate evolving drafts of a document). This method is not very common, so you should check with your hosting provider to see if it is supported. To publish files to WebDAV, you need to know the address to publish to, and the user name and password for your account.

- **FTP**

  FTP, or File Transfer Protocol, is by far the most common method used to transfer files from a local to remote server. To use FTP, you need to know the address to publish to and the user name and password for your account. In addition, you need to know the file path to the directory in which you plan to publish your files. You can usually find these details in the support or help section of your hosting provider's Web site.

- **File System**

  The **File System** option allows you to publish a copy of your site to a folder on the same computer or same network. Consider using this option to publish a copy of your site to another folder for backup purposes before you publish it to a remote site.

FIGURE H-11: Remote Web Site Properties dialog box

Available server types

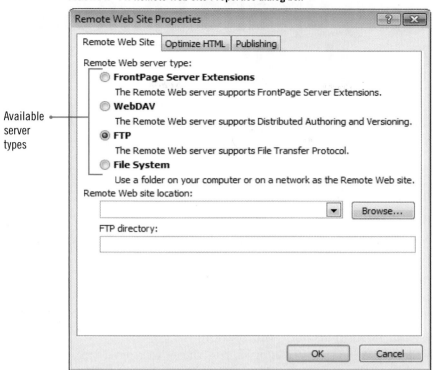

Choosing a hosting provider

With hundreds of Web hosting providers from which to choose, selecting a provider can be overwhelming. If you know people who are involved in creating or running Web sites, it can be helpful to ask which provider they recommend. You also need to be sure the provider and service package meet your needs. The following questions can assist you in selecting a provider:

- Does the provider offer Windows or Unix servers? If you are using any of the ASP.NET tools in Expression Web, you need a Windows server that is running ASP.NET.
- Does the service include access to traffic statistics for your site?
- How many e-mail accounts are included?
- Does the provider offer domain registration services to assist you in securing a domain name?
- How is support provided? By telephone, Internet chat, or e-mail only?

- Does the provider back up their clients' Web site files? If so, how often and how can you access the backup if needed?
- How is the provider's reliability? Don't settle for a company that has less than 95% uptime. **Uptime** is the time during which the servers are running and available.
- How much storage space is included in the packages? To select the package that's right for you, you need to know how much storage space you require. One way to check this is to navigate to your root folder in Windows Explorer, right-click the root folder, click Properties, then note the size of the folder.
- How much bandwidth do you need? Hosting packages usually include a maximum amount of traffic or bandwidth that is allowed to your site each month. Talk to your provider for assistance in determining how much bandwidth you are likely to need.
- What is the pricing structure, and is a contract required?

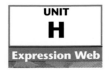

UNIT
H
Expression Web

Setting Up and Connecting to a Remote Site

Before you can publish your Web site, you must set up a remote Web site to tell Expression Web where to place the Web site files. ▄▄▄▄▄ In preparation for publishing the TradeWinds site files, you learn the process for setting up a remote Web site and then connecting to the remote site.

DETAILS

To set up a remote site:

- **Gather information about your remote site**

  Based on the Web hosting service you have arranged, gather your server type, account information, and other account details for easy reference.

- **Open the Remote Web Site Properties dialog box**

  You can access the Remote Web Site Properties dialog box by clicking the Remote Web Site View button at the bottom of the Web site tab, then clicking the Remote Web Site Properties button, as shown in Figure H-12.

- **Enter your hosting account information**

  In the Remote Web Site Properties dialog box, choose your server type, then fill in the information requested. The information needed will vary depending on the publishing method you choose, but it always includes the address to publish to. When you are finished, click OK.

- **Enter your user name and password**

  When the completed Remote Web Site Properties dialog box closes, the Connect to dialog box opens, as shown in Figure H-13. In this dialog box, you enter your user name and password. After entering this information, click OK to connect to your remote site.

TROUBLE
If Expression Web is not able to connect successfully, an error message appears; if this happens, first check that you entered the information correctly, and then contact your hosting provider for help.

- **Verify that you are connected**

  Once you are connected to your remote site, the view changes to Remote Web Site view. In this view, two sets of files are listed: on the left side of the window, under Local Web site, are the files on your local site (your computer); on the right, under Remote Web site, are the files posted to the remote site (your Web server). See Figure H-14. The Remote Web site area will likely be blank if you have not yet published any files. If you see any files on the remote site, don't remove them without first checking with your hosting company. The files might be necessary for your site to function. If you have already published your site at least once, you will see the files that are currently on your remote site listed on the right. The status area provides information about what is currently happening in the publishing process or about the most recent publishing session.

Naming your home page

Web servers are set up to look for a specially named file to display to visitors as the home page when they type in your Web site address. Depending on the server, this file can have various names such as index.html, index.htm, default.htm, or default.html. Expression Web names the home page default.htm, which is the default name for Windows servers. Before you publish your site, though, you should check with your Web hosting company or server administrator to find out if you should use a different name for your home page file. If you need to name it something different, simply open your Web site in Expression Web, right-click default.htm in the Folder List task pane, click Rename, then type in the new name. Expression Web will still recognize it as the home page for your site.

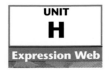

FIGURE H-12: Remote Web Site view

Remote Web
Site Properties
button

Remote Web
Site View
button

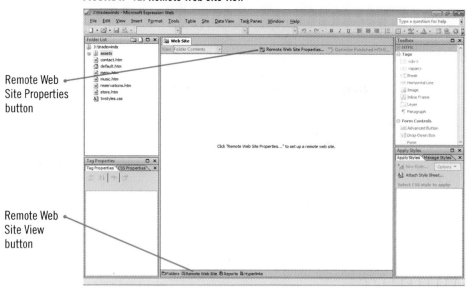

FIGURE H-13: Connect to dialog box

FIGURE H-14: Remote Web Site view when connected to remote site

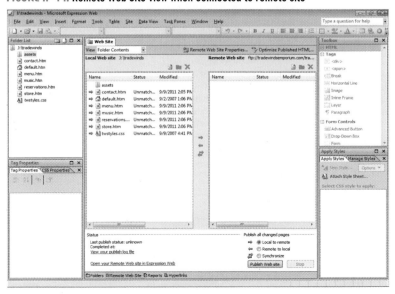

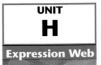
Publishing a Web Site

Once you have set up your remote site, publishing your files is simple. Expression Web includes features for publishing your files for the very first time as well as options for updating a site with additional files when necessary. You will want to publish your files whenever you make a change to the design or content of the site. How often you need to publish files depends on how frequently you are adding or editing content. Some sites are updated several times a day, while others may go months without a change. ░░░░ You are ready to publish the TradeWinds site, so you familiarize yourself with the steps in the publishing process.

DETAILS

To publish your site:

QUICK TIP

You can change which files are listed in the Local Web site area by using the View list arrow to display Folder content (all files), Files to Publish, Files Not to Publish, or Files in Conflict.

- **Choose a publishing option**

  Expression Web offers several options for publishing, which appear in the Status area shown in Figure H-15. The most common option is to publish your files from **local to remote**. This makes sense because you are working on files locally on your computer first and then publishing them to a remote location. You can also choose to publish **from remote to local**. This option can be useful if your local files have gotten lost or corrupted, because you can re-create your local site by copying the remote files. However, use extreme caution with this option; copying older files from the remote server can cause you to lose any intentional changes you made to local files. Finally, you can choose to **synchronize** the files, meaning that Expression Web will copy whichever version of the file is newer to the opposite site so that you end up with a matching set of the newest version of all files at the end. This option is useful when multiple people are working on a site.

QUICK TIP

By default, Expression Web publishes only files that have changed since you last published the site; to publish all files and overwrite all files currently on the remote site, click Remote Web Site Properties, click the Publishing tab, click All pages, overwriting pages already on destination, then click OK.

- **Publish your site**

  After you choose a publishing option, click the Publish Web site button. The status window lists file names as the files are being published, although if you have a fast connection to the server, the status might change so quickly that you can't read the details.

- **Verify that your site was published**

  When your files are published, the status window lists the status of the last publish as successful and your files appear in the Remote Web site area, as shown in Figure H-16. The status window also shows the date and time of the last publish and provides a link to the log files, which offer more details on which files were published, as shown in Figure H-17.

Excluding unfinished files from being published

Sometimes you want to publish a site before you have finished working with all the pages. It's best not to publish files you are still working on, because it can reflect poorly on the site and can be confusing to Web site visitors. By default, Expression Web publishes all changed files to the remote site, but you can exclude files that you are still working on in Remote Web Site view. To exclude a particular file from being published, right-click the file name in the Local Web site area in Remote Web Site view, then click Don't Publish on the shortcut menu. A Don't Publish icon ⊗ appears beside the file in Remote Web Site view and in the Folder List task area, and Expression Web will not include the file when publishing your site. When you are ready to publish the file, right-click the file name, then click Don't Publish to remove the icon.

FIGURE H-15: Publishing options

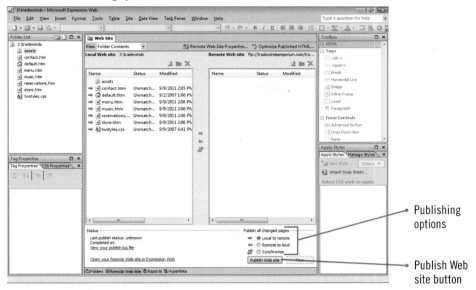

Publishing options

Publish Web site button

FIGURE H-16: Remote Web Site view after publishing files

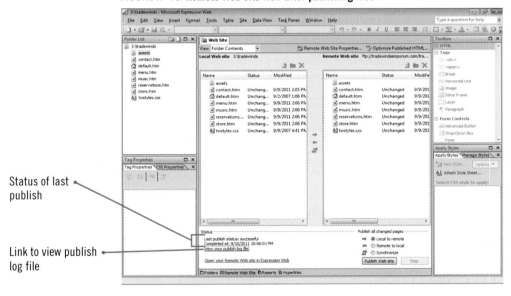

Status of last publish

Link to view publish log file

FIGURE H-17: Publish log file

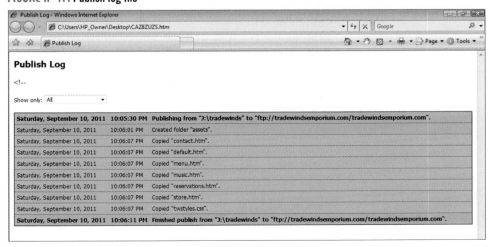

Practice

If you have a SAM user profile, you may have access to hands-on instruction, practice, and assessment of the skills covered in this unit. Log in to your SAM account (http://sam2007.course.com/) to launch any assigned training activities or exams that relate to the skills covered in this unit.

▼ CONCEPTS REVIEW

Refer to Figure H-18 to answer the following questions.

FIGURE H-18

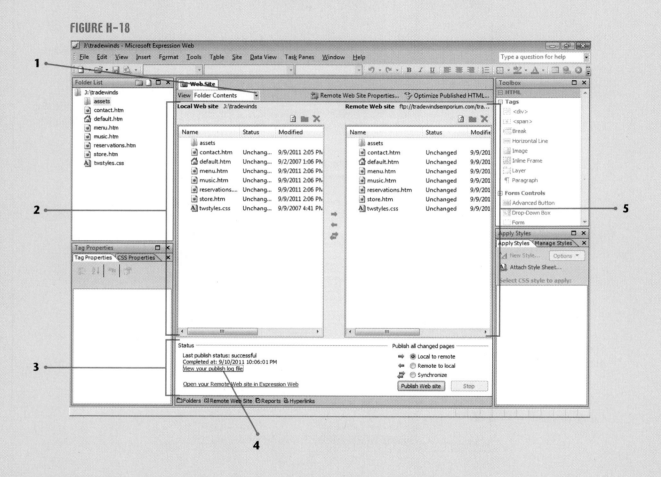

1. Which element shows the files that are on your computer or network drive?
2. Which element shows the files that are on a Web server?
3. Which element do you click to see a list of files that were transferred during the last publish?
4. Which element do you click to change which files are displayed?
5. Which element shows the files currently being transferred during publishing?

Match each server type with the statement that best describes it.

6. **FrontPage Server Extensions**
7. **WebDAV**
8. **FTP**
9. **File system**

a. Allows for a group of people to work on a common set of files
b. Most common server type
c. Used in older Web design software to publish and support interactive features
d. Used to publish to a folder on the same computer or network

Select the best answer from the list of choices.

10. **Which set of accessibility guidelines is used internationally?**
    a. Section 508
    b. WCAG
    c. XHTML 1.0
    d. World Accessibility Forum

11. **Which publishing option is the one most commonly used?**
    a. Local to remote
    b. Remote to local
    c. Synchronize
    d. Delete

12. **If you want to copy all the files from your remote site onto your computer or disk to replace your local files, which option do you choose in the status area?**
    a. Local to remote
    b. Remote to local
    c. Synchronize
    d. Delete

13. **By default, Expression Web publishes:**
    a. All files.
    b. Only changed files.
    c. Only HTML files.
    d. No files.

14. **A company that sells Web server space is known as a:**
    a. File transfer provider.
    b. Data backup provider.
    c. System administrator.
    d. Web hosting provider.

15. **Which of the following should you test before you publish your site?**
    a. Spelling and grammar
    b. Display of site in different browsers
    c. Display of site on different screen resolutions
    d. All of the above

16. **In which view can you easily edit page titles?**
    a. Folders view
    b. Remote Web Site view
    c. Reports view
    d. Hyperlinks view

17. **Which of the following is *not* an assistive technology used by people with disabilities to access Web sites?**
    a. Screen reading software
    b. Headphones
    c. Adaptive keyboard
    d. Mouth stick

18. **In the Accessibility Checker dialog box, which option would you choose to see a list of serious issues that definitely need to be fixed?**
    a. Show Warnings
    b. Show Manual Checklist
    c. Show Errors
    d. Generate HTML report

▼ SKILLS REVIEW

1. Verify hyperlinks.
   a. Launch Expression Web, then open the careers site.
   b. Click the Reports View button on the Web Site tab.
   c. Run the Unverified hyperlinks report, clicking Yes to confirm the process.
   d. Use the Hyperlinks list arrow to return to the Site Summary.

2. View and edit page titles.
   a. Click the Hyperlinks View button on the Web Site tab.
   b. Click the home page in the Folder List task pane.
   c. Right-click in a blank area of the Web Site tab, then click Show Page Titles.
   d. Right-click in a blank area of the Web Site tab, then click Show Page Titles to turn off this setting.
   e. In Hyperlinks view, right-click the about page, click Properties, in the Title box type **About Careers Guaranteed** to replace the highlighted text, then click OK.
   f. In Hyperlinks view, right-click the contact page, click Properties, replace the highlighted text in the Title box with **Contact Careers Guaranteed**, then click OK.
   g. In Hyperlinks view, right-click the services page, click Properties, replace the highlighted text in the Title box with **Careers Guaranteed Services**, then click OK.
   h. Right-click in a blank area of the Web Site tab, click Show Page Titles, then compare your screen to Figure H-19.
   i. Right-click in a blank area of the Web Site tab, then click Show Page Titles to turn off this setting.

FIGURE H-19

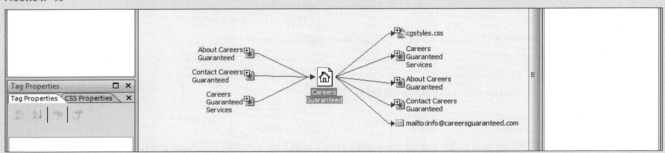

3. Run an accessibility report.
   a. Click the Folders View button on the Web Site tab.
   b. Click the services page to select it.
   c. Click Tools on the menu bar, then click Accessibility Reports.
   d. In the Accessibility Checker dialog box, make sure that Selected pages is selected under Check where; that WCAG Priority 1, WCAG Priority 2, and Access Board Section 508 are selected under Check for; and that only Errors and Warnings are selected under Show.
   e. Click Check.
   f. Right-click the fourth error listed on the report in the Accessibility task pane, then click Learn More.
   g. Close the browser, then return to Expression Web.
   h. Click the Generate HTML Report button, then print the report.
   i. Close the Accessibility task pane, close the careers Web site, then exit Expression Web.

▼ INDEPENDENT CHALLENGE 1

In this project you continue your work on the ConnectUp Web site. You have a meeting scheduled with Tiffany to show her your progress on the site. You decide to do some testing to make sure the links are working, the pages are titled appropriately, and there are no major accessibility problems.

a. Launch Expression Web, then open the connectup Web site.

b. In the Reports view of the Web Site tab, run the hyperlinks report and verify hyperlinks, as shown in Figure H-20.

c. In the Hyperlinks view of the Web Site tab, view the hyperlinks to and from the home page. Show the Page Titles and review the current page titles.

d. In the Hyperlinks view, hide the Page Titles.

e. In the Hyperlinks view, edit the title for the contact page and give it the new title **Contact ConnectUp**.

f. In the Hyperlinks view, edit the title for the faq page and give it the new title **Frequently Asked Questions about ConnectUp**.

g. In the Hyperlinks view, edit the title for the joinup page and give it the new title **JoinUp with ConnectUp**.

h. Show the Page Titles, then deselect Show Page Titles.

i. Switch to Folders view, select the joinup page, then run an Accessibility report on the selected page, checking for WCAG Priority 1, WCAG Priority 2, and Access Board Section 508 , and showing Errors and Warnings.

j. Right-click the fifth error, then click Learn More.

k. Close the browser, then return to Expression Web.

l. Generate an HTML Report, print it, then close the Accessibility task pane.

m. Close the Web site, then exit Expression Web.

FIGURE H-20

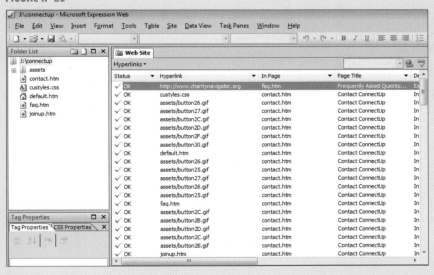

▼ INDEPENDENT CHALLENGE 2

In this project you continue your work on the Memories Restored Web site.

    a. Launch Expression Web and open the memories Web site.

    b. Verify any external hyperlinks in the site.

    c. Working in Hyperlinks view, review and edit page titles for all pages in the site, as shown in Figure H-21.

    d. Run an Accessibility Report on the testimonials page. Generate an HTML Report and print it. Close the Accessibility task pane when you are finished.

Advanced Challenge Exercise

    ■ Run an All Files Report on the memories Web site.

    ■ Press [Print Screen] and paste the image into a word-processing program.

    ■ Add your name at the top of the document and print the document.

    e. Close the memories site and exit Expression Web.

FIGURE H-21

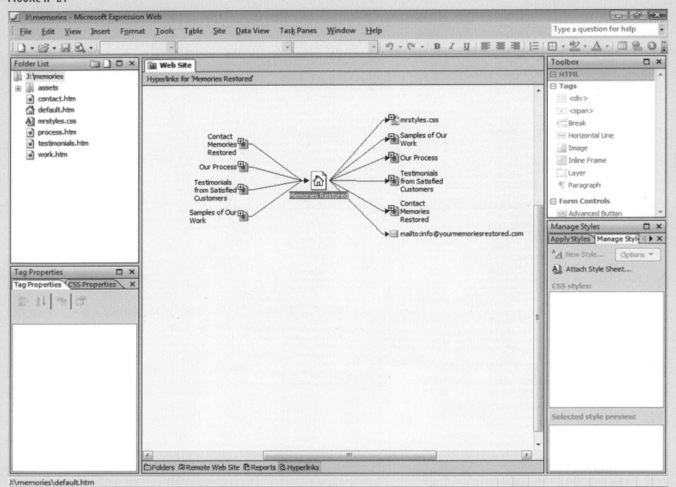

▼ INDEPENDENT CHALLENGE 3

This Independent Challenge requires an Internet connection.

Technology for All wants you to explore new options for hosting their Web site. They feel that their current Web hosting provider has poor technical support and is too expensive. They need 75 GB of space, 1000 GB of bandwidth, and a server that has Windows and ASP.NET installed.

    a. Using your favorite search engine, research Web hosting providers and find three companies to compare.

    b. Visit the companies' Web sites and find the package each company offers that would meet Technology for All's needs.

    c. Create a chart comparing the features and costs for each package.

Advanced Challenge Exercise

    ■ Research the Web site for each company to find out how they provide technical support (phone, e-mail, live chat, etc).

    ■ Research if there are any additional costs for technical support and how quickly customers can expect a response.

    ■ Incorporate this information into your chart.

    d. Conclude your report with a recommendation of which company you would choose for hosting and why.

    e. Add your name to the document, save it, and print it.

▼ REAL LIFE INDEPENDENT CHALLENGE

This assignment builds on the personal Web site you have worked on in previous units. You are ready to verify the site's hyperlinks, view and edit page titles, and check for accessibility problems.

    a. Verify all hyperlinks in your site. Fix any that are not valid.

    b. Review and edit as appropriate all page titles.

    c. Run an accessibility report and use the Learn More feature to visit the WCAG Web site for more information.

    d. Run a Slow pages report on your site.

    e. Test your site in a variety of browsers and screen resolutions.

    f. Proofread your content for spelling and grammatical errors.

▼ VISUAL WORKSHOP

Launch Expression Web, then open the ecotours Web site. Use the appropriate Web Site view and run the report shown in Figure H-22. When you have finished, press [Print Screen], paste the image into a word-processing program, add your name at the top of the document, print the document, close the word-processing program, then close the Web site and exit Expression Web.

FIGURE H-22

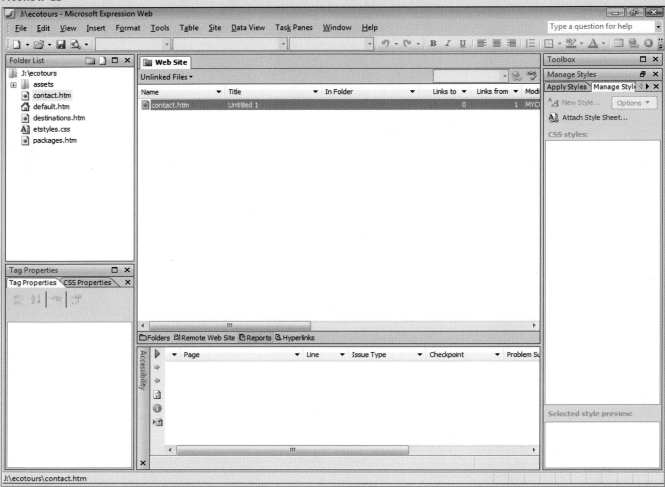

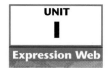

Working with Tables

HTML tables are grid-like containers consisting of columns and rows that are designed to hold tabular data. **Tabular data** is simply content that is displayed in a table format. The intersection of a row and a column in a table creates a rectangular area called a **cell**. You can use tables in your Web site to organize and present content. Expression Web makes it easy not only to create a table, but also to modify its properties to best fit the content and your site design. Designers previously relied on tables to create entire page layouts, but due to their lack of flexibility and limitations for access by people with disabilities, this use is now discouraged in favor of using CSS-based layouts. Catalina has sent you the live music schedule for TradeWinds, and you decide to create a table for the information.

OBJECTIVES

Insert a table and add content

Apply an AutoFormat to a table

Set table properties

Merge cells

Add and resize rows and columns

Modify cell properties

Modify a table style

Make a table accessible

Inserting a Table and Adding Content

Before you add a table to your page, it helps to plan out the table's structure—basically, how many rows and columns you need. You can always add or remove rows or columns later if you change your mind. Once you have created a table, you can add text, images, and other content to it just as you would for other HTML elements. 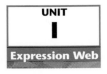 The live music schedule for TradeWinds should include information on the day, date, and artist name for each event. You want each event listed on its own row; in addition, you want to include a row at the top with headings. Three events are currently scheduled, so you need a table with three columns and four rows.

STEPS

1. **Launch Expression Web, open the** tradewinds **site, then open** music.htm

2. **Click to the right of the text** 8:00 p.m.**, click** Table **on the menu bar, then click** Insert Table
   The Insert Table dialog box opens, where you can set size, layout, borders, and background options. When creating a table, it's easiest to just set the size options, and then to modify the other properties later after you add the content.

> **QUICK TIP**
> When you insert a table, it is always placed on a new line.

3. **Type** 4 **in the Rows text box, select the text** 2 **in the Columns text box, press** [Delete]**, type** 3**, compare your screen to Figure I-1, then click** OK
   A table with four rows and three columns is inserted into the music page. Expression Web also creates a new class-based style in the page and applies it to the table. The default width for a table is 100%, meaning the width will stretch to fill the element in which the table is placed, which in this case is the page_content div.

> **QUICK TIP**
> If you wanted this table structure to be the default for new tables, you could click the Set as default for new tables check box to add a check mark.

4. **Click in the** top-left table cell**, type** Day**, then compare your screen to Figure I-2**
   This is the first cell of the **header row**, which lists the headings for the table columns.

5. **Press** [Tab]**, type** Date**, press** [Tab]**, type** Who**, then press** [Tab]
   Pressing [Tab] while in a table moves you to the next cell. If you press [Tab] while your cursor is in the last table cell, a new row is created and the cursor moves to the first cell of the new row.

> **TROUBLE**
> If you accidentally press [Tab] after the last entry, press [Ctrl][Z] to undo the new row.

6. **Type the following text in the table, pressing** [Tab] **after each entry to move to the next cell, but do not press** [Tab] **after the last entry:**

Every	Saturday	Jimmy Gill's Island Orchestra
Tuesday,	June 5	Kat Hollis
Friday,	June 14	The Pan Boys

7. **Compare your screen to Figure I-3, then save your changes**

Recognizing HTML table tags

You will be at an advantage when working with tables if you know the HTML tags involved in constructing them. The **<table>** tag is used to create the table itself. Table rows are designated with a **<tr>** tag and table cells with a **<td>** tag (td stands for table data). The **<th>** tag is used to designate a cell as a table header. HTML does not use tags to designate columns; columns are simply created when cells are added to rows. Expression Web also places the * * code in each cell, which adds a **nonbreaking space**. Some browsers will collapse table cells that do not contain any content. The nonbreaking space keeps this from happening. Once you add your own content, Expression Web removes the nonbreaking space from the cell.

FIGURE I-1: Completed Insert Table dialog box

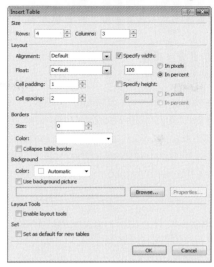

FIGURE I-2: New table with text added

Quick tag selector shows style applied to table tag

New class style created

Text entered into top-left table cell

FIGURE I-3: Table with all content entered

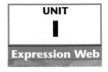

Applying an AutoFormat to a Table

You can quickly change the appearance of a table by using the **Table AutoFormat** feature in Expression Web. Table AutoFormat instantly creates borders, font formatting, background colors, and other effects for your table. When using this feature, you can use all formatting options or you can choose which ones to apply. Expression Web then adds class-based styles to the table to implement the formatting. You are short on time and decide to use the Table AutoFormats feature to quickly style the live music schedule table.

STEPS

1. **Right-click anywhere in the table, point to Modify, then click Table AutoFormat**

   The Table AutoFormat dialog box opens, as shown in Figure I-4. In the Formats list, you can browse through the predesigned Formats, such as Simple 1 and Simple 2. The check boxes in the second section, Formats to apply, allow you to apply or remove individual elements of the selected Format, such as borders or shading. The Apply special formats section allows you to designate certain rows and columns to receive special formatting.

   QUICK TIP
   If you add a check mark to the AutoFit check box, Expression Web resizes the table to be as small as possible while still fitting the table contents.

2. **Click Colorful 2 in the Formats list**

   The Preview area displays a sample table with the Colorful 2 Format applied. The preview is updated whenever you change an option in this dialog box.

3. **Click the Borders check box to remove the check mark, then click the Font check box to remove the check mark**

   The preview changes to show the format applied without border or font formatting.

   QUICK TIP
   The first column in this table is not unique, so there is no need to apply special formatting to it.

4. **Click the First Column check box to remove the check mark, compare your screen to Figure I-5, then click OK**

   See Figure I-6. The table is formatted with the options you chose. Notice the quick tag selector shows new classes have been applied to the table and table cells. These new styles are now also listed in the Manage Styles and Apply Styles task panes. You decide that this design doesn't quite work on the music page, so you want to remove it.

5. **Right-click anywhere in the table, point to Modify, then click Table AutoFormat**

   The Table AutoFormat dialog box opens.

6. **Click None in the Formats list, then click OK**

   The formatting is removed, and the styles associated with the AutoFormat are deleted from the page and no longer appear in the Apply Styles and Manage Styles task panes.

7. **Save your changes**

FIGURE I-4: Table AutoFormat dialog box

Step 2

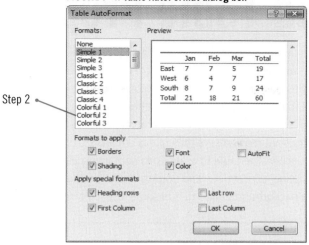

FIGURE I-5: Completed Table AutoFormat dialog box

Borders
check box

First
Column
check box

Font check box

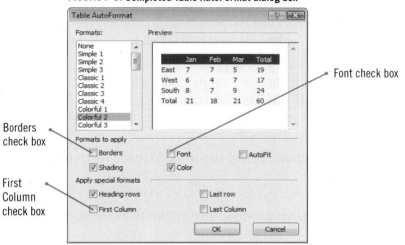

FIGURE I-6: Table with AutoFormat applied

Quick tag
selector
shows new
classes
applied

New class
styles created

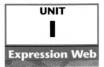

Setting Table Properties

You can change basic table properties using the Table Properties dialog box. Table properties include both structural elements, such as number of rows and columns, and formatting options, such as border size and color. You can use this dialog box instead of or along with the AutoFormat dialog box to customize the look of a table. See Table I-1 for options you can set in this dialog box. One option is table width, which can be dictated in one of two ways—in pixels or as a percentage. Setting a width in pixels creates an absolute width that remains constant regardless of the visitor's screen resolution. Setting a width in percentages creates a relative width that allows the table to scale as its containing element scales. ▰▰▰▰▰ You would like the table centered in its page_content div, and you want it to be the same size on all computer monitors. You also decide to add a background image to add some visual interest to the table.

STEPS

QUICK TIP

The Table Properties dialog box has the same options as the Insert Table dialog box.

1. **Right click** anywhere inside the table, **then click** Table Properties
    The Table Properties dialog box opens.

2. **Click the** Alignment list arrow, **then click** Center

3. **Under the Specify Width check box click the** In pixels option button, **select the text** 100 **in the specify width text box, press** [Delete], **then type** 500

4. **Click the** Use background picture check box **to add a check mark, click the** Browse button **below it, navigate to the folder where you store your Data Files, click** tw_tablebg.gif, **click** Open, **compare your screen to Figure I-7, then click** OK
    The changes have been applied to the table. The table is centered in the page_content div and will always appear with a 500-pixel width.

5. **Save your changes, saving the embedded file when prompted, then preview the page in a browser**
    See Figure I-8. Notice that the table is now a set width and is centered in the page_content div.

6. **Close the browser window, then return to Expression Web**

TABLE I-1: Table Properties dialog box options

option	use to...	option	use to...
Rows	Set number of rows	Borders Size	Set size of the table border
Columns	Set number of columns	Borders Color	Set color of the table border
Alignment	Set horizontal alignment of the table within its containing element; options are default (left), left, right, and center	Collapse table border	Combine adjacent table borders so they appear as one
Specify width	Set table width in pixels or percentages	Background Color	Set a background color for the table
Specify height	Set table height in pixels or percentages; usually not necessary because tables expand their height to accommodate the content you add to them	Use background picture	Set a background image for the table
Float	Float table to right or left relative to surrounding content	Enable layout tools	Draw tables and table cells by clicking and dragging
Cell padding	Set amount of space in pixels between the cell contents and the inside edge of the cell	Set as default for new tables	Save current settings as the default for all new tables
Cell spacing	Set amount of space in pixels between table cells		

FIGURE I-7: Table Properties dialog box with properties changed

Alignment list arrow

In pixels option button

Specify width text box

Use background picture check box

Browse button

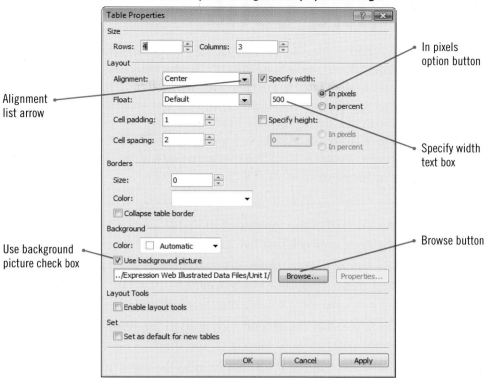

FIGURE I-8: Table with properties changed

Merging Cells

After you have created a table, you may find you need to split or merge cells. **Splitting** cells is the process of dividing a single cell into two or more rows or columns. **Merging** cells is the process of combining two or more cells into a single cell. For example, you might merge cells to create a heading that spans two columns, or when you have two cells whose content you feel would make more sense in a single cell. When you merge two cells that already contain content, you usually find you need to clean up the content a bit by adding spaces or line breaks after the cells are merged. 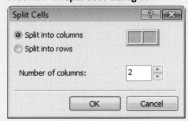 You decide the Day and Date columns would work better as a single column. You merge the Day and Date cells for each listing to create one cell containing the combined content.

STEPS

QUICK TIP

You can also select the two cells by clicking in one, pressing and holding [Ctrl], then clicking in the second cell.

1. **Click in the** first cell in the top row of the table, **press and hold the mouse button, then drag to the right until the first two cells in the top row are selected**

2. **Release the mouse button, right-click** anywhere in the selected cells, **point to** Modify **on the shortcut menu, then click** Merge Cells

   The two cells merge into one and their contents are combined, as shown in Figure I-10.

3. **Click in the** first cell in the second row, **drag to the right to select the first two cells in the row, right-click, point to** Modify **on the shortcut menu, then click** Merge Cells

TROUBLE

When right-clicking, be sure to click within the selected area, not outside it.

4. **Click in the** first cell in the third row, **drag to the right to select the first two cells in the row, right-click, point to** Modify **on the shortcut menu, then click** Merge Cells

5. **Click in the** first cell in the fourth row, **drag to the right to select the first two cells in the row, right-click, point to** Modify **on the shortcut menu, then click** Merge Cells

   See Figure I-11. Because the text in the combined cells now runs together, you need to insert a space in each newly merged cell. You also decide to rename the heading for the first column.

6. **Click in the** first cell in the table, **select the text** DayDate, **press [Delete], then type** When

7. **Click between the** y and S **in** EverySaturday, **then press [Spacebar]**

8. **Click between the** , and J **in** Tuesday,June, **then press [Spacebar]**

9. **Click between the** , and J **in** Friday,June, **press [Spacebar], compare your screen to Figure I-12, then save your changes**

Splitting cells

The process of splitting cells is similar to merging cells. To split a cell, right-click in the cell, point to Modify on the shortcut menu, then click Split Cells. The Split Cells dialog box opens, as shown in Figure I-9. You can indicate whether you want the cells split into columns or rows and the number of columns or rows you would like. If you split a cell that contains content, the content will stay in one cell and the new cell or cells will be empty.

FIGURE I-9: Split Cells dialog box

FIGURE I-10: Merged table cells

Selected cells are merged into one cell

FIGURE I-11: Merged table cells

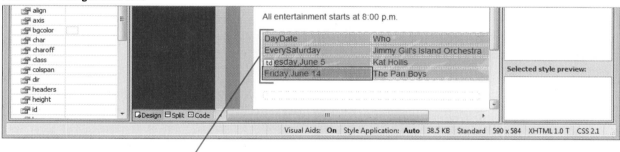

Each pair of cells have been merged into one

FIGURE I-12: Merged cells with text adjusted

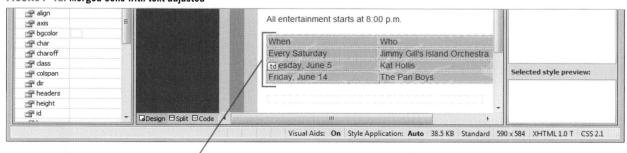

Adjusted text

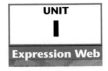

Adding and Resizing Rows and Columns

If you decide to increase the amount of content a table contains, you often need to add new columns or rows. You can add one or more columns or rows at a time. You can also resize the width of any column to better fit the amount of content it contains. You can change the height of a row, also, but it's usually not necessary since row heights expand as you add content. Catalina has sent you a description of the type of music for each event in the music schedule. She has also sent an additional event to add to the listings. You decide to add a new column to accommodate the descriptions. You also need to add a row for the new entry.

STEPS

QUICK TIP

You may have to scroll to the right in the editing window to see the new column.

1. **Right-click in the second cell in the top row of the table, point to Insert, then click Column to the Right on the shortcut menu**

   A new column is inserted on the right side of the table. The column is very narrow but will widen as you add content.

2. **Add the following text to the cells in the new column, pressing [↓] to move to each new cell:**

   What

   Retro island lounge

   Jazz standards and contemporary favorites

   An unforgettable night of steel drums

   The descriptions are added, as shown in Figure I-13.

QUICK TIP

You can also create new rows by right-clicking on a row, pointing to Insert, then choosing one of the row options.

3. **Click after the word drums in the last table cell, then press [Tab]**

   A new row is created.

4. **Add the following text to the cells in the new row, pressing [Tab] to move to each new cell:**

   Every Wednesday

   You!

   Island karaoke. Come on, you know you want to join us!

   See Figure I-14.

5. **Point to the dotted line between the first and second cell in the first row until the pointer changes to ⟺, click and drag to the right until the ScreenTip reads 130px, compare your screen to Figure I-15, then release the mouse button**

6. **Point to the dotted line between the second and third cell in the first row until the pointer changes to ⟺, click and drag to the right until the ScreenTip reads 160px, then release the mouse button**

7. **Save your changes, preview your page in a browser, close the browser window, then return to Expression Web**

FIGURE I-13: Table with additional column and text

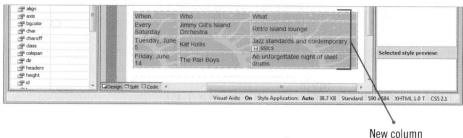

New column

FIGURE I-14: Table with additional row and text

New row

FIGURE I-15: Dragging column to resize

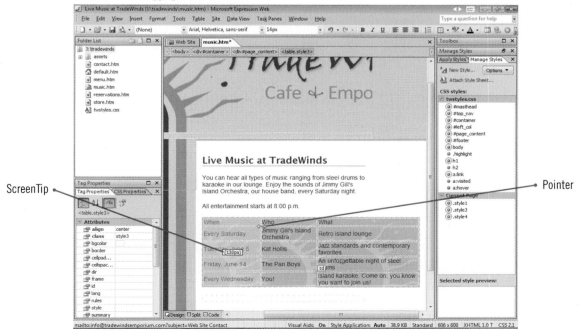

ScreenTip

Pointer

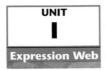

Modifying Cell Properties

In addition to modifying properties for an entire table, you can also modify properties for an individual cell or a group of cells. Using the Cell Properties dialog box, you can set both the horizontal and vertical alignment of cell content, specify the width and height of a cell, and create cells that span columns and rows. (Spanning essentially has the same effect as merging cells.) In addition, you can specify a cell as a header cell and dictate that the content of a cell not wrap inside the cell. You can also set borders and background images on individual or multiple cells. **You decide you want the header row to have centered text and a solid color background.**

STEPS

QUICK TIP

You can also select a row by pointing to its left edge until the mouse pointer changes to ➡, then clicking.

1. **Right-click in the first cell in the top row of the table, point to Select, then click Row**
   The header row is selected, as shown in Figure I-16.

2. **Right-click in the selected row, then click Cell Properties on the shortcut menu**
   The Cell Properties dialog box opens, where you can make changes to the properties of the selected cell or cells. See Figure I-17.

3. **Click the Horizontal alignment list arrow, then click Center**
   This setting centers the text within each selected cell.

4. **Click the Color list arrow in the Background section, click the light tan swatch that matches the page background in the Document Colors section (ScreenTip reads "rgb (229,233,203)"), compare your screen to Figure I-18, then click OK**
   The cells in the top row have centered text and a solid, light tan background. The Document Colors section displays colors already used in the current document. Using one of these colors helps you to accurately match colors with styles you created previously.

5. **Save your changes, preview the page in a browser, close the browser window, then return to Expression Web**

Selecting table elements

Being able to select just the part of a table you want to modify is an important skill in working with tables. You have several options for selecting table elements. You can right-click in a cell or row, point to Select, then choose Table, Column, Row, or Cell. You can also click in a cell, then click the tab on the visual aid to select the cell. To select multiple cells, you can click in a cell, then press and hold [Ctrl] while clicking in other cells. To select multiple adjacent cells, you can

click in a cell, hold down the mouse button, then drag to select adjacent cells. To select a row or column, you can point to the left edge of a row or the top edge of a column until the mouse pointer changes to either ➡ or ⬇, then click to select. Finally, you can use the quick tag selector at the top of the editing window to select a table, tr, or td tag.

FIGURE I-16: Table with top row selected

Selected row

FIGURE I-17: Cell Properties dialog box

Color list
arrow

Horizontal alignment
list arrow

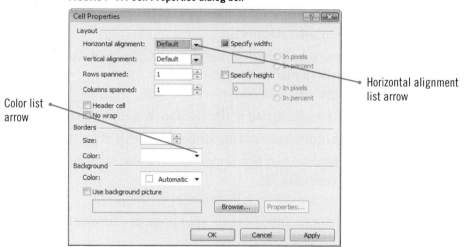

FIGURE I-18: Completed Cell Properties dialog box

Horizontal alignment
set to Center

Background color
set to light tan

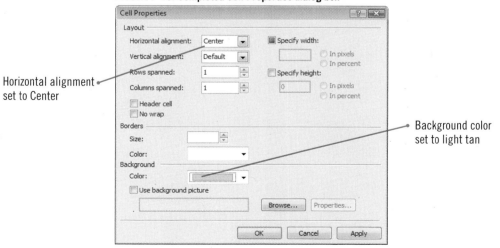

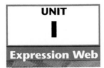
Modifying a Table Style

As you have learned, the Table Properties dialog box provides quick access to modifying many attributes of a table. However, for finer control over a table's appearance, you sometimes need to modify the table's class-based style directly through the Modify Style dialog box. For example, in the Table Properties dialog box, you can set a border width and color, but if you want to specify a border type or create a border that appears on just one side, you need to use the Modify Style dialog box. To modify a table's style, you first need to determine which class style is applied to the table by clicking in the table and looking at the corresponding table tag on the quick tag selector to see which style appears after it (for example, table.style3). To make the live music schedule stand out a bit more, you decide to add a dark red border to the bottom of the table. To do this, you need to modify the table style.

STEPS

1. **Right-click anywhere in the table, click Select, click Table, then look at the visual aid tab to see what style is applied to your table (for example, .style3)**
   See Figure I-19.

2. **In the Manage Styles or Apply Styles task pane, right-click the style that is applied to your table, then click Modify Style on the shortcut menu**
   The Modify Style dialog box opens. The Background and Position categories are bolded, indicating that properties have been set in them. These are the properties you set earlier through the Table Properties dialog box, which Expression Web added to the table style rule.

3. **Click Border in the category list**

4. **Click the Same for all check boxes under border-style, border-width, and border-color to remove the check marks**
   You want to define only a bottom border for the table.

5. **Click the bottom list arrow under border-style, then click solid**

6. **Click in the bottom text box under border-width, then type 2**

7. **Click in the bottom text box under border-color, type #B1012A, compare your screen to Figure I-20, then click OK**
   A dark red border now appears at the bottom of the table.

8. **Save your changes, then preview your page in a browser**
   See Figure I-21.

9. **Close the browser window, then return to Expression Web**

FIGURE I-19: Selected table

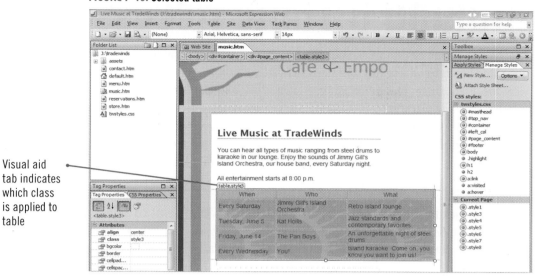

Visual aid tab indicates which class is applied to table

FIGURE I-20: Border style settings for table style

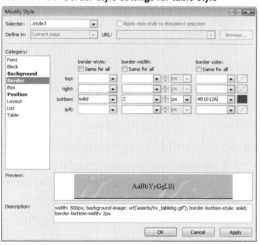

FIGURE I-21: Table with new style applied

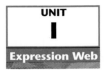

Making a Table Accessible

People with disabilities who visit your site may have a difficult time navigating through the information presented in a table unless you take steps to make your table accessible. Sighted people are easily able to view the arrangement of information in a table and see how it is grouped. But a blind visitor relies on a screen reader that reads the content aloud one cell at a time, which can make it difficult to understand how the information is organized in the table. Improvements you can make include marking the header row so it's not interpreted as a regular row of data, adding a table caption, and adding summary information. You want your Web site to be accessible to all visitors, so you need to make some final modifications to the table.

STEPS

1. **Right-click in the first cell in the top row of the table, point to Select, then click Row**

   One way to make a table more accessible is to format the header row so that a screen reader identifies these cells as column headings rather than as the first row of data.

2. **Right-click in the selected row, then click Cell Properties on the shortcut menu**

   The Cell Properties dialog box opens, where you can mark the cells in the top row with a <th> tag.

> **QUICK TIP**
>
> Most browsers also display the contents of <th> tags as bold, centered text to visually distinguish them for sighted visitors.

3. **Click the Header cell check box in the Layout section, compare your screen to Figure I-22, then click OK**

   The text in these cells is now displayed as bold. The <tr> tags formerly marking up these cells have changed to <th> tags, so a screen reader will interpret them correctly.

4. **Click Table on the menu, point to Insert, then click Caption**

   A visual aid appears on the page above the table, with the tab indicating that it is a caption element. Adding a caption above a table allows you to succinctly state the purpose of the table before the reader scans the table.

5. **Type Live Music Schedule in the caption area**

   The text appears above the table, as shown in Figure I-23. The <caption> tag will be recognized as a caption by screen readers, making it easer for a site visitor to determine whether they are interested in the table data. It also appears on the page for visitors using a standard browser.

6. **Right-click anywhere in the table, point to Select, then click Table**

   A summary appears in the code and provides screen readers with a more detailed description of each type of content in the table. It is read by screen readers but is not visible in a browser.

7. **Click the Tag Properties tab in the CSS Properties task pane, then click in the text box to the right of summary, as shown in Figure I-24**

8. **Type This table lists the date, the artist, and the type of music scheduled in the TradeWinds lounge.**

   This content has been added to the <table> tag as the summary attribute and will be read aloud as a summary by screen readers.

9. **Save your changes, close the tradewinds site, then exit Expression Web**

Using CSS instead of tables for page layout

Before the existence of style sheets, HTML tables were the only means available to position elements on a page. Although they were intended to be used only for presenting data in a tabular format, designers used them to lay out entire Web pages. Now that designers can use CSS for layout, the use of tables is very much discouraged.

Using CSS instead of tables for layout makes your Web pages:
- quicker to load
- easier to update
- more accessible to visitors with disabilities
- more accessible to visitors using handheld devices
- more visible to search engines
- more professional looking to other designers

FIGURE I-22: Cell Properties dialog box

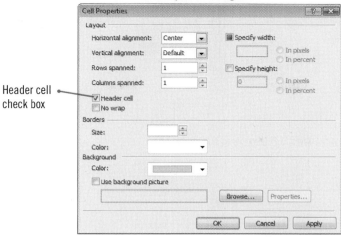

Header cell
check box

FIGURE I-23: Table with caption added

Caption
visual aid

Caption text

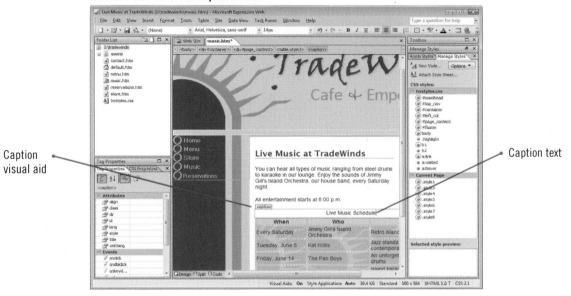

FIGURE I-24: Completed summary tag

Tag Properties
task pane

Summary

Expression Web

Practice

If you have a SAM user profile, you may have access to hands-on instruction, practice, and assessment of the skills covered in this unit. Log in to your SAM account (http://sam2007.course.com/) to launch any assigned training activities or exams that relate to the skills covered in this unit.

▼ CONCEPTS REVIEW

Use Figure I-25 as a guide to answer the questions below.

FIGURE I-25

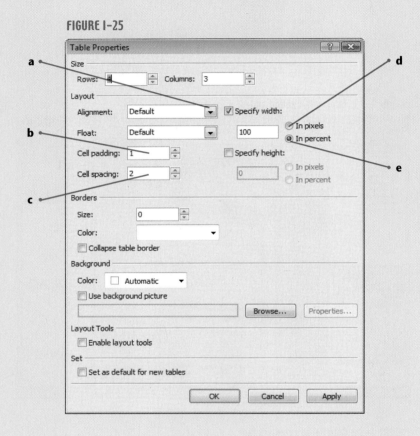

1. Which element do you click to center a table within its containing element?
2. Which element do you click to change the amount of space between cells?
3. Which element do you click to set an absolute table width?
4. Which element do you click to set a relative table width?
5. Which element do you click to change the amount of space between a cell's content and the edge of the cell?

Match each HTML tag with the table element it marks up.

6. <table>   a. table header cell
7. <tr>   b. table
8. <td>   c. table cell
9. <th>   d. table row

Select the best answer from the list of choices.

10. **Which of the following can you *not* do in the Table Properties dialog box?**
    a. Set the table background color
    b. Add a border around the table
    c. Add a border to the right side of the table only
    d. Set the table width

11. **Which feature do you use to combine two cells?**
    a. Merge
    b. Split
    c. Table AutoFormat
    d. Join

12. **Which of the following helps make a table more accessible?**
    a. Designating a header row
    b. Adding a caption
    c. Adding a summary
    d. All of the above

13. **What is the intended function of an HTML table?**
    a. To display tabular data
    b. To control the position of layout elements
    c. To calculate sums
    d. To create graphs

14. **Which of the following is possible to do after you have created a table?**
    a. Add a row
    b. Add a column
    c. Change the width
    d. All of the above

15. **Which of the following is *not* an advantage of using CSS instead of tables for layout?**
    a. More accessible pages
    b. Faster loading pages
    c. Pages that are easier to update
    d. Pages with a better color scheme

16. **What feature allows you to quickly add a predesigned combination of formatting attributes to a table?**
    a. AutoFormat
    b. Table Properties
    c. Cell Properties
    d. QuickStyle

▼ SKILLS REVIEW

1. **Insert a table and add content.**
    a. Launch Expression Web, open the careers site, then open the services page.
    b. Click after the last sentence on the page (which ends "commonly used in businesses."), then open the Insert Table dialog box.
    c. Insert a table with 4 rows and 2 columns, leaving the other settings at their defaults, then click OK to close the Insert Table dialog box.

   d. Enter the following text in the table, pressing [Tab] to move to the next cell, but do not press [Tab] after the last entry: (*Hint*: The last row has no content for the second cell.)

Software	Skill Level
Microsoft PowerPoint	Beginner
Microsoft Word	Beginner, Intermediate, Advanced
More great titles coming soon!	

   e. Save your changes.

2. **Apply an AutoFormat to a table.**
   a. Right-click in the table and open the Table AutoFormat dialog box.
   b. Select the Simple 3 format, deselect the Font option in the Formats to apply section, then click OK to close the dialog box.
   c. View the changes to the table in the Expression Web window.
   d. Right-click in the table, open the Table AutoFormat dialog box, select None in the Formats list, then click OK to close the dialog box.
   e. Save your changes.

3. **Set table properties.**
   a. Open the Table Properties dialog box.
   b. Set the cell padding to 6 pixels and the table width to 600 pixels, then click OK to close the dialog box.
   c. Save your changes, preview the page in a browser, close the browser window, then return to Expression Web.

4. **Merge cells.**
   a. Select the bottom row of cells.
   b. Right-click in the selected area, point to Modify, then click Merge Cells.
   c. Save your changes.

5. **Add and resize rows and columns.**
   a. Right-click in the first cell in the table, point to Insert, then click Row Below.
   b. Add the following text to the new row:

Microsoft Excel	Beginner

   c. Point to the dotted line between the first and second cell in the top row, then press and hold the mouse button and drag to the left until the ScreenTip reads "190 px".
   d. Save your changes, preview the page in a browser, close the browser window, then return to Expression Web.

6. **Modify cell properties.**
   a. Right-click in the first cell in the table, point to Select, then click Row.
   b. Right-click in the selected area, then click Cell Properties.
   c. In the Cell Properties dialog box, set the horizontal alignment to Center, then set a border with a size of 1. Choose the dark blue color from the Document Colors section. (*Hint*: The ScreenTip reads "rgb (0, 41, 128)".)
   d. Set the background color to the light blue swatch chosen from the Document Colors section. (*Hint*: The ScreenTip reads "rgb(204, 221, 255)".) Then click OK to close the dialog box.
   e. Save your changes, preview the page in a browser, close the browser window, then return to Expression Web.

7. **Modify a table style.**
   a. Open the Modify Styles dialog box for the table style and set the font color to black.
   b. Switch to the Block category, set the text-align to center, then click OK to close the dialog box.
   c. Save your changes, preview the page in a browser, close the browser window, then return to Expression Web.

8. Make a table accessible.

a. Select the top row in the table, then open the Cell Properties dialog box.

b. Click the Header cell check box to add a check mark, then click OK.

c. Click Table on the menu bar, point to Insert, then click Caption.

d. Type **Technology Training Videos** in the caption area.

e. Select the entire table.

f. Click the Tag Properties tab in the CSS Properties task pane, click in the text box next to summary, then type **This table lists software video training titles and available skill levels.**.

g. Save your changes, preview the page in a browser, compare your screen to Figure I-26, close the browser window, close the careers site, then exit Expression Web.

FIGURE I-26

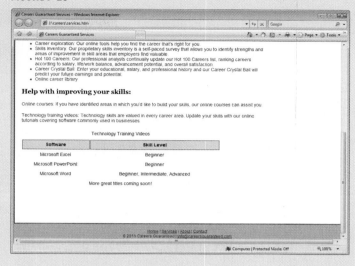

▼ INDEPENDENT CHALLENGE 1

In this project you continue your work on the ConnectUp Web site. Tiffany wants to add information to the contact page that tells visitors which department to contact with different types of questions or inquiries. She wants the table to be accessible to all Web site visitors, so you want to make some additional modifications that facilitate use by screen readers.

a. Launch Expression Web, then open the connectup Web site.

b. Open the contact page.

c. At the bottom of the page, after the e-mail link, insert a table with 4 rows and 2 columns.

d. Add the following content to the table:

For questions about:	Contact:
Membership	Customer service
Technical issues	Technical support
Sponsorship opportunities	Sales

e. Using the Table Properties dialog box, set the cell padding to 4, the table width to 600 pixels, and the background color to the dark gray swatch in the Document Colors section. (*Hint*: The ScreenTip reads "rgb (102, 102, 102)".)

f. Modify the table style to make the font color white and the font weight bold.

g. Add a column to the right of the Contact column and enter the following text:

Email:
service@connectup.com
tech@connectup.com
sales@connectup.com

h. Select the top row, then use the Cell Properties dialog box to set the cells as Header cells and to set the background color to the green in the Document Colors section. (*Hint*: The ScreenTip reads "rgb(111,217, 23)".)

i. Insert a caption and add the following text: **Who to call at ConnectUp.** Note that because the text is white on a white background, it will not be readable on the page, but screen readers will still be able to use it.

Expression Web

j. Select the table and use the Tag Properties task pane to add this summary: **This table lists types of questions, the appropriate department to contact, and that department's e-mail address**.

k. Save your changes, preview the page in a browser, then compare your screen to Figure I-27.

l. Close the browser window, close the connectup site, then exit Expression Web.

FIGURE I-27

▼ INDEPENDENT CHALLENGE 2

In this project you continue your work on the Memories Restored Web site. You decide to add a table to the Our Work page to list services provided by Memories Restored.

a. Launch Expression Web, open the memories Web site, then open the Our Work page.

b. Above the example photos on the Our Work page, add a table that lists services offered by Memories Restored and the turn-around time for each service:

Service:	Turn-Around Time:
Photo restoration	Depends on extent of damage
Photo portrait touch-up	7 business days
Photo DVD	14 business days

c. Adjust the table properties, cell properties, and table style as necessary to fit the page design.

d. Improve the accessibility of the table by setting the first row as a header row and adding a caption and summary you think will clearly identify its purpose.

Advanced Challenge Exercise

- Add a row at the bottom that spans two columns.
- Add the text **Please contact us if you have questions**.
- Format the row with a background color of your choosing.

e. Save your changes, preview your page in a browser, close the browser window, return to Expression Web, close the memories site, then exit Expression Web.

▼ INDEPENDENT CHALLENGE 3

This Independent Challenge requires an Internet connection.

The director of Technology for All would like to know more about how the use of tables for layout can affect the accessibility of a Web site. You need to do some research to provide some insight on this issue.

   a. Visit your favorite search engine and enter "layout tables accessibility" as a search term.

   b. Read at least two articles that you find.

   c. Copy and paste information from each article into a word processor document.

Advanced Challenge Exercise

   ■ Find at least one article or comment that supports the use of tables for page layout.

   ■ Based on your readings, decide whether you agree or disagree with the argument supporting the use of tables for page layout.

   ■ Write a paragraph explaining why you agree or disagree with the argument.

   d. Write a paragraph summarizing the information you found.

   e. Add your name to the document, save it, and print it.

▼ REAL LIFE INDEPENDENT CHALLENGE

This assignment builds on the personal Web site you have worked on in previous units. In this project, you add a table to your site.

   a. Review your site's content and structure and choose an area of the site where a table would make sense. You might use a table to list event information, to describe a collection of items, to identify people or places, or for some other purpose appropriate to your site.

   b. Add the table to the page, then add content to the table.

   c. Change the properties and styles as you like, including table width, alignment, borders, and background colors.

   d. Designate the first row as header cells, and add a caption and summary to the table.

   e. Save your changes to all open files, then preview your page in a browser. When you are finished, close the browser, return to Expression Web, close the site, then exit Expression Web.

▼ VISUAL WORKSHOP

Launch Expression Web, open the **ecotours** Web site, then open the home page. Using Figure I-28 as a guide, add a table to the page, add content, and format it so that your page matches the table shown in the figure. (*Hint*: You can sample colors from elements on the page for the header row background.) When you are finished, save your changes, close the Web site, then exit Expression Web.

FIGURE I-28

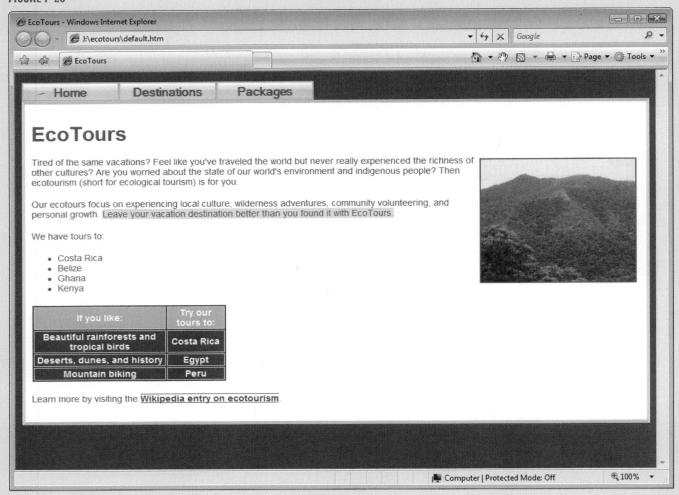

Creating Forms

In a Web site, a **form** is an HTML element that can be placed anywhere on a Web page to collect information from site visitors. Visitors fill out the form and submit it. A script, often called a form handler, sends the information to the Web server to be added to a database, e-mailed to a designated recipient, or processed in some other way. You've probably used an online form to order merchandise, search site content, or provide feedback on a Web site. Catalina would like you to add a form to the reservations page that enables visitors to send reservation requests directly from the Web site. You will create the form so that it's ready to connect to a form handler.

OBJECTIVES

Understand forms and form controls

Add a form to a Web page

Group form controls

Add a text box

Add radio buttons

Add checkboxes

Add a drop-down box

Add a text area

Add buttons

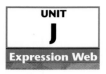

Understanding Forms and Form Controls

Forms can be placed anywhere on a Web page, and can vary considerably in appearance. A form can be as simple as a single search box on a Web page or as complex as a multi-screen, Web-based questionnaire. What all forms have in common is that they provide a way for visitors to enter information and a button for visitors to click to send that information to the server. ▓▓▓▓ You decide to learn more about how forms are created.

DETAILS

Before you create a form, you should understand:

- **Required components of a form**

  A valid HTML form requires at minimum a form element, a form control, and a submit button. A **form element** is like other HTML elements in that it is a container created by wrapping content in an HTML tag. In this case, the <form> tag is used as the container. A form tag can contain almost any type of content except another form tag. A **form control**, also called a **form field**, allows visitors to interact with the form by providing a place to either type information or choose from a set of options. A **submit button** is a special kind of form control that sends the information the visitor entered to the Web server. The form controls and submit button are all contained within the form tag. See Figure J-1 for an example of the code for a simple form.

- **Common form controls**

  You use different types of form controls to gather specific types of information. For example, you might use a drop-down box to provide a list of states for a visitor to choose from. Some common form controls include:

  - **Text input** or **text box**: Displays a single-line text box where visitors can type information, such as their name or e-mail address.
  - **Text area**: Displays a multiple-line text box where visitors can type information.
  - **Radio button**: Displays options as a series of circles that visitors can select. Radio buttons are mutually exclusive, meaning that only one button within a set of options can be selected.
  - **Checkbox**: Displays options as a series of boxes that visitors can select. Checkboxes are not mutually exclusive, so visitors can select as many options in a set as they would like.
  - **Drop-down box**: Displays options within a drop-down list where visitors can click a list arrow to view the choices.
  - **Button**: A submit button is required but you can also provide a button to **reset** the form, which clears any information the visitor entered, allowing them to start over.

  See Figure J-2 for an example of these form controls.

- **Form-handling scripts**

  In order for a form to function and send information to the server, it must be linked to a form-handling script or **form handler**, a file that processes the information entered in the form so that the data can be stored or used to initiate other actions, such as sending an e-mail or searching a database. The form tag includes a required attribute called an **action** that allows you to specify the file path of the form-handling script. Form handlers can be written in any programming language, such as ASP.NET, PHP, or Perl. Expression Web provides tools to help you create the form within the Web page, but it does not create the form handler. Fortunately, you do not need to learn these languages to create your own form handler. Instead, you can download and use one of the many free form-handling scripts available on the Internet. Most Web hosting companies also provide scripts as part of their hosting packages.

FIGURE J-1: Code for a simple form

Opening form tag

Text input form control tag

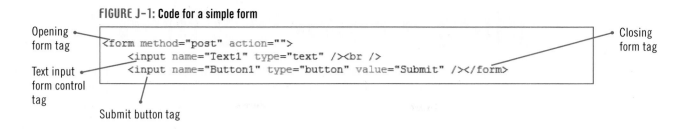

```
<form method="post" action="">
    <input name="Text1" type="text" /><br />
    <input name="Button1" type="button" value="Submit" /></form>
```

Closing form tag

Submit button tag

FIGURE J-2: Sample form

Name

Text box

Reason for contacting us:
- ⦿ Information about a product
- ○ Comment about service received
- ○ Question about an order

Radio buttons

What do you like best about our site?
- ☐ The information
- ☑ The design
- ☑ The interactive tools

Checkboxes

How often do you visit our site?

Please choose one ▼

Drop-down box

Other comments:

Text area

Reset   Submit

Reset and submit buttons

Adding a Form to a Web Page

The first step in building your form is to add a form element to an existing Web page. In Expression Web, all the tools for building forms are accessible in the Toolbox task pane, which by default appears above the Manage Styles and Apply Styles task panes. To add form controls to a page, you can either drag or double-click the items listed on the Toolbox task pane. You are ready to add a form element to the TradeWinds reservations page.

STEPS

1. **Launch Expression Web, open the tradewinds site, then open the reservations page**

2. **Click the Maximize button on the Toolbox task pane, then if necessary click the plus sign next to Tags and the plus sign next to Form Controls**

   The list of Tags and Form controls is displayed on the Toolbox task pane, as shown in Figure J-3.

3. **Click after the text during your meal. at the bottom of the page, then press [Enter]**

   Expression Web creates a new paragraph and a visual aid appears, marking the boundaries of the paragraph.

4. **Click the p tab on the visual aid**

   See Figure J-4. Clicking the tab selects the entire paragraph element. You cannot place a form within a paragraph in Expression Web, but this method allows you to replace the paragraph with a form.

5. **Double-click Form in the Form Controls list on the Toolbox task pane**

   See Figure J-5. A form element replaces the paragraph element, and the visual aid tab changes to indicate this is now a form rather than a paragraph. You can also drag a form control onto the page to add it, but for more accurate placement it's best to double-click to add a control.

6. **Save your changes**

FIGURE J-3: Reservations page with Toolbox task pane maximized

Tags

Form controls

FIGURE J-4: Paragraph element selected

FIGURE J-5: Form element added to reservations page

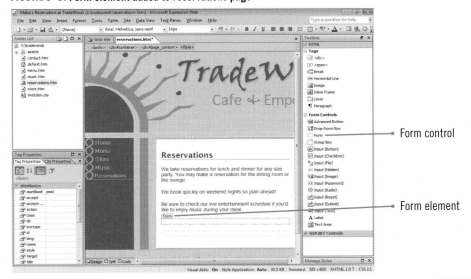

Form control

Form element

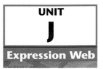

Grouping Form Controls

Using **group boxes** is a convenient way to organize your forms into sections of related fields to make them easier for visitors to fill out. Group boxes are created by wrapping one or more form controls in a <fieldset> tag and are displayed with a box around the entire group. When you add a group box to a form, Expression Web also adds a label with placeholder text, which allows you to customize the text to display a label for that group of form controls. You can cluster controls in an existing form by selecting them and adding a group box, but it's easier to create the group boxes first and then add the controls. 🔲🔲🔲 Catalina wants Web site visitors to be able to enter customer information, reservation information, and additional reservation preferences in the form. This is a lot of information, so you decide to create three separate group boxes to organize the form and make it more manageable for visitors to complete.

STEPS

> **QUICK TIP**
> A group box or field-set label is created in HTML using the <legend> tag.

1. **Click inside the form, then double-click Group Box in the Form Controls list on the Toolbox task pane**

   A group box consisting of a box with a placeholder label is inserted in the form element, and is selected, as shown in Figure J-6. Notice that the visual aid displays a fieldset tab.

2. **Right-click the group box you just inserted, click Group Box Properties, click in the Label text box, type Your Information, then click OK**

   The placeholder text is replaced with the new label you typed. You can also use this dialog box to set the alignment of the label to left, right, or centered.

> **QUICK TIP**
> The new group box appears beneath the first box instead of beside it because group boxes are always displayed on their own lines instead of side by side.

3. **Press [→], then double-click Group Box on the Toolbox task pane**

   A second group box is inserted below the first, as shown in Figure J-7.

4. **Right-click the group box you just inserted, click Group Box Properties, type Reservation Information in the Label text box, then click OK**

5. **Press [→], double-click Group Box on the Toolbox task pane, right-click on the group box you just inserted, click Group Box Properties, type Optional Information in the Label text box, then click OK**

   See Figure J-8.

6. **Save your changes, preview the page in a browser, close the browser window, then return to Expression Web**

Understanding tab order

When visitors fill out a form, they can use the [Tab] key on the keyboard rather than a mouse to move from field to field. For some visitors, this is simply a matter of preference, but for visitors with certain disabilities, using the keyboard is the only means by which they can navigate the form. When you modify a form field's properties, you have the option of setting the tab order. By assigning the first field a tab order of 1, the second a tab order of 2, and so on, you ensure that keyboard users can complete the form in a logical manner. It's important to set the tab order on all fields if you set it on one; otherwise, keyboard users will not proceed through the form as you intended. If you don't assign a tab order to any of the fields, visitors who use the [Tab] key will move through the field in the order in which the fields appear in the HTML code. Depending on how your form is laid out, this can work just fine, as is the case with the form you are building in this lesson. If you're not sure whether you need to assign a tab order, preview the page in a browser, then press [Tab] to move to each field on the form. If you move through the fields in a different order than makes sense, it's a good idea to set the tab order for each field.

FIGURE J-6: First group box added to the form

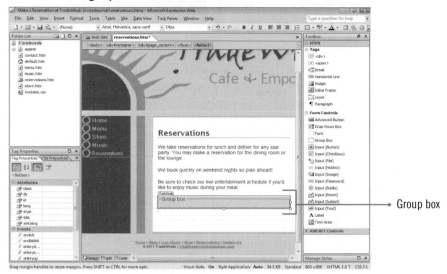

Group box

FIGURE J-7: Second group box added to the form

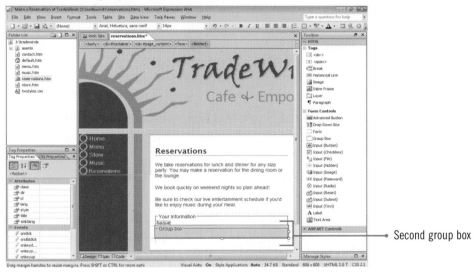

Second group box

FIGURE J-8: Three group boxes with edited labels added to the form

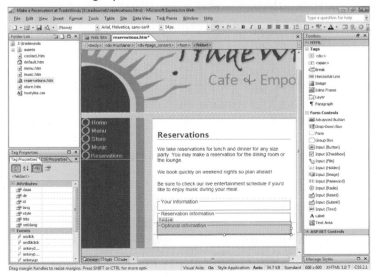

Adding a Text Box

Text boxes are useful when you would like visitors to type in a small amount of freeform text, such as their name or e-mail address. To create a text box in a form, you add an Input (Text) form control to the form element. The HTML code for a text box consists of an <input> tag with a type attribute of text (<input type="text">). Before you add any type of form control that asks for visitor input, you should first add a text label for that control. **[icon]** You are ready to add form controls for visitors to enter their name, e-mail address, and requested reservation date. Before creating each control, you want to add a label that identifies its purpose for Web site visitors.

STEPS

1. **Click inside the Your Information group box, double-click Paragraph in the Tags list on the Toolbox task pane, type Name, then press [Shift][Enter]**
   A label for the name field is added to the form and the insertion point moves to a new line, as shown in Figure J-9.

2. **Double-click Input (Text) in the Form Controls list on the Toolbox task pane**
   A text box control is added to the form.

3. **Right-click the text box you just inserted, then click Form Field Properties**
   You can use this dialog box to designate attributes for the text box, including the name (which is used by form-handling scripts), the initial value (which provides default text that is displayed when the form is loaded), the width in characters (which dictates the width of the displayed text box), and the tab order. You can also designate this as a password field, which means that as a visitor enters information it will be displayed on the screen as asterisks for security reasons.

4. **Type name in the Name text box, compare your screen to Figure J-10, then click OK**
   When choosing a name attribute for a form control, always use only letters and numbers and no spaces. Value attributes can contain spaces.

5. **Press [→], press [Enter], then type Email Address**
   This provides a label for the next form control.

6. **Press [Shift][Enter], double-click Input (Text) in the Form Controls list on the Toolbox task pane, right-click the text box you just inserted, click Form Field Properties, type email in the Name text box, then click OK**

7. **Click inside the Reservation Information group box, double-click Paragraph in the Tags list on the Toolbox task pane, then type Reservation Date**

8. **Press [Shift][Enter], double-click Input (Text) on the Toolbox task pane, right-click the text box you just inserted, click Form Field Properties, type date in the Name text box, click OK, then click outside the visual aid to deselect it**
   See Figure J-11.

9. **Save your changes, preview the page in a browser, type your name in the Name text box, close the browser window, then return to Expression Web**
   Because the form is not connected to a form handler, information you enter will not be saved.

Understanding labels

HTML features a label tag that is available for pairing text labels with form fields when creating forms. The label tag wraps around both the text and the HTML code for the form control, grouping them together in the code. This helps the devices used by visitors with disabilities to identify which text label goes with which form field. Expression Web includes the ability to add a label tag in Design view, but the tag does not wrap around the control unless you manually edit the HTML in Code view.

FIGURE J-9: Label for first text box added to the form

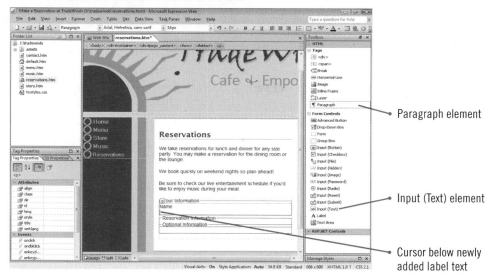

Paragraph element

Input (Text) element

Cursor below newly added label text

FIGURE J-10: Text Box Properties dialog box

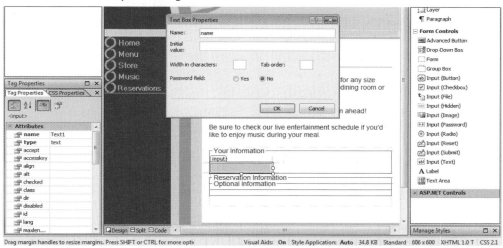

FIGURE J-11: Three text boxes added to form

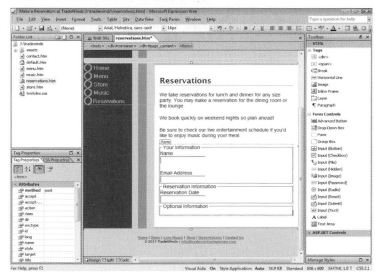

Expression Web

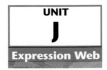

Adding Radio Buttons

Radio buttons, also known as option buttons, are useful when you need to present a list of options and want the visitor to be able to choose only one. Radio buttons are always created in a group with more than one option present. A radio button is created in Expression Web by adding an Input (Radio) form control to the form element. The HTML code for a radio button consists of an <input> tag with a type attribute of radio (<input type="radio">). Catalina wants visitors to indicate whether they want to reserve a table in the dining room or lounge. You decide that radio buttons are the best form control to use because you want a visitor to be able to select just one, not both, of these options.

STEPS

1. **Click to the right of the text box under Reservation Date, press [Enter], double-click Paragraph in the Form Controls list on the Toolbox task pane, type Location, then press [Shift][Enter]**

   The label text is entered and the cursor is on a new line ready for you to add the first radio button.

2. **Double-click Input (Radio) in the Form Controls list on the Toolbox task pane**

   A radio button is inserted into the form under the Location label. A visual aid indicates that this is an input element.

3. **Right-click the radio button you just inserted, then click Form Field Properties**

   The Option Button Properties dialog box opens. The Group name text box allows you to assign your own name to this group of radio buttons. It's a good idea to change the name because this can make it easier to connect the form to a form handler. The value is required and is submitted to the server as a label for the information entered by the visitor.

4. **Type location in the Group name text box, click in the Value text box, type diningroom, click the Not selected radio button, compare your screen to Figure J-12, then click OK**

5. **Click to the right of the radio button you just inserted, type Cafe Dining Room, then press [Shift][Enter]**

   See Figure J-13. When you add a radio button, you not only need to add text above the group of radio buttons, you also need to add text next to each option so the visitor knows what the options are.

6. **Double-click Input (Radio) on the Toolbox task pane, right-click the radio button you just inserted, then click Form Field Properties**

7. **Click in the Value text box, type lounge, click the Not selected radio button, then click OK**

8. **Click to the right of the radio button you just inserted, double-click Paragraph on the Toolbox task pane, then type Lounge**

   The radio buttons are complete, as shown in Figure J-14.

9. **Save your changes, preview the page in a browser, click one of the radio buttons, close the browser window, then return to Expression Web**

FIGURE J-12: Option Button Properties dialog box

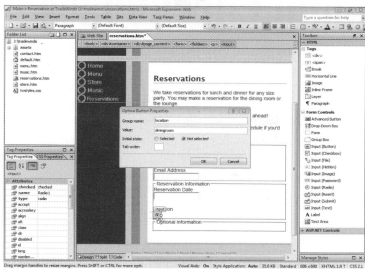

FIGURE J-13: First radio button added to form

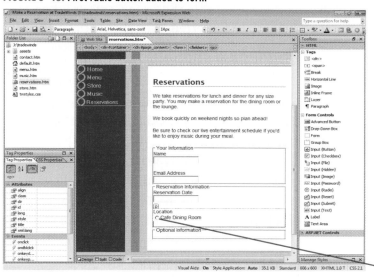

Radio button

FIGURE J-14: Two radio buttons added to form

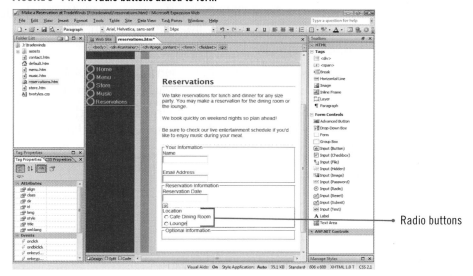

Radio buttons

Adding Checkboxes

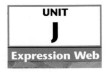

Using checkboxes enables you to present a list of options to visitors and allows them to choose more than one from the list. When a visitor selects a checkbox, a check mark appears in it. Checkboxes are often, but not always, created in a group. Sometimes a single checkbox is used to indicate, for example, that a visitor would like to be added to a mailing list. A checkbox is created in Expression Web by adding an Input (Checkbox) form control to the form element. The HTML code for a checkbox consists of an <input> tag with a type attribute of checkbox (<input type="checkbox">). Catalina wants to find out how visitors heard about TradeWinds. Since a person may have heard about it from more than one source, you decide that checkboxes would be the best form control to use in this situation. That way, visitors can select as many choices as necessary.

STEPS

1. **Click in the Optional Information group box, double-click Paragraph in the Form Controls list on the Toolbox task pane, type How did you hear about us?, then press [Shift][Enter]**
The label text is entered and the cursor is on a new line ready for you to add a checkbox.

2. **Double-click Input (Checkbox) in the Form Controls list on the Toolbox task pane, right-click the checkbox you just inserted, then click Form Field Properties**
The Check Box Properties dialog box opens. You can assign your own name to this checkbox using the Name text box to make it easier for a form handler to identify the control. The Value field is required; the information you enter is submitted to the server as a label for the information entered by the visitor.

QUICK TIP
If you want a checkbox to be selected by default when a visitor fills out the form, click to select the Checked option button.

3. **Type islander in the Name text box, click in the Value text box, type islander, make sure the Not checked option button is selected, compare your screen to Figure J-15, then click OK**

4. **Click to the right of the checkbox, type Islander Newspaper, then press [Shift][Enter]**
See Figure J-16. A checkbox appears on the form with a label to the right.

5. **Double-click Input (Checkbox) on the Toolbox task pane, right-click the checkbox you just inserted, click Form Field Properties, type website in the Name text box, click in the Value text box, type website, make sure the Not checked radio button is selected, then click OK**

6. **Click to the right of the checkbox, type Web Site, then press [Shift][Enter]**

7. **Double-click Input (Checkbox) on the Toolbox task pane, right-click the checkbox you just inserted, click Form Field Properties, type wordofmouth in the Name text box, click in the Value text box, type wordofmouth, make sure the Not checked radio button is selected, then click OK**

8. **Click to the right of the checkbox, then type Word of Mouth**
See Figure J-17. Three checkboxes are now included in the form.

9. **Save your changes, preview the page in a browser, click to add a check mark to at least two of the checkboxes, close the browser window, then return to Expression Web**

FIGURE J-15: Completed Check Box Properties dialog box

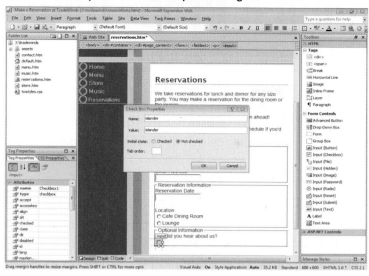

FIGURE J-16: First checkbox added to form

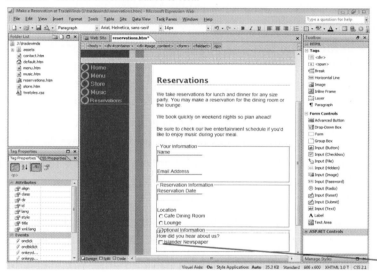

Checkbox

FIGURE J-17: Completed list of checkboxes added to form

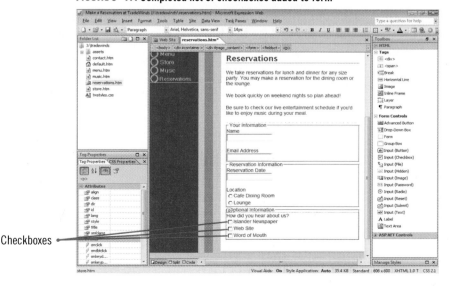

Checkboxes

Expression Web

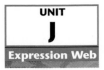

Adding a Drop-Down Box

Drop-down boxes are similar to radio buttons or checkboxes, but they allow you to present a long list of options in much less space on the page because the user clicks to open and close the list. You can create a drop-down box that allows visitors to select only one option, or one that allows visitors to select multiple options. To create a drop-down box in Expression Web, you add a Drop-Down Box form control to the form element. The HTML code for a drop-down box consists of a <select> tag that contains <option> tags within it. The text within the <option> tag determines the items that show in the drop-down box. ██████ Catalina wants to encourage visitors to sign up for specialized e-mail lists. Since the form is getting a bit long, you decide to use a drop-down box for the mailing list choices.

STEPS

QUICK TIP

If you want people to be able to select more than one option, click to select the Yes option button in the Allow multiple selections section.

QUICK TIP

If you want to add your own value, click the Specify Value checkbox and type your own text.

1. **Click after the text** Word of Mouth, **press [Enter], type** If you would like to receive TradeWinds email updates, please choose an area of interest:, **then press [Shift][Enter]**

2. **Double-click Drop-Down Box in the Form Controls list on the Toolbox task pane, right-click the drop-down box you just inserted, then click Form Field Properties**
   The Drop-Down Box Properties dialog box opens, as shown in Figure J-18. In this dialog box, you can add, remove, or modify the options listed in the drop-down box. You can also rearrange them by moving them up or down in the list.

3. **Click in the Name text box, select the text Select1, press [Delete], type interests, then click Add**
   The Add Choice dialog box opens, as shown in Figure J-19. Text you enter in the Choice text box is listed in the drop-down box. Expression Web will automatically fill in a value that is the same as the Choice text.

4. **Type Emporium Products in the Choice text box, then click OK**
   Emporium Products is added to the Choice list in the Drop-Down Box Properties dialog box.

5. **Click the Add button, type Music Events in the Choice text box, then click OK**
   Music Events is now the second option in the Choice list. However, Catalina would like Music Events listed first in the box.

6. **Click Music Events in the Choice list, then click Move Up**
   Music Events now appears first in the Choice list, as shown in Figure J-20.

7. **Click the first line in the Choice list, click Modify, type Select an area of interest: in the Choice list, then click OK**
   The first choice in the list is now text that instructs a visitor to choose another option.

8. **Click OK, then save your changes, preview the page in a browser, click the drop-down list arrow to see the choices, close the browser window, then return to Expression Web**

FIGURE J-18: Drop-Down Box Properties dialog box

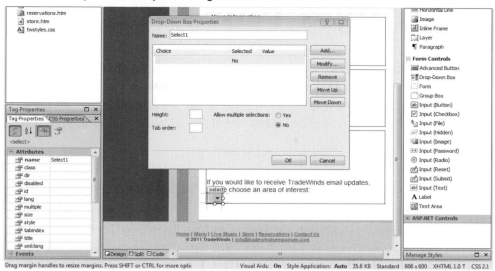

FIGURE J-19: Add Choice dialog box

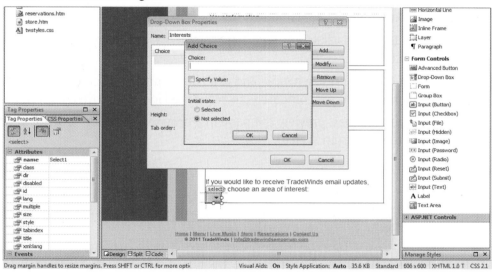

FIGURE J-20: Music Events moved up in the Choice list

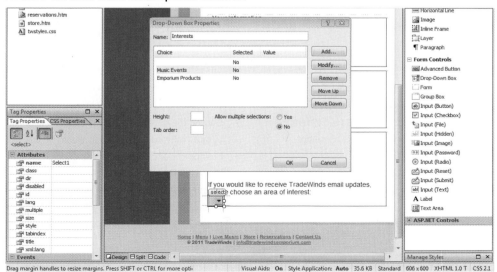

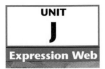

Adding a Text Area

Text areas are similar to text boxes except they display a multiple-line input box, providing a larger area in which visitors can enter text. You can control the height and width of a text area, but visitors can type as much as they'd like into the box. To create a text area in a form, you add a Text Area form control to the form element. The HTML code for a text area consists of a <textarea> tag. Catalina wants visitors to be able to add any type of comments they'd like, so you decide to add a text area to the bottom of the form.

STEPS

1. **Click to the right of the drop-down box you just inserted, press [Enter], type Other Comments, then press [Shift][Enter]**

2. **Double-click Text Area in the Form Controls list on the Toolbox task pane**
   A text area is inserted into the form, as shown in Figure J-21. The visual aid tab indicates that this is a text area.

3. **Right-click the text area you just inserted, then click Form Field Properties**
   The TextArea Box Properties dialog box opens. This dialog box allows you to specify a name, an initial value which is the text that will initially appear in the text area on the Web page, and the width and height.

4. **Type comments in the Name text box**

5. **Click in the initial value box, type Type comments here, compare your screen to Figure J-22, then click OK**

6. **Click the bottom resize handle and drag down until the ScreenTip indicates the height is approximately 90 px, compare your screen to Figure J-23, then release the mouse button**

7. **Save your changes, preview the page in a browser, close the browser window, then return to Expression Web**

> **TROUBLE**
> If you don't see the ScreenTip right away, look far above the actual text area visual aid; sometimes the ScreenTip does not appear near the element itself. The height is also displayed in the status bar at the bottom left of the window.

Creating usable forms

When designing your forms, the layout can make a big difference in how easy the form is for visitors to fill out. Here are some tips for making sure your forms are user friendly:

- Require as few fields as possible; this encourages visitors to complete the form.
- Organize fields in a sequence that is logical for visitors; for example, always place name fields above address fields.
- Group related fields together.

- Choose the right control for the job; for example, don't use a set of radio buttons if checkboxes would be a better choice.
- Use concise and user-friendly language.
- When inserting text elements, provide plenty of space for people to enter information.
- Where possible, place labels above rather than beside fields; research has shown this helps people fill out forms more accurately and quickly.
- If you must place labels beside fields, right-align the labels.

FIGURE J-21: Text area inserted into form

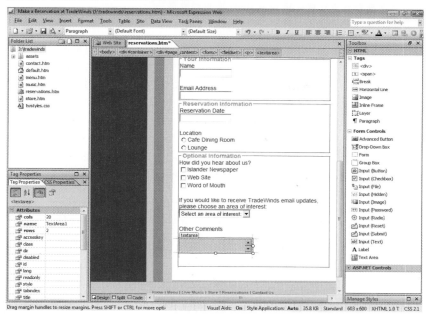

FIGURE J-22: Completed TextArea Box Properties dialog box

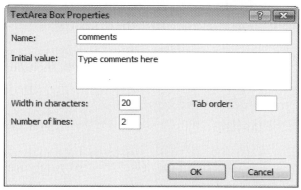

FIGURE J-23: Resizing the text area by dragging the resize handles

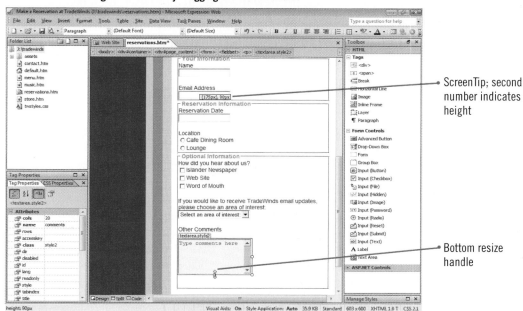

ScreenTip; second number indicates height

Bottom resize handle

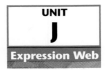
Adding Buttons

A button on a form allows a visitor to submit the information or clear any information already entered. Expression Web includes controls for a Submit button, a Reset button, and a button you can customize for any purpose. The appearance of a form button in the browser varies somewhat depending on the browser defaults. The shape of the button and its text formatting can look quite different in say, Safari, than in Internet Explorer, and on a Mac versus a PC. However, they will still be recognizable as buttons and will still function the same way. The HTML code for a button consists of a <button> tag with optional name and type attributes. ▓▓▓ The form is almost complete. You just need to add submit and reset buttons so that visitors can send their information to the server or clear the form if they want to change their choices.

STEPS

1. **Click to the right of the text area you inserted, then press [Enter]**

2. **Double-click Input (Submit) in the Form Controls list on the Toolbox Task Pane**
   A submit button is added to the form, as shown in Figure J-24. You can customize the text that appears on a submit button to make it more user friendly.

> **QUICK TIP**
> You can also change the type of button from submit to reset, though you should not do so unless you accidentally inserted the wrong type of button.

3. **Right-click the button you just inserted, then click Form Field Properties**
   The Push Button Properties dialog box opens. Here you can change the name, which appears only in the code, and the Value/label, which appears on the button.

4. **Click in the Value/label text box, select the text submit, press [Delete], type Send, compare your screen to Figure J-25, then click OK**
   The button now displays the text Send rather than Submit.

5. **Click to the right of the button you just inserted, then double-click Input (Reset) on the Toolbox Task Pane**
   A reset button is inserted into the form.

6. **Right-click the button you just inserted, then click Form Field Properties**
   The Push Button Properties dialog box opens.

7. **Click in the Value/label text box, select the text reset, press [Delete], type Cancel, then click OK**
   The button now displays the text "Cancel."

8. **Save your changes, preview the page in a browser, then compare your screen to Figure J-26**

9. **Fill out at least one form control, click the Cancel button, close the browser window, return to Expression Web, close the tradewinds site, then exit Expression Web**

Using your own image for a submit button

The standard HTML buttons can look a bit boring; also, they can display differently in different browsers. If you'd like a submit button that coordinates with the look of your site and that displays consistently across browsers, you can use Expression Web to insert any image and have it act as an HTML button. To use a customized submit button, first place your cursor inside the form at the point where you would like the button to appear. Double-click Input (Image) in the Form Controls list on the Toolbox task pane, right-click the placeholder image that's inserted, then click Picture Properties. In the Picture Properties dialog box, click the General tab, click the Browse button next to the Picture box, browse to where the image is located on your disk, click Open, type "Submit form" or other explanatory text in the Alternate Text textbox, then click OK. Note that this method only works with submit buttons, not with reset buttons. (Customizing a reset button requires using JavaScript.)

FIGURE J-24: Submit button added to form

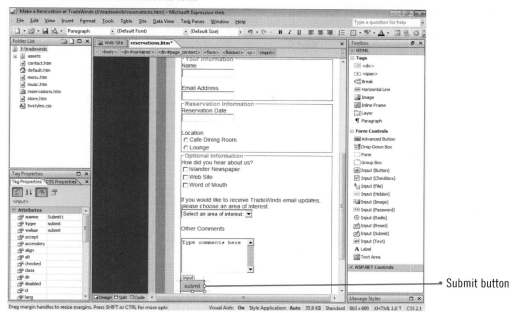

Submit button

FIGURE J-25: Push Button Properties dialog box

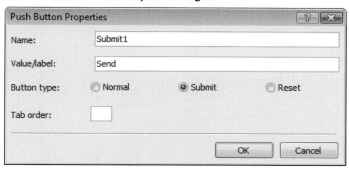

FIGURE J-26: Completed form

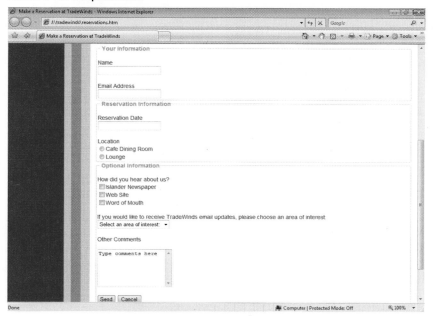

Expression Web

Practice

If you have a SAM user profile, you may have access to hands-on instruction, practice, and assessment of the skills covered in this unit. Log in to your SAM account (http://sam2007.course.com/) to launch any assigned training activities or exams that relate to the skills covered in this unit.

▼ CONCEPTS REVIEW

Label each form control on the sample form shown in Figure J-27.

FIGURE J-27

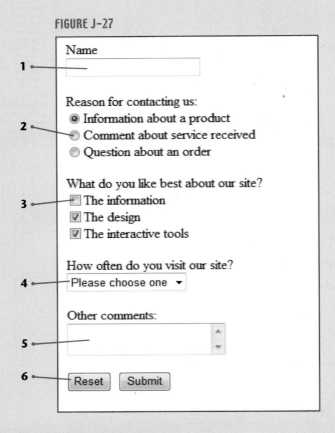

Match each form control with its HTML tag.

7. **Group boxes**
8. **Text box**
9. **Radio button**
10. **Checkbox**
11. **Drop-down box**
12. **Text area**

a. <input type="radio">
b. <option>
c. <input type="checkbox">
d. <fieldset>
e. <textarea>
f. <input type="text">

Select the best answer from the list of choices.

13. **Which form control would you use if you wanted visitors to choose only one option from a list?**
    a. Drop-down box
    b. Radio button
    c. Checkbox
    d. Text area

14. **Which form control would you use if you wanted visitors to be able to see all list options at once and be able to choose more than one?**
    a. Drop-down box
    b. Radio button
    c. Checkbox
    d. Text area

15. **Which form control would you use if you wanted to display a long list of options in a compact manner?**
    a. Drop-down box
    b. Radio button
    c. Checkbox
    d. Text area

16. **Which form control would you use if you wanted to provide a large space for visitors to type in?**
    a. Drop-down box
    b. Radio button
    c. Text area
    d. Text box

17. **Which of the following is *not* an option for creating a form handler?**
    a. Write your own script.
    b. Use one provided by your hosting company.
    c. Use a premade one provided in Expression Web.
    d. Find a free one on the Internet.

18. **How can you improve the usability and accessibility of a form?**
    a. Set tab orders on form controls.
    b. Use the label tag.
    c. Put text labels above form controls.
    d. All of the above

19. **Which form control clears all the information a visitor entered into a form?**
    a. Reset button
    b. Submit button
    c. Checkbox
    d. Hidden field

20. **The legend tag serves as a label for a:**
    a. Checkbox.
    b. Radio button.
    c. Group box.
    d. Drop-down box.

▼ SKILLS REVIEW

1. **Add a form to a Web page.**
    a. Launch Expression Web, open the careers site, then open the contact page.
    b. Click the maximize button on the Toolbox task pane if necessary, then expand the Tags list and Form Controls list if necessary.
    c. Click after the text **Please contact us.**, then press [Enter].
    d. Click the p tab on the visual aid.
    e. Double-click Form in the Form Controls list on the Toolbox task pane.
    f. Save your changes.

2. **Group form controls.**
    a. Click inside the form visual aid, then double-click Group Box in the Form Controls list on the Toolbox task pane.
    b. Open the Group Box Properties dialog box, type **About You** in the Label text box, then click OK to close the dialog box.
    c. Press [➔], then insert a Group Box form control.
    d. Open the Group Box Properties dialog box, type **How Can We Help You?** in the Label text box, then click OK to close the dialog box.
    e. Save your changes, preview the page in a browser, close the browser window, then return to Expression Web.

3. **Add text boxes.**
    a. Click inside the About You group box, double-click Paragraph on the Toolbox task pane, type **Name**, then press [Shift][Enter]. (*Hint*: Be sure to click in the group box and not in the label.)
    b. Double-click Input (Text) on the Toolbox task pane.

c. Open the Text Box Properties dialog box for the text box you just inserted

d. Type **name** in the Name text box, then click OK to close the dialog box.

e. Press [➡], press [Enter], type **Email Address**, then press [Shift][Enter].

f. Double-click Input (Text) on the Toolbox task pane.

g. Open the Text Box Properties dialog box for the text box you just inserted.

h. Type **email** in the Name text box, then click OK to close the dialog box.

i. Save your changes, preview the page in a browser, type your name in the name box, close the browser window, then return to Expression Web.

4. Add radio buttons.

a. Click to the right of the Email Address text box, press [Enter], type **Are you a current Careers Guaranteed customer?**, then press [Shift][Enter].

b. Double-click Input (Radio) on the Toolbox task pane.

c. Open the Option Button Properties dialog box for the radio button you just inserted, assign it a Group name of **customerstatus**, a Value of **current**, and an Initial state of **Not selected**, then click OK to close the dialog box.

d. Click to the right of the radio button you just inserted, type **Yes**, then press [Shift][Enter].

e. Double-click Input (Radio) on the Toolbox task pane.

f. Open the Option Button Properties dialog box for the radio button you just inserted, assign it a Value of **notcurrent** and an Initial state of **Not selected**, then click OK to close the dialog box.

g. Click to the right of the radio button you just inserted, then type **No**.

h. Save your changes, preview the page in a browser, click both of the radio buttons, close the browser window, then return to Expression Web.

5. Add checkboxes.

a. Click in the How Can We Help You? group box, double-click Paragraph in the Form Controls list on the Toolbox task pane, type **My question is about:**, then press [Shift][Enter].

b. Double-click Input (Checkbox) in the Form Controls list on the Toolbox task pane, then open the Checkbox Properties dialog box.

c. Give the checkbox a Name of **services**, a Value of **services**, and an Initial state of **Not checked**, then click OK to close the dialog box.

d. Click to the right of the checkbox, type **Services and products**, then press [Shift][Enter].

e. Add an Input (Checkbox) control, then open the Check Box Properties dialog box for the new control.

f. Give the checkbox a Name of **billing**, a Value of **billing**, and an Initial state of **Not checked**, then click OK to close the dialog box.

g. Click to the right of the checkbox, then type **Billing**.

h. Save your changes, preview the page in a browser, click both of the checkboxes, close the browser window, then return to Expression Web.

6. Add a drop-down box.

a. Click to the right of Billing, press [Enter], type **If you are a current customer, please indicate which service you currently use:**, then press [Shift][Enter].

b. Double-click Drop-Down Box on the Toolbox task pane, open the Drop-Down Box Properties dialog box, then assign it a name of **serviceused**.

c. Click the Add button, type **Personal career matchmakers** in the Choice text box, then click OK.

d. Repeat Step c to add the following choices:
Resume and interview coaching
Online courses and tutorials
Online career planning tools

e. Click Online career planning tools, then click the Move Up button.

f. Click the first line in the Choice list, click Modify, type **Please choose a service:** in the Choice text box, then click OK to close the Modify Choice dialog box.

g. Click OK to close the Drop-Down Box Properties dialog box.

h. Save your changes, preview the page in a browser, click the drop-down box list arrow, close the browser window, then return to Expression Web.

7. **Add a text area.**

a. Click to the right of the drop-down box you just added, press [Enter], type **What is your question?**, then press [Shift][Enter].

b. Double-click Text Area in the Form Controls list on the Toolbox task pane.

c. Open the Text Area Box Properties dialog box.

d. Give it a name of **question** and an initial value of **Type your question here.**, then click OK to close the dialog box.

e. Click the bottom resize handle, drag down until the ScreenTip indicates a height of 100px, then release the mouse button.

f. Save your changes, preview the page in a browser, click in the text area and type some text, close the browser window, then return to Expression Web.

8. **Add buttons.**

a. Click to the right of the text area you inserted, then press [Enter].

b. Double-click Input (Submit) on the Toolbox Task Pane.

c. Open the Push Button Properties dialog box.

d. Give the button a Value/label of **Send my question**, then click OK to close the dialog box.

e. Click to the right of button you just inserted, then double-click Input (Reset) on the Toolbox task pane.

f. Open the Push Button Properties dialog box, give the button a Value/label of **Clear this form**, then click OK to close the dialog box.

g. Save your changes, preview the page in a browser, compare your screen to Figure J-28, close the browser window, return to Expression Web, close the careers site, then exit Expression Web.

FIGURE J-28

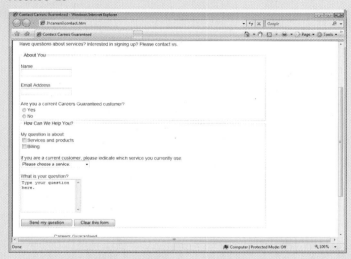

▼ INDEPENDENT CHALLENGE 1

In this project you continue your work on the ConnectUp Web site. The joinup page on the site contains some placeholder text that needs to replaced with a form. After meeting with Tiffany, you have more details about what type of information she wants to collect from visitors when they join. You are now ready to create a form.

a. Launch Expression Web, open the connectup Web site, then open the joinup page.

b. Select the lines of text that begin with **Name** and end with **Career area**, including any blank lines above or below this text, then delete the selection.

c. Use the Toolbox task pane to add a Form to the page.

d. Click inside the form, type **Name**, press [Shift][Enter], then add a text box form control. Use the Text Box Properties dialog box to assign the text box a name of **name**.

e. Press [➤], press [Enter], type **E-mail Address**, press [Shift][Enter], then add a text box control. Use the Text Box Properties dialog box to give the text box a name of **email**.

f. Click to the right of the email text box, then press [Enter].

g. Type **Age**, press [Shift][Enter], and add a radio button form control. Use the Option Button Properties dialog box to give the radio button the following properties: a Group name of **age**, a Value of **18to25**, and an Initial state of **Not selected**. Press [➤], then type **18 to 25 years**.

h. Press [Shift][Enter], then add a radio button. Use the Option Button Properties dialog box to give the radio button the following properties: a Group name of **age**, a Value of **26to35**, and an Initial state of **Not selected**. Press [→], then type **26 to 35 years**.

i. Press [Shift][Enter], then add a radio button. Use the Option Button Properties dialog box to give the radio button the following properties: a Group name of **age**, a Value of **over35**, and an Initial state of **Not selected**. Press [→], then type **Over 35 years**

j. Press [Enter], type **Geographic area**, press [Shift][Enter], then add a drop-down box form control.

k. Open the Drop-Down Box Properties dialog box, then give the box a name of **geographic**. Use the Add button in the Drop-Down Box Properties dialog box to add the following options to the box:

U.S. Northeast

U.S. Southeast

U.S. Mid-Atlantic

U.S. West

U.S. South

Canada

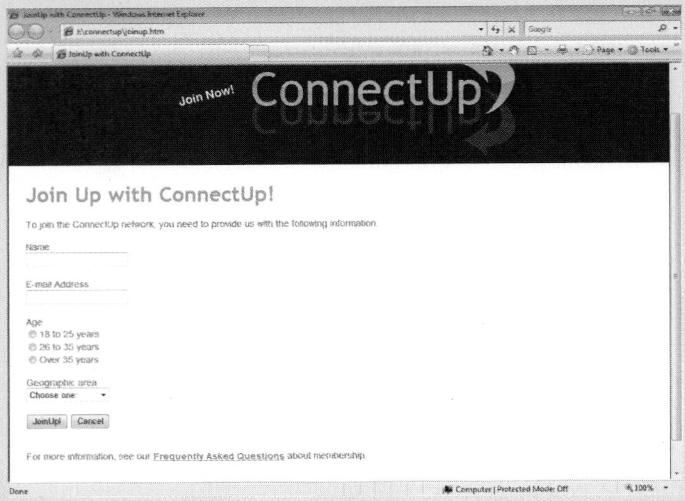

l. Modify the first choice so the text says **Choose one:**, then click OK to close the dialog box.

m. Click to the right of the drop-down box, press [Enter], then add a submit button with a Value/label of **JoinUp!**.

n. Press [→], then add a reset button with a Value/label of **Cancel**.

o. Save your changes, preview the page in a browser, compare your screen to Figure J-29, fill out the form, press the Cancel button, then close the browser window.

p. Return to Expression Web, close the connectup site, then exit Expression Web.

FIGURE J-29

▼ INDEPENDENT CHALLENGE 2

In this project you continue your work on the Memories Restored Web site. Brian, the owner of Memories Restored, asks you to add a form to the contact page where visitors can describe what service they need and request a price quote.

a. Launch Expression Web, then open the memories Web site.

b. Open the contact page, click after the email address info@yourmemoriesrestored.com, press [Enter], type **Request a Quote**, then press [Enter].

c. Add a form to the page. (*Hint*: Select the visual aid for the empty paragraph, then use the Toolbox task pane to add a form.)

d. Add a group box control, give it a label of **Contact Information**, then add a second group box below it and give it a label of **Service Requested**.

e. In the Contact Information group box, add one text box control for name and another for email, along with appropriate text above each text box to identify it.

f. In the Service Requested group box, add the text **Type of service**, then add a series of checkboxes below it that provide the following options:

Photo restoration

Portrait touch-up

Photo DVD

Other

Remember to use the Check Box Properties dialog box to give each option an appropriate name.

▼ INDEPENDENT CHALLENGE 2 (CONTINUED)

g. In a new paragraph, type the text **Is this order time-sensitive?**, then add radio buttons below it that provide the following options:

Yes

No

Remember to use the Option Button Properties Button dialog box to give each an appropriate name, value, and initial state.

Advanced Challenge Exercise

- Add a new paragraph, then type **How would you like your final product delivered?**
- Add a drop-down box with the following choices:

  Digital file via email

  Digital file on DVD

  Printed photo via postal mail
- Allow the option for visitors to select more than one choice.

h. In a new paragraph, type the text **Please describe the service you are requesting**, add a text area below it, use the Text Area Box Properties dialog box to give it an appropriate name, then use the resize handles to adjust the height and width of the text area to your liking.

i. Add submit and reset buttons.

j. Preview your page in a browser, fill out the form, click the reset button, close the browser window, return to Expression Web, close the site, then exit Expression Web.

▼ INDEPENDENT CHALLENGE 3

This Independent Challenge requires an Internet connection.

The staff at Technology for All is interested in having more interaction with the visitors to their Web site. Having just learned about HTML forms, you decide to explore some other Web sites to see how they use forms to gather input from visitors.

a. Choose three Web sites that you frequently visit, and explore each to find an example of a form. Remember that forms can have many fields or just one and can be used for many purposes.

b. Based on your research, write a paragraph about each of the three forms, describing its purpose and the type of form controls used to gather input.

Advanced Challenge Exercise

- Review the layout of each form and the wording of the text labels.
- Write a paragraph describing what you do or do not like about the way each form is designed.

c. Add your name to the document, save it, and print it.

▼ REAL LIFE INDEPENDENT CHALLENGE

This assignment builds on the personal Web site you have worked on in previous units. In this project, you will add a form to your site.

a. Review your site content and find an area where it would be useful to collect visitor input, such as a contact page.

b. Plan a form, considering the type of information you would like to collect and which form control would be best to use for each piece of information. If useful, sketch out a structure for the form.

c. Open the appropriate page in your Web site, then create the form and add the form controls, using group boxes to organize the areas of the form.

d. Preview your page in a browser, save your changes, close your site, then exit Expression Web.

▼ VISUAL WORKSHOP

Launch Expression Web, open the **ecotours** site, then open the contact page. Add text and form controls to the page so that your screen matches Figure J-30. (*Hint*: An H1 tag was applied to the Contact Us text.)

FIGURE J-30

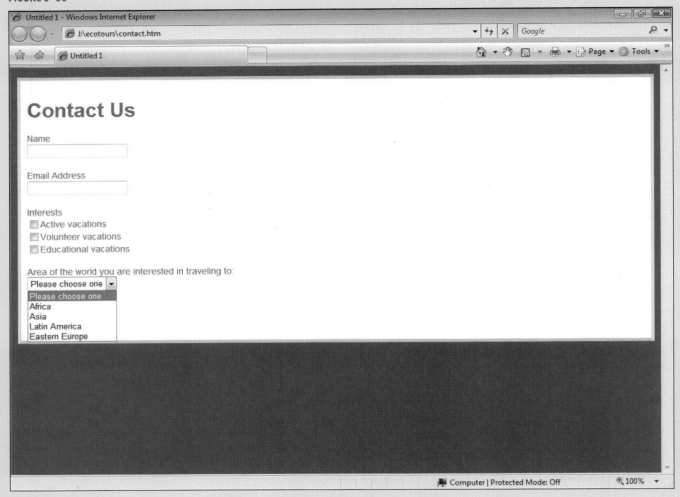

Working with Behaviors

Behaviors let you add interactivity to your Web pages by causing HTML elements to act in a specific way when visitors perform certain actions. For example, a behavior could cause a popup message to be displayed when a visitor clicks a link, or to make a different image appear when a visitor points to a picture with a mouse. Thoughtful use of behaviors can add interest to your Web site and enhance its functionality. Catalina likes the look of the TradeWinds Web site but feels it is too static. You decide to incorporate several behaviors into the site to make it more interactive.

OBJECTIVES

Understand behaviors

Add a popup message

Add a status message

Add a jump menu

Add an image swap

Open a browser window

Modify a behavior

Understanding Behaviors

A **behavior** is a piece of JavaScript code that Expression Web generates and adds to your Web pages. **JavaScript** is a programming language that creates types of interactivity that are not possible with HTML alone. JavaScript is more complex to learn than HTML, so having these prewritten code pieces available is quite convenient when you are beginning to learn Web design. See Table K-1 for a complete list of behaviors available in Expression Web. ▰▰▰ You decide to learn more about how behaviors work.

DETAILS

To use behaviors effectively, it is important to understand:

- **The components of a behavior**

  A behavior consists of two parts—an event and an action. An **event** is an act that triggers a result. The event is usually something a visitor does, such as scrolling, clicking, resizing a window, or submitting a form. A few events, such as an HTML page loading, don't require the visitor to do something first. Events are designated with special names in JavaScript. For example, when a visitor clicks an element, the event is called *onclick*; when a visitor exits a page, the event is called *onunload*. The second part of a behavior is the **action**, a specific result triggered by the event such as opening a new browser window or displaying a new image.

  Most behaviors are attached to a particular HTML element. For example, a link or anchor element can have a behavior attached to it that causes a window to open (the action) when the link is clicked (the event).

- **The Behaviors task pane in Expression Web**

  > **QUICK TIP**
  >
  > The Behaviors task pane is not open by default in Expression Web.

  The Behaviors task pane provides access to all Behaviors available in Expression Web, as shown in Figure K-1. When an element is selected on a page, the task pane displays any behaviors currently attached to that element. In this task pane, you can also add, delete, and modify behaviors, and change the order in which behaviors are attached to an element.

- **The right time to use a behavior**

  > **QUICK TIP**
  >
  > Not all browsers display all behaviors consistently, so make sure to test your behaviors in several browsers.

  When deciding whether to use a behavior, carefully consider the effect it will have on your visitors' experiences. Will it help visitors complete a task or find information? Will it interfere with the visitors' ability to easily navigate the site? Will it increase download times for the page? Before incorporating a behavior into your site, evaluate these factors to be sure that the behavior will be a help rather than a hindrance to your audience.

Adding more behaviors

The set of behaviors available in Expression Web is a good foundation for adding interactivity to your site. You may discover, though, that you would like a wider range of options. Third-party companies have developed sets of behaviors for Expression Web that you can purchase and add to the program. Using the behaviors included in these packages, you can easily add such features as slide shows, bread crumb navigation, and rotating ad banners to your Web pages.

FIGURE K-1: Behaviors task pane

Element to which
behavior is
attached

Event

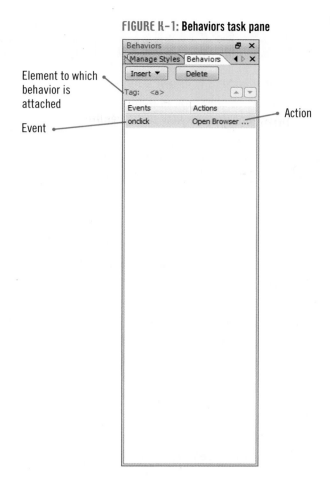

Action

TABLE K-1: Behaviors available in Expression Web

behavior	description
Call Script	Triggers JavaScript that is written outside of Expression Web
Change Property	Changes properties of the element such as font, position, borders, and visibility
Change Property Restore	Restores original properties of element
Check Browser	Detects what browser type and version a visitor is using; useful for customizing pages to specific browsers
Check Plug-in	Detects if a visitor has special software installed for playing multimedia and other features; useful for displaying pages customized to visitors who do or do not have the plug-in installed
Go To URL	Opens a link
Jump Menu	Creates a dropdown menu of links
Jump Menu Go	Sends visitor to a selected link in a jump menu when the specified action is performed
Open Browser Window	Opens a new browser window that can be a particular size
Play Sound	Plays an audio file
Popup Message	Opens a small window with a text message
Preload Images	Load images for image swaps onto the visitor's computer when the page loads; this prevents any delay in the image appearing when a visitor points to a rollover image
Set Text	Sets text in a status bar or specified frame, layer, or text field
Swap Image	Replaces one image with another
Swap Image Restore	Restores original image after an image swap

Adding a Popup Message

A **popup message** is text that appears in its own window. A visitor must click the OK button on a popup message in order to proceed. A common use of popup messages is to alert visitors when they click links that will take them off the current site to a new site. Overuse of popup messages can annoy visitors and make your site difficult to use, so exercise good judgment in their use. The TradeWinds emporium stocks many more beads than are listed on the store page. Catalina is concerned that visitors will think the emporium has a limited inventory. You suggest adding a popup message when visitors click the store link from the home page alerting them to the fact that not all beads are listed on the Web site.

STEPS

1. **Launch Expression Web, open the tradewinds site, then open the home page**

2. **Click Task Panes on the menu bar, click Behaviors, then if necessary click the Maximize button on the Behaviors task pane**
   The Behaviors task pane opens in the same window as the Manage Styles and Apply Styles task panes.

> **QUICK TIP**
> Remember that a link is created by using <a> tags and is called an anchor element.

3. **Click anywhere in the selection of beads link in the last paragraph, then click Insert on the Behaviors task pane, as shown in Figure K-2**
   A list of actions that are available for the selected element, an anchor, are displayed. By attaching the action to the anchor tag, it will be triggered when visitors click the link. Any behaviors that cannot be attached to the element you have selected are dimmed on the Insert menu.

4. **Click Popup Message**
   The Popup Message dialog box opens.

> **QUICK TIP**
> To edit the message, double-click Popup Message in the Actions column of the Behaviors panel.

5. **Click in the Message box if necessary, type Our Web site shows only a small selection of the beads we have in stock!, compare your screen to Figure K-3, then click OK**
   The Behaviors panel indicates that an onclick event and a Popup Message action are now attached to the anchor tag.

6. **Save your changes, then preview the home page in a browser**
   If you are using Internet Explorer, a security message may open in a yellow bar at the top of the browser window.

> **TROUBLE**
> If you are using a different Web browser, such as Mozilla Firefox, skip Step 7.

7. **If necessary, click the yellow bar containing the security message, click Allow Blocked Content, then click Yes**

8. **Click the selection of beads link**
   A popup message opens, as shown in Figure K-4.

9. **Click OK, then leave the browser window open**
   Clicking OK closes the dialog box, and the store page opens in the browser window.

FIGURE K-2: Insert menu on Behaviors task pane

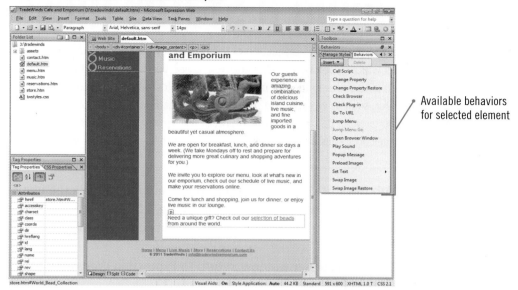

Available behaviors for selected element

FIGURE K-3: Completed Popup Message dialog box

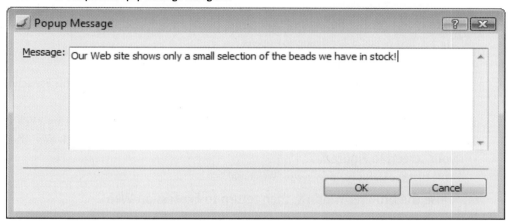

FIGURE K-4: Popup message on home page

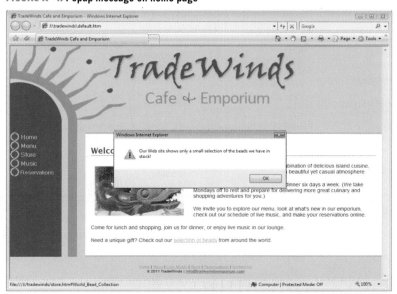

Adding a Status Message

The area in the bottom-left section of the browser window is called the **status bar**. To review the parts of a browser window, see Table K-2. Using a behavior, you can replace the default text, or **status message**, that appears in this area with your own message. The default status messages provide important information to the visitor, such as whether the page is finished loading, the URL of a link, or alerts that there are errors on a page, so exercise discretion in overriding this with your own information. 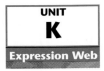 Catalina has asked you to add a welcome message that will appear in the browser status bar when visitors load the home page.

STEPS

1. **With the store page open in the browser window, click the home page button, then notice the status bar, as shown in Figure K-5**
   The status bar displays the word "Done"; this is the default text that appears in the status bar when a page is finished loading in a browser.

2. **Close the browser window, return to Expression Web, then select <body> on the quick tag selector**
   See Figure K-6. The entire body of the page is selected so that you can attach a behavior to it. When you attach a behavior to the body element, the action will be triggered when the page loads, rather than when a visitor performs a specific action.

3. **Click Insert on the Behaviors task pane, point to Set Text, then click Set Text of Status Bar**
   The Set Text of Status Bar dialog box opens.

4. **Type Welcome! in the Message box, then click OK**
   The Behaviors panel now indicates that an onload event and a Set Text of Status Bar action are attached to the body tag.

5. **Save your changes, preview the home page in a browser, if necessary click the yellow bar containing the security message, click Allow Blocked Content, click Yes, then compare your screen to Figure K-7**
   Note that the status bar now reads "Welcome!"

6. **Close the browser window, then return to Expression Web**

TABLE K-2: Parts of a browser window

name	description
Navigation toolbar	Area that contains navigational elements such as back, forward, and refresh buttons
Location toolbar	Area where the URL is typed and displayed
Status bar	Bottom-left part of the window; displays status information
Menu bar	Area that displays menus such as File, Edit, and Tools; usually located in the top part of the window but not shown by default in Internet Explorer 7
Scrollbars	Areas on bottom and right side of window that allow visitors to scroll through page content
Resize handles	Icons that appear when mouse points to a corner or side of the browser window; dragging a handle resizes the window
Title bar	Topmost area of browser window; displays page title as designated by HTML <title> tags

FIGURE K-5: Status bar

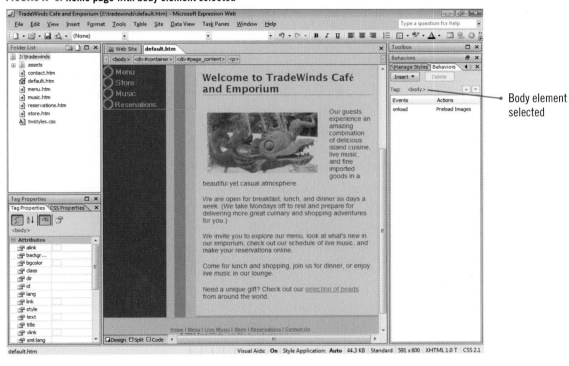

Status bar displays default browser message

FIGURE K-6: Home page with body element selected

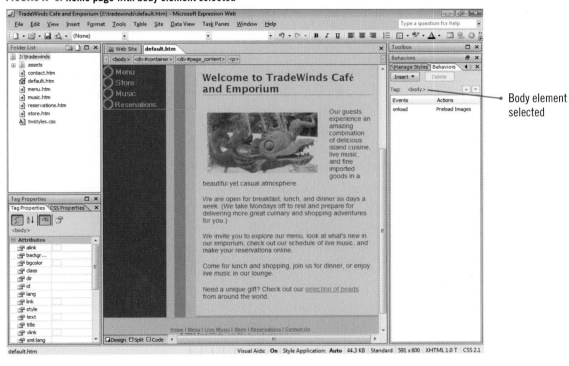

Body element selected

FIGURE K-7: Customized status bar message

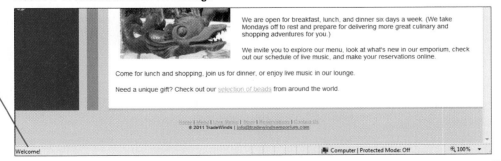

Status bar displays customized message

Adding a Jump Menu

A **jump menu** is a drop-down menu that lists a selection of navigation links. When visitors click a link in the menu, they are taken to the corresponding page. Jump menus are a convenient way to pack a lot of navigation into a small amount of space. In talking to customers who visit the TradeWinds emporium, Catalina has discovered that many of them did not realize that TradeWinds also has a café and live music. She asks you to add a feature that encourages visitors who browse the store page to also view the café menu and live music schedule. You decide to add a jump menu to the bottom of the store page that will allow visitors to quickly access the menu and music pages.

STEPS

1. **Open the store page, click after the text** spend some time with us. **in the last paragraph, press [Enter], type** Check out our cafe and live music:, **then press [Shift][Enter]**

QUICK TIP
Unlike most behaviors, jump menus are not attached to a particular HTML element.

2. **Click** Insert **on the Behaviors task pane, then click** Jump Menu
   The Jump Menu dialog box opens. You can add, modify, and remove items in the jump menu here. Using the Open URLs in list arrow, you can choose whether the pages open in the same browser window or a new window.

3. **Click** Add
   The Add Choice dialog box opens. The text you add to the Choice text box is listed in the jump menu, and the Value text box lists the URL the visitor will go to when they click that choice.

4. **Type** Select one **in the Choice text box, compare your screen to Figure K-8, then click** OK
   When you create a jump menu in Expression Web, a Go button is not included. This means that visitors will not have a button to click to initiate the first choice in a jump menu. Because of this, it's a good idea to make the first choice instructional text such as "Choose One" rather than one of the link choices.

QUICK TIP
You can also link to external Web sites from a jump menu; links to external Web sites will automatically open in a new browser window.

5. **Click** Add, **type** Cafe Menu **in the Choice text box, click** Browse, **click** menu.htm, **click** OK, **then click** OK
   The new choice and value are listed in the dialog box.

6. **Click** Add, **type** Live Music Schedule **in the Choice text box, click** Browse, **click** music.htm, **click** OK, **then click** OK
   See Figure K-9.

7. **Click** OK, **save your changes, preview the page in a browser, if necessary click the** yellow bar containing the security message, **click** Allow Blocked Content, **then click** Yes
   See Figure K-10.

QUICK TIP
Some jump menus require visitors to click a Go button after they choose an option, but the menus that Expression Web creates require that visitors only click the option.

8. **Click the** jump menu list arrow, **then click** Cafe Menu
   The menu page loads.

9. **Click the** Store button **on the navigation bar, click the** jump menu list arrow, **click** Live Music Schedule, **close the browser window, then return to Expression Web**

FIGURE K-8: Add Choice dialog box

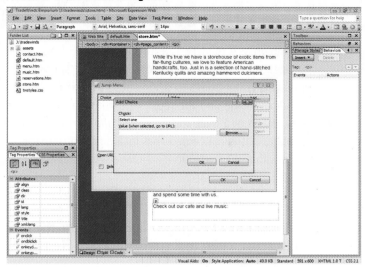

FIGURE K-9: Completed Jump Menu dialog box

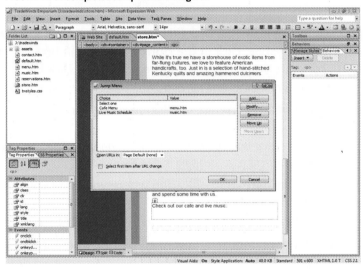

FIGURE K-10: Completed jump menu on the store page

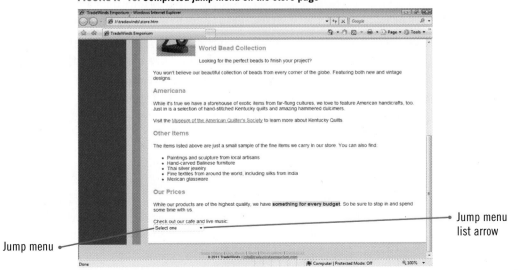

Jump menu

Jump menu list arrow

Adding an Image Swap

An image swap, also known as a rollover, is a fun way to add some interactivity to your site. The **image swap** behavior replaces one image with another upon a specified event, usually a mouseover. A **mouseover** occurs when a visitor points to the image with the mouse pointer. In order for this behavior to work properly, the original image and the replacement image must have the same dimensions. 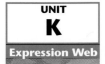 Catalina would like an image of a quilt and an image of a handmade basket to appear in the Americana section of the store page, but is concerned that including both images will make the that section look crowded. You come up with a clever solution: an image swap that enables you to feature both images, one at a time.

STEPS

1. **Make the store page the active page, click just before the heading Americana, click Insert on the menu bar, point to Picture, then click From File**
   The Picture dialog box opens.

2. **Navigate to the location where you store your Data Files, click quilt.jpg, click Insert, type Kentucky Quilt in the Alternate text text box, then click OK**
   The picture is inserted into the page.

3. **Right-click the quilt image, click Picture Properties, click the Appearance tab, click Right under Wrapping style, click in the Horizontal margin text box, delete the current text 0, type 10, compare your screen to Figure K-11, then click OK**
   The quilt picture is now aligned to the right, with white space on the left and right sides.

> **QUICK TIP**
> It can be difficult to tell the images apart in this list, so it's helpful that Expression Web always automatically selects the image in the list that you have selected on the page.

4. **Click the quilt image to select it, click Insert on the Behaviors task pane, then click Swap Image**
   The Swap Images dialog box opens, with the quilt image selected. All images that are referenced in the HTML code of the current page are listed in this dialog box.

5. **Click Browse, navigate to the location where you store your Data Files, click basket.jpg, then click OK**
   The file path to the basket image appears in the Swap Image URL text box.

> **QUICK TIP**
> It's a good idea to always leave the Preload Images option checked to ensure that there is no delay between the time a visitor points to an image and the time the second image is displayed.

6. **Click the Restore on mouseout event check box, compare your screen to Figure K-12, then click OK**
   Because you chose to restore the image on mouseout, Expression Web added two behaviors to the image: one swaps the image when a visitor points to it (on mouseover); the other restores the original image when the visitors stops pointing to the image (on mouseout). You could leave this check box unchecked if you want the swapped image to stay on the page even after a visitor moves the mouse pointer away from the picture.

7. **Save your changes, save the images to the assets folder when prompted, preview the page in a browser, if necessary click the yellow bar containing the security message, click Allow Blocked Content, click Yes, then point to the quilt image**
   The image changes to display the basket image, as shown in Figure K-13.

8. **Close the browser, then return to Expression Web**

Changing the order of behaviors

If you have more than one behavior attached to an element, you may wish to change the order in which these behaviors are triggered. To change the order, select the behavior in the Behaviors task pane, then click the up arrow button ▲ or the down arrow button ▼ to move the behavior up or down in the list. The behaviors at the top of the list will be triggered first.

FIGURE K-11: Completed Picture Properties dialog box

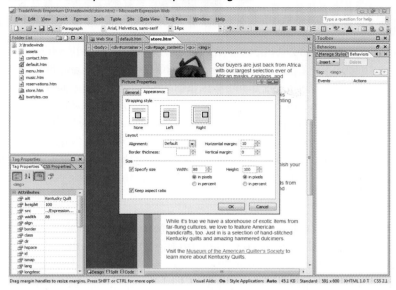

FIGURE K-12: Swap Images dialog box

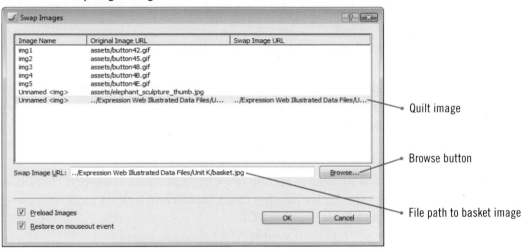

Quilt image

Browse button

File path to basket image

FIGURE K-13: Basket image displayed on mouseover

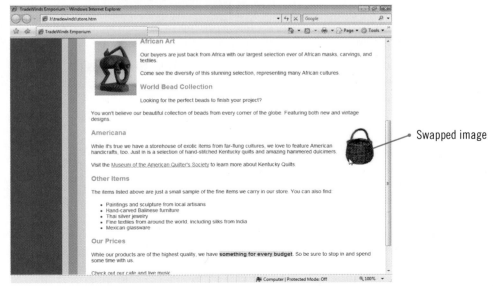

Swapped image

Expression Web

Opening a Browser Window

As you have learned, you can open a link in a new window by setting the target frame on the link to New Window. Attaching an Open Browser Window behavior to a link is another way to open a link in a new window. Using the behavior rather than the target frame offers you greater control over the appearance of the new window. You can specify the dimensions and other options such as whether scrollbars, a location toolbar, or resize handles appear. Web designers will often open a new browser window without address or status bars to display a small amount of related information. 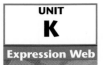 Catalina wants visitors to be able to check the live music schedule as they're making a reservation, but she does not want them to leave the reservations page. You create a link from the reservations page to the music page that opens in a new window.

STEPS

1. **Open the reservations page, select the text live entertainment schedule, right-click the selected text, then click Hyperlink on the shortcut menu**
   The Insert Hyperlink dialog box opens.

QUICK TIP
Sometimes a # is used instead of javascript:; as a placeholder.

2. **Click in the Address text box if necessary, type javascript:;, then click OK**
   The text javascript:; is used as a placeholder to indicate that the link will be controlled by JavaScript.

3. **In the Behaviors task pane, click Insert, then click Open Browser Window**
   The Open Browser Window dialog box opens, as shown in Figure K-14.

4. **Click Browse, click music.htm, then click OK**
   The music.htm file name appears in the Go to URL text box.

5. **Type schedule in the Window name text box, click in the Window width text box, delete the text 200, type 800, click in the Window height text box, delete the text 200, then type 600**
   The window name is used by JavaScript to identify the window. It is not displayed anywhere on the page or in the browser window.

QUICK TIP
It's a good idea to always display scrollbars to ensure that visitors can scroll to see content if needed; otherwise some content might be hidden from view.

6. **In the Attributes section, click the Scrollbars as needed check box to add a check mark, click the Resize handles check box to add a check mark, compare your screen to Figure K-15, then click OK**
   The new behavior is listed in the Behaviors task pane.

7. **Save your changes, preview the page in a browser, if necessary click the yellow bar containing the security message, click Allow Blocked Content, click Yes, then click the live entertainment schedule link**
   As shown in Figure K-16, the music page opens in a new window, with scrollbars displayed. The scrollbars allow visitors to access all the content on the page.

8. **Close both browser windows, then return to Expression Web**

FIGURE K-14: Open Browser Window dialog box

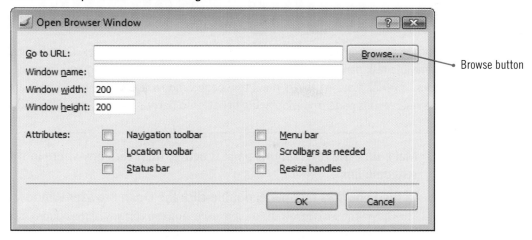

Browse button

FIGURE K-15: Completed Open Browser Window dialog box

Go to URL linked to music page

Window name

Window width

Window height

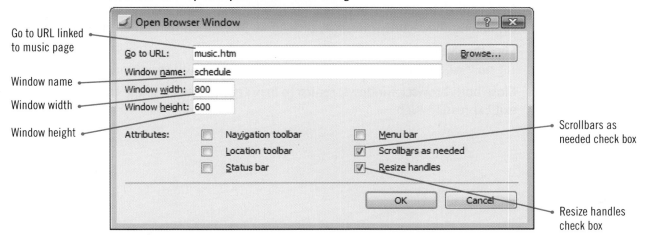

Scrollbars as needed check box

Resize handles check box

FIGURE K-16: Music page opened in new window from reservations page

New window

Scrollbar

Modifying a Behavior

Once you've added a behavior to a page, it's easy to make changes. Double-clicking the behavior on the Behaviors task pane opens the corresponding dialog box, allowing you to make any necessary modifications. ▰▰▰ Catalina thinks the music page window that opens is too large and obscures too much of the reservations page. You modify the behavior to decrease the height of the music page window.

STEPS

1. **Make sure the reservations page is active, then click anywhere in the** live entertainment schedule **link**

2. **In the Behaviors task pane, double-click the** Open Browser Window action
   The Open Browser Window dialog box opens. You can edit any of the options here to modify the behavior.

QUICK TIP
You can also change the window width to reduce the size of a window, but doing so would mean that visitors might have to scroll from side to side, which would make reading the page difficult.

3. **Click in the** Window height text box, **delete the text** 600, **then type** 400

4. **Compare your screen to Figure K-17, then click** OK

5. **Save your changes, preview the page in a browser, if necessary** click the yellow bar containing the security message, **click** Allow Blocked Content, **then click** Yes

6. **Click the** live entertainment schedule **link**
   The music page now opens in a window with a smaller height, as shown in Figure K-18.

7. **Close both browser windows, return to Expression Web, close the tradewinds site, then exit Expression Web**

Modifying a behavior's event

When you insert a behavior, Expression Web automatically chooses the event that is most commonly used for the specified HTML element. For example, if you are attaching a behavior to a link or anchor element, the onclick event is selected by default. You can modify which event triggers a behavior's action by pointing to the event in the Behaviors task pane, clicking the list arrow, then choosing a new event. Usually the default event is the best option, so if you choose to change the event, test the behavior in multiple browsers to be sure it works as you expect.

FIGURE K-17: Open Browser Window dialog box

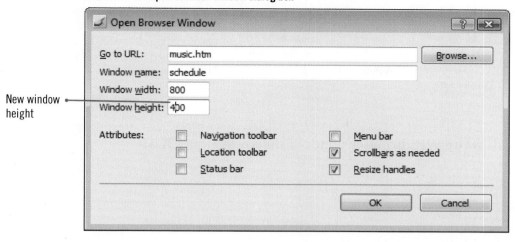

New window
height

FIGURE K-18: Music page opened in modified browser window

New window
now has a
shorter
height

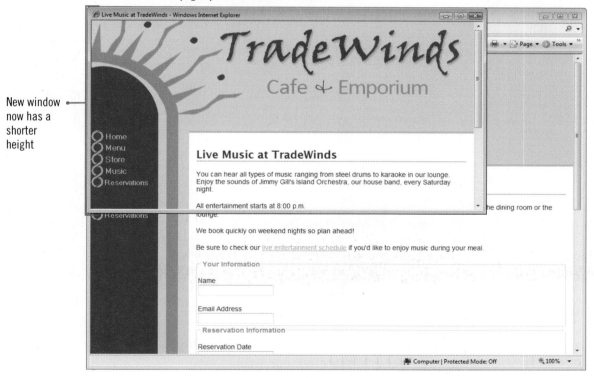

Practice

▼ CONCEPTS REVIEW

Label each element in the Web browser window shown in Figure K-19.

FIGURE K-19

Match each term with the statement that best describes it.

6. Jump menu

7. Popup message

8. Status bar message

9. Image swap

10. Action

11. Event

a. The part of a behavior that triggers a result

b. Text that appears in the bottom-left of a browser window

c. A behavior that replaces one image with another

d. A drop-down menu that lists a selection of navigation links

e. Text that appears in its own window

f. The part of a behavior that results when triggered

Select the best answer from the list of choices.

12. **In what language are behaviors written?**
    a. JavaScript
    b. HTML
    c. CSS
    d. ASP.NET

13. **What is the advantage of using the open browser window behavior rather than setting the target frame of a link to New Window?**
    a. It is easier to implement.
    b. It works in more browsers.
    c. It provides more control over size and features in new window.
    d. It is easier for visitors to use.

14. **By default, the Behaviors task pane is docked with the:**
    a. Tag Properties and CSS Properties task panes.
    b. Folders list task pane.
    c. Toolbox task pane.
    d. Manage Styles and Apply Styles task panes.

15. **Which of the following statements is true?**
    a. Behaviors are always attached to an HTML element.
    b. Behaviors are usually attached to a HTML element.
    c. Behaviors are never attached to an HTML element.
    d. None of the above

16. **When creating an image swap behavior, the two images must have the same:**
    a. File format.
    b. File size.
    c. Dimensions.
    d. Color profile.

17. **What is the advantage of preloading images?**
    a. More consistent page display in browser
    b. Less delay in displaying the image rollover
    c. More accessible to visitors with disabilities
    d. More compliant with Web standards

▼ SKILLS REVIEW

1. **Add a popup message.**
    a. Launch Expression Web, open the careers site, then open the home page.
    b. Open and maximize the Behaviors task pane, if necessary.
    c. Click the career exploration tools link, then click Insert on the Behaviors task pane.
    d. Insert a Popup Message behavior that reads **We have a brand new set of online tools coming soon!**.
    e. Save your changes, preview the page in a browser, then click the career exploration tools link.
    f. Click OK to close the popup message, close the browser window, then return to Expression Web.

2. **Add a status message.**
    a. On the home page, select all of the body tag using the quick tag selector.
    b. Click Insert on the Behaviors task pane.
    c. Insert a Set Text of Status Bar behavior that reads **We guarantee your success!**.
    d. Save your changes, preview the page in a browser, then read the status message.
    e. Close the browser window, then return to Expression Web.

3. **Add a jump menu.**
    a. On the home page, click just after the text **career exploration tools can help!**, then press [Enter].
    b. Type **What would you like to do?**, then press **[Shift][Enter]**.
    c. Use the Behaviors task pane to insert a jump menu behavior.
    d. In the Jump Menu dialog box, click Add, type **Choose one** in the Choice text box, then click OK.
    e. Click Add button, type **Learn about our services** in the Choice text box, click Browse, click services.htm, then click OK.
    f. Click Add, type **Contact us** in the Choice text box, click Browse, click contact.htm, click OK, then click OK to close the Jump Menu dialog box.
    g. Save your changes, preview the page in a browser, then compare your screen to Figure K-20.
    h. Click the jump menu list arrow, click Learn about our services, close the browser window, then return to Expression Web.

4. Add an image swap.

  a. Open the about page, click just before the text **Tina Russo, Chief Technology Officer**, click Insert on the menu bar, point to Picture, then click From File.

  b. Navigate to the location where you store your Data Files, click tina_bw.jpg, then click Insert.

  c. Type **Tina Russo** in the Alternate text text box, then click OK.

  d. Right-click the image, click Picture Properties, click the Appearance tab, set the wrapping style to Right, set the Horizontal margin to 10, then click OK to close the dialog box.

  e. With the image selected, use the Behaviors task pane to insert a Swap Image behavior.

  f. In the Swap Images dialog box, click Browse, navigate to the location where you store your Data Files, click tina_sepia.jpg, then click OK.

  g. Click the Restore on mouseout event check box, then click OK to close the dialog box.

  h. Save your changes, saving the images to the assets folder when prompted.

  i. Preview the page in a browser, point to the image you inserted, close the browser window, then return to Expression Web.

5. Open a browser window.

  a. Open the contact page, then select the text **about services** in the first sentence.

  b. Right-click the text, click Hyperlink on the shortcut menu, type **javascript:;** in the address text box, then click OK.

  c. Use the Behaviors task pane to insert an Open Browser Window behavior.

  d. Click Browse, click services.htm, then click OK.

  e. Give the window a Window name of **services**, a window width of **800**, and a window height of **400**, then click OK to close the dialog box.

  f. Save your changes, preview the page in a browser, then click the about services link.

  g. Close both browser windows, then return to Expression Web.

6. Modify a behavior.

  a. Make the contact page the active page, then click the about services link.

  b. Double-click the Open Browser Window action in the Behaviors task pane.

  c. Click the Scrollbars as needed check box, then click OK.

  d. Save your changes, preview the page in a browser, then click the about services link.

  e. Close both browser windows, return to Expression Web, close the careers site, then exit Expression Web.

FIGURE K-20

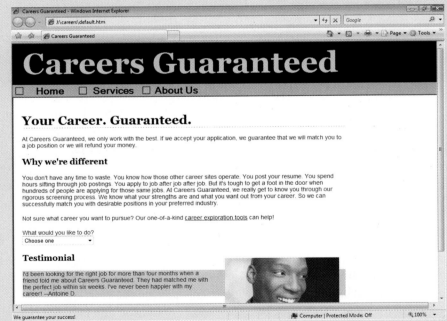

▼ INDEPENDENT CHALLENGE 1

In this project you continue your work on the ConnectUp Web site. Tiffany has requested that you add some interactivity to the site, such as a popup message on the joinup page, a jump menu on the home page, and a rollover image on the faq page.

a. Launch Expression Web, open the connectup Web site, then open the joinup page.

b. Select the body tag in the quick tag selector, and insert a Popup message behavior that reads **We're so happy you're joining up!**.

c. Click anywhere on the Frequently Asked Questions link, then insert an Open Browser Window behavior with the following properties: Go to URL of faq.htm, Window name of faq, Window width of 500, Window height of 400, and Scrollbars as needed.

d. Modify the Open Browser Window behavior to change the Window width to 400.

e. Save your changes to the joinup page, preview in a browser, compare your screen to Figure K-21, click the Frequently Asked Questions link, then close the browser windows and return to Expression Web.

f. Open the home page, use the quick tag selector to select the body tag, then insert a Set Text of Status Bar behavior that reads **ConnectUp today!**.

g. Click just after the text **socialize your way to success**, press [Enter], then insert a Jump Menu behavior.

h. Add a choice to the jump menu with text that reads **I want to:** with no link.

i. Add a choice to the jump menu with text that reads: **Join ConnectUp now!** that links to the joinup page.

j. Add a choice to the jump menu with text that reads: **Learn more!** that links to the faq page.

k. Save your changes, preview the page in a browser, click the Learn more! link, close the browser window, then return to Expression Web.

l. Open the faq page, click just before the text **Frequently Asked Questions about ConnectUp**, click Insert, point to Picture, click From File, navigate to where you store your Data Files, click questions.jpg, click Insert, type **Got Questions?** in the alternate text text box, then click OK.

m. Right-click the image, click Picture Properties, click the Appearance tab, then give the image a wrapping style of Left and a horizontal margin of 15.

n. Click the image to select it, then insert a Swap Image behavior. In the Swap Images dialog box, click the Browse button, navigate to the location where you store your Data Files, click answers.jpg, then click OK.

o. Click the Restore on mouseout event check box, then click OK to close the dialog box.

p. Save your changes, save the images to the assets folder when prompted, preview the page in a browser, then point to the questions image.

q. Close the browser window, return to Expression Web, save changes to all open pages, close the connectup site, then exit Expression Web.

FIGURE K-21

Expression Web

▼ INDEPENDENT CHALLENGE 2

In this project you continue your work on the Memories Restored Web site. The site is intended to look old-fashioned, but Brian wants the functionality to be very up-to-date. He is especially interested in a more interactive presentation of the before and after photos on the Our Work page. You decide to impress him by adding some behaviors.

a. Launch Expression Web, then open the memories Web site.

b. Open the home page, then add a Popup Message behavior to the historical societies and museums link that reads **This is just a sample of hundreds of testimonials we have received!**.

c. On the home page, add a Set Text of Status Bar behavior to the body tag with text that reads **Become one of our satisfied customers.**.

d. Save your changes, then preview the page in a browser.

e. On the home page, add a jump menu after the bulleted list with the following choices:

Text	URL
What would you like to do next?	None
Read testimonials	testimonials page
See examples of our work	our work page
Learn about our process	our process page

(*Hint*: You may have to press [Enter] more than once to start a new paragraph that is separate from the bulleted list.)

f. Save your changes, preview the page in the browser, click the testimonials link, return to the home page, then click one of the links in the jump menu. Close the browser, then return to Expression Web.

g. Open the our work page, click after the text, **Here are some examples of the fine work that we do:**, click [Backspace] to delete the :, then type **. Point to each image to see the final result.**.

h. Click the image under Example One, press [Delete], then insert the image example_one_before.jpg from the location where you store your Data Files, giving it appropriate alternate text.

i. Adjust the picture properties as you like, then select the image and insert a Swap Image behavior to swap the image with example_one_after.jpg. Be sure to set the option to restore the image on mouseout.

j. Repeat Steps h and i for the Example Two image, using example_two_before.jpg for the original image and example_two_after.jpg for the swapped image.

k. Repeat Steps h and i for the Example Three image, using example_three_before.jpg for the original image and example_three_after.jpg for the swapped image.

l. Save your changes, save the images to the assets folder when prompted, preview the page in a browser, and point to each example image.

Advanced Challenge Exercise

- On the home page, use the Behaviors task pane to change the event for the Popup Message behavior so that it is triggered onmouseout.
- Save your changes, preview the page in a browser, then test the behavior by pointing your mouse to the link, then moving the pointer away.

m. Save your changes, preview the page in a browser, click the services link, close both browser windows, return to Expression Web, close the memories site, then exit Expression Web.

▼ INDEPENDENT CHALLENGE 3

This Independent Challenge requires an Internet connection.

The director for Technology for All loves the idea of using popup windows. In fact, he would like for you to use popup windows on every page of the Web site. While you agree that popup windows can be useful, you are curious as to whether using them presents any problems. You need to do some research to provide some insight on this issue.

a. Visit your favorite search engine and enter "popup window usability" as a search term.

b. Read at least two articles that you find.

c. Copy and paste information from each article into a word processing document.

d. Write a paragraph summarizing the pros and cons of using popup windows.

Advanced Challenge Exercise

■ Based on your readings, decide whether you think Technology for All should use popup windows on every page.

■ Write a paragraph explaining your position.

e. Add your name to the document, save it, then print it.

▼ REAL LIFE INDEPENDENT CHALLENGE

This assignment builds on the personal Web site you have worked on in previous units. In this project, you will add some behaviors to your site.

a. Review your site content and find at least two areas where it would be useful to add one of the behaviors available in Expression Web.

b. Add at least two behaviors to your site.

c. Save your changes, preview the pages you edited in a Web browser, then test the behaviors to make sure they work correctly.

d. Close the browser, close your site, then exit Expression Web.

▼ VISUAL WORKSHOP

Launch Expression Web, then open the ecotours Web site. Modify the contact page so that as soon as the contact page opens, your screen matches Figure K-22. To accomplish this, you need to add two behaviors to the page. (*Hint*: You may need to reorder the behaviors to achieve the results shown.) When you are finished, save your changes, close the Web site, then exit Expression Web.

FIGURE K-22

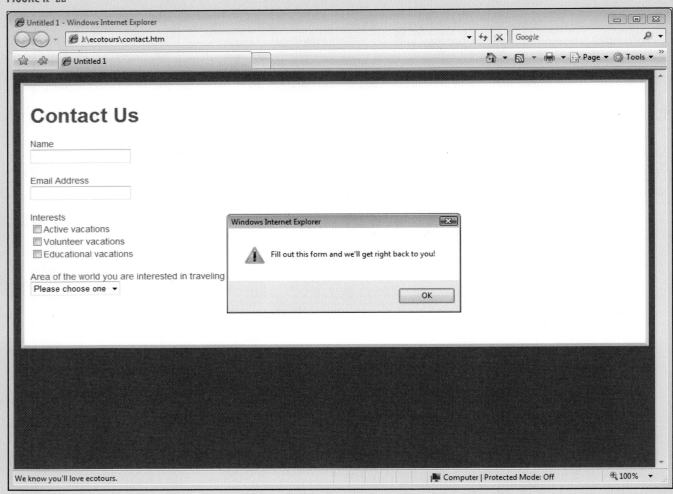

Using Code Tools

It's entirely possible to create a complete Web site in Expression Web without ever working in Code view. However, for making small changes or for ensuring exact placement of tags and page elements, working directly with the code can be more convenient than working solely in Design view. You can use the code tools in Expression Web to safely edit code, so there's no need to be intimidated by the thought of working "under the hood" of your pages. Also, the more you work with the code, the more comfortable you will feel and the better you will understand the HTML and CSS underpinnings of your Web pages.  Catalina has several small changes she would like you to make to the TradeWinds site. You decide to explore ways to make these edits using Expression Web's code tools.

OBJECTIVES

Work in Code view

Remove a tag

Use the Quick Tag Editor

Insert HTML comments

Use the Find and Replace feature

Use the Tag Properties task pane

Use code hyperlinks to locate
  CSS code

Use the CSS Properties task pane

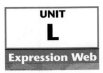
Working in Code View

Many features of Code view in Expression Web, such as color coding, line numbering, and code highlighting, make it easier for you to work directly with the code. You decide to learn more about Expression Web's Code view.

When working in Code view, it helps to understand:

- **Color coding**

  In Expression Web, HTML, CSS, and other types of code are highlighted to make it easier to locate and edit specific bits of code. Compare the two screens shown in Figures L-1 and L-2 to see how color coding improves the readability of the code. By default, as shown in Figure L-2, element names (such as p, h1, or div) are purple, attribute names (such as alt, style, or height) are red, and attribute values (such as numbers or colors) are blue.

- **Line numbering**

  A line number appears beside each line of code in Code view. Line numbers are referenced in error reports and in other code tools to refer you to specific areas of the code.

- **Code highlighting**

  If you are typing code directly into Code view, any code that is incorrect or not understood by Expression Web is highlighted in yellow and/or marked with a red wavy line. See Figure L-3.

- **HTML and white space**

  When you work in Design view, pressing [Enter] creates a paragraph element and a line of white space. When working directly in Code view, white space is ignored. This is because HTML itself ignores white space. This means you can add 50 spaces between words but only one will be reflected in the page when viewed in the browser. If you want to add whitespace that will appear in the browser window, such as line breaks and paragraph tags, you can either use Design view or add the tags themselves in Code view.

- **HTML tag order and nesting**

  Remember that in HTML, the content of an element is surrounded by an opening tag and a closing tag. A common cause of errors in Web page elements is a missing opening or closing tag.

Setting Code view options

You can fine-tune the Code view settings by clicking Tools on the menu bar, then clicking Page Editor Options. On the General tab of the Page Editor Options dialog box, the Code View Options section allows you to set an option to have code wrap in the window so you do not have to scroll back and forth to see it. You can also turn line numbering on and off, as well as the highlighting of invalid code. On the Color Coding tab, you can change which colors Expression Web uses to mark HTML elements, attribute names, attribute values, and other parts of the code. If you find yourself frequently working directly with the code, you may also find it useful to explore the options on the Code Formatting and IntelliSense tabs.

FIGURE L-1: HTML code with no color coding applied

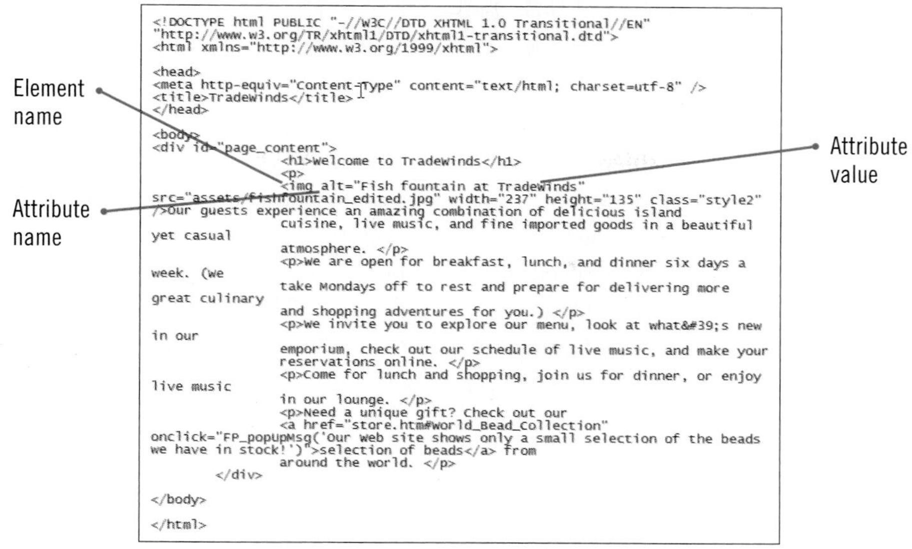

Element name

Attribute name

Attribute value

```
<!DOCTYPE html PUBLIC "-//W3C//DTD XHTML 1.0 Transitional//EN"
"http://www.w3.org/TR/xhtml1/DTD/xhtml1-transitional.dtd">
<html xmlns="http://www.w3.org/1999/xhtml">

<head>
<meta http-equiv="Content-Type" content="text/html; charset=utf-8" />
<title>Tradewinds</title>
</head>

<body>
<div id="page_content">
                <h1>Welcome to Tradewinds</h1>
                <p>
                <img alt="Fish fountain at Tradewinds"
src="assets/fishfountain_edited.jpg" width="237" height="135" class="style2"
/>Our guests experience an amazing combination of delicious island
                cuisine, live music, and fine imported goods in a beautiful
yet casual
                atmosphere. </p>
                <p>We are open for breakfast, lunch, and dinner six days a
week. (We
                take Mondays off to rest and prepare for delivering more
great culinary
                and shopping adventures for you.) </p>
                <p>We invite you to explore our menu, look at what&#39;s new
in our
                emporium, check out our schedule of live music, and make your
                reservations online. </p>
                <p>Come for lunch and shopping, join us for dinner, or enjoy
live music
                in our lounge. </p>
                <p>Need a unique gift? Check out our
                <a href="store.htm#world_Bead_Collection"
onclick="FP_popupMsg('Our web site shows only a small selection of the beads
we have in stock!')">selection of beads</a> from
                around the world. </p>
        </div>

</body>

</html>
```

FIGURE L-2: HTML code with color coding applied

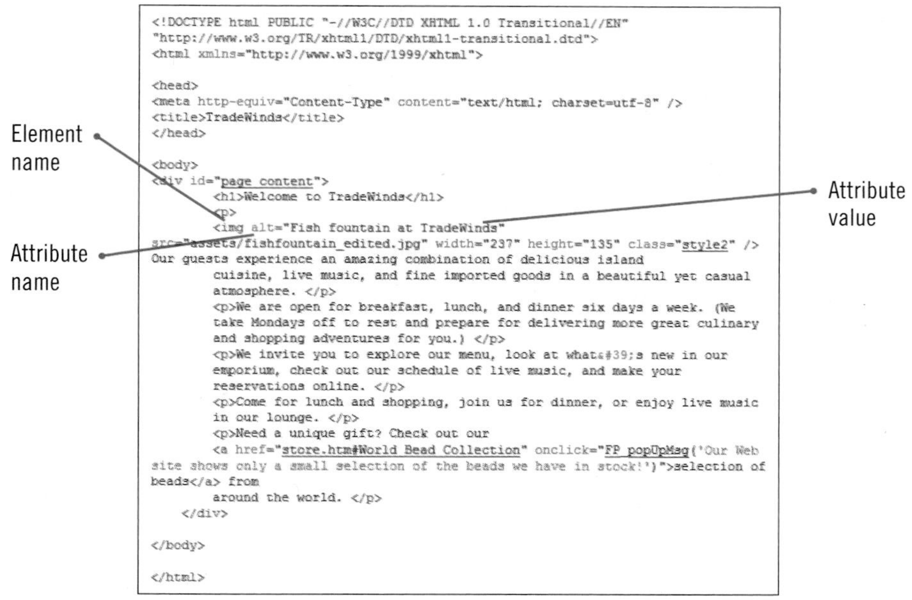

Element name

Attribute name

Attribute value

```
<!DOCTYPE html PUBLIC "-//W3C//DTD XHTML 1.0 Transitional//EN"
"http://www.w3.org/TR/xhtml1/DTD/xhtml1-transitional.dtd">
<html xmlns="http://www.w3.org/1999/xhtml">

<head>
<meta http-equiv="Content-Type" content="text/html; charset=utf-8" />
<title>TradeWinds</title>
</head>

<body>
<div id="page_content">
                <h1>Welcome to TradeWinds</h1>
                <p>
                <img alt="Fish fountain at TradeWinds"
src="assets/fishfountain_edited.jpg" width="237" height="135" class="style2" />
Our guests experience an amazing combination of delicious island
                cuisine, live music, and fine imported goods in a beautiful yet casual
                atmosphere. </p>
                <p>We are open for breakfast, lunch, and dinner six days a week. (We
                take Mondays off to rest and prepare for delivering more great culinary
                and shopping adventures for you.) </p>
                <p>We invite you to explore our menu, look at what&#39;s new in our
                emporium, check out our schedule of live music, and make your
                reservations online. </p>
                <p>Come for lunch and shopping, join us for dinner, or enjoy live music
                in our lounge. </p>
                <p>Need a unique gift? Check out our
                <a href="store.htm#World Bead Collection" onclick="FP_popupMsg('Our Web
site shows only a small selection of the beads we have in stock!')">selection of
beads</a> from
                around the world. </p>
        </div>

</body>

</html>
```

FIGURE L-3: Invalid code highlighted in Code view

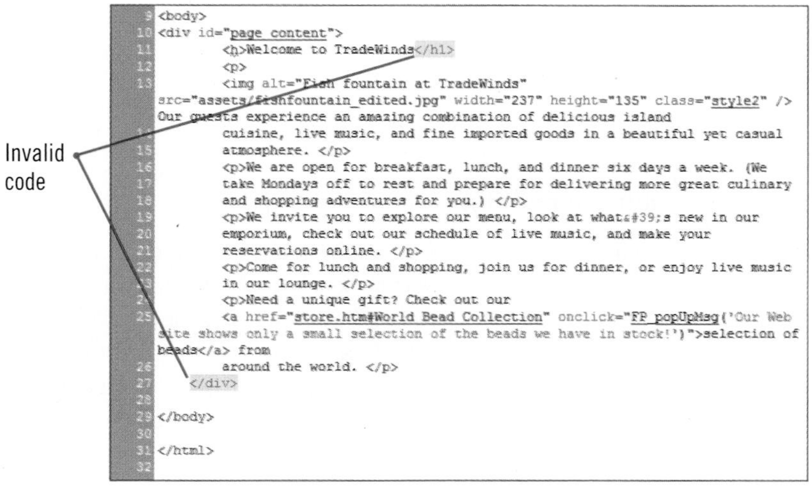

Invalid code

```
 9  <body>
10  <div id="page_content">
11                  <h>Welcome to TradeWinds</h1>
12                  <p>
13                  <img alt="Fish fountain at TradeWinds"
    src="assets/fishfountain_edited.jpg" width="237" height="135" class="style2" />
    Our guests experience an amazing combination of delicious island
                    cuisine, live music, and fine imported goods in a beautiful yet casual
15                  atmosphere. </p>
16                  <p>We are open for breakfast, lunch, and dinner six days a week. (We
17                  take Mondays off to rest and prepare for delivering more great culinary
18                  and shopping adventures for you.) </p>
19                  <p>We invite you to explore our menu, look at what&#39;s new in our
20                  emporium, check out our schedule of live music, and make your
21                  reservations online. </p>
22                  <p>Come for lunch and shopping, join us for dinner, or enjoy live music
                    in our lounge. </p>
24                  <p>Need a unique gift? Check out our
25                  <a href="store.htm#World Bead Collection" onclick="FP_popupMsg('Our Web
    site shows only a small selection of the beads we have in stock!')">selection of
    beads</a> from
26                  around the world. </p>
27          </div>
28
29  </body>
30
31  </html>
32
```

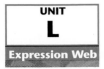

Removing a Tag

On occasion, you may find you need to remove an HTML tag from a portion of content. The most straight-forward way to do this is to open the page in Code view and delete the tag manually. However, by deleting directly in Code view without using any of the code tools, you run the risk of accidentally removing more or less code than you intended. This can cause everything from minor display flaws to major page structure problems. By using Code view in combination with the quick tag selector's Remove tag feature, you can safely remove HTML tags from your content. The Remove tag feature removes both opening and closing tags while leaving the content between the tags intact. ▰▰▰▰▰ Catalina pointed out that the é at the end of Café in the heading on the home page has a font that is different from the other text in the heading. She has asked you to fix this. To find out the cause, you view that text and its accompanying code in Code view.

STEPS

1. **Launch Expression Web, open the tradewinds site, then open the home page**
   Notice the é in the word Café in the heading is displayed in a different font.

QUICK TIP

Expression Web added the span tag and style when you inserted the é symbol.

2. **Select the word Café in the page heading that reads Welcome to TradeWinds Café and Emporium, then click the Show Code View button**
   The page is displayed in Code view, as shown in Figure L-4. The é has a span tag with a class attribute applied to it. This causes the é to be displayed in a Times New Roman font. You want to remove the span tag.

TROUBLE

Your quick tag selector may display a different style number on the span tag.

3. **Click anywhere in the span tag, point to the span tag in the quick tag selector, click the selector list arrow, then click Remove Tag, as shown in Figure L-5**
   The span tag is removed, but the é, which is the content of the tag, remains, as shown in Figure L-6.

4. **Click the Show Split View button**
   Notice the é now is displayed in the same font as the other heading text.

5. **Save your changes**

Creating a larger Split view with multiple monitors

If you like working in Split view, but find you need more room to work in each pane, you can open your page in two Expression Web windows at once, and work in Design view in one window and Code view in the other. If you have two monitors connected to your computer, you can view the window displaying the Design view of your page on one monitor, and the window displaying the Code view of the page on the other monitor. To do this, open a page in Expression Web, click Window on the menu bar, then click Open in New Window. You will now have two editing windows open and can use the Design view of the page in one window and the Code view of the page in the other window. If you don't have multiple monitors, you can open two windows and use [Alt][Tab] to switch between them, but you won't be able to see both the Code and the Design views at once.

FIGURE L-4: Home page in Code view with Café text selected

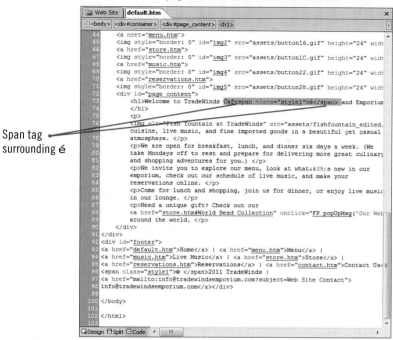

Span tag
surrounding é

FIGURE L-5: Span tag menu in quick tag selector

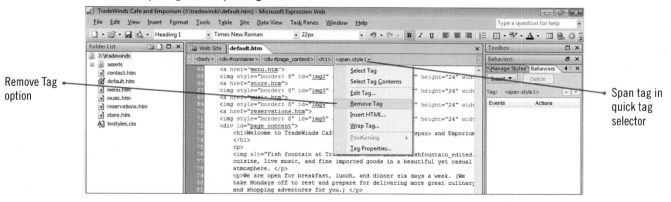

Remove Tag
option

Span tag in
quick tag
selector

FIGURE L-6: Code after removal of span tag

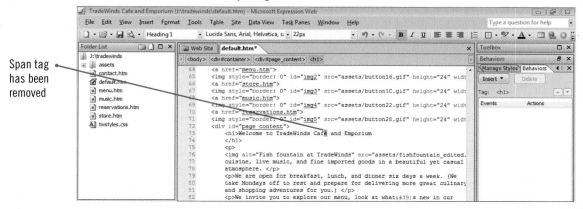

Span tag
has been
removed

Using the Quick Tag Editor

The Quick Tag Editor allows you to quickly edit an existing HTML tag, wrap a new HTML tag around content, or insert HTML into your page. You can also perform these tasks directly in Code view but, like using the quick tag selector, using the editor provides some safeguards against accidentally deleting important code from your pages. It's also usually faster than looking through Code view and editing manually. Catalina wants you to mark up the menu page with some subheadings to break up the text and make it easier to read.

STEPS

1. Open the menu page, click the Show Code View button to display the page in Code view, then click anywhere in the text `Salads &amp; Starters`

The insertion point is positioned in the tag, as shown in Figure L-7.

> **QUICK TIP**
> You can also press [CTRL][Q] to open the Quick Tag Editor.

2. Click Edit on the menu bar, then click Quick Tag Editor

In the Quick Tag Editor window, you can edit the selected HTML tag, wrap a new tag around the existing tag and content, or insert a new bit of HTML into the page. To indicate which action you want to take, you click the list arrow on the left side of the window. You want to edit the paragraph tag and make it an h2 tag instead. To accomplish this, you need to edit the tag that appears in the Quick Tag Editor window.

> **QUICK TIP**
> You can also press [Enter] to accept the change and close the window.

3. Click the list arrow, click Edit Tag, click between `p` **and** `>` **in the window, press [Backspace], then type** `h2`

4. Compare your screen to Figure L-8, then click the Enter button ☑

Both the opening and closing p tags have been replaced by h2 tags.

> **QUICK TIP**
> The Quick Tag Editor can be used in any view. This means you can use it to quickly insert HTML code while working in Design view without having to switch to Code view.

5. Click the Show Split View button

Notice the text is now formatted as a heading rather than as a regular paragraph.

6. Click the Show Code View button

7. Scroll down if necessary, click anywhere in the word `Entrees`, **then repeat Steps 2 through 4**

8. Click anywhere in the text `Desserts &amp; Coffees`, **then repeat Steps 2 through 4**

9. Click the Show Design View button, compare your screen to Figure L-9, then save your changes

---

Understanding character entities

The characters that can be used as part of HTML are limited to a set called the **standard ASCII character set**. (This is the same set of characters you see on the keys of your keyboard.) Characters outside this set as well as certain characters that are reserved for code (such as <, &, or ") are replaced with a **character entity** in the HTML code. For example, when you type & in Design view, Expression Web inserts the character entity & into the HTML code. The browser then interprets the character entity and displays it as an ampersand. Many characters also have equivalent **numeric entities** that yield the same results. A nonbreaking space, for example, can be written as   or .You do not need to know which character entries or numeric entries correspond to which characters, because Expression Web automatically converts them. If you're interested, though, just type "character entity" into your favorite search engine to access one of the many reference charts available online.

FIGURE L-7: Insertion point inserted in the text Salads & Starters

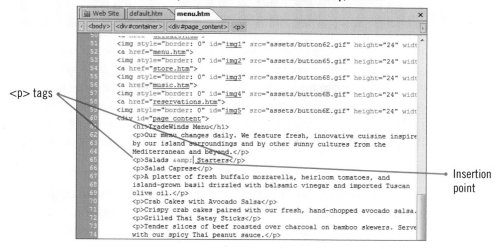

<p> tags

Insertion point

FIGURE L-8: Quick Tag Editor window with tag edited

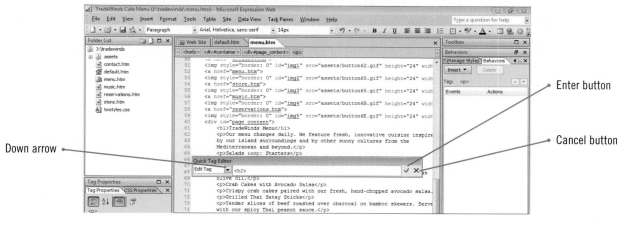

Down arrow

Enter button

Cancel button

FIGURE L-9: Level 2 headings in Design view

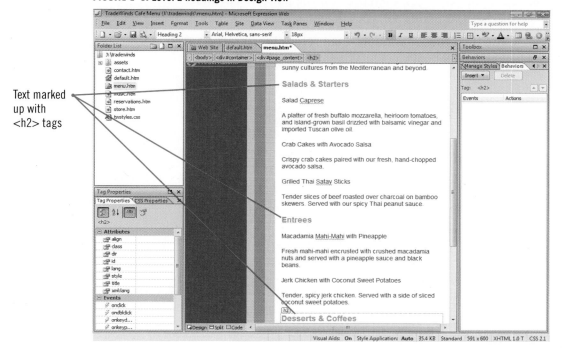

Text marked up with <h2> tags

Expression Web

Inserting HTML Comments

Any text or code surrounded by the HTML comment tag is displayed in Code view but not in the browser or in Design view. It's a good idea to use comments liberally in your code so that if other designers need to work on your pages in the future, they can use your comments to guide them. Comments can also be helpful reminders for you if you return to a site you have not worked on in several months. ▰▰▰ You decide to add comments to the menu page to mark where the navigation buttons begin and end in the code. Then you and other designers can easily understand the page structure in the future.

STEPS

TROUBLE

Be sure to click after this code's closing angle bracket and not within the code.

1. **Working in Design view, click the home button on the menu page, click div#left_col on the quick tag selector, then click the Show Code View button**

   The entire div element is selected and highlighted in Code view, as shown in Figure L-10. This helps guide your placement of the HTML comments.

2. **Click just after the code `<div id="left_col">` on the top line of the selected code**

   The navigation buttons begin here in the code. The comment will be inserted wherever your cursor is placed.

QUICK TIP

Even though comments don't show up in a Web browser, they are not entirely hidden. Visitors can see them if they view the page's source code in a browser.

3. **Click Edit on the menu bar, point to Code View, then click Insert Comment**

   An empty comment tag is inserted. The comment tag looks different from other HTML tags, but the principle is the same. The element is opened by a <! - - tag and closed by a - -> tag.

4. **Type Navigation buttons start here**

   The text is inserted in the comment tag, as shown in Figure L-11. Expression Web displays comments in Code view as gray text.

QUICK TIP

You can also move large pieces of code and content inside a comment to make it invisible on the page. This can be helpful if you want to temporarily hide something on the page but think you might want to make it visible again later.

5. **Click just before the code `<div id="page_content">` near line 60, click Edit on the menu bar, point to Code View, then click Insert Comment**

6. **Type Navigation buttons end here**

   Compare your screen to Figure L-12.

7. **Click the Show Design View button**

   The comments do not appear in Design view.

8. **Save your changes, then preview the page in a browser**

   The comments also do not appear in the browser.

9. **Close the browser window, then return to Expression Web**

FIGURE L-10: left_col div selected in Code view

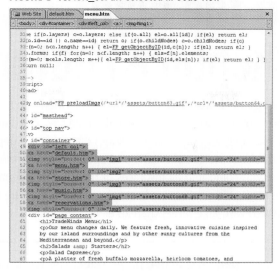

FIGURE L-11: First comment inserted in menu page

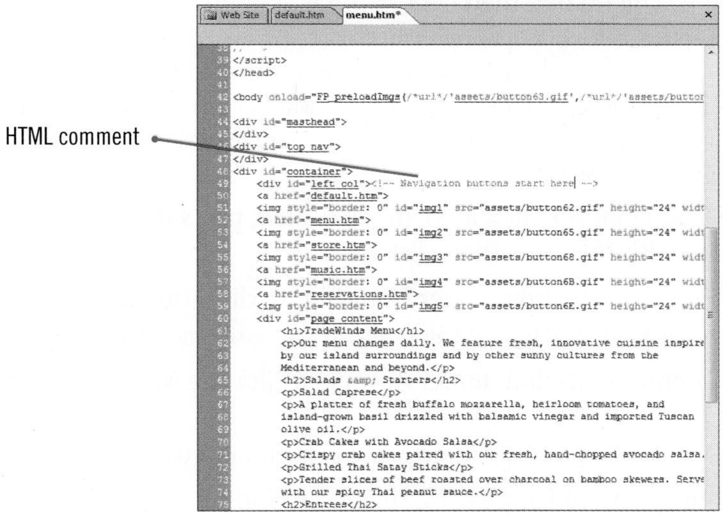

HTML comment

FIGURE L-12: Both HTML comments added to menu page

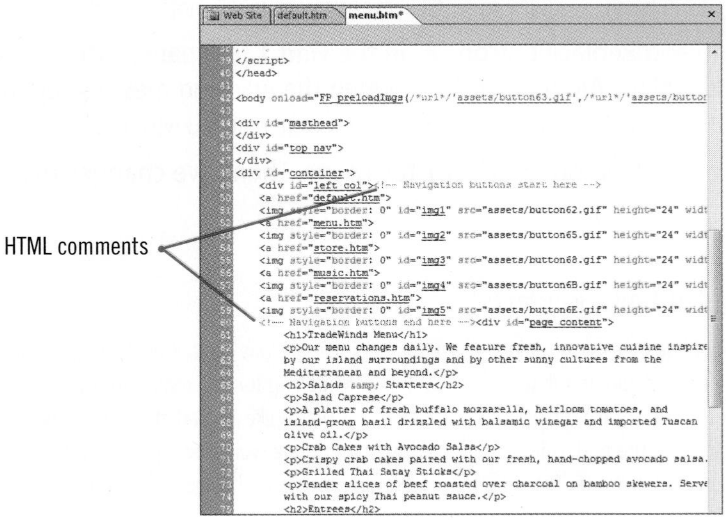

HTML comments

Using the Find and Replace Feature

The **Find and Replace feature** is extremely useful when you're working with text or code. You can search for any piece of text or code in one file, multiple files, or an entire site, and replace it with different text or code. For example, let's say a client changes the name of a department. Looking through each page of a site for any references to the old name and updating it with the new one could take hours. But using Find and Replace, you could find all instances of the outdated department name and replace it with the new name in one step. ▰▰▰▰ Catalina has asked you to make sure that on the TradeWinds site, the word Café is always spelled with an é rather than an e.

STEPS

1. **Make the home page the active page, select the word** Café **in the Welcome to TradeWinds Café and Emporium heading, click the** Show Code View button, **click** Edit **on the menu bar, then click** Copy

QUICK TIP

To replace the lower-case instances of the word cafe, you would need to perform the find and replace twice, once for the capitalized word and once for the lowercase word.

2. **Click** Edit **on the menu bar, then click** Replace

The Find and Replace dialog box opens with the Replace tab in front and with the copied text entered in the Find what text box. To use Find and Replace effectively, you need to think ahead about exactly what you want to find and exactly what you want to replace it with. In this case, some instances of the word cafe in the Web site are capitalized and some are not. You only want to replace the capitalized instances of the word Cafe, not the lowercase instances.

3. **Click in the** Find what text box after the text Café, **press** [Backspace], **type e, right-click in the** Replace with text box, **then click** Paste

4. **In the Search options section, under Find Where, click the** All pages option button

This tells Expression Web to find the text Cafe in all pages of the site, including pages that are not currently open.

QUICK TIP

If the Match case check box does not contain a check mark, case is ignored.

5. **In the Search options section, under Advanced click the** Match case check box **to add a check mark**

Checking the Match case option tells Expression Web to only find occurrences of Cafe and not of cafe.

6. **Compare your screen to Figure L-13, then click** Find All

The Find 1 task pane opens under the editing window, as shown in Figure L-14. It lists each page on which the term was found, the line number in which the term is located, and a snippet of the surrounding text and code. It's a good idea to do a Find All before a Replace All just to make sure you're not inadvertently changing something that shouldn't be changed. If you replace text in a page that is not currently open, you cannot undo it.

QUICK TIP

You can choose to have the results open in either the Find 1 or Find 2 task panes. You could also perform two searches and have one open in each so you can compare them.

7. **Click the** Find and Replace button ▶ **in the Find 1 task pane, click the** All Pages option button, **click** Replace All, **then click** Yes **when the warning message opens**

The Find 1 task pane lists all occurrences of Cafe that were replaced with Café.

8. **Click the** Close button **on the Find 1 task pane, then save changes to all pages**

Exercising caution when using Find and Replace

Find and replace is a powerful tool, but it should be used with caution. If you don't do a Find All before a Replace All, you could find that your replacements have unintended consequences. For example, to ensure that café was always spelled with the é on the end, one strategy could be to find the text afe and replace it with afé. That way, whether café was capitalized or not wouldn't matter; Expression Web is only looking for and replacing the end of the word. At first glance, this seems like a smart strategy. However, this means that all occurrences of safe would be replaced with safé. Always do a Find All and review the results before you complete a replacement.

FIGURE L-13: Completed Find and Replace dialog box

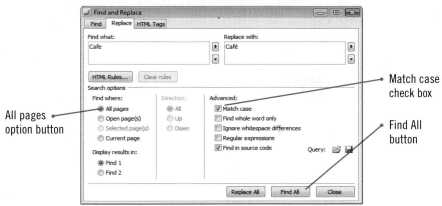

All pages option button

Match case check box

Find All button

FIGURE L-14: Results of Find All displayed in Find 1 task pane

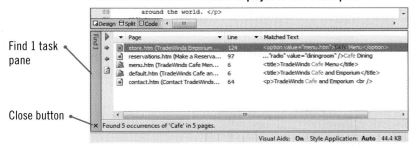

Find 1 task pane

Close button

TABLE L-1: Commonly used options on the Replace tab

option	specifies...
Find what	The text you want to find
Replace with	The text with which you want to replace the found text
HTML Rules button	A complex set of conditions for searching and replacing HTML
Find where	Where to perform the find—in all pages in the site, all open pages, selected pages, or the current page
Display results in	Whether to show results in the Find 1 or Find 2 task pane, so you can compare two sets of results
Direction	Whether to search above the cursor's current placement in the page, below it, or both
Match case	To find only those instances where the case matches the case of the text in the Find what text box
Find whole word only	To ignore text found that is part of a word rather than a whole word
Ignore white space differences	Find similar text even if the white space is different; used mostly for code and tag searches
Regular expressions	Use search terms to find patterns rather than just exact matches
Find in source code	To search in source code rather than just the text visible in Design view
Query	To save the current options as a reusable query or to open a previously saved query
Replace All	Replace all found instances
Replace	Replace next occurrence found
Find Next	Find next occurrence
Find All	Find all occurrences
Close	Close the dialog box

Using the Tag Properties Task Pane

The Tag Properties task pane provides easy access to all attributes of a selected HTML tag. All of these attributes can also be changed by other means, by opening the properties dialog box for that tag, for example. But the Tag Properties provides a shortcut to these properties. ▰▰▰▰ You want to change the alternate text attribute on the photo of the fish fountain on the home page. You could right-click the image in Design view and click Picture Properties, but you decide to try using the Tag Properties task pane.

STEPS

1. **Make the home page the active page if necessary, click Show Split View, then click the fish fountain photo in the Design view pane**

   See Figure L-15. The picture is highlighted in Design view, and the code for the image is highlighted in Code view.

2. **If necessary, click the Tag Properties tab to make it the active task pane**

   The task pane shows the attributes for the selected image tag. Attributes can be sorted using the buttons along the top of the task pane. You can choose to sort the attributes by category as an A–Z list. Clicking the Show Tag Properties button opens the properties dialog box associated with the selected element. See Table L-2 for all options available on this task pane.

3. **In the Tag Properties task pane, click in the text box to the right of the alt attribute**

   To change an attribute, you click in the text box to the right of the attribute name. Clicking in the text box selects all the text in the text box so that you can replace it.

QUICK TIP

Remember, you can drag the border between the right edge of the task pane and the editing window to expand the task pane and make editing easier.

4. **Press [Delete], type Exotic fish fountain, compare your screen to Figure L-16, then press [Enter]**

   The alternate text changes in the code as well, as shown in Figure L-17.

5. **Click the Show Tag Properties button 🔲 on the Tag Properties task pane**

   The Picture Properties dialog box opens. The edited alternate text is reflected there, too.

6. **Click OK to close the Picture Properties dialog box, then save your changes**

TABLE L-2: Tag Properties task pane options

button	name	function
	Show categorized list	Shows properties organized by categories, such as Attributes and Events
	Show alphabetized list	Shows properties organized alphabetically
	Show set properties on top	Shows properties that have had attributes specified at the top of the list
	Show tag properties	Opens the related dialog box to show properties for the tag

FIGURE L-15: Home page in Split view with image selected

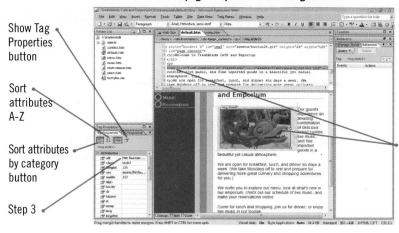

Show Tag
Properties
button

Sort
attributes
A-Z

Sort attributes
by category
button

Step 3

Image is
selected in
Code and
Design views

FIGURE L-16: Edited alt attribute

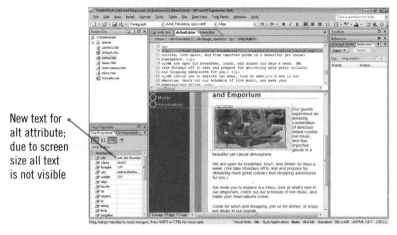

New text for
alt attribute;
due to screen
size all text
is not visible

FIGURE L-17: New alt text reflected in Code view

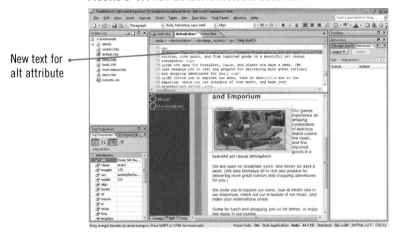

New text for
alt attribute

Locating text and code in Code view

It can be tricky sometimes to locate what you're looking for in Code
view. To make it easier, here are some tips:

- To quickly locate text, switch to Design view, select the text
  there, then switch back to Code view; or work in Split view.
- To quickly select or locate a div, use the quick tag selector at the
  top of the editing window.

- To select other HTML elements such as headings or paragraphs,
  switch to Design view, click anywhere in the text contained by
  that element, then click the tab on the visual aid.
- To find any text or code quickly, use the tools on the Find tab in
  the Find and Replace dialog box to locate text or code on the
  current page.

Using Code Hyperlinks to Locate CSS Code

When working in Code view, you can quickly jump from code in the page to the corresponding style rule in the external style sheet. This makes it quick and easy to go from viewing the HTML code to editing the CSS code. To take advantage of this feature, you press [Ctrl] while clicking a code hyperlink. This opens the style sheet file and highlights the corresponding style rule. Looking at the Code view on the menu page reminds you that Catalina wants to make the text size in the footer slightly larger. You decide to use a code hyperlink to locate the #footer style and edit it.

STEPS

QUICK TIP

When you return to an opened file, it always remains open in the view you last used.

1. **Make the menu page the active page, click the Show Code View button if necessary, scroll to the bottom of the page, then locate the code** `<div id="footer">`
   See Figure L-18. Code hyperlinks are blue and underlined.

2. **Press and hold [Ctrl], click the code footer, then release [Ctrl]**
   The twstyles.css page opens in the editing window in a new tab, as shown in Figure L-19. The #footer rule is selected.

3. **On the font-size line, click between** 0 **and** p
   You want to change the size from 10 to 11.

4. **Press [Backspace], type 1, then compare your screen to Figure L-20**
   The style rule now specifies a text size of 11 pixels instead of 10.

5. **Save your changes**

QUICK TIP

Use the tabs at the top of the editing window to return to the menu page.

6. **Make the menu page the active page, click Show Design View, note the change in footer text size, then click Show Code View**

FIGURE L-18: Menu page in Code view

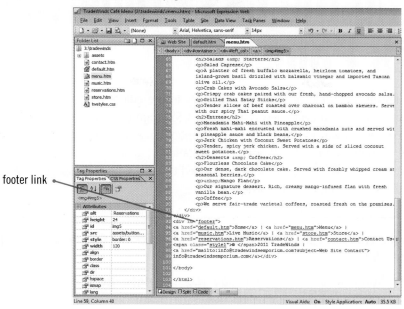

footer link

FIGURE L-19: CSS file with #footer style rule selected

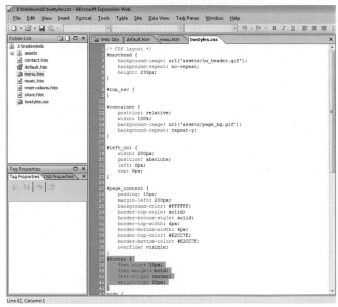

FIGURE L-20: #footer style with font-size edited

font-size
is now 11

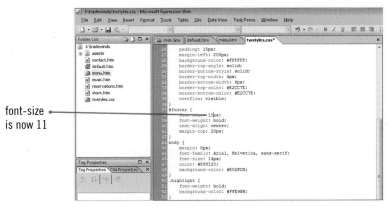

Using the CSS Properties Task Pane

In the last lesson, you modified CSS code directly in the editing window. A safer way to change CSS properties quickly while in Code view is to use the CSS Properties task pane. The CSS Properties task pane provides a convenient way to change all possible options in a style rule without opening the Modify Styles dialog box. It's similar to the Tag Properties task pane but allows you to edit CSS style rules rather than HTML tag attributes.  Catalina has requested that there be more space below the footer text. You add a bottom margin to the #footer style rule.

STEPS

QUICK TIP

You can also use code hyperlinks to locate and select the style rule.

QUICK TIP

You can drag the border between the property and text box columns to enlarge your view of the text box.

1. **Make the twstyles.css file the active tab, then click the CSS Properties tab to make it the active task pane**

2. **In the editing window, click the code #footer near line 37**
   The CSS Properties task pane now lists #footer as the current rule, as shown in Figure L-21.

3. **In the CSS Properties task pane, scroll down to the Box category, then click in the text box to the right of margin-bottom**

4. **Type 20px, then press [Enter]**
   A new line has been added to the #footer rule in the CSS file to include this new property, as shown in Figure L-22.

5. **Save your changes to the twstyles.css file**

6. **Make the home page active, then click the Show Design View button**

7. **Click inside the footer, then click the div#footer tab on the visual aid**
   See Figure L-23. Note the diagonal stripes at the bottom of the visual aid, indicating a bottom margin.

8. **Save changes to all open pages, preview the home page in a browser, use the site navigation to view the other pages in the site, then close the browser window**

9. **Return to Expression Web, close the tradewinds site, then exit Expression Web**

Using different methods to accomplish the same task

Expression Web is such a flexible program that you can choose many ways to perform the same task. For example, to modify an existing rule, you can edit the style sheet directly, use the CSS Properties task pane, or right-click the style in the Apply Styles or Manage Styles task pane and choose Modify Style. As you work in Expression Web, you will learn which ways of working suit your style and will naturally gravitate toward those methods. Experiment with the various methods until you settle on a workflow that's right for you.

FIGURE L-21: CSS Properties task pane displaying #footer properties

CSS Properties tab

#footer is current rule

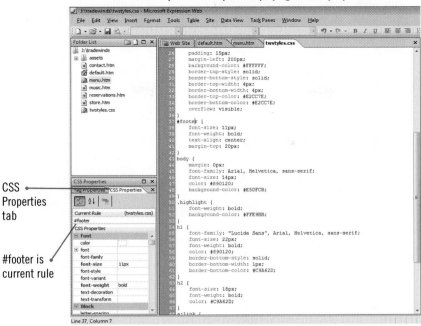

FIGURE L-22: #footer style with margin-bottom set to 20px

A new line has been added to the #footer style

margin-bottom is now 20px

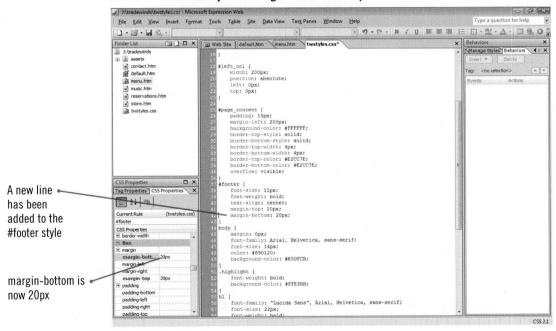

FIGURE L-23: Footer in Design view with visual aid selected

Visual aid indicates a bottom margin has been applied

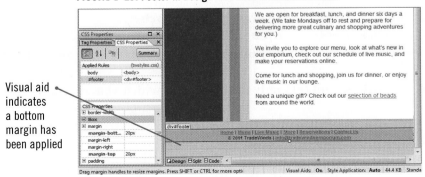

Practice

▼ CONCEPTS REVIEW

Refer to Figure L-24 to answer the following questions:

FIGURE L-24

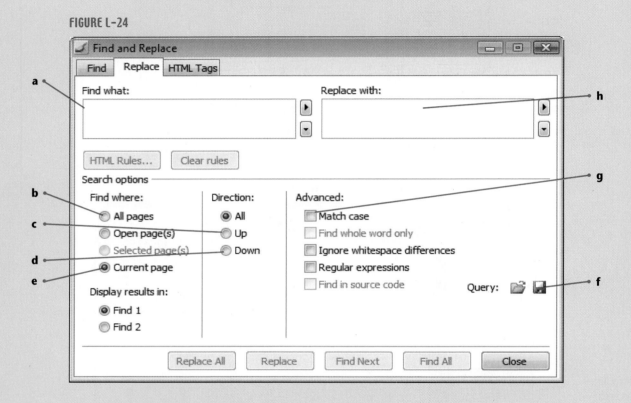

1. Which element would you click to find text with the same case as the text in the Find what box?
2. Which element would you click to enter text you want Expression Web to use as a substitute for the found text?
3. Which element would you click to find text only if it occurs after the current location of the insertion point?
4. Which element would you click to find text only if it occurs before the current location of the insertion point?
5. Which element would you click to find text in every page of a Web site?
6. Which element would you click to enter text you want Expression Web to find?
7. Which element would you click to save the currently selected options so you can use them to find text in the future?
8. Which element would you click to find text only in the page in which you are currently working?

Match each term with the statement that best describes it.

9. **Character entities**
10. **HTML comment tag**
11. **Code hyperlink**
12. **CSS Properties task pane**
13. **Tag Properties task pane**

a. Provides access to edit attributes of a selected HTML tag
b. Provides one-click access to specific code in a style sheet
c. Contents are visible in the HTML code but not when viewed normally in a browser
d. Provides access to edit properties of a selected style rule
e. Codes that are used to specify characters outside the standard HTML character set

Select the best answer from the list of choices.

14. **& and   are examples of what?**
    a. HTML tags
    b. Attributes
    c. Character entities
    d. Elements
15. **HTML characters are limited to:**
    a. The Roman alphabet.
    b. The standard ASCII character set.
    c. Letters, numbers, and underscores.
    d. Character entities.
16. **What feature allows you to locate all occurrences of a word or phrase and update it with new text?**
    a. Quick Tag Editor
    b. Code hyperlinks
    c. Tag Properties task pane
    d. Find and Replace
17. **If you wanted to easily change some properties in the #masthead style rule, you could use:**
    a. The CSS Properties task pane.
    b. The Tag Properties task pane.
    c. The Quick Tag Editor.
    d. Find and Replace.
18. **If you wanted to add HTML code to a page while working in Design view, you could use:**
    a. The CSS Properties task pane.
    b. Code hyperlinks.
    c. The Quick Tag Editor.
    d. Find and Replace.
19. **If you want to remove a tag from a piece of content, you could use:**
    a. The CSS Properties task pane.
    b. The quick tag selector.
    c. The Quick Tag Editor.
    d. The Tag Properties task pane.
20. **The line numbers in Code view are used:**
    a. To assist in locating specific pieces of code.
    b. To rearrange code.
    c. To organize code.
    d. As reference when writing JavaScript code.

▼ SKILLS REVIEW

1. **Remove a tag.**
   a. Launch Expression Web, open the careers site, then open the home page.
   b. Click the Show Design View button if necessary, then select the © at the bottom of the page.
   c. Switch to Code view, click in the span tag surrounding the ©, point to the span tag in the quick tag selector, click the down arrow, then click Remove Tag.
   d. View page in Split view, then save your changes.

2. **Use the quick tag editor.**
   a. Open the about page, then switch to Code view.
   b. Click in the text **Ken Lee, Chief Executive Officer**.
   c. Click Edit on the menu bar, then click Quick Tag Editor.
   d. Select Edit Tag in the drop down menu, then delete the p between the angle brackets (< >), type **h2** between the angle brackets, then click the Enter button.
   e. Click in the text **Tina Russo, Chief Technology Officer**, then repeat Steps c and d to edit the <p> tag to **<h2>**.
   f. Click in the text **Nelson Ferraz, VP of Marketing**, then repeat Steps c and d to edit the <p> tag to **<h2>**.
   g. View the page in Design view, then save your changes.

3. **Insert HTML comments.**
   a. On the about page, click in the text **Our Management team**, click the h2 tag in the quick tag selector, then switch to Code view.
   b. Click just before the selected code <h2>Our Management Team</h2>.
   c. Click Edit on the menu bar, point to Code View, then click Insert Comment.
   d. Type **Management bios begin**.
   e. Click after the code several area non-profit organizations. </p>, click Edit on the menu bar, point to Code View, then click Insert Comment.
   f. Type **Management bios end**.
   g. Click in the second paragraph before the code out from your career, select the word out, then press [Delete].
   h. View the page in Design view, then save your changes.
   i. Preview the page in a browser, close the browser window, and return to Expression Web.

4. **Use the Find and Replace feature.**
   a. Click Edit on the menu bar, then click Replace.
   b. Select and delete the text in the Find what text box, then type **tutorials**.
   c. Select and delete the text in the Replace with text box, then type **videos**.
   d. Click the All pages option button, then click Find All.
   e. Click the Find and Replace icon on the Find 1 task pane.
   f. Click the All pages option button, click Replace All, then click Yes.
   g. Close the Find 1 task pane, then save changes to all open pages.

5. **Use the Tag Properties task pane.**
   a. Make the home page the active page, view the page in Split view, then click the photo of the man.
   b. Click the Tag Properties task pane, if necessary, to display this task pane.
   c. Click in the box to the right of alt, delete the text, type **Satisfied Customer**, then press [Enter].
   d. Click the Show Tag Properties button.
   e. Click OK to close the dialog box, then save your changes.

6. **Use code hyperlinks to locate CSS code.**
   a. View the home page in Code view, then scroll down and find the code <div id="footer">.
   b. Press and hold [Ctrl] while clicking the word footer.
   c. Change the padding-top value from 15px to **25px**.
   d. Save the change to the style sheet, make the home page the active page, then view the home page in Design view.

▼ SKILLS REVIEW (CONTINUED)

7. Use the CSS Properties task pane.

a. Make the cgstyles.css file the active tab, then click the CSS Properties tab to make it the active task pane.

b. In the editing window, click the code `.testimonial`.

c. In the CSS Properties task pane, scroll to font-weight, click in the box to the right, click the down arrow, then click Bold.

d. Save your changes to the cgstyles.css file.

e. Make the home page the active page, then view it in Design view.

f. Save changes to all open pages, preview the home page in a browser, compare your screen to Figure L-25, use the site navigation to view the other pages in the site, then close the browser window.

g. Return to Expression Web, close the careers site, then exit Expression Web.

FIGURE L-25

▼ INDEPENDENT CHALLENGE 1

In this project you continue your work on the ConnectUp Web site. Tiffany has asked for some changes to the site, such as making the company contact information stand out more on the contact page, replacing the word "professional" on the site with the word "business," and making the text size in the footer slightly larger. You also have some clean-up you would like to finish on the site, such as removing unnecessary span tags and adding some comments to the code.

a. Launch Expression Web, open the connectup Web site, then open the contact page.

b. In Design view, select the © in the footer, then switch to Code view.

c. Click within the span tag that surrounds the ©, then use the quick tag selector to remove the span tag.

d. Click in the paragraph that starts **ConnectUp 481 Broad Street**, then use the Quick Tag Editor to change the p tag to an **h2** tag. (*Hint*: You may have to choose Edit Tag in the drop-down menu.)

e. Switch to Design view, review the change, then save your changes.

f. Open the joinup page, click in the form, click the form tag on the quick tag selector, switch to Code view, insert an HTML comment before the code
   `<form method="post" action="">`, then type **JoinUp form begins**.

g. Insert an HTML comment after the code `</form>` and type **JoinUp form ends**.

h. View the page in Design view, then save your changes.

i. Open the Find and Replace dialog box, then find all occurrences of the word **professional** in all pages.

j. Review the results, then open the Find and Replace dialog box and replace all occurrences of the word **professional** with the word **business**. (*Hint*: Make sure the All pages option button is selected.) Close the Find 1 task pane.

k. Make the joinup page the active page, then switch to Code view. Find the code `<div id="footer">`, then press [Ctrl] while clicking it to open the custyles.css page at the location of the #footer rule.

l. Using the CSS Properties task pane, change the font size in the #footer rule from 10px to **12px**.

m. Save the changes to the custyles.css file.

n. Open the faq page, view the page in Split view, then select the Got Questions? image.

▼ INDEPENDENT CHALLENGE 1 (CONTINUED)

o. Click the Tag Properties task pane, click to the right of the alt property, then change the text to **Got Questions? We've Got Answers!**.

p. Save your changes to all pages, preview the contact page in a browser, compare your screen to Figure L-26, then use the site's navigation buttons to view the other pages.

q. Close the browser window, return to Expression Web, close the site, then exit Expression Web.

FIGURE L-26

▼ INDEPENDENT CHALLENGE 2

In this project you continue your work on the Memories Restored Web site.

a. Launch Expression Web, then open the memories Web site.

b. Open the our work page, then use the quick tag selector to remove the span tag that surrounds the ©.

c. Also on this page, use the Quick Tag Editor to change the tags surrounding the text **Example One**, **Example Two**, and **Example Three** from p tags to **h2** tags. View in Design view and save your changes.

d. Open the contact page and, working in Code view, insert HTML comments to mark where the contact form begins and ends. (*Hint*: Use the <form> and </form> tags to guide you. You can also work in Design view to select the form first to make it easier to find.) Preview in Design view and save your changes.

e. Open the home page, then, working in Split view, use the Tag Properties task pane to change the alternate text for the photo on the home page from **Couple in antique car** to **One of our successful restorations**. Save your changes.

f. Open the testimonials page, then use a code hyperlink to locate the .testimonialname style rule in the mrstyles.css file.

g. Use the CSS Properties task pane to set the font-style property on the .testimonialname style rule to **italic**. Save your changes to the mrstyles.css file, then view the testimonials page in Design view.

h. Use the Find and Replace feature to replace the term **specialists** with the the word **technicians** on all pages in the site. Save your changes to all open pages, then close the Find 1 task pane when you are finished.

Advanced Challenge Exercise

■ Make the home page the active page.

■ Use the Find and Replace feature to replace the term **photo** with the term **photograph** only on the home page. Do not replace the term Photo. (*Hint*: You will need to select options under the Find Where and the Advanced sections of the Find and Replace dialog box.)

■ Close the Find 1 task pane, save your changes, then view the page in Design view.

▼ INDEPENDENT CHALLENGE 2 (CONTINUED)

i. Preview the home page in a browser, use the site's navigation buttons to view all other pages in the site, then close the browser window.

j. Return to Expression Web, close the memories site, then exit Expression Web.

▼ INDEPENDENT CHALLENGE 3

This Independent Challenge requires an Internet connection.

Over lunch, you and your techie friend (who works as a Web designer) were discussing Expression Web's code tools. During the conversation, your friend mentioned HTML code validation tools. Intrigued, and thinking that validation tools might be useful in redesigning the Technology for All Web site, you decide to research this topic. You want to prepare some information describing validation tools and the purpose they serve, so that you can introduce this topic to the Technology for All director.

a. Enter the phrase **importance of valid code** into your favorite search engine.

b. From the search results, choose at least three articles that explain why valid code is or is not important. See if you can find one that argues it is and one that says it is not.

c. Write at least one paragraph explaining what valid code is and a second paragraph explaining whether or not you think valid code is important.

Advanced Challenge Exercise

- Type the words **HTML code validator** into your favorite search engine.
- Visit at least three of the validating tools and read the instructions for them.
- Write at least one paragraph describing whether you think these tools do a good job explaining their purpose and how to use them. Include any suggestions you have for improving the way they present their information to make them more user friendly.

d. Add your name to the document, save it, and print it.

▼ REAL LIFE INDEPENDENT CHALLENGE

This assignment builds on the personal Web site you have worked on in previous units. In this project, you will use Expression Web's code tools to make some changes of your choice to your site.

a. Use the quick tag selector to remove at least one set of HTML tags on a page.

b. Insert at least two HTML comments in a page.

c. Use the Quick Tag Editor to edit or insert at least one HTML tag into your site's code. (*Hint*: You may need to use the list arrow to change the selection in the drop-down menu.)

d. Use the Find and Replace dialog box to search for and make some text substitutions in your site.

e. Use a code hyperlink to locate and edit at least one style rule.

f. Use the CSS Properties task pane to edit at least one property in a style rule.

g. Use the Tag Properties task pane to edit an attribute of at least one HTML element.

h. Save your changes, then preview all your site's pages in a browser.

▼ VISUAL WORKSHOP

Launch Expression Web, open the ecotours site, then open the home page. Use the Tag Properties task pane to modify the table attribute so your screen matches Figure L-27. When you have finished, save your changes, close the ecotours site, then exit Expression Web.

FIGURE L-27

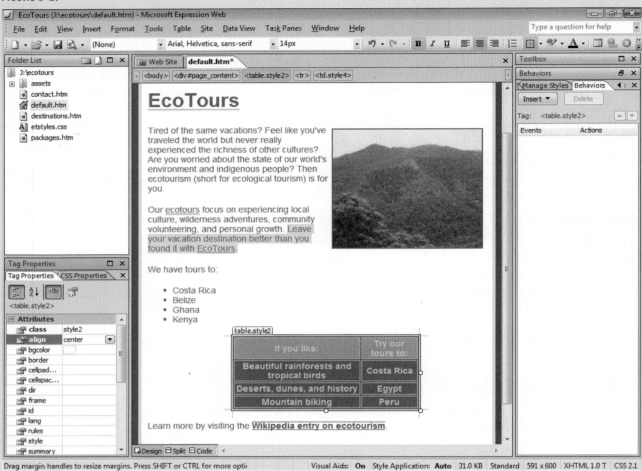

Advanced Typography Using CSS

In previous units, you learned the fundamentals of formatting text with CSS. In this unit, you go beyond the basics to explore more powerful typographical capabilities. **Typography** is simply the arrangement of text on the page or screen. It includes the use of font families, sizes, and colors as well as managing white space through the use of padding and margins. Setting CSS text properties in Expression Web is very straightforward, but with a little creativity, properties can be combined in ways that have a dramatic visual effect. Catalina is extremely pleased with the work you have done so far on the TradeWinds site. She is happy with the content, structure, and graphic design of the site and now wants you to focus on the site's typography to help make the site easier to read and more visually appealing.

OBJECTIVES

Understand the importance of typography

Control line length

Use the line-height property

Use the text-transform property

Use the letter-spacing property

Create and apply a drop cap style

Create and apply a pull quote style

Create advanced typography effects

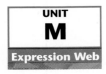

Understanding the Importance of Typography

The effect of typography on Web site visitors is often overlooked. The choice and formatting of type affects both the visual design of a site as well as the ability of visitors to read and understand your site's content. CSS offers significant control over text formatting options. You decide to learn more about the importance of typography.

Your typography choices affect:

- **Visual design**

  The typography of your site is an important part of the site's visual design. A beautiful site design filled with ugly text will never achieve its full potential. The text on your site should be styled in accordance with the overall site design. Font families, sizes, colors, and other details should coordinate with the colors and images used on the site. You should also ensure that the tone of the site's typography is appropriate. If the tone of your site is serious, avoid using a childish font in bright primary colors. Conversely, if you want to convey a light-hearted tone, avoid typography that consists solely of stodgy fonts in somber colors.

- **Eye fatigue**

  Reading content on a screen is more tiring to the human eye than reading the same content on a printed page. However, by paying attention to how your content is formatted, you can help your visitors have a more pleasant, less fatiguing visit to your site.

- **Legibility**

  The styles you apply to your content have a marked impact on visitors' ability to read and understand your content. In striving to coordinate your site's typography with its design, don't forget the importance of legibility. **Legibility** describes how well pieces of text can be recognized and read. Some important factors that affect legibility are font size, font family, the contrast between the font color and background color, and the amount of white space between letters, between words, and between lines. See Figures M-1 and M-2 for an example of how attention to typography can improve the legibility of site content.

- **Accessibility and download times**

  Smart use of CSS-based typography can even affect download times and accessibility. By using CSS to style headers and other text elements, rather than using images containing text, your pages will download more quickly and will also be accessible to visitors with disabilities and those using handheld devices and cell phones.

FIGURE M-1: Typography that decreases legibility

CHAPTER 1

Down the Rabbit-Hole

Alice was beginning to get very tired of sitting by her sister on the bank, and of having nothing to do: once or twice she had peeped into the book her sister was reading, but it had no pictures or conversations in it, 'and what is the use of a book,' thought Alice 'without pictures or conversation?'

So she was considering in her own mind (as well as she could, for the hot day made her feel very sleepy and stupid), whether the pleasure of making a daisy-chain would be worth the trouble of getting up and picking the daisies, when suddenly a White Rabbit with pink eyes ran close by her.

FIGURE M-2: Typography that improves legibility

CHAPTER 1

Down the Rabbit-Hole

Alice was beginning to get very tired of sitting by her sister on the bank, and of having nothing to do: once or twice she had peeped into the book her sister was reading, but it had no pictures or conversations in it, 'and what is the use of a book,' thought Alice 'without pictures or conversation?'

So she was considering in her own mind (as well as she could, for the hot day made her feel very sleepy and stupid), whether the pleasure of making a daisy-chain would be worth the trouble of getting up and picking the daisies, when suddenly a White Rabbit with pink eyes ran close by her.

Researching typography and layout

Research labs around the world study how typography affects people's ability to read and understand content. Some research looks at print-based materials or reading on-screen, while some research compares the two. To assess the readability and legibility of content, researchers ask subjects how comfortable or uncomfortable they were while reading; researchers can track the amount of time it takes for subjects to read a particular passage, and researchers can test subjects' understanding of the passage after reading. In addition, some labs use eyetracking cameras and software to track people's eye movements as they read a page or screen of material. The software produces "heatmaps" with spots of color indicating the areas of the page that people viewed most. This provides valuable information on the success of different page layouts and the effects of different text formatting on people's reading behaviors. To find out more about this fascinating area of research, type *eyetracking study* into your favorite search engine.

Expression Web

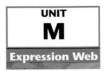

Controlling Line Length

In typography, **line length** is the width of a block of text. Line length is important for two reasons. First, line length affects the aesthetics of your page; creating a narrower or wider block of content has a visual impact on the page design. Even more important, very short or very long lines of text decrease reading comprehension and increase eye strain. A convenient way to set a comfortable line length is to control the width of the element containing the text. That way, you have to change a property in only one style rule rather than setting the width on all text-containing elements such as paragraphs and headings. See Table M-1 for a complete list of CSS properties related to formatting text and how they are organized in Expression Web. ▓▓▓▓▓ You want to adjust the line length throughout the TradeWinds site. You decide to set a value on the width property for the page_content div, which contains the site's content on each page.

STEPS

1. **Launch Expression Web, open the** tradewinds **site, open the** menu page, **then click the Show Design View button** if necessary

> **QUICK TIP**
> Remember that style rules can be inherited from one element to another; this is why multiple rules applying to the page_content div are listed.

2. **Preview the page in a browser, observe the line length of the content, close the browser window, then return to Expression Web**
   The text stretches almost all the way across the screen, as shown in Figure M-3, making for a very long line. This long line length makes the text difficult to read at a glance.

3. **Click** anywhere in the first paragraph of text, **click <div#page_content> on the quick tag selector bar, then if necessary click the CSS Properties tab to make it the active task pane**
   When you select content or an element on the page, the Applied Rules section of the CSS Properties task pane lists all the rules that apply to the selected content. Because you selected the page_content div, all rules applying to that div are listed, but only the last one in the list, #page_content, is selected. This is the one you want to modify.

> **QUICK TIP**
> Be sure *not* to type a space between 600 and px.

4. **Scroll down to the Position category, locate the width property, click in the** width text box, **type** 600px, **compare your screen to Figure M-4, then press [Enter]**
   The twstyles.css file opens and the file name displays an asterisk, indicating that a change has been made.

5. **Save changes to all open files, then preview the page in a browser**
   See Figure M-5. The entire page_content div is narrower, which makes the block of text narrower as well, shortening the line length.

6. **Close the browser, then return to Expression Web**

TABLE M-1: CSS properties related to typography

property	specifies	category	property	specifies	category
color	font color	Font	text-transform	display text as written or capitalized, uppercase, or lowercase	Font
font-family	font	Font	letter-spacing	amount of space between letters in a word	Block
font-size	font size	Font			
font-style	display text as normal, oblique, or italic	Font	line-height	amount of space between lines within a paragraph	Block
font-variant	display text as normal or small caps	Font	text-align	alignment of text to the right, center, or justified	Block
font-weight	display text as normal, light, bold, or bolder	Font	text-indent	indentation of the first line of a paragraph or other element	Block
text-decoration	display text with underline, overline, line-through, blink, or no decoration	Font	vertical-align	alignment of text to the top, center, or bottom of an element as well as superscript and subscript	Block

FIGURE M-3: Menu page

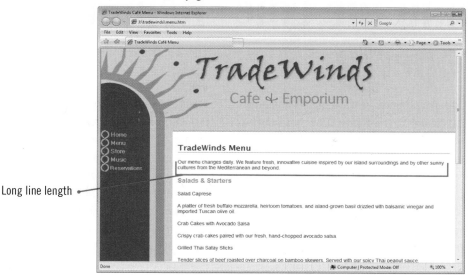

Long line length

FIGURE M-4: Menu page with page_content div selected

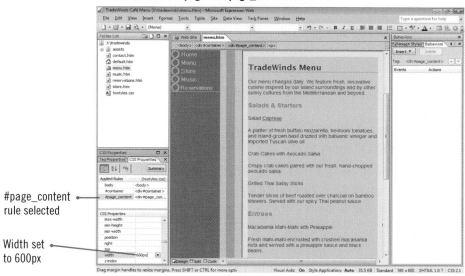

#page_content
rule selected

Width set
to 600px

FIGURE M-5: Menu page with reduced line length

Using the Line–Height Property

The line-height property in CSS controls the amount of space between lines of text within a paragraph. In typographical terms, this is also known as **leading** (rhymes with wedding). The line-height value in a style rule can be specified in the same units of measurement that are available for specifying fonts, such as pixels, ems, and percentages. However, it's best to specify line-height as a percentage, rather than in an absolute measurement such as a pixel. That way, if you change the font size in a paragraph, the amount of white space changes proportionally. Because it's based on a percentage of the font size rather than on an absolute unit such as a pixel, it appears to be the same and you don't have to make any adjustments to it. If no line height is specified, most browsers use a setting of approximately 120–130%. 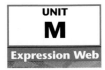 You decide to make the text on the TradeWinds page more readable by specifying a line-height value on all paragraph elements.

STEPS

1. **Click the** Manage Styles tab **to make it the active task pane, then click the** New Style button
   The New Style dialog box opens.

2. **Click the** Selector list arrow, **scroll down, then click** p
   You are defining this style rule based on the p tag so that it will apply to all text that is contained within a paragraph element on the site.

3. **Click the** Define in list arrow, **click** Existing style sheet, **click the** URL list arrow, **then click** twstyles.css
   See Figure M-6.

4. **Click** Block **in the category list**

5. **Type** 150 **in the** line-height text box, **click the** measurements list arrow, **click** %, **compare your screen to Figure M-7, then click** OK
   All text within paragraph elements now displays more white space between the lines of text. Setting the line height to 150% does not have a huge visual impact on the page, but it does improve readability. Setting a line height that is less than 100% or fewer pixels than the text size results in text lines running together on the screen.

6. **Save your changes to all open pages, then preview the page in a browser**
   See Figure M-8. The change is subtle but makes the text easier to read. Note that this change in line height will apply only to text within a paragraph element. This means it will not apply to text marked up as a list or other nonparagraph element.

7. **Close the browser window, then return to Expression Web**

Justifying text

Justified text is text that is spaced so that both the left and right margins are even, unlike normal text, which usually has a ragged-right margin. CSS includes a text-align property that allows you to dictate that text be aligned to the left, aligned to the right, centered, or justified. Some formal print publications feature justified text because it has a clean-edged, orderly appearance. However, without any means to control hyphenation and with all the variations in visitors' computer configurations, justified text on screen can end up having large ribbons of white space running through it. This makes it fairly strange in appearance and difficult to read, so using the Justified text-align property is not recommended.

FIGURE M-6: Font category for p style in New Style dialog box

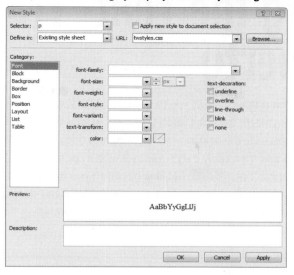

FIGURE M-7: Block category for p style

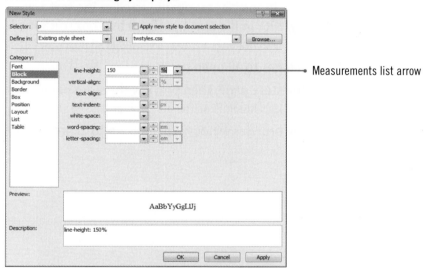

Measurements list arrow

FIGURE M-8: Menu page with increased line spacing

Increased line spacing

Using the Text-Transform Property

The text-transform property allows you to specify that text be displayed in uppercase, lowercase, or capitalized (which in this case means the first character of every word is uppercase and the rest of each word is lowercase). This setting will override the case in which the text was originally entered. For example, if you enter a heading as CONTACT US and then apply a style rule to it with a text-transform property set to lowercase, it will appear on the page as contact us. ████ Catalina has asked you to change all the second-level headings on the site so they are displayed in all uppercase letters. Both the menu and store pages feature second-level headings, so several changes must be made. You realize that rather than retyping the headings, you can use the text-transform property.

STEPS

1. **Click in the text Salads and Starters**
   In the CSS Properties task pane, the h2 style rule is now selected, as shown in Figure M-9.

QUICK TIP

Text set in all upper-case letters can be difficult to read, so use this property judiciously.

2. **In the CSS Properties task pane, scroll to the text-transform property in the font category, click in the text-transform text box, click the list arrow, then click uppercase**
   The second-level headings are now displayed in all uppercase letters, as shown in Figure M-10.

3. **Save changes to all open pages**

4. **Open the store page, then preview the store page in a browser**
   The second-level headings on the store page are also displayed in uppercase letters, as shown in Figure M-11.

QUICK TIP

You can also keep the browser window open, then click the refresh button or [F5] to reload the page after you've made a change.

5. **Close the browser window, then return to Expression Web**

Experimenting with type tester tools

Because so many CSS properties can be combined to format text, deciding on all the options can be a little overwhelming. Fortunately, several online tools are available that allow you to easily experiment with different text formatting options. You can use a standard text sample or paste in your own text, then change the font size, font family, color, spacing, and other properties. Some tools also allow you to create different sets of styles and compare them side-by-side. As a bonus, you can usually also export the CSS, copy it, and paste it into your style sheet. To try it out, enter *type tester* into your favorite search engine.

FIGURE M-9: h2 rule selected

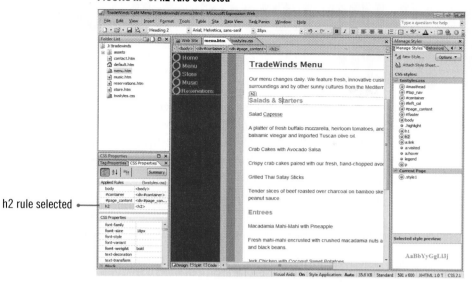

h2 rule selected

FIGURE M-10: Menu page with uppercase second-level headings

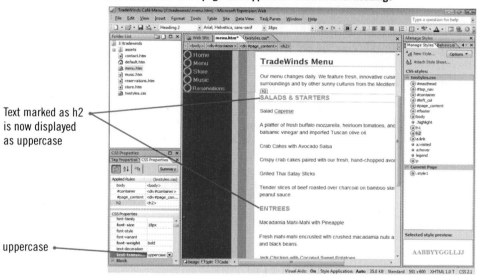

Text marked as h2
is now displayed
as uppercase

uppercase

FIGURE M-11: Store page with uppercase second-level headings

Using the Letter-Spacing Property

The letter-spacing property controls the amount of white space between letters in a word. Setting a negative value decreases spacing between letters; setting a positive value increases the spacing. This effect can be used to make text easier to read. It can also add visual interest to headings and other text elements by spreading out the letters or giving them a more crowded look. The font that you are using makes a big difference in what effect letter-spacing values have on your text. Some fonts normally are displayed with their letters farther apart than others, so if you are using the letter-spacing property and you change the font, you may find you need to adjust the value of the letter-spacing. 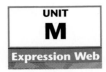 Now that the second-level headings are displayed in all uppercase letters, you decide to experiment with changing the letter spacing on these headings.

STEPS

1. **Make the menu page the active page, then click in the text Salads & Starters**
   Because this text is contained in an h2 element, clicking it selects the h2 style rule in the CSS Properties task pane.

QUICK TIP
To more easily navigate through the task pane, you can click the plus sign next to a category to collapse it.

2. **In the CSS Properties task pane, scroll to the Block category if necessary, click in the letter-spacing text box, type 2px, then press [Enter]**
   The text in the headings is now stretched out with more space between letters, as shown in Figure M-12. You decide you don't like the way it looks.

3. **In the Block section of the CSS Properties task pane, click in the letter-spacing text box, press [Delete], type -2px, then press [Enter]**
   The text in the headings is now more compact with less space between the letters, as shown in Figure M-13. You're happy with the look of these headings.

4. **Save changes to all open pages**

5. **Click the store page tab, then preview the store page in a browser**
   The change applies to the level-two headings on all pages including the store page, as shown in Figure M-14.

6. **Close the browser window, then return to Expression Web**

FIGURE M-12: Second-level headings with increased letter spacing

Increased letter spacing

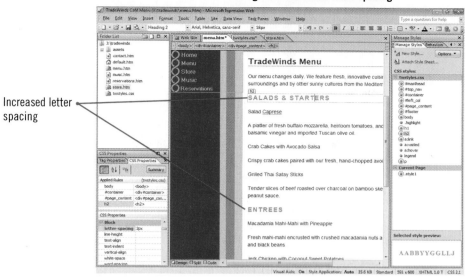

FIGURE M-13: Second-level headings with decreased letter spacing

Negative value for letter-spacing

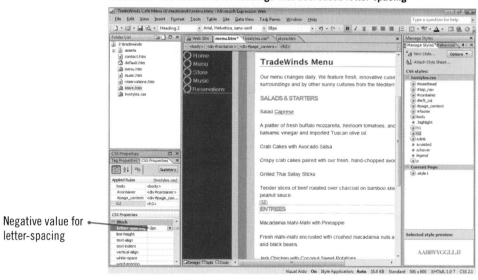

FIGURE M-14: Store page with new letter spacing

Decreased letter spacing

Expression Web

Creating and Applying a Drop Cap Style

A **drop cap** is the first letter of a paragraph that has been styled to be larger in size and to drop down into the text of the paragraph. Drop caps are commonly used in print, but you can also create a drop cap style in a Web page. Using drop caps can add drama to your site and give it a professional polish. The three key elements in creating a drop cap are: to increase the font size compared to the normal paragraph text; to make the letter drop down on the left side so that the paragraph text wraps to the right around it; and to increase the line height to give the letter room to drop down. 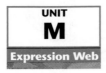 You want to add a drop cap to the first paragraph on each page of the TradeWinds site, so you need to create a class-based drop cap style and apply it to the appropriate paragraphs.

STEPS

1. **Click the** Apply Styles tab, **click the** New Style button **on the Apply Styles task pane, type** dropcap **in the** Selector text box, **click the** Define in list arrow, **click** Existing style sheet, **click the** URL list arrow, **then click** twstyles.css

2. **Click the** font-family list arrow, **click** Times New Roman, Times, serif, **type** 75 **in the** font-size text box, **type** #C6B98C **in the** color text box, **then compare your screen to Figure M-15**

3. **Click** Block **in the category list, type** 55 **in the** line-height text box, **click** Box **in the category list, click the** Same for all check box **next to padding to remove the check mark, then type** 2 **in the** top text box
   See Figure M-16.

4. **Click** Layout **in the category list, click the** float list arrow, **click** left, **then click** OK
   The float property causes anything with this style applied to it to move to the designated side, causing the other content to wrap around it. You will learn more about floats in a future unit.

5. **Select the** O **in** Our intrepid buyers, **then click** .dropcap **in the Apply Styles task pane**
   See Figure M-17. Because this is a class-based style, rather than a style that is based on an HTML element, you need to manually apply it to the first letter of each page. Expression Web applies a span tag to the letter with a class of dropcap.

6. **Make the menu page the active page, select the** O **in** Our menu changes daily, **click** .dropcap **in the Apply Styles task pane, open the** contact page, **select the** P **in** Please contact us, **then click** .dropcap **in the Apply Styles task pane**

7. **Open the** home page, **select the** O **in** Our guests experience, **click** .dropcap **in the Apply Styles task pane, open the** music page, **click the** Y **in** You can hear, **click** .dropcap **in the Apply Styles task pane, open the** reservations page, **select the** W **in** We take reservations, **then click** .dropcap **in the Apply Styles task pane**

8. **Save changes to all open pages, preview the home page in a browser, use the navigation buttons to view all the pages, close the browser, then return to Expression Web**

Understanding the first letter element

The official CSS specification outlines a pseudo-element called first letter, although it's not yet fully supported in all browsers. Theoretically, it allows you to create an element-based style, rather than a class-based style, based on the first letter selector, which is then automatically applied to the first letter of every paragraph in the site. A first-line selector would act similarly on the first line of each paragraph. Unfortunately, these pseudo-elements are not well-supported by browsers. Until they are, designers continue to create class-based styles and apply them one-by-one to the first letters they wish to style.

FIGURE M-15: Completed Font category for .dropcap style

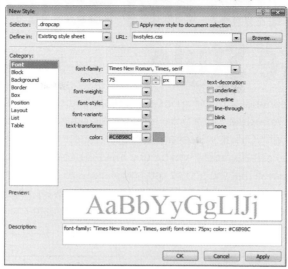

FIGURE M-16: Completed Box category for .dropcap style

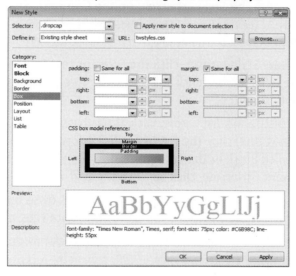

FIGURE M-17: Letter with .dropcap style applied

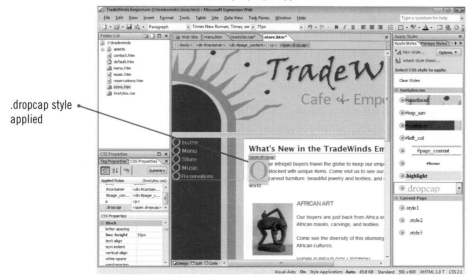

.dropcap style applied

Expression Web

Creating and Applying a Pull Quote Style

Pull quotes are commonly used in print publications and on the Web. A **pull quote** is a quote or excerpt summary that is formatted with a larger font size and placed on the page to draw visitors' attention. To create a pull quote with CSS, it is necessary to float the quote to the side, make the font size larger, and adjust the padding. You can also add a background image or color, borders, and additional text effects.  You have just learned that the photos you had planned to add to the menu page will not be ready in time for the site launch. The menu page looks a bit plain without the photos, so you decide to use CSS typography to add some visual interest to the page. You start by adding a testimonial from a customer to the page and creating a pull quote style for it.

STEPS

QUICK TIP
A blockquote is an HTML element used to indicate that the text is a quote.

1. **Close all pages except the menu page, click just before the text** Grilled Thai Satay Sticks, **type** TradeWinds serves the best food on the island!, **press [Enter], click in the** text you just typed, **click the** Style list arrow **on the Common toolbar, then click** Block Quote
   See Figure M-18. The <blockquote> tag is added to the selection. Because this is a quote, marking it up as a block quote identifies it as a quote to screen readers and also gives you a selector to use for the style rule.

QUICK TIP
If you wanted to add the source of the quote, you could create a second class-based style, add the text, then apply the new style to it.

2. **Click the** New Style button, **click the** Selector text box list arrow, **click** blockquote, **click the** Define in list arrow, **click** Existing style sheet, **if necessary click the** URL list arrow, **then click** twstyles.css

3. **Click the** font-family list arrow, **click** Times New Roman, Times, serif, **type** 30 **in the** font-size text box, **click the** font-style list arrow, **click** italic, **type** #EFAA21 **in the** color text box, **click** Block **in the category list, type** 90 **in the line-height text box, click the** measurement list arrow, **click** %, **click the** text-align list arrow, **then click** center

4. **Click** Background **in the category list, click the** Browse button **next to background-image, browse to the location where you store your Data Files, click** quotebg.gif, **then click** Open

5. **Click the** background-repeat list arrow, **then click** no-repeat
   You want the quotation marks to show up only once in the background.

6. **Click** Box **in the category list, click the** Same for all check box **next to padding to remove the check mark, type** 40 **in the** top text box **under padding, type** 20 **in the** left text box **under padding, then compare your screen to Figure M-19**
   This makes the text start slightly down and to the right and gives the background image some space.

7. **Click** Position **in the category list, type** 150 **in the width text box, click** Layout **in the category list, click the** float list arrow, **click** right, **then click** OK
   This setting will cause the quote to float to the right of the page content.

8. **Save changes to all open pages, save the image to the assets folder when prompted, preview the menu page in a browser, compare your screen to Figure M-20, close the browser window, then return to Expression Web**

FIGURE M-18: Text with blockquote tags applied

Style list arrow

Text in blockquote element

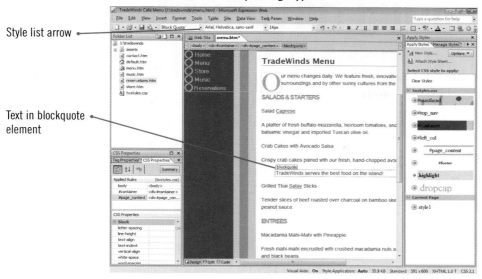

FIGURE M-19: Box category of blockquote style

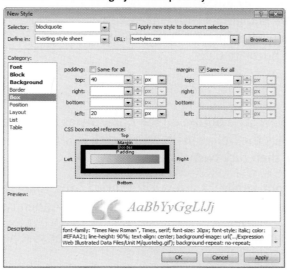

FIGURE M-20: Menu page with styled pull quote

Pull quote

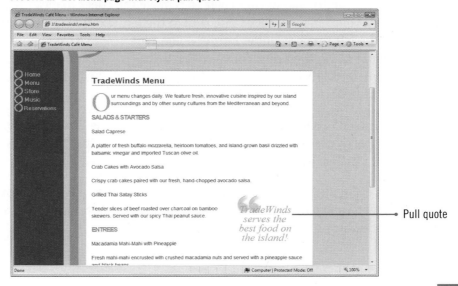

Expression Web

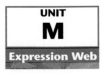

Creating Advanced Typography Effects

As you have learned, you can combine simple CSS properties in ways that can create interesting effects. These combinations can also be applied to regular headings on your site to provide another way to dress up your pages. ▰▰▰▰ The menu item names don't stand out on the page, so you decide to mark them up as third-level headings and then create a style that calls attention to them.

STEPS

QUICK TIP
To scroll to selectors that start with h, press [h].

1. **Select the text Salad Caprese, click the Style list arrow on the Common toolbar, then click Heading 3 <h3>**
   This applies an <h3> tag to the selected text, as shown in Figure M-21.

QUICK TIP
Remember to select the text, click the Style list arrow, then click the Heading <H3> tag.

2. **Apply the Heading <h3> tag to the following text:**
   Crab Cakes with Avocado Salsa
   Grilled Thai Satay Sticks
   Macadamia Mahi-Mahi with Pineapple
   Jerk Chicken with Coconut Sweet Potatoes
   Flourless Chocolate Cake
   Mango Flan
   Coffee

3. **Click the New Style button on the Apply Styles task pane, click the Selector list arrow, click h3, click the Define in list arrow, click Existing style sheet, if necessary click the URL list arrow, then click twstyles.css**

4. **Click the font-family list arrow, click Lucida Sans, Arial, Helvetica, sans-serif, type 14 in the font-size text box, click in the color text box, then type #666633**

5. **Click Block in the category list, type -1 in the letter-spacing text box, click the measurement list arrow, then click px**

6. **Click Border in the category list, click the Same for all check boxes under border-style, border-width, and border-color to remove the check marks, click the left list arrow under border-style, click solid, click in the left text box under border-width, type 4, click in the left text box under border-color, type #C9A62D, compare your dialog box to Figure M-22, then click OK**
   Setting the border properties creates a block of color to the left of the heading. However, the text is too close to the border.

7. **In the CSS Properties task pane, scroll down to the Box category, locate the padding-left property, click in the padding-left text box , type 2px, then press [Enter]**
   This adds some white space between the border and the left edge of the text.

8. **Save changes to all open pages, preview the menu page in a browser, compare your screen to Figure M-23, close the browser window, return to Expression Web, close the tradewinds site, then exit Expression Web**

FIGURE M-21: Text with h3 tags applied

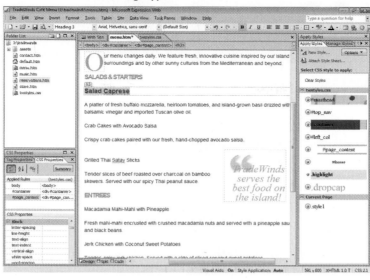

FIGURE M-22: Completed Border category of h3 style

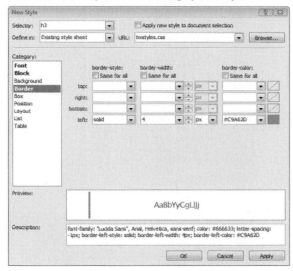

FIGURE M-23: Menu page with new h3 styles

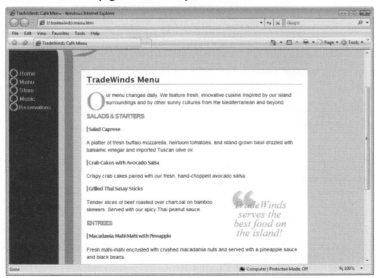

Expression Web

Practice

▼ CONCEPTS REVIEW

Refer to Figure M-24 to answer the following questions:

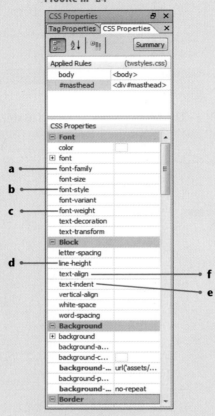

FIGURE M-24

1. **Which property would you change to specify the amount of space between lines of text?**
2. **Which property would you change to specify the font family?**
3. **Which property would you change to display text in italics?**
4. **Which property would you change to display text as bold?**
5. **Which property would you change to center text within an element?**
6. **Which property would you change to indent the first line of a paragraph?**

Match each term with the statement that best describes it.

7. **Leading**
8. **Drop cap**
9. **Pull quote**
10. **Justified text**

a. Text with even margins on both the right and left sides
b. Another term for line height
c. First letter of a paragraph styled differently from surrounding text
d. An excerpt from text highlighted on a Web or print page

Select the best answer from the list of choices.

11. **Which type of text alignment is best avoided on the Web?**
    a. Center
    b. Left
    c. Right
    d. Justify

12. **Which of the following affects the way we read on the Web?**
    a. Our eyes tire less easily when reading from a screen.
    b. Our eyes tire more easily when reading from a screen.
    c. Our brains have evolved to read print materials.
    d. Our brains have not evolved to read screen-based materials.

13. **What effect does the float property have?**
    a. Causes elements to float to the top of the page
    b. Causes elements to float to one side or the other relative to other content
    c. Causes elements to float in front of text and images
    d. None of the above

14. **Which of the following can improve legibility?**
    a. Using all uppercase letters
    b. Decreasing letter-spacing
    c. Using justified text
    d. Decreasing line length

▼ SKILLS REVIEW

1. **Control line length.**
   a. Launch Expression Web, open the careers site, then open the services page.
   b. Preview the page in a browser, observe the line length, then close the browser window.
   c. Click anywhere in the first line of text, then select the page_content div in the quick tag selector bar.
   d. In the CSS Properties task pane, locate the width property in the Position category, set the width to **650px**, then press [Enter].
   e. Save changes to all open files, preview the page in a browser, close the browser window, then return to Expression Web.

2. **Use the line-height property.**
   a. Open the New Style dialog box.
   b. Choose the p element as a selector, and define the rule in the cgstyles.css style sheet.
   c. Switch to the Block category and set the line-height property to 160%.
   d. Click the OK button to close the dialog box.
   e. Save your changes to all open pages, preview the page in a browser, close the browser window, then return to Expression Web.

3. **Use the text-transform property.**
   a. Click in the text Careers Guaranteed Services.
   b. Using the CSS Properties task pane, set the text-transform property for the h1 rule to uppercase.
   c. Save changes to all open pages.
   d. Open the home page, preview the page in a browser, close the browser window, then return to Expression Web.

4. **Use the letter-spacing property.**
   a. Make the services page the active page, then click in the text Careers Guaranteed Services.
   b. Use the CSS Properties task pane to set the letter-spacing property in the Block category to -1.5px.
   c. Save changes to all open pages.
   d. Click the home page tab, preview the page in a browser, close the browser window, then return to Expression Web.

5. **Create and apply a drop cap style.**

   a. Click the Apply Styles tab, then open the New Style dialog box.

   b. Type **dropcap** in the Selector text box. (*Hint*: Be careful not to type over the period.)

   c. Define the style in the existing style sheet (cgstyles.css).

   d. Set the font-family to Lucida Sans, Arial, Helvetica, sans-serif, the font-size to 50px, and the font-color to #CCDDFF.

   e. Switch to the Block category, then set the line-height to 35px.

   f. Switch to the Box category, then set the top padding only to 2px.

   g. Switch to the Layout category and set the float to left.

   h. Click OK to close the dialog box.

   i. Click the Apply Styles tab, select the **A** in **At Careers Guaranteed**, then click .dropcap in the Apply Styles task pane.

   j. Make the home page the active page, select the **A** in **At Careers Guaranteed**, then use the Apply Styles task pane to apply the .dropcap style.

   k. Open the about page, then apply the .dropcap style to the C in Careers Guaranteed.

   l. Open the contact page, then use the Apply Styles task pane to apply the .dropcap style to the H in Have questions.

   m. Save changes to all open pages, preview the about page in a browser, close the browser window, then return to Expression Web.

6. **Create and apply a pull quote style.**

   a. Close all pages except the services page.

   b. Click after the text **target it to desirable employers**, press [Enter], then type **"Careers Guaranteed's online personal services helped me polish my skills and resume."**

   c. Select the text you just typed, then apply the blockquote tag. (*Hint*: Use the Style list arrow.)

   d. Open the New Style dialog box.

   e. Choose the blockquote element as the selector and define the style in the existing style sheet (cgstyles.css).

   f. Set the font-family to Arial, Helvetica, sans-serif, the font-size to 20px, the font-style to italic, and the color to #265B91.

   g. Switch to the Block category, then set the line-height to 90%.

   h. Switch to the Background category, then set the background color to #EAE1D5.

   i. Switch to the Box category, then set the padding on all four sides to 20px.

   j. Switch to the Position category, then set the width to 200px.

   k. Switch to the Layout category, then set the float to right.

   l. Click OK to close the New Style dialog box. Save changes to all open pages, preview the services page in a browser, compare your screen to Figure M-25, close the browser window, then return to Expression Web.

7. **Create advanced typography effects.**

   a. Open the about page, click in the text Ken Lee, then use the Style list arrow to apply an h3 tag.

   b. Click in the text Tina Russo, then use the Style list arrow to apply an h3 tag.

   c. Click in the text Nelson Ferraz, then use the Style list arrow to apply an h3 tag.

   d. Open the New Style dialog box.

   e. Choose the h3 element as the selector and define the style in the existing style sheet (cgstyles.css).

   f. Set the font-size to 14px and the color to #666666.

   g. Switch to the Block category, then set the letter spacing to -1px.

   h. Switch to the Border category, then set the left border to a border-style of dashed, a border-width of 3px, and a border-color of #CCDDFF. Click OK to close the New Style dialog box.

FIGURE M-25

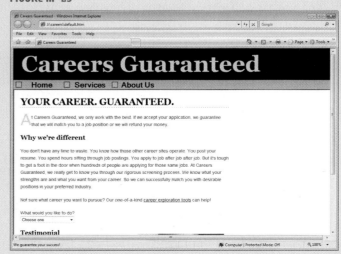

i. Click in the text Ken Lee, then use the CSS Properties task pane to set the padding-left in the Box category to 5px for the h3 rule.

j. Save all open pages, preview the about page in a browser, close the browser, return to Expression Web, close the careers site, then exit Expression Web.

▼ INDEPENDENT CHALLENGE 1

In this project you continue your work on the ConnectUp Web site. Tiffany has sent you some changes she'd like to make to the site. She would like to add a drop cap and an eye-catching quote to the home page and change the styles of some of the headings.

a. Launch Expression Web, open the connectup Web site, then open the faq page.

b. Create a new style in the existing style sheet (custyles.css), using the p element as the selector. For the new style, set the line-height to 170%.

c. Use the CSS Properties task pane to set the text-transform property for the h2 heading to uppercase and the letter-spacing property to -2px. (*Hint*: First click in an h2 heading such as Services.)

d. Save changes to all open pages, preview the faq page in a browser, close the browser, then return to Expression Web.

e. Open the home page, then create a class-based style rule named .dropcap in the existing style sheet (custyles.css) that sets the font-family to Trebuchet MS, Arial, Helvetica, sans-serif, the font-size to 36px, and the color to #FF8800. Set the line-height to 15px. Set the top padding to 3px. Set the float to left.

f. Select the letter **Y** in **You don't separate**, then click .dropcap in the Apply Styles task pane.

g. Click before the text **You don't separate**, type **"You won't regret joining up with ConnectUp!!"**, press Enter, click in the text you just typed, then use the Style list arrow to apply a blockquote tag.

h. Create a new style in the existing style sheet (custyles.css) using blockquote as the selector, and set the following properties: font-size 24px; font-style italic; color #03C4EC, border on all four sides with a border-style of solid, border-width of 2px, border-color of #6FD917, padding on all sides of 5px, width of 150px, and float right.

i. Preview the home page in a browser, compare your screen to Figure M-26, close the browser, return to Expression Web, close the connectup site, then exit Expression Web.

FIGURE M-26

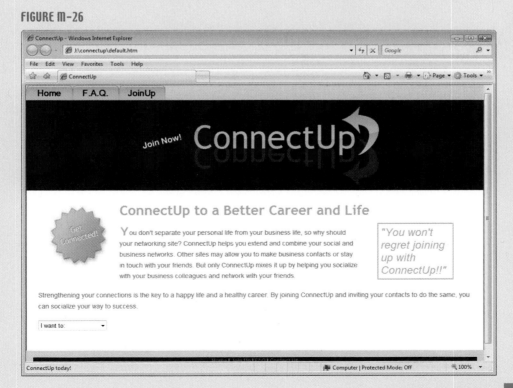

▼ INDEPENDENT CHALLENGE 2

In this project you continue your work on the Memories Restored Web site. Brian has sent you some changes he'd like you to make to the site.

a. Launch Expression Web, open the memories Web site, then open the home page.

b. Set the width of the page_content div to 600px.

c. Using the p element as a selector, create a style in the existing style sheet setting the line-height to 150%.

d. Create a class-based style rule named .dropcap in the mrstyles.css style sheet. Using the skills you have learned in this unit, set properties for the dropcap that you think coordinate well with the Memories Restored site. Apply the style to the first letter on each page. Use your judgment in deciding which pages lend themselves to a drop cap. Some of them may not. (*Hint*: If you create a style and you're not completely satisfied with it, you can right-click the style in the Apply Styles task pane, then click Modify Style to change the properties.)

e. Open the process page, click after the text **We send you a quote**, press [Enter], then type *"We are thrilled with our restored photos!"*

f. Apply a blockquote tag to the text you just typed, then create a style in the external style sheet based on the block-quote element to highlight the quote. (*Hint*: Remember to set the float to either the left or the right, and to set a width in pixels.)

Advanced Challenge Exercise

■ Open the process page, then apply an h3 tag to the following lines of text:
  You send us your photo
  We send you a quote
  We send you a proof
  You approve the proof and send payment
  We mail you the photos
■ Create a style based on the h3 element that adds visual interest to these headings.

g. Save your changes, preview each page of the site in a browser, close the browser, return to Expression Web, close the memories site, then exit Expression Web.

▼ INDEPENDENT CHALLENGE 3

This Independent Challenge requires an Internet connection.

At a recent design meeting with the staff of Technology for All, you voiced concerns about the importance of making the content on the site legible and easy to read. The employees did not see this as an important issue and asked you to focus on the graphics for the redesign instead. You want to convince the staff of the importance of attention to typography, so you decide to do some research that will help you drive this point home at the next meeting.

   a. Identify three Web sites that include a fair amount of text-based content. These can include news sites, shopping sites, or other general-interest sites.

   b. Visit each site and spend a few minutes analyzing the typography and its effect on your experience in the site.

   c. Write a paragraph on each site, describing what you like or don't like about the typography, how easy it is to read the content, and how well the typography supports the site design.

Advanced Challenge Exercise

    ■ Choose the site that fared the worst in your evaluation.

    ■ Write a paragraph recommending changes you would make to improve the site. Include specific changes to CSS properties such as line spacing or font size.

   d. Add your name to the document, then print it.

▼ REAL LIFE INDEPENDENT CHALLENGE

This assignment builds on the personal Web site you have worked on in previous units. In this project, you will create and modify style rules to refine the typography for your site.

   a. Assess the line length of the text in your site and, if necessary, adjust it to a comfortable length by setting the width on the containing element.

   b. Using the p element as the selector, create a style in your external style sheet that changes the line height.

   c. Modify the text-transform property and the letter-spacing property in an existing or new style rule.

   d. Using the skills you have learned in this unit, create a dropcap class-based style rule and apply it to the first letter on each page of your site.

   e. Add a quote or excerpt to a page in your site, apply a blockquote tag, then, using the settings from the lessons as a guide, create a pull quote style based on the blockquote element.

   f. Create a new heading style or edit an existing one to add some of the properties you have learned about in this unit.

Expression Web

▼ VISUAL WORKSHOP

Launch Expression Web, open the site, then open the contact page. Use the CSS Properties task pane to modify the h1 attributes so your screen matches Figure M-27. When you have finished, save your changes, close the ecotours site, then exit Expression Web.

FIGURE M-27

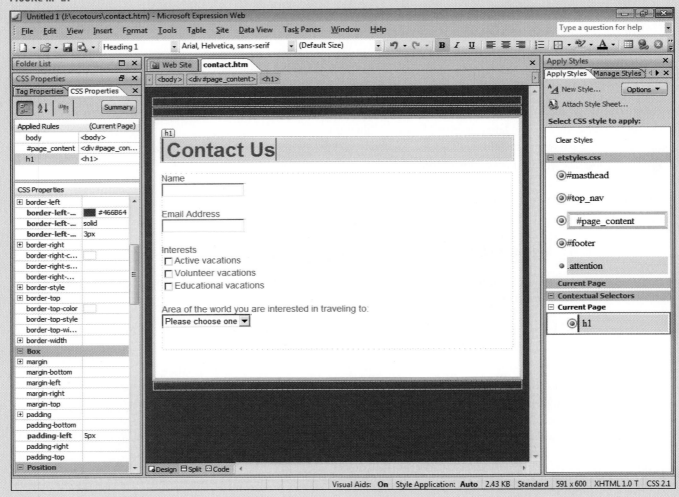

Creating a Layout with CSS

Because browsers differ in the way they display CSS layout elements, designing your own CSS layouts can be challenging. Designing a successful layout requires much experimenting and a fair bit of knowledge about the nuances of CSS. However, learning some layout basics will help you start creating your own page layouts.  Catalina is holding an arts festival at TradeWinds, and she'd like you to create some Web pages promoting it. These pages will be part of the TradeWinds site but will have their own look and feel. You decide to create a simple layout for the new pages using CSS.

OBJECTIVES

Understand CSS layouts

Create the HTML file

Create divs and assign IDs

Create ID-based style rules

Use a container div

Create floating columns

Clear floats

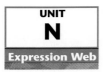

Understanding CSS Layouts

CSS has many properties you can use to control the positioning of divs and other elements on a page. Achieving the layout you want is a matter of becoming familiar with these properties and combining them to create the design you desire. Using CSS to position elements is not as straightforward as using it for typography or other purposes. For example, if you want to create a multi-column layout, you cannot simply specify this in CSS, because CSS does not include a column property that allows you to dictate the number of columns. Instead, you need to use a different method, such as using the float property to achieve the effect of multiple columns. Using floats is just one way to create a two-column layout. The more you know about CSS properties and how they affect the flow of elements on a page, the more flexibility you will have in creating your layouts. ██████ You want to create a simple fixed-width, two-column layout with a footer for the new festival pages. Before you begin, you decide to learn more about creating CSS-based Web page layouts.

DETAILS

Before you create a CSS-based layout, you should understand:

- **The process of creating CSS layouts**

  When creating a CSS layout from scratch, you should first sketch out what you want the page to look like, then determine how many divs you will need to create the layout and what you want to call the divs. Figure N-1 shows the sketch for the tradewinds festival page. Next, you create a blank HTML page, then add the necessary divs to the page and assign them each a unique id. The divs act as containers for the content, and the ids provide a way to attach the style rules that control the way the divs will be positioned on the page. Next, you create a style rule for each div using its id as the selector. Finally, you modify the properties of each element to create the layout you desire.

- **The flow of HTML elements**

  HTML elements flow in a defined way relative to other elements within a page. The way an element interacts with other elements on the page is determined by what type of element it is. The two basic types of elements are block-level and inline. **Block-level elements** are larger elements such as divs, tables, and paragraphs. They can contain other block-level elements or they can contain inline elements. By default, block-level elements always appear on their own line, stacked one on top of the other, on the page. That means you would not have two tables side-by-side or a paragraph beside a table unless you create a special style rule to display them that way. Block-level elements appear on the page in the order in which they appear in the code.

  Inline elements are smaller elements such as images, lists, or hyperlinks. They can only contain text or other inline elements. By default, inline elements are not displayed on their own separate lines; they are displayed side-by-side. So if you place an image element on a page and then a list element, they would not stack on top of each other.

- **How floats work**

  Floats are a mainstay of CSS layouts. As you learned in previous units, when you use the **float** property on an element, you can set the attribute to float left or right. An element with the float property set will exist outside the normal flow of HTML. It does not behave as a normal block-level element or as an inline element. Instead, it floats on top of all the other elements around it and pushes the content in those elements to the side. For example, if the element is floated to the right, it takes up the right side and pushes other content to the left. See Figure N-2 for a demonstration of how floated elements act in the flow of a page.

- **The importance of testing**

  Every browser available today has a few bugs that affect the way CSS layouts are displayed. This is what makes CSS layouts so challenging to design. You can understand the properties, follow the rules, and have a design that is technically correct, but a browser bug could cause it to be displayed incorrectly in one or more browsers. It is critical that you test in one browser as you design and that you also test in other browsers that your visitors are likely to be using.

FIGURE N-1: Sketch of festival home page

FIGURE N-2: Floated element in the flow of a page

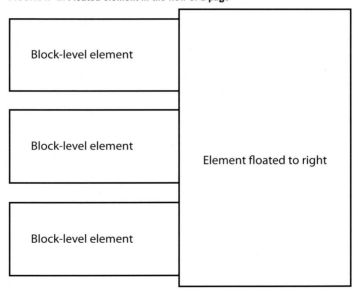

TABLE N-1: CSS Layout Properties

property	specifies
Visibility	Whether an item is visible or not
Display	How or if an element is displayed on the page; this property can be used to display a block-level element as inline or vice versa
Float	That an element should float to the right or left outside the normal flow of elements
Clear	That floating should not occur on specified sides of the element
Cursor	The type of cursor to be displayed when pointing to an element
Overflow	What happens if an element's contents overflow its area; can be visible, hidden, or displayed with scrollbars in element
Clip	The shape and dimensions of an element; content that overflows these dimensions will not be visible

Creating the HTML file

When you need to build a separate section of a Web site, it is usually best to create a separate folder within the site's root folder to hold the files for that section, in order to keep your files organized. ▚▚▞▞ You need to create a festival folder inside the tradewinds folder and create a blank HTML file for the festival home page. You also want to set some options to make it easier to work with the divs later.

STEPS

1. **Launch Expression Web, then open the tradewinds site**

2. **Right-click the tradewinds root folder in the Folder List task pane, point to New, then click Folder**
   A new folder is created and the name is selected and highlighted in blue in the Folder List task pane.

3. **Type festival, then press [Enter]**
   The default folder name is replaced with the new name, as shown in Figure N-3.

> **QUICK TIP**
> Make sure the Page tab is selected, then make sure General and HTML are selected.

4. **Click File on the menu bar, point to New, then click Page**
   The New dialog box opens, as shown in Figure N-4. You want to use the default setting, which creates a blank HTML page from the General category.

5. **Click OK**
   A new, blank HTML page opens in the editing window. This will be the home page for the festival pages. The home page for each folder or subfolder should have an appropriate file name such as default.htm or index.htm.

> **QUICK TIP**
> You can also save a page by pressing [CTRL][S].

6. **Click File on the menu bar, click Save, double-click the festival folder, select Untitled_1.htm in the File name text box, press [Delete], then type default.htm**
   See Figure N-5. You can also use this dialog box to change the title of the page. Changing the title when you save a page is a good habit to get into, because you don't have to remember to make the change later.

7. **Click Change title, type TradeWinds Arts Festival in the Page title text box, click OK, then click Save in the Save As dialog box**

8. **Click Tools on the menu bar, click Page Editor Options, click the IntelliSense tab, in the Auto Insert section click the Close tag check box to remove the check mark, then click OK**

FIGURE N-3: Festival folder inside Tradewinds root folder

tradewinds
root folder

festival
folder

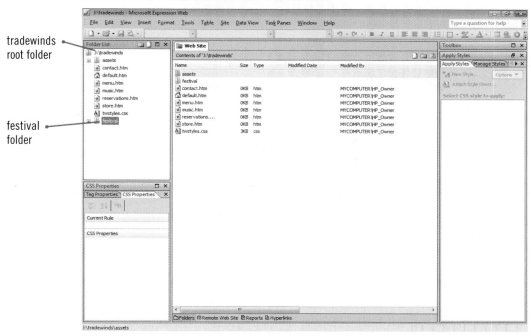

FIGURE N-4: New dialog box

HTML is
selected

General is
selected

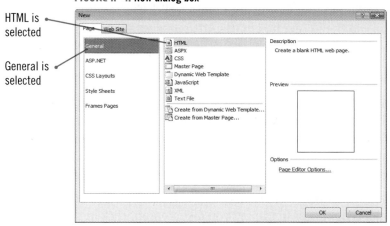

FIGURE N-5: Save As dialog box

Saving in
festival folder

File name
text box

Change title
button

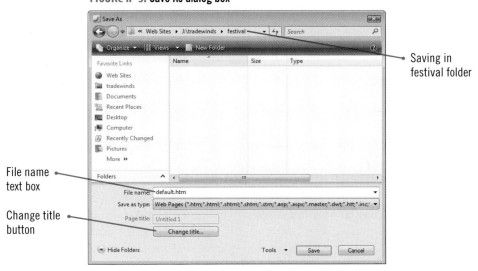

Expression Web

Creating Divs and Assigning IDs

The first step in creating a CSS layout is to create div elements in the HTML page. The divs hold content and allow you to position it on the page. To position a div, the div must have an id assigned to it. As you have learned, it's best to assign a semantic id that describes the function or content of the div rather than its placement on the page. For example, if you add a div to the left column that will contain branding content, such as a logo, it's better to assign the id "branding" rather than the id "left column." The divs and their assigned ids are all contained in the HTML code. ▰▰▰▰ You're ready to create divs for the festival pages. The basic layout requires three divs: one to contain the branding area for the pages, one to hold the main content of the page, and one for the footer content.

STEPS

QUICK TIP

The festival home page is the default.htm file within the festival folder; it should already be open.

1. **Click the** Maximize button **on the Toolbox task pane, if necessary double-click the** plus sign **next to HTML, then if necessary double-click the** plus sign **next to Tags**

2. **Click in the** top left of the festival home page, **then double-click** <div> **under Tags in the HTML section on the Toolbox task pane**

   A visual aid appears, indicating that a div element has been inserted into the festival home page.

3. **Type** branding **in the div you just created, click the** Tag Properties tab **to open this task pane, click in the** id text box **in the Attributes category, type** branding, **then press [Enter]**

   The branding div appears on the page, as shown in Figure N-6. Adding some placeholder text to the div can help you visually identify the div when working in design view and when previewing it in a browser. If you don't enter any text, it's easy to confuse the various divs on a page.

4. **Click the** div#branding tab **on the visual aid, press [→], compare your screen to Figure N-7, double-click** <div> **on the Toolbox task pane, type** content **in the div you just created, click in the** id text box **in the Attributes section of the Tag Properties task pane, type** content, **then press [Enter]**

   The content div appears on the page beneath the branding div.

QUICK TIP

Remember that the # indicates that the element has an id assigned to it; the id name follows the #.

5. **Click the** div#content tab **on the visual aid, press [→], double-click** <div> **on the Toolbox task pane, type** footer **in the div you just created, click in the** id text box **in the Attributes section of the Tag Properties task pane, type** footer, **press [Enter], then click anywhere on the page outside of the div#footer element**

   The three divs appear on the page, as shown in Figure N-8. Until you create styles to position the divs, they stack on top of each other like other block-level HTML elements.

6. **Save your changes to the page**

Ordering divs in the HTML code

Using the positioning and layout properties of CSS, it is possible to display divs in one order in your HTML code, but have them appear in a different order on the page. For example, you might want to have main content appear first in the source code, but have your navigation or masthead appear first on the page. Putting your main content at the top of the HTML code can help your site rank higher in search engine results. It can also be helpful for visitors with disabilities and those browsing on handheld devices.

FIGURE N-6: Branding div inserted

Visual aid tab

id assigned

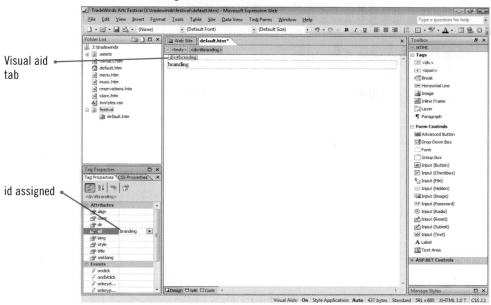

FIGURE N-7: Insertion point positioned for next div

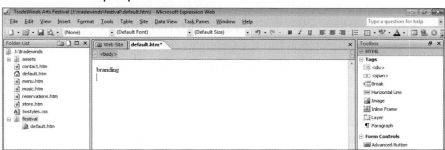

FIGURE N-8: Three divs added to page

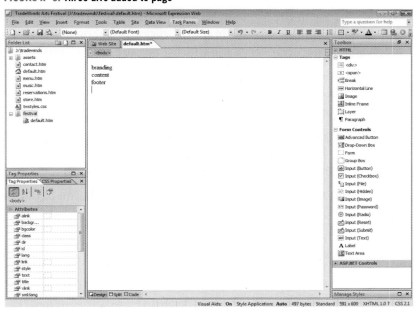

Expression Web

Creating ID-Based Style Rules

Creating CSS layouts requires that you create id-based style rules. By creating a style rule and using a selector that consists of the # followed by an id name, the properties of the style are automatically applied to the element on the page that is using the id. When creating CSS layouts, it can be helpful to temporarily assign background colors to each div so that you can see how the divs are being positioned on the page. You should choose background colors that are easy to distinguish from each other. They do not have to look nice or match your site's design because you will be removing the colors once you have created and tested the basic layout structure. ▰▰▰▰ You decide to create an id-based style rule for each div on the festival home page and give each div a background color for testing purposes. When you create your first style rule, you also need to create a new style sheet and attach it to the festival home page.

1. **Click the** Maximize button **on the Apply Styles task pane, click the** Manage Styles tab, **then click** New Style

2. **Delete the text in the Selector text box**
   Now the Selector text box is empty and ready for you to type in it.

QUICK TIP
Hex codes are not case-sensitive, so you can use either uppercase or lowercase letters when defining colors.

3. **Type** #branding **in the Selector text box, click the** Define in list arrow, **click** New style sheet, **click** Background **in the Category list, type** #FFFFCC **in the background-color text box, compare your screen to Figure N-9, then click** OK
   A dialog box opens asking if you want to attach the new style sheet to the page. In order for the styles to be applied to the elements on that page, the style sheet must be attached to the page.

4. **Click** Yes, **click** File **on the menu bar, click** Save All, **type** festival_style.css **in the File name text box, compare your screen to Figure N-10, then click** Save
   The branding div now has a light yellow background color, making it easier to see the div boundaries. The new style also appears in the Manage Styles task pane. The new style sheet is open in a new tab behind the festival home page tab.

5. **Click** New Style **in the Manage Styles task pane, delete the text in the Selector text box, type** #content **in the Selector text box, click the** Define in list arrow, **click** Existing style sheet, **then if necessary click the** URL list arrow **and click** festival_style.css

6. **In the Category list click** Background, **type** #CCCCCC **in the background-color text box, then click** OK
   The content area now has a gray background.

7. **Click** New Style **in the Manage Styles task pane, delete the text in the Selector text box, type** #footer **in the Selector text box, click the** Define in list arrow, **click** Existing Style Sheet, **click the** URL list arrow, **then click** festival_style.css

8. **In the Category list click** Background, **type** #FF9933 **in the background-color text box, then click** OK
   See Figure N-11. The footer div now has an orange background.

9. **Save changes to all open pages**

FIGURE N-9: New Style dialog box for #branding style rule

Defined in
New style
sheet

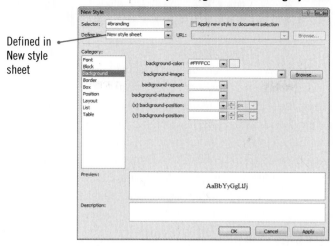

FIGURE N-10: Save As dialog box

Saving in
festival
folder

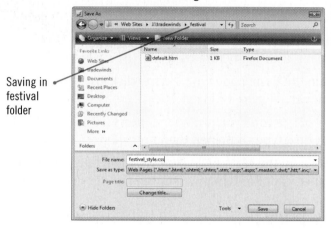

FIGURE N-11: Divs with background colors

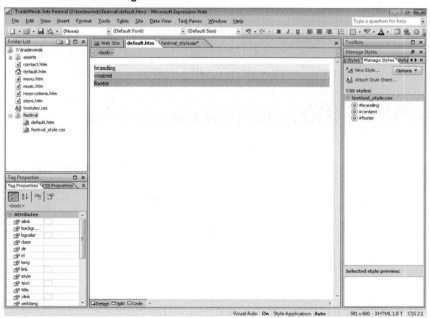

Expression Web

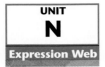

Using a Container Div

When creating a CSS-based layout, it's a good idea to first create and style a div that will act as a container for the others on the page. Styling this container div allows you to control the overall width and placement of all page divs at once. Once the container div is in place, you create each div in the order in which it should appear on the page. The container div holds the other divs and allows you better control over the page layout. By setting a width, margins, and other properties on the container div, you can define the overall parameters of the page layout. When building your CSS layout, it's important to preview your layout in a browser often because Expression Web and other WYSIWYG editors don't always accurately render the layouts. ████ You decide you want the festival page to be a fixed width of 700 pixels and to be centered vertically on the page. As you modify the #container style rule to achieve this, you preview it in a browser to see the effects your modifications are having.

STEPS

1. **Preview the festival home page in a browser**
   The elements are stacked on top of each other and extend all the way across the browser window, as shown in Figure N-12. If you were to resize your window to make it smaller or larger, the divs would resize as well.

QUICK TIP
You can also use the CSS Properties task pane to modify these properties.

2. **Close the browser, return to Expression Web, click the Show Split View button, in the Code View pane click just before the code `<div id="branding">`, then type `<div>`**

3. **Scroll down in the Code pane if necessary, click just before the code `</body>`, then type `</div>`, as shown in Figure N-13**

4. **Click in the `</div>` code you just added, press [F5], in the Tag Properties task pane click in the id text box, type container, then press [Enter]**

QUICK TIP
Pressing [F5] refreshes the screen.

5. **Click New Style on the Manage Styles task pane, delete the text in the selector text box, type #container, click Position in the Category list, type 700 in the width text box, then click OK**
   This sets the width of the container div to 700 pixels. Because the other divs are inside the container, they will also be constrained to 700 pixels.

6. **Save your changes to all pages, then preview the page in a browser**
   The layout is now narrower and does not extend across the entire page. However, all the content is on the left side of the browser window.

7. **Close the browser window, return to Expression Web, right-click #container in the Manage Styles task pane, click Modify Style on the shortcut menu, click Box in the Category list, click the top list arrow under margin, click auto, compare your screen to Figure N-14, then click OK**
   The auto setting for the margins makes the margins the same on both the left and right sides, which has the effect of centering the div horizontally on the page.

8. **Save your changes to the style sheet, then preview the page in a browser**
   The content is now centered horizontally on the page.

9. **Close the browser window, then return to Expression Web**

FIGURE N-12: Previewing the festival page in a browser

Divs stretch across page

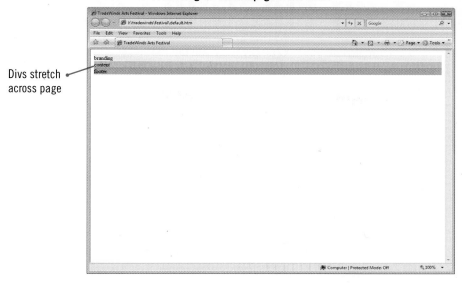

FIGURE N-13: Festival home page in Split View with new div tags inserted

New div tags

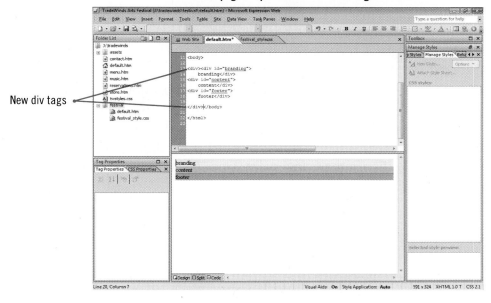

FIGURE N-14: Completed Modify Style dialog box

Top list arrow

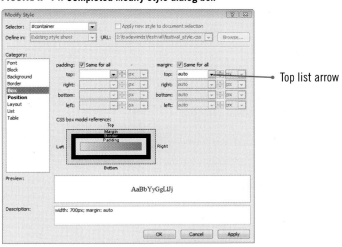

Expression Web

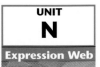
Creating Floating Columns

To create a two-column layout, you can simply float one div to the left and a second div to the right. But whenever you add a float property to an element, you should also give it a width. If you neglect to do this, the browser doesn't know how much space to set aside for that element, so the results are unpredictable. You're ready to create styles that will position the branding and content columns side-by-side on the page. First, you decide to try simply floating the divs without setting widths for them.

1. **Click the** Show Design View button, **right-click** #branding **in the Manage Styles task pane, then click** Modify Style **on the shortcut menu**
    The Modify Style dialog box opens.

2. **Click** Layout **in the Category list, click the** float list **arrow, click** left, **then click** OK
    The div#branding element is now floated to the left, as shown in Figure N-15.

3. **Right-click** #content **in the Manage Styles task pane, click** Modify Style **on the shortcut menu, in the Modify Style dialog box click** Layout **in the Category list, click the** float list **arrow, click** right, **then click** OK

4. **Save the changes to your style sheet, then preview the festival home page in a browser**
    See Figure N-16. The layout does not look as you intended. You want the branding div on the left, the content div on the right, and the footer beneath both of them. The layout is not working correctly because the divs do not have defined widths.

5. **Close the browser window, return to Expression Web, right-click** #branding **in the Manage Styles task pane, click** Modify Style **on the shortcut menu, click** Position **in the Category list, type** 150 **in the width text box, then click** OK

6. **Right-click** #content **in the Manage Styles task pane, click** Modify Style **on the shortcut menu, click** Position **in the Category list, type** 550 **in the width text box, then click** OK

7. **Save the changes to your style sheet, then preview the page in a browser**
    The layout now looks as you intended, with the branding and content columns side-by-side and the footer beneath both of them. See Figure N-17.

8. **Close the browser window, then return to Expression Web**

Deciding which browsers to test in

If your Web site is already up and running, you can look at your server logs to find out which browsers your visitors are using. This information can help you decide which browsers to use to test your designs. If you are creating a new site, you will not have access to existing server logs. In that case, a good place to start is to find out which browsers are the most popular and test in those. To find statistics for browser popularity, type **browser statistics** into your favorite search engine. New versions of browsers are always being released, so the statistics do change over time.

FIGURE N-15: branding div floated to the left

branding div

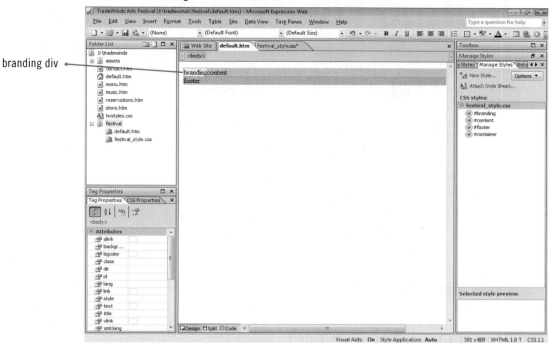

FIGURE N-16: Footer before widths are defined

FIGURE N-17: Floating divs with widths set

Expression Web

Clearing Floats

The CSS clear property allows you to specify that when an element is placed on a page, no floating content is allowed to be displayed on either the right side, left side, or both sides of the element (depending on what you specify). Essentially, it "clears" the floats from around that element. Think of it as cancelling the float. ▓▓▓▓ You decide to test the design and make an adjustment to the footer.

STEPS

1. **Click after the text content on the festival home page, then press [Enter] twice**
   It's a good idea to always add more content to your divs, even if it's just placeholder text, to see how it affects the design before you declare your layout complete.

QUICK TIP
If you had made the branding div longer than the content div, it would have pushed the footer to the right and its content would have floated to the left of the div.

2. **Save your changes, then preview the festival home page in a browser**
   The footer is not behaving as you intended. See Figure N-18. Because the content div has the float property set to right, the content div is also floating to the right of the footer. But you want the footer to extend fully below the other two divs, no matter how much content is in either div.

3. **Close the browser, return to Expression Web, right-click #footer in the Manage Styles task pane, click Modify Style on the shortcut menu, click Layout in the Category list, click the clear list arrow, click both, compare your screen to Figure N-19, then click OK**
   This clears any floats away from both sides of the footer, meaning that no content should float to the left or the right.

4. **Save the changes to your style sheet, then preview the festival home page in a browser**
   See Figure N-20. The footer now extends across both columns, as you intended. The clear property has kept any of the other divs from appearing to the right or left. Your layout is complete. You will add actual content to this page in the next unit.

5. **Close the browser, return to Expression Web, close the tradewinds site, then exit Expression Web**

Using CSS layout templates

If you do not want to create your own CSS layouts but would like more options than are provided in Expression Web, many Web sites provide free basic layouts that you can download and modify for your site. To find these sites, type **CSS layout** into your favorite search engine. You can find layouts with different numbers of columns, with and without headers and footers, and with flexible and liquid widths. Make sure you choose designs that have been tested in the most popular browsers. (Most sites indicate exactly which browsers were used to test the layouts.) Using these basic layouts can save you a lot of time and provide a basis for customizing your own designs.

FIGURE N-18: Content div floating to the right of the footer

Footer should
extend beneath
both branding
and content divs

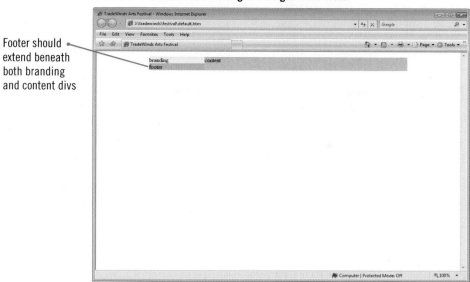

FIGURE N-19: Modify Style dialog box

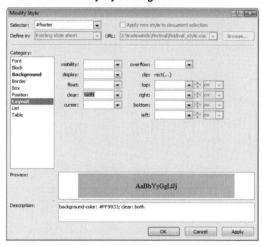

FIGURE N-20: Footer with clear property set

Expression Web

Practice

▼ CONCEPTS REVIEW

Refer to Figure N-21 to answer the following questions:

FIGURE N-21

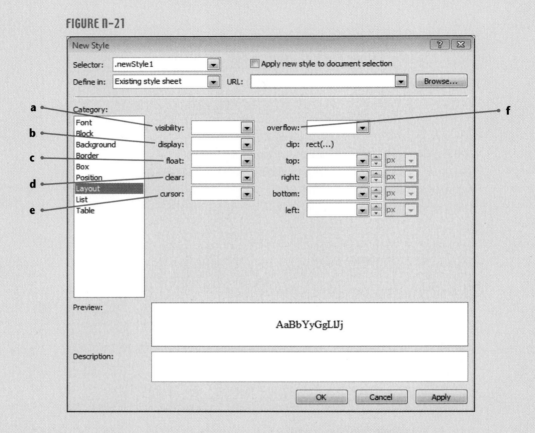

1. Which property controls whether an element is outside the normal flow?
2. Which property allows you to scroll content within an element?
3. Which property allows you to dictate that content cannot be floated to the side of an element?
4. Which property allows the display of a block-level element as inline and vice versa?
5. Which property controls whether an element is visible on the page?
6. Which property allows you to change the type of cursor that appears when an element is pointed to?

Match each term with the statement that best describes it.

7. **Block-level element**
8. **Inline element**
9. **Floated element**
10. **Cleared element**

a. An element that is moved to the right or left of other elements and is outside the normal flow of the page
b. An element that by default is displayed on its own line
c. An element that other elements are not allowed to float to the side of
d. An element that by default is displayed side-by-side with other similar elements

Select the best answer from the list of choices.

11. **Which of the following can you *not* specify by using a single CSS property?**
    a. Type of cursor to display
    b. Number of columns on a page
    c. Whether content scrolls within an element
    d. Whether an element is visible on a page

12. **If you are redesigning an existing Web site, you can find out which browsers your visitors are using by:**
    a. Viewing the HTML code.
    b. Searching the Web for browser statistics.
    c. Reviewing the server logs.
    d. None of the above

13. **Why is it important to assign background colors to each div when designing a CSS layout?**
    a. To allow you to clearly see how the divs are positioned on the page
    b. To keep the divs from collapsing
    c. To coordinate with your design
    d. To help search engines find your page

14. **What is the advantage of having your divs in a different order in the source code compared to the way they are displayed on a page?**
    a. May improve search engine ranking
    b. Helpful for visitors with disabilities
    c. Helpful for visitors using handheld devices
    d. All of the above

▼ SKILLS REVIEW

1. **Create the HTML file.**
   a. Launch Expression Web, then open the careers Web site.
   b. Right-click the careers root folder, then add a subfolder named **featured**.
   c. Click File on the menu bar, point to New, click Page, then add a new HTML page from the General category.
   d. Click File on the menu bar, click Save, navigate to the featured folder, then type **default.htm** in the File name text box.
   e. Click the Change title button and change the title to **Featured Products at Careers Guaranteed**.
   f. Click Save.

2. **Create divs and assign IDs.**
   a. Maximize the Toolbox task pane if necessary.
   b. Click in the top left of the featured home page, then double-click **<div>** on the Toolbox task pane.
   c. Type **branding** in the div you just created, then type **branding** in the id text box on the Tag Properties task pane.
   d. Click the div#branding tab on the visual aid, press [→], then double-click **<div>** on the Toolbox task pane.
   e. Type **content** in the div you just created, then type **content** in the id text box on the Tag Properties task pane.
   f. Click the div#content tab on the visual aid, press [→], then double-click **<div>** on the Toolbox task pane.
   g. Type **footer** in the div you just created, then type **footer** in the id text box on the Tag Properties task pane.
   h. Save your changes.

3. **Create ID-based style rules.**
   a. Maximize the Manage Styles task pane, then click New Style.
   b. Delete the text in the Selector text box, then type **#branding**.
   c. Define the new style in a New style sheet.
   d. Switch to the Background category, type **#99CCFF** in the background-color text box, then click OK to close the New Style dialog box.
   e. Click Yes, click File on the menu bar, then click Save All.
   f. Save the style sheet in the featured folder with the file name **featured_style.css**.

g. Click New Style on the Manage Styles task pane, delete the text in the selector text box, type **#content** in the Selector text box, switch to the Background category, type **#CCFF99** in the background-color text box, then click OK.

h. Click New Style on the Manage Styles task pane, delete the text in the selector text box, type **#footer** in the Selector text box, switch to the Background category, type **#CCCCCC** in the background-color text box, then click OK.

i. Save changes to all open pages.

4. Use a container div.

a. Preview the featured page in a browser.

b. Close the browser, return to Expression Web, click the Show Split View button, in the Code view pane click just before the code `<div id="branding">`, then type **`<div>`**.

c. In the Code View pane, click just before the code `</body>`, then type **`</div>`**.

d. Click in the `</div>` code you just added, press [F5], click in the id text box on the Tag Properties task pane, type **container**, then press [Enter].

e. Click New Style on the Manage Styles task pane, delete the text in the Selector text box, then type **#container** in the selector text box.

f. Switch to the Position category, type **750** in the width text box, then click OK.

g. Save your changes to all open files, preview the featured home page in a browser, then close the browser and return to Expression Web.

h. Right-click #container in the Manage Styles task pane, click Modify Style, switch to the Box category, click the top list arrow under margin, click auto, then click OK.

i. Save your changes to the style sheet, then preview the page in a browser.

5. Create floating columns.

a. Switch to Design View, open the Modify Style dialog box for the #branding style rule, switch to the Layout category, set the float property to left, then click OK.

b. Open the Modify Style dialog box for the #content style rule, switch to the Layout category, set the float property to right, then click OK.

c. Save the changes to the style sheet, preview the featured home page in a browser, then close the browser window and return to Expression Web.

d. Open the Modify Style dialog box for the #branding style rule, switch to the Position category, then set the width to 250 px.

e. Open the Modify Style dialog box for the #content style rule, switch to the Position category, then set the width to 500 px.

f. Save your changes, preview the page in a browser, then close the browser and return to Expression Web.

6. Clear floats.

a. Click after the text content on the featured home page, then press [Enter] three times.

b. Save your changes, preview the page in a browser, then close the browser and return to Expression Web.

c. Open the Modify Style dialog box for the #footer style rule, switch to the Layout category, set the clear property to both, then click OK.

d. Save the changes to the style sheet, preview the featured home page in a browser, then compare your screen to Figure N-22.

e. Close the browser, return to Expression Web, close the careers site, then exit Expression Web.

FIGURE N-22

▼ INDEPENDENT CHALLENGE 1

In this project, you continue your work on the ConnectUp Web site. Tiffany has asked you to design some special pages for a contest they are running called the ConnectUp Challenge.

a. Launch Expression Web, then open the connectup Web site.

b. Right-click the connectup root folder and create a new folder named **challenge**. Inside the challenge folder, create a new blank HTML page from the General category.

c. Save the page in the challenge folder with the file name **default.htm** and the page title **Take the ConnectUp Challenge!**.

d. Click in the challenge home page, then use the Toolbox task pane to add a div to the page.

e. Type **banner** in the div you created, then type **banner** in the id text box on the Tag Properties task pane.

f. Click the div#banner tab on the visual aid, press [→], then use the Toolbox task pane to add a second div to the page.

g. Type **content** in the div you created, then type **content** in the id text box on the Tag Properties task pane.

h. Click the div#content banner on the visual aid, press [→], then use the Toolbox task pane to add a third div to the page.

i. Type **footer** in the div you created, type **footer** in the id text box on the Tag Properties task pane, then save your changes.

j. Maximize the Manage Styles task pane, create a new style using #banner for the selector, create it in a new style sheet, switch to the Background category, specify a background color of #99FF66, switch to the Layout category, set the float property to left, switch to the Position category, set the width to 300 px, then click OK.

k. Click Yes, then save the style sheet in the challenge folder as challenge_style.css.

l. Create a new style in the challenge_style style sheet using #content for the selector, switch to the Background category, specify a background color of #66FFFF, switch to the Layout category, set the float property to right, switch to the Position category, set the width to 500 px, then click OK.

m. Create a new style in the challenge_style sheet using #footer for the selector, switch to the Background category, specify a background color of #FFFF99, switch to the Layout category, set the clear property to both, then click OK.

n. Save changes to all pages, preview the challenge home page in a browser, then close the browser and return to Expression Web.

o. Switch to Split view, in the Code view pane click before the code `<div id="banner">`, type `<div>`, click before the code `</body>`, then type `</div>`.

FIGURE N-23

p. Click in the `</div>` code you just entered, press [F5], then type **container** in the id text box in the Tag Properties task pane.

q. Switch to Design view, create a new style using #container as the selector, switch to the Position category, specify a width of 800 px, switch to the Box category, set margins to auto, then click OK.

r. Save changes to all pages, preview the challenge home page in a browser, compare your screen to Figure N-23, close the browser window, return to Expression Web, close the connectup site, then exit Expression Web.

▼ INDEPENDENT CHALLENGE 2

In this project, you continue your work on the Memories Restored Web site. Brian would like to start targeting historical societies to get more business from that audience. His idea is to create a few additional pages with their own design especially targeted to historical society directors.

a. Launch Expression Web, then open the memories Web site.

b. Inside the root folder, create a subfolder called **historical** and create a new blank HTML page and save it in that folder with the file name **default.htm**.

c. In the historical page, add a div, type the text **branding** into it, and assign it an id of branding.

d. Click the div#branding visual aid tab, press [→], add a div, type the text **content** into it, and assign it an id of content.

e. Click the div#content tab on the visual aid, press [→], add a div, type the text **footer** into it, assign it an id of footer, then save your changes.

f. Create a new style rule in a new style sheet using #branding as the selector, assign it a background color of your choosing, a width of 200 px, and a float property of left. When prompted, click Yes to attach the new style sheet to the HTML page and then save it in the historical folder using an appropriate name. (Remember the rules of naming files—use only numbers, letters, and underscores and do not use spaces.)

g. Create a new style rule in the new style sheet using #content as the selector, assign it a background color of your choosing, a width of 500 px, and a float property of right.

h. Create a new style rule in the new style sheet using #footer as the selector, assign it a background color of your choosing, and set the clear property to both.

i. Save your changes and preview the page in a browser.

j. Working in Split view, click in the Code view pane before the code `<div id="branding">` and type `<div>`, then click before the code `</body>` and type `</div>`. Click in the `</div>` code you just typed, press [F5], then assign the div an id of container.

k. Create a new style rule in the new style sheet using #container as the selector, then assign it a width of 700 pixels and auto margins.

l. Click in the branding div, press [Enter]four times, click in the content div, then press [Enter] three times.

Advanced Challenge Exercise

- Change the footer style so that the floats only clear on the left side of the footer.

m. Save your changes and preview the page in a browser.

n. Close the browser, return to Expression Web, close the memories site, then exit Expression Web.

▼ INDEPENDENT CHALLENGE 3

This Independent Challenge requires an Internet connection.

The director of Technology for All is interested in experimenting with different page layouts for the site. You know you want to use CSS rather than tables to achieve these layouts, but you also know that CSS layouts can be challenging to design. You decide to research and see what pre-made CSS layouts are available for free on the Internet.

   a. Visit your favorite search engine and type in **CSS layouts** as the search term.
   b. Find at least two sites that offer CSS layouts for free.
   c. Visit each site and review the types of designs and layouts that are available (for example, two-column with footer, three-column with header) as well as the instructions for how to use the layouts.
   d. Write one paragraph describing the designs available, and another paragraph describing how you would go about using these as a starting point for your own page design.

Advanced Challenge Exercise

   ■ Find a similar design offered by the two sites. For example, choose the two-column fixed width layout with header from each site.
   ■ Review the CSS code and the explanations of the design from each site.
   ■ Write a paragraph describing the differences and similarities in the CSS used to achieve the two designs.

   e. Add your name to the document and print it.

▼ REAL LIFE INDEPENDENT CHALLENGE

This assignment builds on the personal Web site you have worked on in previous units. In this project, you will create a new folder, HTML page, and style sheet, then create a simple CSS-based layout.

   a. Think of an area of content you can add to your Web site that would benefit from its own look and feel.
   b. Create a folder inside the root folder for this content, then create a blank HTML file inside the subfolder.
   c. Add the appropriate divs to your HTML page and assign an id to each. Be sure to add some unique text to each div so you can distinguish the divs.
   d. Create a style rule for each div in a new external style sheet, using the id as the selector. Assign a different background color to each div, and modify the layout and positioning properties to achieve your desired layout.
   e. Save your changes, then preview the page in a browser. Based on your review, make any necessary modifcations to the new page.
   f. Close your site, then exit Expression Web.

Expression Web

Launch Expression Web, open the ecotours site, then open the home page. Modify the home page so your screen matches Figure N-24. (*Hint*: You will need to assign an id to the image and then create an id-based style rule to achieve the effect.) When you are finished, save your changes, close the ecotours site, then exit Expression Web.

FIGURE Π-24

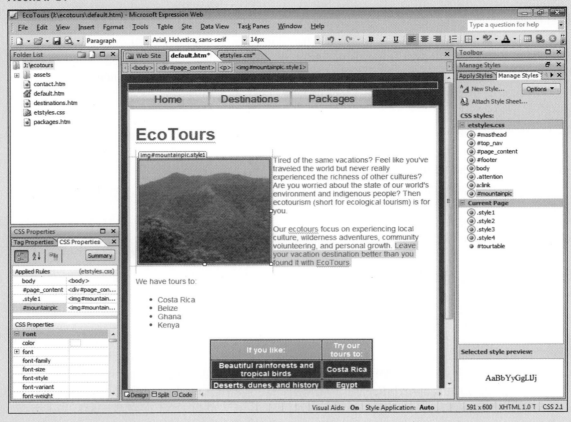

Designing Like a Pro

When professional Web designers create sites, they take into account not only the overall visual design of the site, but also the details that make it more polished and easier to navigate. These include colorful text-based navigation links, sidebars that include scroll bars for easier reading, and print style sheets to facilitate printing a Web page. In this unit, you learn to use some advanced CSS methods to enhance the look and feel of a Web site. Catalina has asked you to finish the design for the festival page and to add content to it. To complete the design, you'll employ some professional-level design tools and techniques.

OBJECTIVES

Import files into a site
Use the faux column technique
Create list-based navigation
Create CSS-based rollovers
Create a scrolling sidebar
Create an attached image
Create a print style sheet

Importing Files into a Site

You have learned to *insert* a file into a Web page, which adds the content of that file to the page. However, you can also *import* files such as graphics and style sheets, into a Web site. Importing a file simply adds a copy of that file to your Web site folder, making it available for you to use in your Web pages. If you have a file such as a style sheet that contains references to supporting image files, you need to import the referenced image files, too. ▓▓▓▓▓ Catalina has sent you two text files containing information about the festival. You need to insert these files into the festival page, import a new style sheet that uses the actual colors of the festival page design, and import some images that are used in the imported style sheet.

STEPS

QUICK TIP
Remember that the festival home page is the default.htm file in the festival subfolder.

1. **Launch Expression Web, open the tradewinds site, then open the festival home page**
   The festival page you created in the previous unit opens. It includes temporary background colors that you added in order to see the page layout.

2. **Switch to Design view if necessary, click anywhere in the content div, select the word content, then press [Delete]**
   The content div is now empty.

3. **Click Insert on the menu bar, click File, in the Select Files dialog box click the file type list arrow, click All Files (*.*), navigate to the location where you keep your Data Files, click twf_content.txt, click Open, then click OK**
   The content is inserted into the content div, as shown in Figure O-1.

4. **Click anywhere in the branding div, select the word branding, then press [Delete]**

QUICK TIP
Inserting the file as plain text allows you to apply your own styles to the content and prevents any conflicting styles from being added along with the content.

5. **Click anywhere in the footer div, select the word footer, press [Delete], click Insert on the menu bar, navigate to the location where you store your Data Files, click File, click twf_footer.txt, click Open, then click OK**
   The twf_footer file is inserted as plain text into the footer div.

6. **In the Folder List task pane expand the festival folder if necessary, right-click festival_style.css in the list, click Delete, then click Yes**
   Deleting the style sheet removes all layout and formatting from the page.

7. **Click File on the menu bar, point to Import, click File, click Add File, in the Add File to Import List dialog box, navigate to the location where you store your Data Files, press and hold [Ctrl], click twf_body_bg.gif, twf_branding_bg.gif, and festival_style.css, then click Open**
   The file path and name for the three files appear in the Import dialog box, as shown in Figure O-2.

8. **Click OK, save your changes, click anywhere in the editing window, then press [F5] to refresh the screen**
   The styles from the style sheet you imported are now reflected in the page layout and design.

9. **Preview the festival home page in a browser, compare your screen to Figure O-3, then keep the browser window open for the next lesson**

FIGURE O-1: Text file inserted into festival page

FIGURE O-2: Completed Import file dialog box

Theses files will be imported

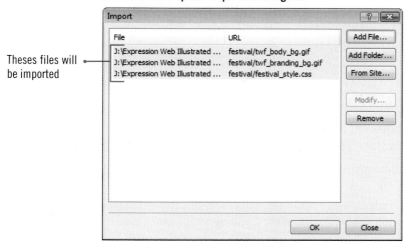

FIGURE O-3: Festival page with imported text, images, and style sheet

Reusing style sheets

You can create a style sheet containing rules for a page layout and basic formatting and use it as a starting point for multiple designs. Many Web designers have a foundational style sheet containing basic formatting that they use to start each design. Once you've created the style sheet, you can just import it into your new site, attach it to each page, then modify it as needed. Using this method can save time and prevent you from having to repeatedly create the same styles for each site.

Using the Faux Column Technique

A common problem with column-based CSS layouts is that a column is really just a div, and divs are only as tall as the content they contain. This means that if a page contains a short column, the column background color will stop at the end of the content, leaving a bit of a "hole" in your design. To get around this problem, designers use what's called the **faux column technique**. To create the illusion of a column, designers insert a background image that mimics the color of the column in the container div and repeat it vertically. The background image fills the holes left when the column's actual background color ends.  You examine the festival home page and notice a gap in the branding column's background color. You decide to use the faux column technique to fix this problem.

STEPS

1. **Review the festival home page in the browser**

   See Figure O-4. Notice that because the branding div on the left is shorter than the content div, the blue color does not extend all the way down and the wave background image from the body style is showing through.

2. **On the Manage Styles task pane, right-click #container, then click** Modify Style

   The Modify Style dialog box opens.

3. **Click** Background **in the Category list, click** Browse, **navigate to the drive and folder where you store your Data Files, click** twf_container_bg.gif, **then click** Open

4. **Click the** background-repeat list arrow, **click** repeat-y, **compare your screen to Figure O-5, then click** OK

   The image is added, with a vertical repeat setting. Notice the thin border that appears between the bottom of the branding div and the top of the repeating background image.

5. **Save changes to all open pages, save the embedded file when prompted, then preview the page in a browser**

   See Figure O-6. Notice that the columns now appear to be of equal length. This is because the background image repeats down the page and fills in the colors.

6. **Close the browser, then return to Expression Web**

Creating a faux column background image

Modifying a style to implement the faux column technique is not difficult. What can be tricky is creating a background image to use in the technique. The image must be sized correctly and must work seamlessly with the CSS background color. To create a faux column background image, you need to use a graphics editing program such as Microsoft Expression Design or Adobe Photoshop. First, create an image that is exactly as wide as the area that your columns cover. (The faux columns technique works only with a fixed-width design.) Then, for each column in your design, create a block of color on the image that matches the background color and width of each column. To match the color, you can use a color picker tool in your image editing program to sample from a background image, or type the hex code directly if you're trying to match a background color that's defined in the style sheet. Finally, crop the image so that you save only a thin horizontal slice of it. Because you are going to repeat it down the page, the image can have a very small height of, say, 5 pixels or so. That way, you won't end up with a column that is too long rather than too short, and the image will also download more quickly in the visitor's browser.

FIGURE O-4: Background image used to create faux column effect

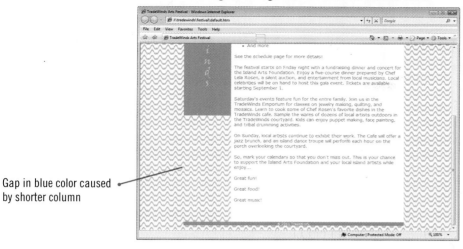

Gap in blue color caused by shorter column

FIGURE O-5: Modifiy style box for #container

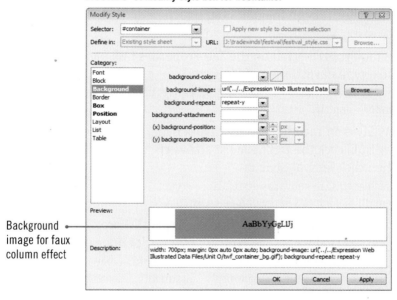

Background image for faux column effect

FIGURE O-6: Festival page with faux column background image

Columns now appear to be of equal length

Creating List-Based Navigation

When designing sites with text-based navigation (rather than image-based navigation), most professional designers mark up the navigation bar as an unordered list, because it is essentially a list of navigation options. This provides semantic meaning to the navigation options and increases the accessibility of the site. However, unordered lists with no style rules applied result in a look that may not suit the overall design; items are stacked on top of one another, and each item has a bullet in front of it. If you want the navigation options to blend into the site design, you need to add an id to the list and then write style rules for the items that appear in that list. ▓▓▓▓▓ The navigation list was imported into the page with the page content. You decide to create a style rule that will make the list look more like a horizontal navigation bar. You also want to create the links for each list item.

STEPS

1. **In the first bulleted list on the festival home page, click anywhere in the text** Festival Home, **then click** <ul> **on the quick tag selector bar**
   The unordered list is selected.

2. **Click the** Tag Properties tab **on the Tag Properties task pane if necessary, click in the id text box, type** navlist, **then press** [Enter]
   See Figure O-7. The quick tag selector bar now displays ul#navlist, indicating that the navlist id has been attached to the unordered list.

   QUICK TIP
   Be sure to leave a space between #navlist and li.

3. **Click** New Style **on the Manage Styles task pane, delete the text in the Selector text box, type** #navlist li, **click the** Define in list arrow, **click** Existing style sheet, **click the** URL list arrow, **then click** festival_style.css
   Selectors such as this are known as descendant selectors. A **descendant selector** applies the style rule to any list item (li) that appears in the unordered list that is marked with an id of navlist.

4. **Click** Layout **in the Category list, click the** display list arrow, **click** inline, **click** List **in the Category list, click the** list-style-type list arrow, **click** none, **then click** OK
   See Figure O-8. The navigation items now all appear on the same line and without bullets in front of the list items. The style rule causes the list to be displayed as an inline element (with the text all on one line) rather than as a block-level element (with each list item on its own line). Setting the list-style-type to none causes the bullets in front of each list item to not be displayed.

5. **Click between the word** Home **and the word** Schedule, **then press** [Spacebar]

6. **Click between the word** Schedule **and the word** Sponsors, **then press** [Spacebar]

7. **Select the text** Festival Home, **right-click the** selected text, **click** Hyperlink **on the short-cut menu, click in the** Address text box, **double-click the** festival folder, **click** default.htm, **then click** OK

   QUICK TIP
   When entering an address ahead of time, make sure that when you create the page, you name the file exactly what you typed into the address bar.

8. **Select the text** Schedule, **right-click the** selected text, **click** Hyperlink **on the shortcut menu, click in the** Address text box, **type** schedule.htm, **then click** OK
   Because the schedule page has not been created yet, you must type the filename.

9. **Select the text** Sponsors, **right-click the** selected text, **click** Hyperlink **on the shortcut menu, click in the** Address text box, **type** sponsors.htm, **click** OK, **then save changes to all open pages**
   The list items are now links, as shown in Figure O-9.

FIGURE O-7: Unordered list with navlist id applied

Quick tag selector displays ul with #navlist applied

List id is designated as navlist

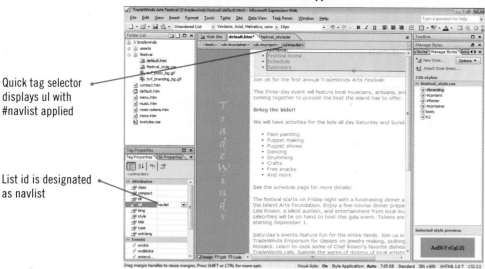

FIGURE O-8: List with style rules applied

List items appear as inline elements and without bullets

FIGURE O-9: List items with hyperlinks added

Three hyperlinks

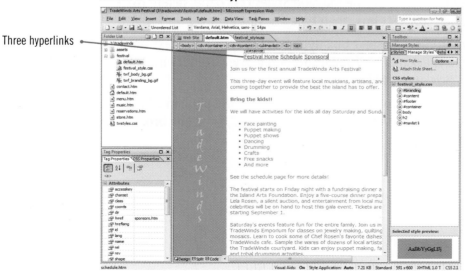

Expression Web

Creating CSS-Based Rollovers

You have learned how to create rollover images in Expression Web. If you prefer to use text-based navigation on your page, though, you don't have to give up rollovers. By applying different background colors to the a:hover state, you can create a CSS-based rollover that changes the look of the text when the user points to it or clicks it. ▄▄▄▄ You want to create rollovers for the text-based navigation on the festival page. To do this, you need to create style rules for the navigation links.

QUICK TIP

Make sure to type a space between navlist and a.

1. **Click** New Style **on the Manage Styles task pane, select the** text and period in the Selector text box, **press** [Delete], **then type** #navlist a
   Using this descendent selector creates a style rule that applies to every link in the navlist list, but to no other links in the site.

2. **Click** Box **in the Category list, click the** padding Same for all checkbox **to remove the checkmark, type** 10 **in the padding top text box, type** 3 **in the padding right text box, type** 10 **in the padding bottom text box, type** 3 **in the padding left text box, compare your screen to Figure O-10, then click** OK
   Adding some padding around the list items will help to make them look a bit more like buttons.

QUICK TIP

Do not type a space between a and the colon.

3. **Click** New Style **on the Manage Styles task pane, delete the** existing period and text **in the Selector text box, then type** #navlist a:link

4. **Click in the** color text box, **type** #FFFFFF, **click the** text-decoration none checkbox **to add a checkmark, click** Background **in the Category list, click in the** background-color text box, **type** #49B3E4, **then click** OK
   The background color of the navigation links is now blue, the text is white, and they are no longer underlined.

5. **Right-click** #navlist a:link **on the Manage Styles task pane, click** New Style Copy, **in the Selector text box delete the text** link, **type** visited **to replace it, compare your screen to Figure O-11, then click** OK
   The visited links style now matches the unvisited links style, which ensures visual consistency for the navigation bar.

6. **Click** New Style **on the Manage Styles task pane, delete the existing period and text in the Selector text box, then type** #navlist a: hover

7. **Click in the** color text box, **type** #24A3DF, **click the** text-decoration none check box **to add a check mark, click** Background **in the Category list, click in the** background-color text box, **type** #FEEF38, **then click** OK

8. **Save changes to all open pages, preview the page in a browser, point to the navigation links, compare your screen to Figure O-12, close the browser window, then return to Expression Web**

FIGURE O-10: Completed New Style dialog box for #navlist a style rule

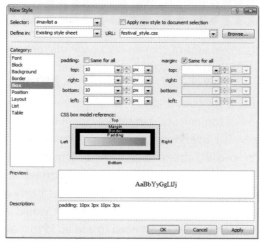

FIGURE O-11: Completed New Style dialog box for #navlist a:visited style rule

Edited style name •

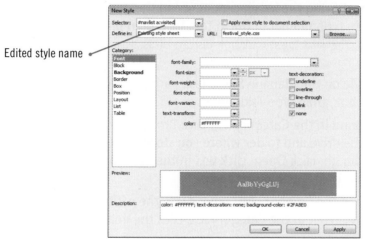

FIGURE O-12: Navigation links with CSS rollovers

Background changes when user points to link

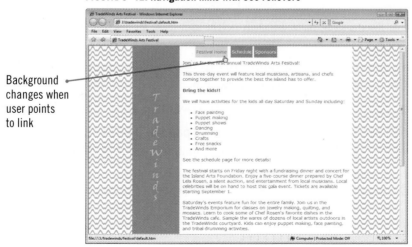

Getting creative with CSS rollovers

CSS rollovers can be much more elaborate than just changing the background colors. You can create style rules that swap out background images, change the location of background images, change the size and location of text, and more. Taking the time to experiment and creatively combine these properties can yield text links that are as visually interesting as image-based ones.

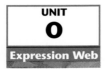
Creating a Scrolling Sidebar

A **sidebar** is a short, boxed area of content on a page that provides additional information about a topic. To create a sidebar on a Web page, you place the desired content inside a div and assign an id to the div, and then you write an id-based style rule that floats the sidebar to one side or the other and also dictates the visual design, such as the background color or borders. If you want a sidebar that is a consistent height no matter the amount of content, you can set the height to your desired number of pixels and then set the CSS overflow property. The **overflow property** determines how the browser should handle content that doesn't fit within the specified size of its containing element. Setting this property to the value of "auto" causes scrollbars to appear when there is more content than will fit. This allows visitors to scroll to view the rest of the text or images. See Table O-1 for all overflow property values. ░░░░ You and Catalina decide that the content about kids' activities on the home page would work better as a sidebar. The content is already marked up with a div, so you just need to add an id to it and create a style rule based on that id.

STEPS

1. **Click in the text Bring the kids!!, click <div> on the quick tag selector bar, click the Tag Properties tab, type sidebar in the id text box, then press [Enter]**
   See Figure O-13. The quick tag selector now displays div#sidebar, indicating that an id of sidebar has been assigned to the div.

2. **Click New Style on the Manage Styles task pane, delete all the existing text in the Selector text box, then type #sidebar**

3. **Click Background in the Category list, click Browse next to the background-image field, navigate to the drive and folder where you store your Data Files, click twf_sidebar_bg.gif, click Open, click Box in the Category list, type 10 in the padding top box, then type 10 in the margin top box**

4. **Click Position in the Category list, type 200 in the width text box, type 100 in the height text box, click Layout in the Category list, click the float list arrow, click right, then click OK**

5. **Save changes to all files, saving embedded files when prompted, then preview the page in a browser**
   The sidebar div does not have sufficient height to display all the content, as shown in Figure O-14. One option is to increase the height of the sidebar; another option is to use the overflow auto property.

6. **Close the browser window, return to Expression Web, on the Manage Styles task pane right-click #sidebar, then click Modify Style**

QUICK TIP

You can also set the overflow to auto on the main content div of a page, to control the height of the entire page.

7. **Click Layout in the Category list, click the overflow list arrow, click auto, then click OK**

8. **Save changes to all files, then preview the page in a browser**
   See Figure O-15. All the text is now contained within the sidebar. Scrollbars are displayed on the sidebar, allowing visitors to scroll through the sidebar text.

9. **Close the browser window, then return to Expression Web**

FIGURE O-13: Div with sidebar id applied

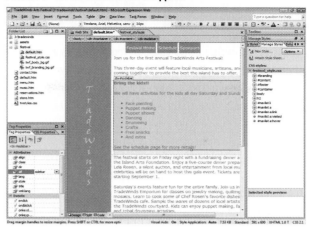

FIGURE O-14: Sidebar with content overflowing the div

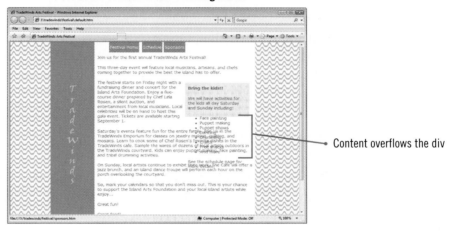

Content overflows the div

FIGURE O-15: Sidebar div after overflow auto property is applied

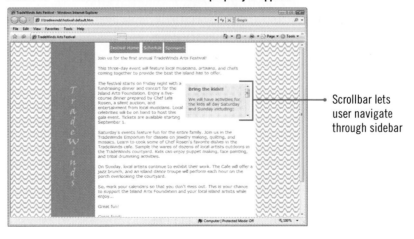

Scrollbar lets user navigate through sidebar

TABLE O-1: CSS overflow values

value	effect
visible (default)	Content overflow is visible but appears outside the containing element
hidden	Content overflow is hidden from the visitor
scroll	Content overflow is hidden, but scrollbars appear to allow visitors to view the content
auto	If content overflows, scrollbars appear; if content does not overflow, scrollbars do not appear

Creating an Attached Image

Using the CSS position property with a value of fixed creates an element that remains stationary when visitors scroll the page. This is a nice effect that can be used if you have a visual element or a navigation area that you want to be sure is always visible on the page. ▰▰▰▰ You decide to add an Arts Festival image to the top left of the festival page and to create a style rule to attach the image to the page so it remains fixed.

STEPS

TROUBLE
Be sure to click in the blue area above the TradeWinds banner, at the top left of the page, rather than in the top left of the content div.

1. **Click in the branding div in the top-left corner of the festival home page, click Insert on the menu bar, point to Picture, click From File, navigate to the folder where you store your Data Files, double-click twf_arts_side.gif, type Arts Festival in the Alternate text field, then click OK**

2. **Save your changes, saving embedded files when prompted, preview the page in a browser, then use the browser scrollbar if necessary to scroll up and down the page**
   Currently, the Arts Festival image scrolls with the rest of the page.

TROUBLE
When creating a class-based style, you should leave the period in front of the selector.

3. **Close the browser window, return to Expression Web, click New Style on the Manage Styles task pane, then type artsimg to replace the highlighted text in the Selector text box**
   This creates a class-based style you can apply to the Arts Festival image.

4. **Click Position in the Category list, click the position list arrow, then click fixed**

5. **Click in the top text box, type 25, compare your screen to Figure O-16, then click OK**
   This sets the position of the image 25 pixels from the top of the page, giving it a bit of a top margin.

6. **In the editing window, click the Arts Festival image, click the Tag Properties task pane, click in the class text box, click the class list arrow, then click artsimg**
   Compare your screen to Figure O-17.

7. **Save changes to all pages, preview the page in a browser, then use the scroll bar to scroll up and down the page; if your screen is large enough that scroll bars do not appear, resize the window until it is small enough that a vertical scroll bar appears**
   The image remains fixed in the top-left corner while the rest of the page content scrolls. See Figure O-18.

TROUBLE
If you are using Internet Explorer version 6, be aware that due to a browser bug, the position fixed property may not work correctly.

8. **Leave the browser window open for the next lesson**

FIGURE O-16: Completed New Style dialog box for .artsimg style rule

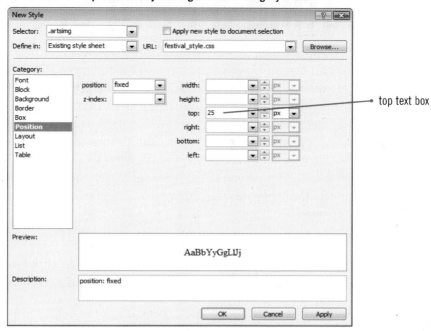

top text box

FIGURE O-17: Arts festival image with .artsimg class applied

Selected image with .artsimg class applied

class list arrow

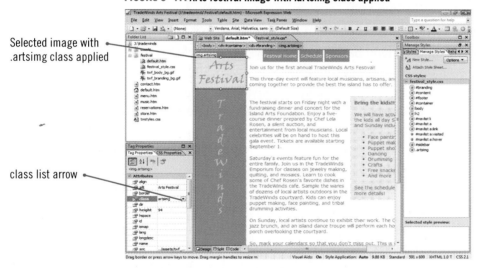

FIGURE O-18: Arts festival image in fixed position

Image does not scroll with page content

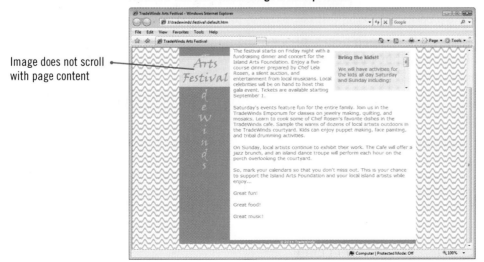

Expression Web

Creating a Print Style Sheet

Up until this point, you have created style rules that dictate how a Web page should be displayed in a visitor's browser on a screen. However, you can attach more than one style sheet to a page, to target each style sheet to a different type of display, such as print, TV, handheld, or Braille readers. The **media property** tells the browser when to display each style sheet and is designated in the HTML code. Many designers create print style sheets and add them to their Web pages. A **print style sheet** controls what a page looks like when a visitor prints the page and often contains rules that hide unnecessary images or change the font size and color to a more print-friendly format. ⬛⬛⬛ You want to hide the Arts Festival image when people print. You have an existing screen style sheet already attached to the page, so you'll create a new CSS file to use for the print style sheet, attach it to the festival home page, then create the rule to hide the image when printed.

STEPS

TROUBLE

If you are using Internet Explorer and do not see the menu bar, press [Alt].

1. **Click** File **on the menu bar in your Web browser, then click** Print Preview

   Print Preview opens, as shown in Figure O-19. This is the Print Preview window for Internet Explorer 7; if you are using a different Web browser your screen will look different from the one shown here. Notice that the Arts Festival image appears.

2. **Click the** Close button **on the Print Preview window, close the browser window, then return to Expression Web**

3. **Click** File **on the menu bar, point to** New, **then click** CSS

4. **Click** File **on the menu bar, then click** Save, **double-click the** festival folder, **click in the** File Name text box, **type** print_festival_style.css, **then click** Save

5. **Click the** default.htm tab, **click** Attach Style Sheet **on the Manage Styles task pane, click** Browse **in the Attach Style Sheet dialog box, double-click the** festival folder, **click** print_festival_style.css, **click** Open, **then click** OK

   The style sheet is now attached to the festival home page and is displayed in the Manage Styles task pane.

QUICK TIP

The code is located near line 9; remember that you can also use the Find feature to locate the code.

6. **Switch to** Code View, **click after the code** `href="print_festival_style.css"`, **press** [Spacebar], **type** media=, **then double-click** print **on the shortcut menu**

   Setting this property tells the browser to use only these styles when a visitor prints the page.

7. **Switch to** Design View, **click** New Style **on the Manage Styles task pane, type** artsimg **in the Selector text box to replace the selected text, click the** Define in list arrow, **click** Existing style sheet, **click the** URL list arrow, **click** print_festival_style.css, **click** Layout **in the Category list, click the** display list arrow, **click** none, **then click** OK

   Setting this property tells the browser not to display the image on a printed copy of the page.

8. **Save changes to all open pages, preview the page in a browser, then view the page in Print Preview within your browser program**

   The image no longer appears, as shown in Figure O-20.

9. **Close the Print Preview window, close the browser window, return to Expression Web, close the tradewinds site, then exit Expression Web**

FIGURE O-19: Print Preview of festival home page

Arts Festival
image is
displayed

Close button

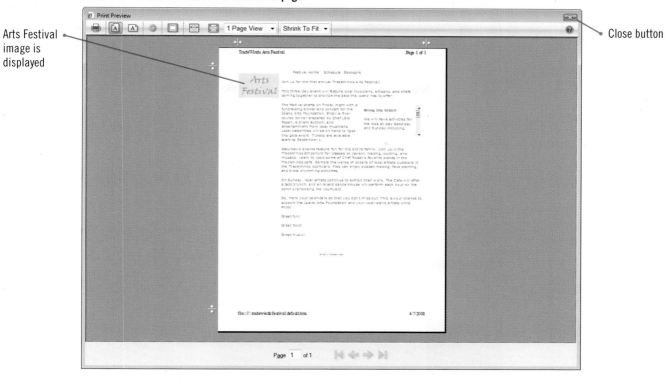

FIGURE O-20: Print Preview with print style sheet applied

Arts Festival
image
is hidden

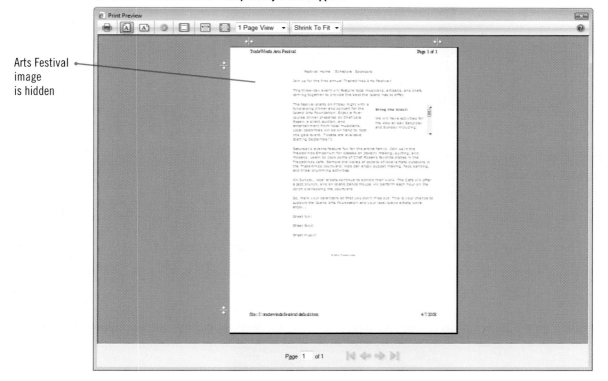

Practice

▼ CONCEPTS REVIEW

Label each element in the Expression Web window shown in Figure O-21.

FIGURE O-21

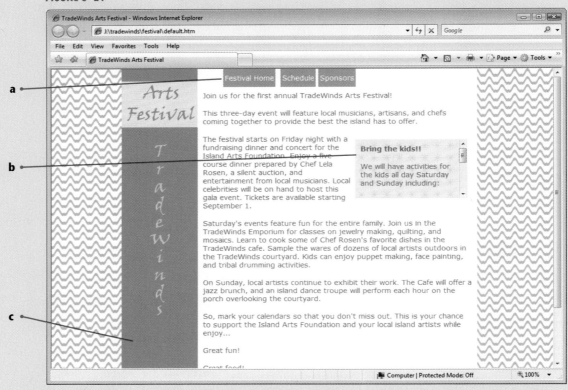

1. Which element uses the faux column technique?
2. Which element constitutes text-based navigation?
3. Which element uses the overflow auto property?

Match each CSS overflow property with the statement that best describes it.

4. **visible**   a. Scrollbars appear if content overflows the containing element.

5. **hidden**   b. Overflow content is not visible.

6. **scroll**   c. Overflow content appears outside of containing element.

7. **auto**   d. Scrollbars appear on containing element regardless of whether or not content overflows.

Select the best answer from the list of choices.

8. **What CSS limitation does the faux column technique solve?**
   - **a.** Divs cannot be taller than the content they contain.
   - **b.** Columns of unequal length have gaps in background.
   - **c.** Columns of unequal width have gaps in background.
   - **d.** Divs hold only a limited amount of content.

9. **What is the advantage of marking up text-based navigation as a list?**
   - **a.** Increases accessibility for users with disabilities
   - **b.** Allows you to create style rules
   - **c.** Looks better on the page
   - **d.** Both a and b are correct.

10. **What effect does setting the CSS display property to inline have on a list?**
    - **a.** It lines up the list items on top of each other.
    - **b.** It creates rollover effects.
    - **c.** It places the list items side by side on the same line.
    - **d.** It adds padding and margins.

11. **The effect of changing background colors in CSS rollovers is created by changing the property of which link state?**
    - **a.** a
    - **b.** a:link
    - **c.** a:visited
    - **d.** a:hover

▼ SKILLS REVIEW

1. **Import files into a site.**
   - **a.** Launch Expression Web, open the careers site, then open the featured home page.
   - **b.** Click anywhere in the content div, delete the word content, click Insert on the menu bar, click File, in the Select File dialog box click the File type list arrow, click All Files (*.*), navigate to the location where you store your Data Files, then open the file cgf_content.txt.
   - **c.** Click anywhere in the branding div, then delete the word branding.
   - **d.** Click anywhere in the footer div, delete the word footer, click Insert on the file menu, click File, then insert the file cgf_footer.txt as plain text.
   - **e.** In the Folder List task pane, expand the featured folder if necessary, then delete the file featured_style.css.
   - **f.** Click File on the menu bar, point to Import, click File, click Add File, select the files cgf_body_bg.gif, cgf_branding_bg.gif, and featured_style.css, open the files, then click OK to import all three files. (*Hint*: Press and hold the [Ctrl] key while clicking the files to select them all.)
   - **g.** Save your changes, press [F5] to refresh the screen, then preview the page in a browser. Leave the browser window open.

2. **Use the faux column technique.**
   - **a.** Review the bottom-left area of the featured home page in the browser, then close the browser window and return to Expression Web.
   - **b.** Right-click #container on the Manage Styles task pane, then click Modify Style.
   - **c.** Switch to the Background category, click Browse next to the background-image field, navigate to the drive and folder where you store your Data Files, then open the file cgf_container_bg.gif.
   - **d.** Set the background-repeat to repeat-y, then click OK.
   - **e.** Save changes to all open pages, saving any embedded files when prompted, then preview the page in a browser.
   - **f.** Close the browser, then return to Expression Web.

3. **Create list-based navigation.**
   - **a.** In the first bulleted list in the page, click anywhere in the text Featured Products, then click <ul> on the quick tag selector bar.
   - **b.** Click in the id text box on the Tag Properties task pane, type **navlist**, then press [Enter].
   - **c.** Open the New Style dialog box, select and delete the text in the Selector text box (including the period), type **#navlist li** in the Selector text box, then define the style in the featured_style.css style sheet.
   - **d.** Switch to the Layout category, set the display property to inline, switch to the List category, set the list-style-type to none, then click OK to close the dialog box.
   - **e.** Click between the word Products and the word Services and press [Spacebar], then click between the word Specials and the word Product and press [Spacebar].

    f. Select the text Featured Products, right-click, click Hyperlink, navigate to and click the default.htm file in the featured folder, then click OK.

    g. Select the text Services Specials, right-click the selected text, click Hyperlink, type **services_specials.htm** in the Address text box, then click OK.

    h. Select the text **Product Specials**, right-click the selected text, click Hyperlink, type product_specials.htm in the Address text box, then click OK.

    i. Save changes to the page, saving any embedded files when prompted.

4. Create CSS-based rollovers.

    a. Open the New Style dialog box, select and delete the text in the Selector text box (including the period), then type **#navlist a** in the Selector text box.

    b. Switch to the Box category, remove the check mark in the padding Same for all check box, set the top and bottom padding to **8px** and the right and left padding to **3px**, then click OK.

    c. Open the New Style dialog box, delete all text in the Selector text box, type **#navlist a:link** in the Selector text box, type **#EDEAE7** in the color text box, add a check mark to the text-decoration none check box, switch to the Background category, type **#693C17** in the background-color text box, then click OK.

    d. Right-click #navlist a:link on the Manage Styles task pane, click New Style Copy, delete the text link in the Selector text box, type **visited** to replace the deleted text, then click OK.

    e. Open the New Style dialog box, delete all text in the Selector text box (including the period), type **#navlist a:hover** in the Selector text box, type **#693C17** in the color text box, add a check mark to the text-decoration none check box, switch to the Background category, type **#CCDDFF** in the background-color text box, then click OK.

    f. Save your changes, saving embedded files when prompted, preview the page in a browser, point to each navigation link, close the browser window, and return to Expression Web.

5. Create a scrolling sidebar.

    a. Click anywhere in the text Feeling blue about your career?, click <div> on the quick tag selector bar, then type **sidebar** in the id text box on the Tag Properties task pane.

    b. Open the New Style dialog box, delete all text in the Selector text box, then type **#sidebar** to replace the deleted text.

    c. Switch to the Background category, type **#CCDDFF** in the background-color text box, switch to the Box category, type **10** in the padding top box, then type **10** in the margin top text box.

    d. Switch to the Position category, type **150** in the width text box, type **200** in the height text box, switch to the Layout category, set the float property to right, then click OK.

    e. Save your changes, saving embedded files when prompted, preview the page in a browser, close the browser window, then return to Expression Web.

    f. Open the Modify Style dialog box for the #sidebar style, switch to the Layout category, set the overflow property to **auto**, then click OK.

    g. Save all changes to the page, preview the page in a browser, close the browser window, then return to Expression Web.

6. Create an attached image.

    a. Click in the top-left corner of the featured home page (the branding div), click Insert on the menu bar, point to Picture, click From File, navigate to the drive and folder where you store your Data Files, double-click the file cgf_ticket.gif, type **Your ticket to success** in the Alternate text field, then click OK.

    b. Save your changes, saving any embedded files when prompted, preview the page in a browser, scroll down the page, close the browser window, then return to Expression Web.

    c. Open the New Style dialog box, then type **ticketimg** to replace the highlighted text in the Selector text box. (*Hint*: Do not type over the period.)

    d. Switch to the Position category, set the position to fixed, set the top property to 15px, then click OK.

    e. Click the ticket image in the editing window to select it, click in the class text box in the Tag Properties task pane, click the class list arrow, then click ticketimg.

    f. Save changes to the page, preview the page in a browser, scroll up and down the page, compare your screen to Figure O-22, then leave the browser window open.

7. Create a print style sheet.

  a. Click Print on the File menu, click Print Preview, view the page, close the Print Preview window, then close the browser window and return to Expression Web.

  b. Click File on the menu bar, point to New, then click CSS.

  c. Save the CSS file in the featured folder with the name **print_featured_styles.css**.

  d. Make the featured home page the active page, click Attach Style Sheet on the Manage Styles task pane, navigate to the print_featured_styles.css file, click Open, then click OK.

  e. Switch to Code view, locate the code **href="print_featured_styles.css"**, click just after the code, press [Spacebar], type **media=**, double-click print on the shortcut menu, then switch back to Design view.

  f. Open the New Style dialog box, type **ticketimg** in the selector text box to replace the highlighted text. (*Hint*: Be careful not to type over the period.) Define the style in the print_featured_styles.css style sheet.

  g. Switch to the Layout category, set the display to **none**, then click OK.

  h. Save changes to all open pages, preview the pages in a browser, click the Print list arrow, click Print Preview, close the Print Preview window, close the browser window, return to Expression Web, close the careers site, then exit Expression Web.

FIGURE O-22

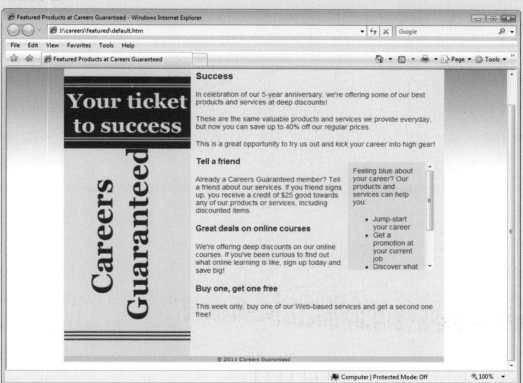

▼ INDEPENDENT CHALLENGE 1

In this project you continue your work on the ConnectUp Web site. You have been working on the design for the new ConnectUp Challenge site and have some images and a style sheet ready to import. Tiffany has also sent you the content for the first page. You need to import those files and then add some finishing touches to the design, such as evening up the columns, creating a scrolling sidebar, and adding an attached image.

a. Launch Expression Web, open the connectup Web site, then open the challenge home page.

b. Select and delete the words banner, content, and footer.

c. Expand the challenge folder in the Folder List task pane if necessary, then delete the challenge_style.css file.

d. Insert the file cuc_content.txt, located in your Data Files folder, in the content div.

e. Insert the file cuc_footer.txt, located in your Data Files folder, as plain text in the footer div.

f. Import the files cuc_banner_bg.gif and challenge_style.css, located in your Data Files folder.

g. Save your changes, press [F5] to refresh the screen, preview the page in a browser, then close the browser window and return to Expression Web.

h. Open the Modify Style dialog box for the #container style, switch to the Background category, set the background image to cuc_container_bg.gif and the background-repeat to repeat-y. (*Hint*: To insert the background image, navigate to the location where you store your Data Files.) Save your changes, saving any embedded files when prompted, preview the page in a browser, then close the browser and return to Expression Web.

i. Click anywhere in the text TAKE THE CHALLENGE AND, select the <div> tag on the quick tag selector bar, then use the Tag Properties task pane to assign the div an id of sidebar.

j. Create a new style in the challenge_style.css style sheet, using a selector of #sidebar. In the Background category, set a background-color of #A2E2F3. In the Box category, set the padding to 5px on all sides, in the Position category, set the width to 150px and the height to 200px. In the Layout category, set the float to right and the overflow to auto. Click OK, save your changes, preview the page in a browser, close the browser window, and return to Expression Web.

k. Click in the banner div in the top-left corner of the challenge home page, then insert the image cuc_badge.jpg from the location where you store your Data Files. Enter **Take the Challenge!** as the alternate text when prompted.

l. Create a new style rule in the challenge_style.css file, using a selector of .challengebadge. In the Position category, set the position to fixed and the top to 30px.

m. Select the badge image in the editing window and use the Tag Properties task pane to assign it a class of challengebadge.

n. Save changes to all your pages, preview the page in a browser, scroll up and down the page, compare your screen to Figure O-23, close the browser window, return to Expression Web, close the connectup site, then exit Expression Web.

FIGURE 0–23

▼ INDEPENDENT CHALLENGE 2

In this project you continue your work on the Memories Restored Web site. You have been working on the design for the new pages targeted to historical society directors and have some images and a style sheet ready to import. Brian has also sent you the content for the first page. You import those files and then add some finishing touches to the design, such as evening up the columns and creating the navigation.

a. Launch Expression Web, open the memories Web site, then open the home page in the historical folder.

b. Delete the placeholder text in each div. Insert the file mrh_content.txt into the content div, then insert the file mrh_footer.text as plain text into the footer div.

c. Delete the file historical_style.css from the historical folder in the Folder List task pane.

d. From the location where you store your Data Files, import the files historical_style.css and mrh_branding_bg.gif. Save your changes, then press [F5] to refresh the screen.

e. Create faux columns by modifying the #container style to add mrh_container_bg.gif as a background image to the container div. Set the background-repeat property to the appropriate value. Save your changes, saving changes to embedded files when prompted. Preview your page in a browser.

f. Click in the list text at the top of the page, use the quick tag selector to select it, then assign it an id of navlist.

g. Create a new style in the historical_style.css style sheet using **#navlist li** as the selector. Set the display to inline and list-style-type to none.

h. Add space as necessary between the intended links in the navigation text.

i. Select the text for each navigation option and link it to the appropriate page. (*Hint*: The only linked page that currently exists is the default page for the Historical Home link. For the other links, you need to type the likely page name into the address bar manually.)

j. Create a new style in historical_style.css, using #navlist a as the selector and set values of your choosing for the padding.

k. Create a new style in historical_style.css, using #navlist a:link as the selector and set values of your choosing for the color, text-decoration, and background-color.

l. Use the New Style Copy command to copy the #navlist a:link style rule. For the copied rule, change the selector #navlist a:visited, and leave the other properties the same.

m. Create a new style in historical_style.css using #navlist a:hover as the selector, and set appropriate values for color, text-decoration, and background-color. (*Hint*: Remember these properties are displayed when a visitor points to the link.)

n. Save your changes, preview the page in a browser, and point to each navigation option.

Advanced Challenge Exercise

- Create a print style sheet, attach it to the historical home page, then change the media type to print in Code view.
- Create a style rule that will cause the body text to print in black, Times New Roman font. (*Hint*: You will need to use the body tag as the selector.)
- Save changes to your files, preview the page in a browser, and use the browser's print preview function to view your page. Close the print preview window.

o. Close the browser window, save your changes, return to Expression Web, close the memories site, then exit Expression Web.

▼ INDEPENDENT CHALLENGE 3

This Independent Challenge requires an Internet connection.

The director of Technology for All has expressed concerns about the download speed of the new Web site. Many people who visit the Technology for All Web site work for nonprofits and schools, and use older, slower computer equipment to access the Internet. Because of this, the director wants to find ways to make the new Web site download as quickly as possible. You know that using text-based navigation instead of image-based navigation would be one way to cut download times. You decide to see if there are any tools online that could help generate more sophisticated-looking list-based navigation.

    a. Type **list-based navigation** into your favorite search engine.

    b. Review the resulting links to find at least two tools that generate HTML and CSS code for list-based navigation.

    c. Use at least two of these tools to generate HTML and CSS code.

    d. Write a paragraph explaining what each rollover you generated looked like, then copy and paste the code from each tool into a word-processing document.

Advanced Challenge Exercise

    ■ Review the code you saved and analyze what CSS properties were used to create the effect.

    ■ Write a paragraph explaining any new techniques you learned from this exercise.

    e. Type your name on the document and print it.

▼ REAL LIFE INDEPENDENT CHALLENGE

This assignment builds on the personal Web site you have worked on in previous units. In this project, you will add some professional design touches to the new section of your site that you added in the previous unit. To accomplish this, you'll modify the existing style sheet for the new section.

    a. Modify the style rules for each div of your new page layout to add suitable background colors, background images, borders, or other decorative elements.

    b. Add content to the divs where appropriate.

    c. Add navigation text, mark it up as a list, then add CSS rules to style the list so that it looks more like a navigation bar.

    d. Style the navigation links to create CSS-based rollovers.

    e. Add at least one element to the page that uses a position:fixed property so that it does not scroll with the page.

    f. Create a print style sheet, attach it to the page, add a media="print" attribute to the link in Code view, then create style rules to modify at least one element to display differently when printed than when displayed on screen.

    g. Save the changes to your files, preview the page in a browser, then use the browser's Print Preview window to view the effects of the print style sheet.

VISUAL WORKSHOP

Launch Expression Web, open the **ecotours** site, then open the home page. Create a new print style sheet, attach it to the page, change the media property value to print, then write a style rule so your screen matches Figure O-24 when you view the page in the Print Preview of your browser. When you have finished, save your changes, print a copy of the home page, close the ecotours site, then exit Expression Web.

FIGURE O-24

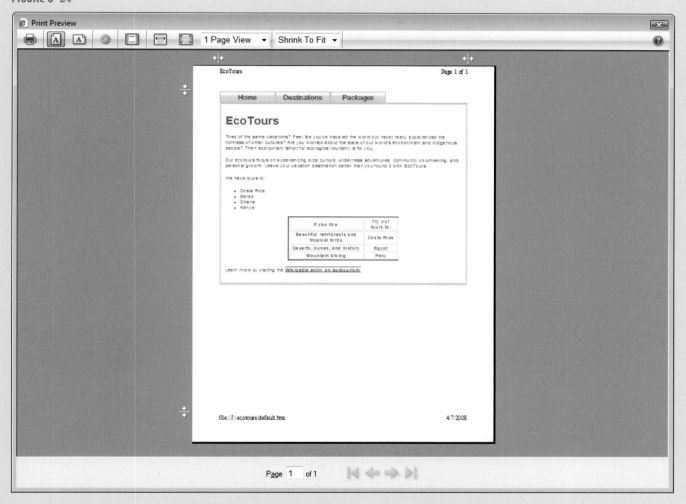

Working with Dynamic Web Templates

Maintaining a consistent look across all pages in your Web site can become tedious. If you decide to change a navigation button, for example, you need to make that change on every page. Using Find and Replace can help save time when making changes across multiple pages, but it's not suitable for every task. Another strategy you can use is to build a page using the Dynamic Web Templates feature available in Expression Web. A Dynamic Web Template allows you to create one master copy of your Web page design, make updates to a single file, and then update all the other pages in your site at once.  Catalina has sent you the complete schedule for the TradeWinds Arts Festival. You decide to create a Dynamic Web Template from the Festival home page to use for the other festival pages.

OBJECTIVES

Understand Dynamic Web Templates

Create a template from an
  existing page

Add an editable region to a template

Create a new page from a template

Apply a template to an existing page

Change a template and update pages

Use the Dynamic Web Template
  toolbar

Understanding Dynamic Web Templates

If you are creating a site with more than two or three pages, it's best to use Dynamic Web Templates. Not only does this feature save you hours of time, it also ensures consistency across your site. Without using Dynamic Web Templates, you need to make changes to each page individually. If you accidentally miss a page or edit some pages differently from others, your site's design and usability can suffer. 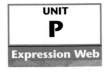 You decide to learn more about Dynamic Web Templates and how they work.

DETAILS

In order to work with Dynamic Web Templates, it's helpful to understand:

- **How Dynamic Web Templates work**

  A Dynamic Web Template is an HTML file that is saved in Expression Web with a .dwt extension. This file can then act as a master template for other HTML files. The Web designer can lock certain areas of the page design and allow others to be edited. The locked areas usually contain the branding, navigation, footer, and other elements that are common across all pages of your site. To make changes to locked areas, you need to edit the .dwt file on which the page is based, rather than editing the page itself.

  When you save a file as a .dwt file, Expression Web adds HTML comments in the code to convert the page from a simple HTML file to a template file. Expression Web uses this extra code to determine which areas of a template-based page can be edited and which cannot.

- **How to create a Dynamic Web Template**

  You can create a Dynamic Web Template either by saving an existing HTML file as a .dwt file or by creating a new blank .dwt file and creating a page design the same as you would in an HTML file.

- **Advantages of using Dynamic Web Templates**

  Using Dynamic Web Templates helps make site maintenance more efficient and accurate. The templates also can be helpful when redesigning an existing site. If your current site is based on a template, you can simply create a new template file and apply that new template to all existing pages, changing the design of all pages in the site at once. See Figures P-1 and P-2 for an example of the same site content shown in two different templates. Templates can also help simplify the management of sites with multiple designers or editors by ensuring that the design is consistent for everyone working on the site.

FIGURE P-1: Web page with template applied

FIGURE P-2: Same page with a different template applied

Creating a Template from an Existing Page

If you already have an existing HTML page in a Web site that you want to use for an overall site design, you can create a Dynamic Web Template based on that page. You can then use the resulting .dwt file to create other pages for the site. ▨▨▨▨ You want to use the festival home page as the basis for other pages about the festival, so you decide to create a festival template based on the page. To do this, you need to save the HTML file as a .dwt file, then delete any content specific to the home page.

STEPS

1. **Launch Expression Web, open the** tradewinds **site, open the** festival home page, **then switch to Design view if necessary**

QUICK TIP

If the festival folder is not open, double-click the festival folder in the Folder List task pane.

2. **Click** File, **click** Save As; **click the** Save as type list arrow, **then click** Dynamic Web Template (*.dwt)

QUICK TIP

Follow the file naming conventions for template files: don't use spaces, and only use letters or numbers.

3. **Select and delete the text** default.dwt **in the File name box, type** main.dwt, **compare your screen to Figure P-3, then click** Save

4. **Click before the text** Join us for the first annual, **hold down the mouse button, then drag down to select all the subsequent text on the page, ending with** Great music!
   All body text describing the details of the event is selected, as shown in Figure P-4.

5. **Press [Delete]**
   The content that is specific to the home page is deleted, as shown in Figure P-5, but the template still contains the navigation, branding, and footer areas.

6. **Save your changes to the main.dwt file**

FIGURE P-3: Save As dialog box for Dynamic Web Template

Make sure your save location is the festival folder

Save as type list arrow

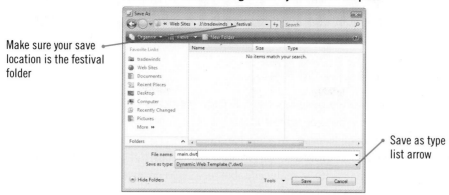

FIGURE P-4: Content selected for deletion

All text below this line is also selected

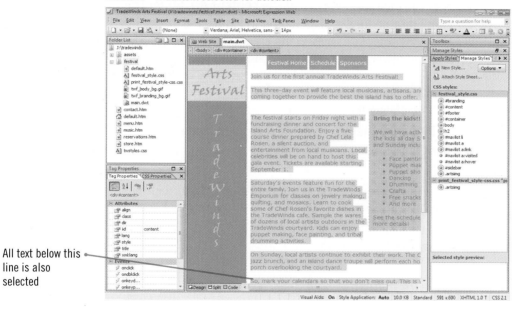

FIGURE P-5: Content deleted from main template

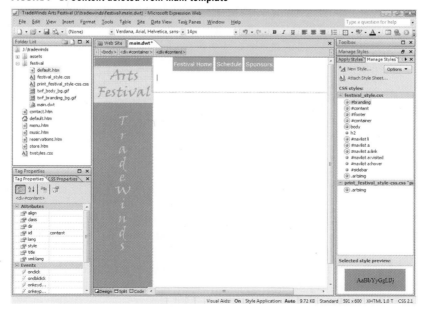

Adding an Editable Region to a Template

By default, all areas of a template-based HTML page are locked down and are only editable by directly editing the template file. While you want consistency in your pages, some areas, such as the main page content, will vary from page to page. To allow for this, you need to add one or more editable regions to your template. An **editable region** is simply an area that can be directly edited and present different content on each page. You can create as many editable regions as necessary in a template. 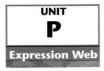 You create an editable region in the main festival template so that you can add content to each page.

STEPS

1. **Right-click in the lower-left corner of the content div, under the navigation area, then click Manage Editable Regions, as shown in Figure P-6**

   The Editable Regions dialog box opens. In this dialog box, you can add new editable regions to a template, remove editable regions, or rename editable regions. When you create a template, Expression Web automatically creates an editable region for the title so that each page can have a distinctive title. It's important to note that editable regions can be created only in the template file. They are then available in individual HTML pages based on the template.

   > **QUICK TIP**
   > Name editable regions with lowercase letters, no spaces, and no special characters.

2. **Click in the Region name box, type pagecontent, then click Add**

   The pagecontent editable region appears in the list below the doctitle editable region, as shown in Figure P-7.

3. **Click Close**

   See Figure P-8. The pagecontent editable region is outlined in the editing window with a visual aid. Expression Web has also added the placeholder text (pagecontent). You can delete this when you add your own text to the pages you create based on this template.

4. **Save your changes to the page**

Finding more Dynamic Web Templates online

In addition to creating your own Dynamic Web Templates, you can purchase predesigned templates online and then add your own content. If you enter **Expression Web Dynamic Web Templates** into your favorite search engine, you will find dozens of sites that offer templates for sale. Usually the templates are categorized by the type of Web site or business for which they would be suitable, such as a medical site, music site, or small business. Once you have purchased the template, you can add your own content and also modify the design as you'd like. Starting with one of these templates can be a great way to create a site design quickly.

FIGURE P-6: Manage Editable Regions menu option

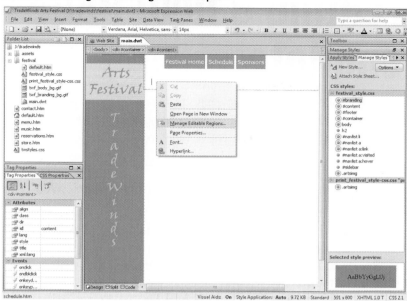

FIGURE P-7: Editable Regions dialog box

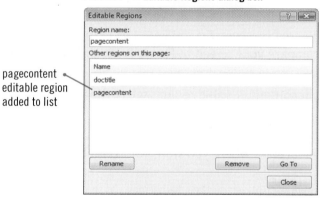

pagecontent
editable region
added to list

FIGURE P-8: Main template after pagecontent editable region added

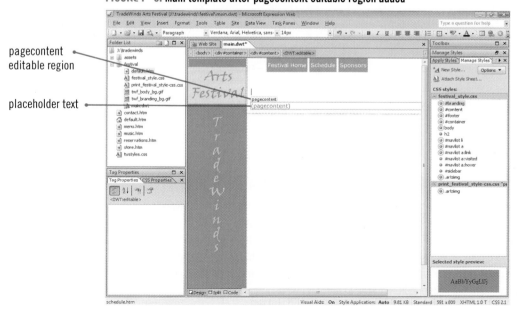

pagecontent
editable region

placeholder text

Creating a New Page from a Template

Once your template is ready, you can easily create new HTML pages based on the template. You need to create a schedule page for the festival using the main template you created. You give the page a title and add text to the pagecontent editable region.

1. **Click File, point to New, then click Create from Dynamic Web Template**
   The Attach Dynamic Web Template dialog box opens.

Remember, if you wanted to edit these locked areas, you'd need to edit the main.dwt file rather than this HTML file.

2. **Click the festival folder, click Open, click main.dwt, click Open, then click Close**
   The new page has the same design as the template you created, as shown in Figure P-9. Any areas outside the editable region are grayed out. If you point to a gray area with your mouse, the cursor changes to ⊘ to indicate that the area is locked and you cannot type or edit anything there.

3. **Click File, then click Save, navigate to the festival folder if necessary, delete the text festival_home_schedule_sponsors.htm in the File name box, type schedule.htm, then click Change title**
   The Set Page Title dialog box opens, with the current page title selected in the Page title text box.

4. **In the Page title text box type TradeWinds Arts Festival: Schedule to replace the highlighted text, compare your screen to Figure P-10, click OK, then click Save**
   Expression Web indicates in the top-right corner that this file is attached to the main.dwt template.

5. **Click in the pagecontent editable region, select the text (pagecontent), then press [Delete]**

6. **Click Insert on the menu bar, click File, click the Files of type list arrow and click All Files, navigate to the location where you store your Data Files, click twf_schedule.txt, then click Open**
   The schedule content is displayed on the schedule page, as shown in Figure P-11.

7. **Save your changes, preview the page in a browser, close the browser window, then return to Expression Web**

Using Dynamic Web Templates in other programs

Dynamic Web Templates are used not only by Expression Web, but also by other Web design software programs. This cross-compatibility allows you flexibility to move between design programs and still use your templates. Some software companies have also created simple WYSIWYG editing tools for use by people who want the ability to update site content but don't have the skills or comfort level to use complex Web design software. Many of these tools integrate with Dynamic Web Templates by allowing users access only to editable regions. This is another advantage of using templates and allows the designer to lock down key parts of the page design while still enabling others to maintain the content.

FIGURE P-9: **New page based on main template**

pagecontent
editable region

cursor indicates
this area is not
editable

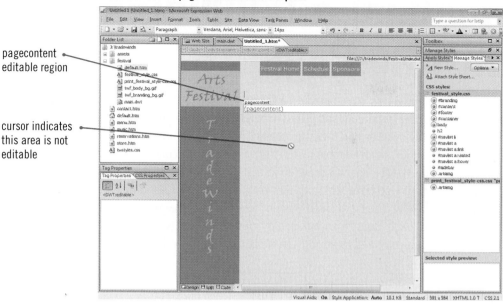

FIGURE P-10: **Changing the page title**

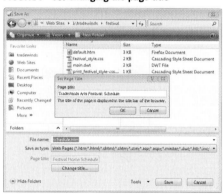

FIGURE P-11: **Schedule page with template applied and content inserted**

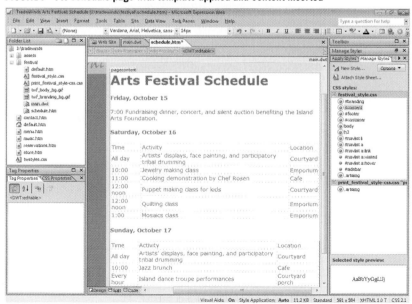

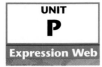

Applying a Template to an Existing Page

In addition to creating a new page based on a Dynamic Web Template, you can also take an existing HTML page that already contains content and attach a template to it. In a simple template, you may only have two editable regions—the doc title and the page content. When you attach the template to a page, you need to tell Expression Web into which editable region the page's existing content should be placed. Because everything in the existing HTML page will show up in that region, it's best if the page contains only the content you want to add to the editable region. If that page also contains design elements, you can end up with design conflicts. **⬛⬛⬛⬛** You have been working on an HTML page that contains text for the sponsors page. Luckily, this page does not contain any design elements. Currently, the file is not inside the tradewinds folder, so you need to import the file and then attach the main festival template to the page.

STEPS

1. **Click File on the menu bar, point to Import, then click File**
    The Import dialog box opens.

QUICK TIP

If the sponsors.htm file appears in the tradewinds folder instead of the festival folder, drag the file into the festival folder.

2. **Click Add File, navigate to the location where you store your Data Files, click sponsors.htm, click Open, then click OK**
    The file sponsors.htm appears in the Folder List task pane.

3. **Open the sponsors.htm file**
    See Figure P-12. The page contains text marked up with some basic HTML, such as paragraphs and headings, but it contains no design elements.

QUICK TIP

You can use this same menu to detach a template from a page.

4. **Click Format on the menu bar, point to Dynamic Web Template, click Attach Dynamic Web Template, double-click the festival folder to open it if necessary, click main.dwt, then click Open**
    A warning message prompts you that some content will be moved. Because two HTML pages are being merged together, it is necessary for Expression Web to remove some redundant code.

5. **Click Yes**
    The Match Editable Regions dialog box opens, as shown in Figure P-13. In this dialog box, you can choose in which editable region you want the existing content in the sponsors page to be placed, once the template is applied. The default is pagecontent and that is where you would like the content to be.

6. **Click OK, then click Close**
    See Figure P-14. The sponsors page now has the same design as the festival home and schedule pages.

7. **Save your changes to the sponsors page, preview the page in a browser, use the navigation links to view the home and schedule pages, then close the browser and return to Expression Web**

FIGURE P-12: Sponsors page without template applied

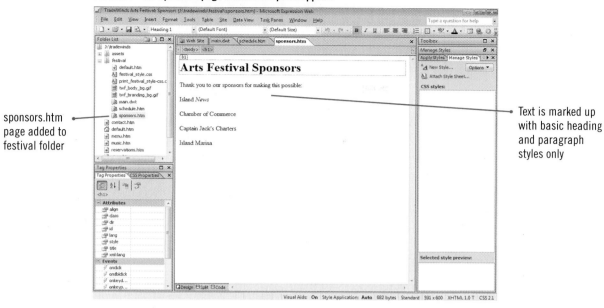

sponsors.htm page added to festival folder

Text is marked up with basic heading and paragraph styles only

FIGURE P-13: Match Editable Regions dialog box

Page that is being attached to template

Template to which page is being attached

Body content of current page is being placed in pagecontent region of template

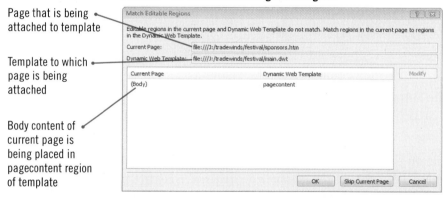

FIGURE P-14: Sponsors page with template applied

Expression Web

Changing a Template and Updating Pages

The biggest advantage of using Dynamic Web Templates is the ability to make a change in the .dwt file and have all the pages based on that template update automatically. Whenever you make a change to a .dwt file and save the file, Expression Web asks you if you want to update attached pages. If you want the changes you made to be reflected in all the site pages, all you have to do is choose yes when prompted. You decide to change the wording of the first navigation option on the schedule and sponsors pages. You could manually make this change on each page, but you decide to take advantage of the fact that they are attached to the main.dwt template. You modify the template and then update the attached pages automatically.

STEPS

1. **Make main.dwt the active page**

2. **Select the word Home and the space following it in the top navigation, then press [Delete]**

   The first navigation option now reads Festival, as shown in Figure P-15.

QUICK TIP

You can update individual pages at a later time by selecting one or more pages in the Folder List task pane, clicking Format on the menu bar, pointing to Dynamic Web Templates, then clicking Update Selected Page.

3. **Click File on the menu bar, then click Save**

   See Figure P-16. A dialog box opens, asking if you would like to update the files attached to the template.

4. **Click Yes**

   A message opens confirming that the files were updated.

5. **Click the Show Log check box**

   A list of all the files that were updated is displayed, as shown in Figure P-17.

6. **Click Close**

7. **Click File on the menu bar, then click Save All**

   Any attached files that were open in Expression Web need to be saved because changes were made to them. Any attached files that were closed when you made the updates are automatically saved.

8. **Make schedule.htm the active page, preview the page in a browser, then click the Festival link to view the home page**

   Notice that the navigation has been changed on the schedule page but not on the festival home page. That's because the festival home page has not been attached to the template.

9. **Close the browser window and return to Expression Web**

FIGURE P-15: Main template with navigation changed

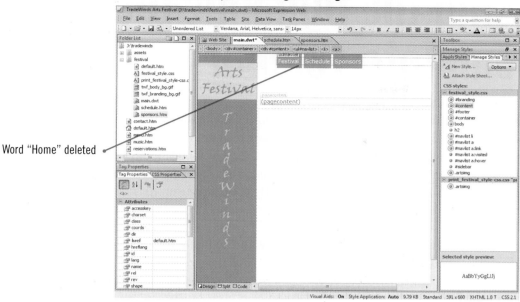

Word "Home" deleted

FIGURE P-16: Dialog box prompting updates to attached files

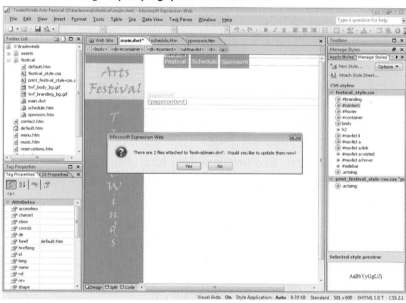

FIGURE P-17: Log file showing which attached files were updated

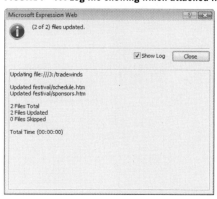

Using the Dynamic Web Template Toolbar

Expression Web features a Dynamic Web Template toolbar that provides easy access to a few commonly used tools for working with templates, such as adding editable regions and immediately updating attached pages. Opening this toolbar when you're working with a template can speed up your work. ▓▓▓▓ You want to add an editable region above the footer text. Once you publish this Web site and begin making maintenance updates to the site, you'll be able to use this editable region to enter information about when each page was last updated. You decide to use the Dynamic Web Template toolbar to add the region.

STEPS

1. **Make main.dwt the active page, click View on the menu bar, point to Toolbars, then click Dynamic Web Template**

   The Dynamic Web Template toolbar opens. The toolbar includes four commands: the Regions list arrow allows you to switch between editable regions; the Manage Editable Regions button opens the Editable Regions dialog box, where you can add, remove, or rename regions; the Update Attached Pages button triggers an update to all HTML pages based on the current template, even before you save changes to the template; and the Template Region Labels button toggles the visual aids for the editable regions on and off.

2. **Click the Template Region Labels button** 🔧

   The visual aids for the editable regions are visible in Design view, as shown in Figure P-18.

3. **Click** 🔧 **again**

   The editable region visual aids are no longer visible.

4. **Click in the footer div just before the text © 2011 TradeWinds, then click the Manage Editable Regions button** 🔧 **on the Dynamic Web Template toolbar**

   The Editable Regions dialog box opens.

5. **Type updated in the Region name text box, click Add, then click Close**

   A new editable region with the name updated is visible above the footer text.

6. **Click the Update Attached Pages button** 🔧, **then click Close**

   Expression Web updates both pages that are based on this template.

7. **Click the Close button on the Dynamic Web Template toolbar**

   The toolbar closes.

8. **Save changes to all pages, then make schedule.htm the active page**

   The schedule page has been updated with the new editable region, as shown in Figure P-19. You don't need to add information to this region yet, so you can leave it as is.

9. **Close the tradewinds site, then exit Expression Web**

FIGURE P-18: Visual aids toggled off for editable regions

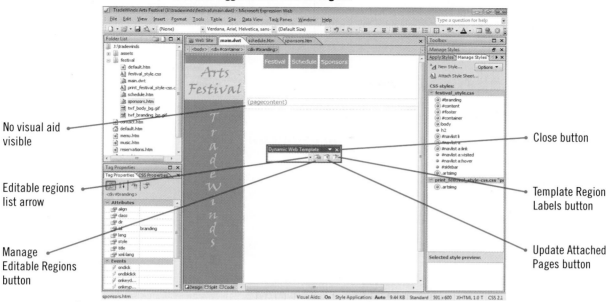

No visual aid visible

Editable regions list arrow

Manage Editable Regions button

Close button

Template Region Labels button

Update Attached Pages button

FIGURE P-19: Schedule page with new editable region

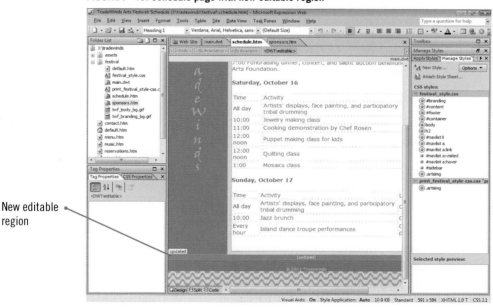

New editable region

Using multiple editable regions

You can use as many editable regions in a template as you like, but in general it's best to keep your template simple. If you use just one large editable region for all the page content, for example, it gives you and others who will be maintaining the site more flexibility and will minimize the complexity of the code. However, if you have several areas that need to be edited and aren't adjacent to one another, you will want to use multiple editable regions to ensure that the necessary updates can be made.

Practice

▼ CONCEPTS REVIEW

Refer to Figure P-20 to answer the following questions:

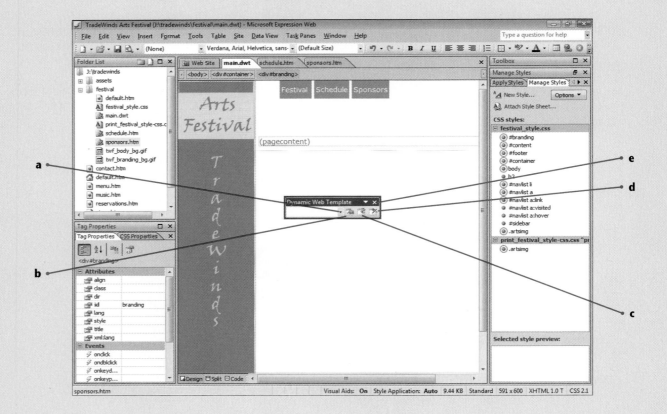

1. Which element would you click to close the toolbar?
2. Which element would you click to update attached pages?
3. Which element would you click to jump to an editable region?
4. Which element would you click to display or hide the visual aids for the editable regions?
5. Which element would you click to manage the editable regions?

Match each term with the statement that best describes it.

6. **Dynamic Web Template**
7. **Editable region**
8. **Attached page**
9. **.dwt**

a. An area of the template that is editable on the HTML page and allows content to vary from page to page.
b. A page that is based on a template
c. The file extension for a Dynamic Web Template
d. A master file that allows you to make changes in one file and then update other files all at once

Select the best answer from the list of choices.

10. **Which is *not* a benefit of using Dynamic Web Templates?**
    a. Easier site maintenance
    b. Maintains consistency across the site
    c. Saves time making updates
    d. Improves accessibility

11. **Before you can add content to a template-based HTML page, it must contain**
    a. A style sheet.
    b. An editable region.
    c. A content div.
    d. An attached page.

12. **How many editable regions can you have per page?**
    a. One
    b. Two
    c. Three
    d. Unlimited

13. **Which of the following is *not* a good name for a .dwt file?**
    a. Festival Template.dwt
    b. main_festival.dwt
    c. Festival#1.dwt
    d. a and c

14. **When you update pages that are attached to a template**
    a. All changes made to the template are also made to the attached pages.
    b. Some changes made to the template are also made to the attached pages.
    c. None of the changes made to the template are made to the attached pages.
    d. None of the above.

15. **When attaching a template to a page, it is best if the page**
    a. has brand new content.
    b. contains only content.
    c. does not contain any design elements.
    d. b and c.

▼ SKILLS REVIEW

1. Create a template based on an existing page.

   a. Launch Expression Web, open the careers site, then open the featured home page.

   b. Click File, click Save As, click the Save as type list arrow, then click Dynamic Web Template (*.dwt).

   c. Type **featured_main.dwt** as the file name, then save the file in the featured folder.

   d. Click before the text **Careers Guaranteed Featured Products**, then drag to select all the subsequent text through the text **get a second one free!**.

   e. Delete the selected text, then save your changes to featured_main.dwt.

2. Add an editable region to a template.

   a. Right-click in the lower-left corner of the content div under the navigation, then click Manage Editable Regions.

   b. Type **pagecontent** in the Region name box, click Add, then click Close.

   c. Save your changes.

3. Create a new page from a template.

   a. Click File, point to New, then click Create from Dynamic Web Template.

   b. Click the featured folder, click Open, click featured_main.dwt, click Open, then click Close.

   c. Click File, click Save, then type **services_specials.htm** as the file name.

   d. Click the Change title button, type **Careers Guaranteed Services Specials** in the Page title text box to replace the highlighted text, click OK, then click Save.

   e. Click in the pagecontent editable region, then delete the text (pagecontent).

   f. Click Insert on the menu bar, click File, navigate to the location where you store your Data Files, click the Files of type list arrow, click All Files, click cgf_services.txt, then click Open.

   g. Save your changes, preview the page in a browser, close the browser window, then return to Expression Web.

4. Apply a template to an existing page.

   a. Click File on the menu bar, point to Import, then click File.

   b. Add the file product_specials.htm from the location where you store your Data Files.

   c. Open the product_specials.htm file, click Format on the menu bar, point to Dynamic Web Template, click Attach Dynamic Web Template, click featured_main.dwt, click Open, then click Yes.

   d. Click OK, then click Close.

   e. Preview the product_specials.htm page in a browser, compare your screen to Figure P-22, use the navigation links to view the featured home and services_specials.htm pages, close the browser window, then return to Expression Web.

5. Change a template and update pages.

   a. Make featured_main.dwt the active page, in the navigation entry Services Specials select the word Specials and the space following it, then delete the selection.

   b. Save the changes to featured_main.dwt, click Yes when prompted whether to update attached files, click Show Log, then click Close.

   c. Save changes to all pages.

   d. Make services_specials.htm the active tab, preview the page in a browser, then click the Product Specials navigation link.

   e. Close the browser window, then return to Expression Web.

6. **Use the Dynamic Web Template toolbar.**

   a. Make featured_main.dwt the active tab, click View on the menu bar, point to Toolbars, then click Dynamic Web Template.

   b. Click the Template Region Labels button, then click it again.

   c. Click in the footer div before the text © 2011 Careers Guaranteed, then click the Manage Editable Regions button on the Dynamic Web Template toolbar.

   d. Type **contact** in the Region name text box, click Add, then click Close.

   e. Click the Update Attached Pages button, click Close, then close the Dynamic Web Template toolbar.

   f. Save changes to all open pages, updating attached files when prompted.

   g. Make the product_specials.htm page the active tab, preview the page in a browser, then close the browser window and return to Expression Web.

   h. Close the careers Web site, then exit Expression Web.

FIGURE P-21

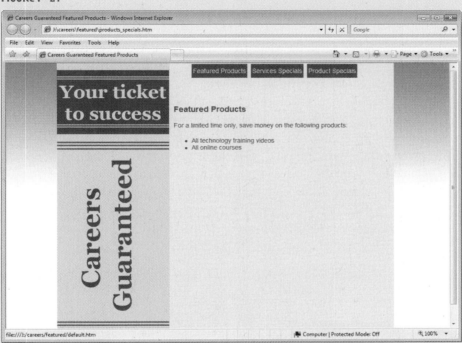

▼ INDEPENDENT CHALLENGE 1

In this project you continue your work on the ConnectUp Web site. You need to add a page that provides information on how to join the ConnectUp Challenge. You want this page to match the Challenge home page, so you decide to create a template from that page that you can then attach to the new page. You start by creating the template, then you'll create the join page, and finally you'll add a link in the template to the join page.

a. Launch Expression Web, open the connectup Web site, then open the challenge home page.

b. Save the challenge home page as a Dynamic Web Template in the challenge folder with a file name of **challenge_main.dwt**.

c. Delete the content that is specific to the challenge home page, starting with Take the ConnectUp Challenge and ending with Better get moving.

d. Save your changes, click after Who Will Benefit, press [Shift][Enter], right-click in the content div under the navigation, then click Manage Editable Regions.

e. Add a region named **main_content**, close the Editable Regions dialog box, click in the main_content editable region, click the p tab on the visual aid, click the <p> list arrow on the quick tag selector bar, click Remove Tag, then save changes to the template file.

f. Create a new page based on the template. (*Hint*: Use the Create from Dynamic Web Template command on the File menu.) Save the new page as **join.htm** in the challenge folder with a title of **How to Join the ConnectUp Challenge**.

g. Delete the (main_content) placeholder text, then insert the file cuc_join.txt from the location where your Data Files are stored.

h. Save the changes to the join page, then preview the page in a browser. Close the browser window and return to Expression Web.

i. Make the challenge_main.dwt file the active page, select the text How to Join in the navigation area, right-click, click Hyperlink, link it to join.htm within the challenge folder, then click OK to close the dialog box.

j. Save your changes to challenge_main.dwt, updating attached pages when prompted.

k. Save your changes to the join page, preview the page in a browser, compare your screen to Figure P-22, close the browser window, return to Expression Web, close the connectup site, then exit Expression Web.

FIGURE P-22

▼ INDEPENDENT CHALLENGE 2

In this project you continue your work on the Memories Restored Web site. You need to add two pages to the Historical section of the site. First you'll create a page that contains information about available historical services, then you'll create a page with information about the staff.

a. Launch Expression Web, open the memories Web site, then open the historical home page.

b. Create a template based on the historical home page. Be sure to save the template with a name that follows the file naming conventions. After you create the template, remove any content from it that is specific to the historical home page.

c. Add an editable region to the template, just under the navigation text.

d. Create a new page based on the template. This page will contain information about historical services. Give the page an appropriate file name and page title, and add the mrh_services.txt content to the editable region. (*Hint*: Be sure to name the file with the same file name you used as a target for the Services navigation link in the last unit. To check this link, right-click the link on the historial home page or the historical template, click Hyperlink Properties, then check the Address text box.)

e. Import the staff.htm file into the historical folder and attach the template to it. (*Hint*: Before importing this file, check the file name you used in the last unit as the target for the Our Staff navigation link and rename the staff.htm file if necessary, so that your navigation link works.)

Advanced Challenge Exercise

- Add an additional editable region of your choosing to the template you created.
- Save the template changes, update all attached pages, then add content to the new editable region in each page.
- Save your changes.

f. Save changes to all pages, preview the pages in a browser, close the browser, return to Expression Web, close the memories site, then exit Expression Web.

▼ INDEPENDENT CHALLENGE 3

This Independent Challenge requires an Internet connection.

In addition to being able to create your own Expression Web Dynamic Web Templates, you can purchase many templates from companies offering this service for sale. For people who don't want to or aren't able to design their own site, these templates can offer a convenient alternative. The director of Technology for All has asked you to go online and look to see if there are any commercially available Expression Web templates that they could possibly use for the site redesign.

a. Type **Expression Web Dynamic Web Templates** into your favorite search engine and find at least two sites that sell templates.

b. Visit the sites and choose one design from each that you think would be suitable to use for a nonprofit organization such as Technology for All.

c. For each of the templates you chose, copy and paste the URL from the browser's address bar to a word-processing document, so that you have a list of URLs for possible template locations.

Advanced Challenge Exercise

- Review the instructions on each site that explain how to use the templates, and find out the cost of using each template. Find out whether any of the templates you found are free for nonprofit use.

- Write a paragraph explaining whether or not you would consider using these templates and the reasons for your decision.

d. Put your name on your document and print it or save it.

▼ REAL LIFE INDEPENDENT CHALLENGE

This assignment builds on the personal Web site you have worked on in previous units. In this project, you will create a Dynamic Web Template based on a current page design, add editable regions, and create new pages based on the template.

   a. Open the page for the new section of the site you created, then save it as a Dynamic Web Template.
   b. Add an editable region of your choosing to the template.
   c. Create at least one new page based on the template. Make sure to save the page(s).
   d. Edit the template file to remove any text that is too specific for use as a template, then update all attached pages.
   e. Save your changes, preview all attached pages, close the browser window, then return to Expression Web.
   f. Close the Web site, then exit Expression Web.

▼ VISUAL WORKSHOP

Launch Expression Web, open the **ecotours** site, then create a template so your screen matches Figure P-23. (*Hint*: You may have to select the paragraph tab on the visual aid and delete the empty paragraph element before adding the editable region.) When you have finished, save your changes, close the ecotours site, then exit Expression Web.

FIGURE P-23

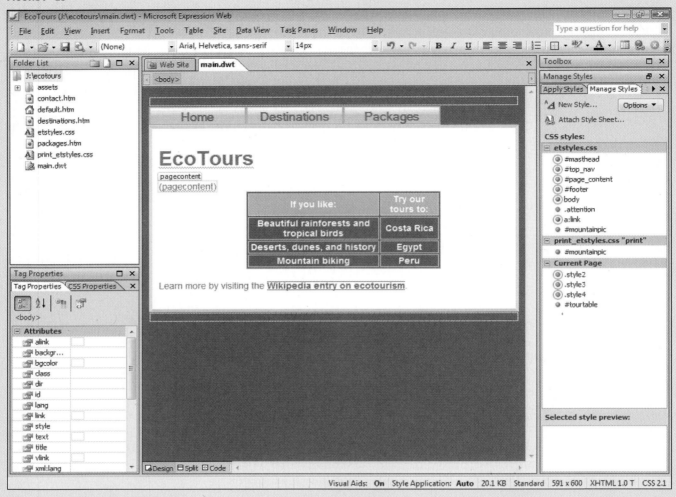

Data Files List

To complete the lessons and practice exercises in this book, students need to use Data Files that are supplied by Course Technology. Once they obtain the files, students choose where to store the Web site files they create, such as on a hard disk drive, network server, or USB storage device.

Below is a list of the Data Files that are supplied, the Web site folders and files students create, and the unit and practice exercise to which the files correspond. For information on how to obtain Data Files, please refer to the inside back cover of this book.

Data File Supplied	Student Creates File	Used In
Unit A		
a_1.htm		Lesson 4
images/banner.gif		
images/fishfountain.jpg		
a_2.htm		Skills Review
images/smilingman.jpg		
images/cgstyles.css		
a_3.htm		Independent Challenge 1
Unit B		
	tradewinds/default.htm	Lesson 4
	tradewinds/twstyles.css	
	tradewinds/store.htm	Lesson 6
	tradewinds/music.htm	
	tradewinds/menu.htm	
	tradewinds/reservations.htm	
	tradewinds/contact.htm	
	tradewinds/assets/	Lesson 7
	careers/about.htm	Skills Review
	careers/contact.htm	
	careers/default.htm	
	careers/services.htm	
	careers/cgstyles.css	
	careers/assets	
	connectup/contact.htm	Independent Challenge 1
	connectup/default.htm	
	connectup/faq.hm	

Data File Supplied	Student Creates File	Used In
	connectup/joinup.htm	
	connectup/custyles.css	
	connectup/assets	
	memories/contact.htm (*Student filename may differ*)	Independent Challenge 2
	memories/default.htm (*Student filename may differ*)	
	memories/process.htm (*Student filename may differ*)	
	memories/testimonials.htm (*Student filename may differ*)	
	memories/work.htm (*Student filename may differ*)	
	memories/mrstyles.css (*Student filename may differ*)	
	memories/assets (*Student filename may differ*)	
	memories_ace/tips.htm (*Student filename may differ*)	
	Student folder and filenames will differ	Independent Challenge 4
	ecotours/contact.htm	Visual Workshop
	ecotours/default.htm	
	ecotours/destinations.htm	
	ecotours/packages.htm	
	ecotours/etstyles.css	
	ecotours/assets	
Unit C		
tw_home.txt		Lesson 1
tw_contact.txt		
tw_music.txt		
tw_reservations.txt		
tw_store.txt		
cafe_menu.doc		Lesson 2
cg_home.txt		Skills Review
cg_contact.txt		
cg_about.txt		
cg_career_services.doc		
cu_home.txt		Independent Challenge 1

Data File Supplied	Student Creates File	Used In
cu_contact.txt		
cu_faq.txt		
cu_joinup.doc		
mr_ace_tips.txt		Independent Challenge 2
mr_contact.txt		
mr_home.txt		
mr_process.txt		
mr_our_work.doc		
mr_testimonials.doc		
et_home.txt		Visual Workshop
Unit D		
No data files supplied		
Unit E		
Fish Fountain.jpg	fishfountain.jpg	Lesson 2
Elephant Sculpture.jpg	elephant_sculpture.jpg	Lesson 7
	elephant_sculpture_thumb.jpg	
Testimonial Picture.jpg	testimonial_pic.jpg	Skills Review
Careers Map.jpg	careers_map.jpg	
	careers_map_thumb.jpg	
Connected Badge.jpg	connected_badge.jpg	Independent Challenge 1
Car Couple.jpg	car_couple.jpg *(Student filename may differ)*	Independent Challenge 2
Example One.jpg	example_one.jpg *(Student filename may differ)*	
	example_one_thumb.jpg *(Student filename may differ)*	
Example Two.jpg	example_two.jpg *(Student filename may differ)*	
	example_two_thumb.jpg *(Student filename may differ)*	
Example Three.jpg	example_three.jpg *(Student filename may differ)*	
	example_three_thumb.jpg *(Student filename may differ)*	
Tips Banner.jpg	tips_banner.jpg *(Student filename may differ)*	
Rain Forest.jpg	rain_forest.jpg *(Student filename may differ)*	Visual Workshop
Unit F		
tw_header.gif tw_page_bg.gif		Lesson 1
cg_logo.gif		Skills Review

Data File Supplied	Student Creates File	Used In
cu_logo.jpg		Independent Challenge 1
	cu_footer_bg.gif	
mr_logo.gif		Independent Challenge 2
	mr_bg.gif	
Unit G		
No data files supplied		
Unit H		
No data files supplied		
Unit I		
tw_tablebg.gif		Lesson 3
Unit J		
No data files supplied.		
Unit K		
quilt.jpg		Lesson 5
basket.jpg		
tina_bw.jpg		Skills Review
tina_sepia.jpg		
questions.jpg		Independent Challenge 1
answers.jpg		
example_one_before.jpg		Independent Challenge 3
example_one_after.jpg		
example_two_before.jpg		
example_two_after.jpg		
example_three_before.jpg		
example_three_after.jpg		
Unit L		
No data files supplied.		
Unit M		
quotebg.gif		Lesson 7
Unit N		
No data files supplied.		
Unit O		
twf_content.txt		Lesson 1

Data File Supplied	Student Creates File	Used In
twf_footer.txt		Lesson 1
festival_style.css		
twf_body_bg.gif		
twf_branding_bg.gif		
twf_container_bg.gif		Lesson 2
twf_sidebar_bg.gif		Lesson 5
twf_arts_side.gif		Lesson 6
cgf_body_bg.gif		Skills Review
cgf_branding_bg.gif		
cgf_container_bg.gif		
cgf_content.txt		
cgf_footer.txt		
featured_style.css		
cuc_badge.jpg		Independent Challenge 1
cuc_banner_bg.gif		
cuc_container_bg.gif		
cuc_content.txt		
cuc_footer.txt		
challenge_style.css		
mrh_branding_bg.gif		Independent Challenge 2
mrh_container_bg.gif		
mrh_content.txt		
mrh_footer.txt		
historical_style.css		
Unit P		
twf_schedule.txt		Lesson 4
sponsors.htm		Lesson 5
cgf_services.txt		Skills Review
product_specials.htm		
cuc_join.txt		Independent Challenge 1
mrh_services.txt		Independent Challenge 2
staff.htm		

Glossary

A:active The state of a link when it has been clicked but the mouse button has not been released.

Absolute URL Contains the protocol (such as http://), the domain name (such as centraluniversity.com), and the file path (such as /library/hours.htm) to make up a complete URL; used to create an external link.

Accessible Usable by all visitors, including people with disabilities or those using non-standard devices such as cell phones to access a Web site.

Action A required attribute of the form tag that allows you to specify the file path of the form-handling script; also, the second part of a behavior that consists of a specific result such as opening a new browser window or displaying a new image.

a:hover The state of a link when a visitor's cursor is pointing to the link.

algorithm A method a search engine uses to decide how search engine results are ranked; the algorithms search engines use are very sophisticated, change frequently, and take into account factors such as the number of times the search term shows up in your content, where the search term occurs on your page, and how many other reputable sites link to your site.

a:link The normal, unvisited state of a link.

Alt text *See* Alternate text.

Alternate text An attribute of the <img> tag that describes the image in words; visitors who use screen reader software hear this text read aloud.

Anchor Another term for a link; also, the name of the HTML element that is used to create a link.

Assets Image, media, sound and other non-HTML Web site files.

Attribute The part of an HTML element that provides additional information about that element.

a:visited The state of a link when it has been clicked in the visitor's browser and is present in the browser's history.

Background-attachment A CSS property that controls whether a background image scrolls with the element's content or stays fixed as the content scrolls over it.

background-repeat A CSS property that controls whether and how a background image repeats across the element.

Behavior A piece of JavaScript code that Expression Web generates and adds to a Web page in order to add interactivity.

Block-level elements Larger HTML elements such as divs, tables, and paragraphs that, by default, always appears on their own line, stacked one on top of the other, on the page.

Bookmark A marker at a specific spot on a Web page that can be used as a destination anchor.

Borders In CSS, a line that that encloses both the padding and content areas.

Breadcrumbs or breadcrumb trails A navigation feature that indicates where the current Web page is in the site's organizational structure.

Browser defaults The built-in styles each Web browser uses to determine the display of HTML elements.

Button An element in an HTML form that allows a user to submit or reset the data.

Cascading Style Sheets (CSS) Rules that describe the presentation and visual design of a Web page, including fonts, colors, and often the layout and positioning of elements on the page.

Cell In an HTML table, a rectangular area created by the intersection of a row and a column.

Character entity A set of characters that are used in HTML to represent special symbols.

Checkbox A form control that displays options as a series of boxes a visitor can select. Checkboxes are not mutually exclusive, so visitors can select as many options in a set as they like.

Class-based style rule A style rule that can be created and applied to any selected content or element.

Code view The view that displays the HTML code that a Web page is written in; useful for writing and revising code, as well as for troubleshooting.

Cognitive disabilities Include learning disabilities, memory impairments, and intellectual impairments.

Common toolbar Provides access to common tasks including creating a new page, saving and opening files, and common text formatting options such as font, font size, bold, and italic.

Content area The innermost box in the CSS box model which contains the text, image, or other content.

Cropping Trimming or removing unwanted parts of a picture.

CSS box model The model on which CSS presentation and layout is based; this model states that every element on a page is a rectangular box with a content area and optional padding, border, and margin areas.

CSS positioning Using CSS to position elements on a Web page.

Declaration The part of a style rule consisting of a property and a value that describes what properties you want to change and how you want to change them.

Definition list HTML element used to list a word or phrase along with its definition or description.

Demographics Characteristics of population such as age, gender, or income level.

Description HTML element containing a description of a Web page and displayed by some search engines in search results.

Design view The view that displays a page as it will look like when viewed in a browser; most commonly used view when designing pages.

Destination anchor The part of a link that is the file or page that opens when a visitor clicks the link.

Dimensions The height and width of an image, usually measured in pixels; determines how large the image looks on a screen.

Div HTML element consisting of a rectangular area you can position on the page to hold your content, including text and images.

Domain name A name that identifies a particular Web site and is part of that site's URL.

Download time Amount of time it takes a Web page to load into a browser; determined by the file size of the page and its referenced files (including image files), and by the speed of the visitor's Internet connection.

Drop cap The first letter of a paragraph that has been styled to be larger in size and to drop down into the text of the paragraph.

Drop-down box A form control that displays options within a drop-down list where visitors can click a list arrow to view the choices.

Editable region An area in a Dynamic Web Template that can be directly edited and can present different content on each page.

Editing window Large area under the Common toolbar where most design work is accomplished.

Element In HTML, the combination of an opening tag, content, and a closing tag; elements identify structural parts of an HTML document.

Element-based style rule A rule that redefines the display of an HTML element.

E-mail link A link that opens an e-mail message in the visitor's default e-mail program, with a designated e-mail address already entered in the To line.

Event The first part of a behavior consisting of an act such as a visitor scrolling, clicking, resizing a window, or submitting a form.

External links Links to Web pages or files on a different Web site.

External style sheet A separate file with a .css extension that contains style rules.

Eyedropper tool Tool that allows you to or select a color by clicking anywhere on your screen.

Faux column technique Inserting a background image that mimics the color of a column in a container div and repeats vertically, to create the illusion of a full column in the gaps left when a column's actual background color ends.

Fieldset tag A tag used to denote group boxes in an HTML form.

File size The physical size of a file, measured in kilobytes (KB); affects how long it takes the picture to display in a visitor's browser.

Find and Replace A feature that allows you to search for any piece of text or code in one file, multiple files, or an entire site, and replace it with different text or code.

Fixed page design A design in which the page is the same width on every visitor's computer no matter how large the visitor's screen is.

Float A CSS property that positions an element to the left or right and outside the normal flow of HTML elements.

Folders view Default view in the Web Site tab, which displays a list of files and folders in the site.

Font family A prioritized list of fonts specified in a style rule that allows fonts to be substituted in case the visitor's computer doesn't have a particular font installed.

Footer An area at the bottom of each Web page; usually contains contact information and a copyright statement.

Form An HTML element that allows visitors to send information from a Web site.

Form control An HTML element that allows visitors to interact with the form by providing a place to either type in information or choose from a set of options.

Form element The element of an HTML form that contains the form controls; denoted by a <form> tag.

Form handler A file that processes the information entered in the form so that the data can be stored or used to initiate other actions, such as sending an e-mail or searching a database; form handlers can be written in any programming language, such as ASP.NET, PHP, or Perl.

Form field *See* form control.

Generic font family A font that is displayed if no other fonts in a font family list are available; only three generic font families are consistently understood by browsers and therefore safe to use—serif, sans serif, and monospace.

GIF Image format best used for images that are drawings, simple graphics, navigation buttons, or that contain large areas of solid color; GIFS can also be animated and can have a transparent background color.

Global navigation Navigation that appears on each page, usually at the top or left side.

Graphics Pictures.

Group boxes Sets of related controls, which make it easier for visitors to fill out related fields in a form.

Headings Six different levels of HTML elements that can be used to define text meant to act as a heading or subheading on a Web page.

Hearing disabilities Deafness and hearing loss.

Hex code Abbreviation of hexadecimal code, a numeric value used to define a specific color in CSS rules.

Home page The first page a visitor sees after entering a Web site address in a browser.

Hover state Image state that appears when a visitors points to or hovers over the image.

HTML Acronym for HyperText Markup Language, the language used to create Web pages.

HTML tags Text enclosed in angle brackets that surround pieces of Web page content and describe its structure or meaning.

Hyperlink Text or an image that visitors click to open another Web page, Web site, or file.

Hyperlinks view Illustrates how one file is linked to other files in a site.

IA *See* Information architect.

Image swap A behavior that replaces one image with another upon a specified event, usually a mouseover.

Images Pictures.

Information architect A person who creates structures, navigation systems, and search systems for Web site; may work as independent consultants or as part of in-house Web design teams within organizations.

Inheritance A characteristic of style sheets that causes a style applied to an element on the page to also be applied to any elements it contains.

Inline elements Smaller HTML elements such as images, lists, or hyperlinks that are, by default displayed side-by-side.

Inline styles Style rules that are placed directly around content similar to the way HTML tags are placed.

Internal links Links between pages or files within the same Web site.

Internal style sheet A set of style rules enclosed in the head of an HTML document in a <style> tag.

JavaScript A programming language that creates types of interactivity that are not possible with HTML alone; used in behaviors.

JPEG Image format best used for photographs and other images that contain many different colors, such as detailed artwork.

Jump menu A drop-down menu that lists navigation links; when visitors click a link in the menu, the corresponding page opens.

Justified text Text that is spaced so that both the left and right margins are symmetrical, unlike normal text which usually has a ragged right margin.

Keywords An HTML element consisting of a list of terms, separated by commas that describe the content of a Web site.

Leading The amount of space between lines of text within a paragraph; controlled by the CSS line-height property.

Legibility Describes how well pieces of text can be recognized and read; factors affecting legibility include font size, font family, the contrast between font color and background color, and the amount of white space between letters, between words, and between lines.

Line length The width of a block of text.

Liquid page design A type of design that that shrinks or expands to fit the size of the visitor's screen.

Local navigation Navigation used on large sites that features links related to a subcategory of the site.

Local site The folder on a hard drive, USB drive, or network drive that contains all files for a Web site.

Long description An attribute of the img tag that provides a more detailed description of an image than the alternate text.

Margins In the CSS box model, the area that creates space surrounding the other three components (borders, padding, and content).

Markup The use of tags to describe the structure of a document; accounts for the "M" in HTML (HyperText Markup Language).

Media property An HTML property that tells the browser under which circumstances to display each style sheet attached to the Web page.

Menu bar Located under the title bar, includes all Expression Web commands organized into menus such as File and Edit.

Merging The process of combining two or more table cells into a single cell.

Monospace font A font with equal space between the characters; an example is the Courier font.

Motor disabilities Includes conditions that may affect the ability to use a standard-issue mouse and/or keyboard to navigate a site.

Mouseover Occurs when a visitor points to an image on a Web page with the mouse pointer.

Named anchor *See* Bookmark.

Navigation bar A set of related navigation links; can be either text or images.

New from Existing Page A command that creates a new page that is a copy of an existing page.

Numeric entities A set of numbers that are used in HTML to represent special symbols.

Original state The image state that appears when a page initially opens.

Ordered lists Used to display items where sequence is important; items appear numbered by default.

Overflow property CSS property that determines how the browser should handle content that doesn't fit within the specified size of its containing element.

Padding area In the CSS box model, the area that creates space between the content and the border.

Page layout The placement of content, graphics, and navigation on a Web page.

Paste Options button Provides options for controlling how much, if any, formatting to include with pasted text.

Pixel The basic unit of measurement for anything displayed on a computer screen.

PNG Image format created specifically for Web graphics; produces very high quality images with small file sizes but is not well-supported by all browsers.

Pop-up blocker Ad-blocking software that prevents unintended new browser windows, such as those containing ads, from opening.

Popup message Text that appears in its own window; a visitor must click the OK button on a popup message in order to proceed.

Pressed state The image state that appears while a visitor is clicking an image.

Preview Feature that allows you to view your pages in a Web browser as you are designing them in Expression Web.

Print style sheet Controls what a page looks like when a visitor prints the page; often contains rules that hide unnecessary images or change the font size and color to a more print-friendly format.

Property The part of a style rule declaration that defines which aspect of an element's formatting to change.

Pseudo-class Defines properties for a particular state of an element, such as hover or active.

Public domain Work that is not protected by copyright law and is free to use and copy.

Publish To copy Web pages and related files from a local computer to a Web server so that visitors can view the files.

Pull quote A quote or excerpt summary that is formatted with a larger font size and placed on the page to draw visitors' attention.

Quick tag selector Located just below the tab area; allows you to easily select and edit specific HTML tags on Web page.

Radio button A form control that displays options as a series of circles that visitors can select; radio buttons are mutually exclusive, so only one button within a set of options can be selected.

Related navigation Set of navigation links that usually appears within the content area and displays links related to that page's content.

Relative URL Describes the location of the file being linked relative to the source file; used for internal links.

Remote site A folder on a Web server that contains all files for a particular Web site.

Remote Web Site view Displays a dual list of files, those on the local Web site and those on the remote Web site.

Reports view Provides an overview of available Web site reports, including reports of broken hyperlinks, slow pages, recently changed pages, and more.

Resampling Removes extra pixels from an image, changing the dimensions and file size; also decreases file size and download time.

Resizing Changing the height and width attributes in the <img> tag to make an image display differently on the page; the image dimensions themselves don't change and neither does the file size.

Root folder A folder that stores all the files that make up a Web site, including HTLM files, CSS files, and images.

Sample To select a color by clicking on it on the screen with an eyedropper tool.

Sans-serif font A font, such as Arial, that has no strokes at the beginning or end of a character.

Search engine optimization The process of adjusting a Web site so it ranks higher than competing sites on search engine pages.

Screen reader Software that uses a synthesized voice to read on-screen text aloud for people with vision-related disabilities.

Section 508 guidelines Accessibility guidelines issued by the United States government in Section 508 of the Rehabilitation Act.

Select tool *See* eyedropper tool.

Selector The part of a style rule that defines which elements a style should apply to; there are three basic types of selectors—IDs, elements, and classes.

Semantic markup Marking up Web page elements with HTML tags in a meaningful and descriptive way.

Serif font A font, such as Times New Roman, that has visible strokes at the ends of the character.

Sidebar A short, boxed area of content on a page that provides additional information about a topic.

Site map A diagram depicting how a Web site's pages are related within the site.

Source anchor The part of a link that is the word, phrase, or image on a Web page that, when clicked, opens another page or file.

Spam Bulk unsolicited e-mail.

Split view A combination view that displays both a Code pane and a Design pane at once.

Splitting The process of dividing a single table cell into two or more rows or columns.

Standard ASCII character set The set of characters that can be used as part of HTML; this is the same set of characters you see on the keys of your keyboard.

Status bar Located along the bottom of the program window, it provides helpful information such as the file size, the page dimensions, and which versions of HTML and CSS Expression Web is using to create your Web page.

Status message The text that appears in the status bar of a browser.

Stock photos Photos taken by professional photographers and then offered for sale to Web designers, graphic designers, and others who need images for Web sites, print advertisements, and other projects.

Style *See* Style rule.

Style rule Describes how a particular element or piece of content should be displayed. A style rule has two parts, the selector and the declaration.

Submit button A form control that sends the information submitted by a visitor to the Web server.

Table A grid-like container with rows and columns that can be used to display data or to lay out elements on a page.

Table AutoFormat A set of coordinated formatting attributes you can apply to a table at once; can include borders, font formatting, background colors, and other effects.

Tabular data Content that is displayed in a table format.

Target The browser window or frame in which the destination file opens.

Task panes Small, resizable windows appearing on either side of the Expression Web window that provide access to tools for specific tasks.

Text area A form control that displays a multiple-line text box where visitors can type in information.

Text box *See* text input.

Text input A form control that displays a single-line text box where visitors can type in information, such as their name or e-mail address.

Text file File with a .txt extension consisting of basic text without formatting such as font faces, colors, and sizes; bold; or italics.

Thumbnails Small images, usually linked to larger versions of the same image; used to save space on the page and minimize download time.

Title HTML element that contains the title of a page; the title is not displayed on the page itself but appears in the title bar of the visitor's browser and as the title in a browser's list of favorites or bookmarks if a visitor has added it to that list.

Title bar Appears at the very top of the program window and shows the title of the current Web site (if a site is open) or the current Web page (if only a page is open), the file path of the current site or page enclosed in parentheses, and the name of the program. Buttons for minimizing, resizing, and closing the program window are located on the right side of the title bar.

Typography The arrangement of text on the page or screen, including the use of font families, sizes and colors as well as managing white space through the use of padding and margins.

Unordered lists Used to display items where order is not important; list items appear with bullets beside them by default.

URL Acronym for Uniform Resource Locator; the address for a Web site, consisting of a domain name, a file name, and sometimes folder names.

Value Options for a property in a style rule.

Verifying links Checking links to ensure that they are working correctly.

Visual aids A feature that displays and allows edits to empty or invisible page elements while in Design view.

Visual disabilities Include legal blindness, low vision, and color blindness.

Visual hierarchy Varying the size of text elements in relationship to their importance to help readers quickly scan the page.

WCAG A set of international Web Content Accessibility Guidelines issued by the World Wide Web Consortium; the guidelines are based on research, expert opinion, and observations of people with disabilities using the Web.

Web browser Software that interprets HTML code and displays the text and images on a Web page.

Web page An HTML document on the World Wide Web.

Web-safe colors Colors that display reliably on all computer monitors that support 256 colors or less; these were more important in the early days of Web design than they are now, since most visitors' monitors now display millions of colors.

Web-safe fonts Fonts likely to be available on Windows, Mac, and Linux-based computer systems.

Web server A computer connected to the Internet that stores Web pages and other Web content and displays it to a Web browser.

Web site A collection of related Web pages, linked together.

Web standards Recommendations for creating Web pages that allow content to be viewed by all browsers and devices.

Windows clipboard A temporary storage area in your computer's memory.

World Wide Web Consortium (W3C) The main standards-setting organization for the World Wide Web.

Wrapping style Dictates how a picture will be positioned relative to its surrounding text.

WYSIWYG An acronym for What You See Is What You Get, meaning that as you're designing, Expression Web displays what your page will look like in a Web browser.

(X) background-position A CSS property that controls where a background image is placed relative to the element's left edge.

XHTML Acronym for eXtensible HyperText Markup Language, a newer version of HTML that has slightly different rules and tags, but still uses the extension .htm or .html.

(y) background-position A CSS property that controls where a background image is placed relative to the element's top edge.

Index

X

 Y